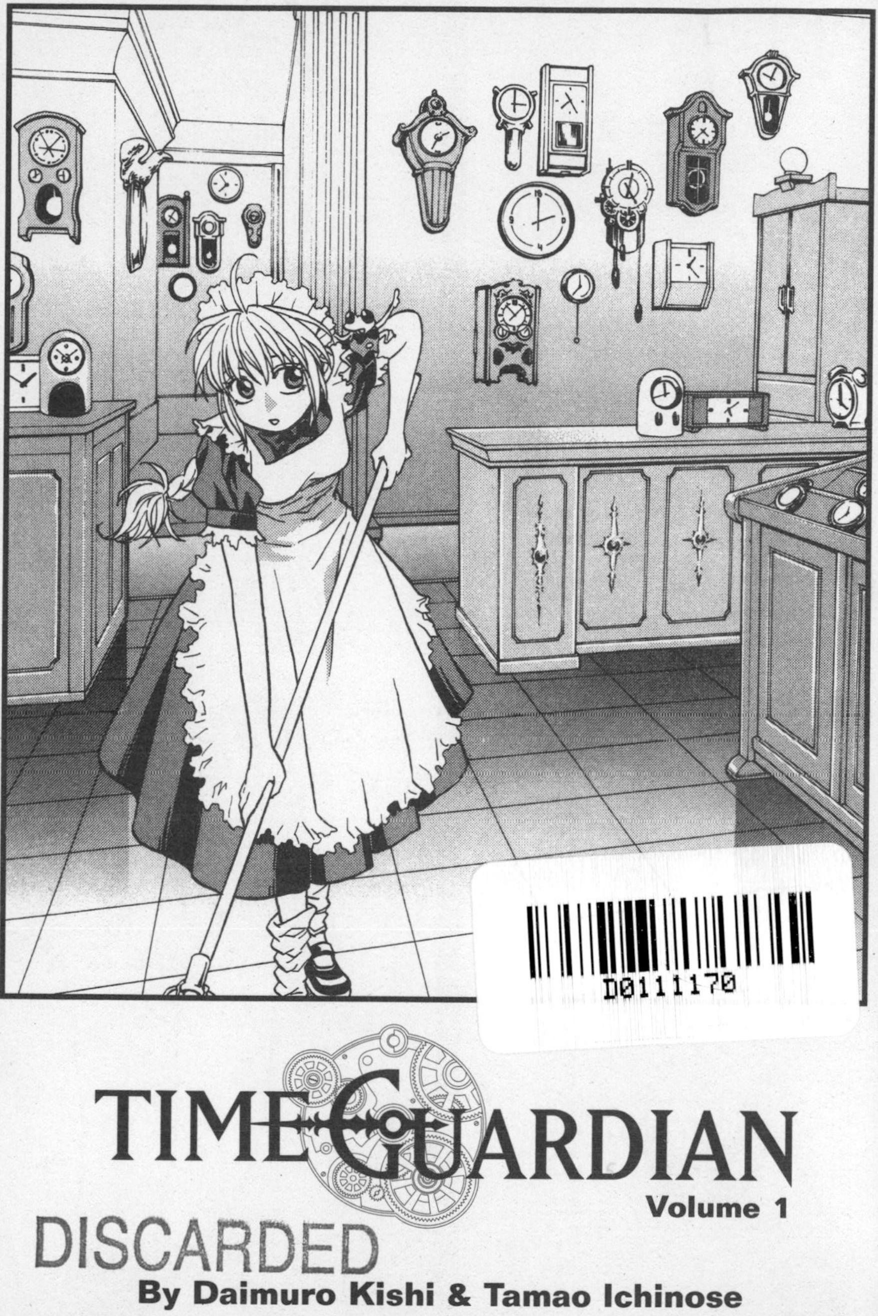

TIME GUARDIAN

Volume 1

By Daimuro Kishi & Tamao Ichinose

CONTENTS

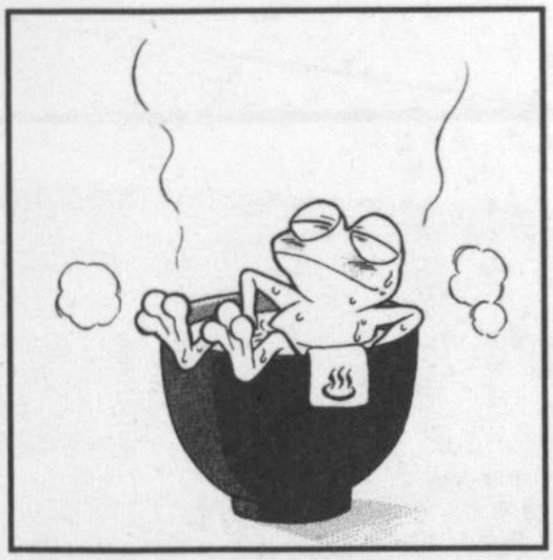

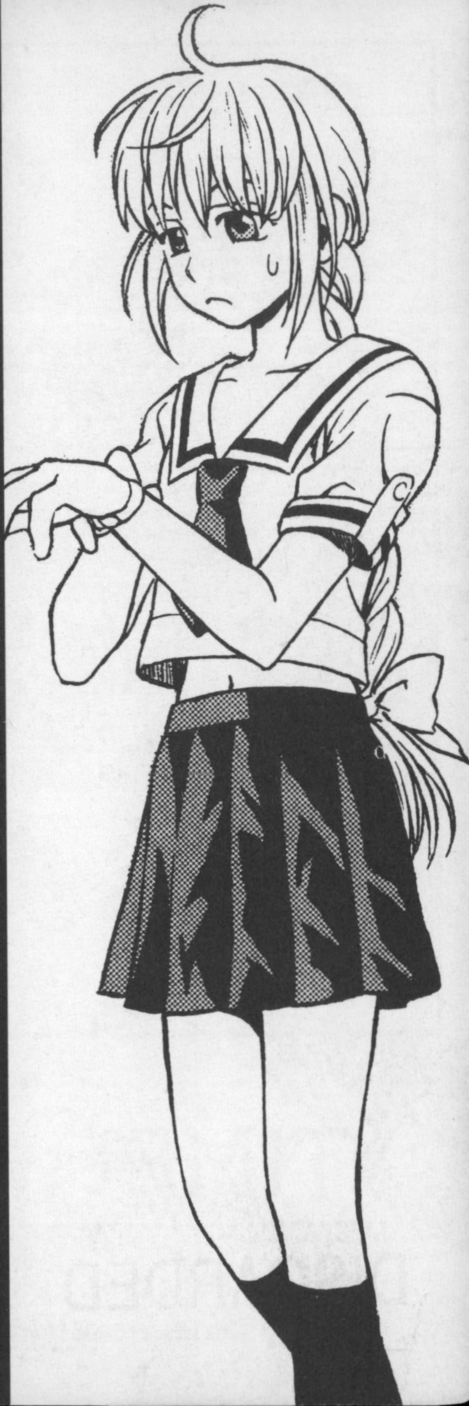

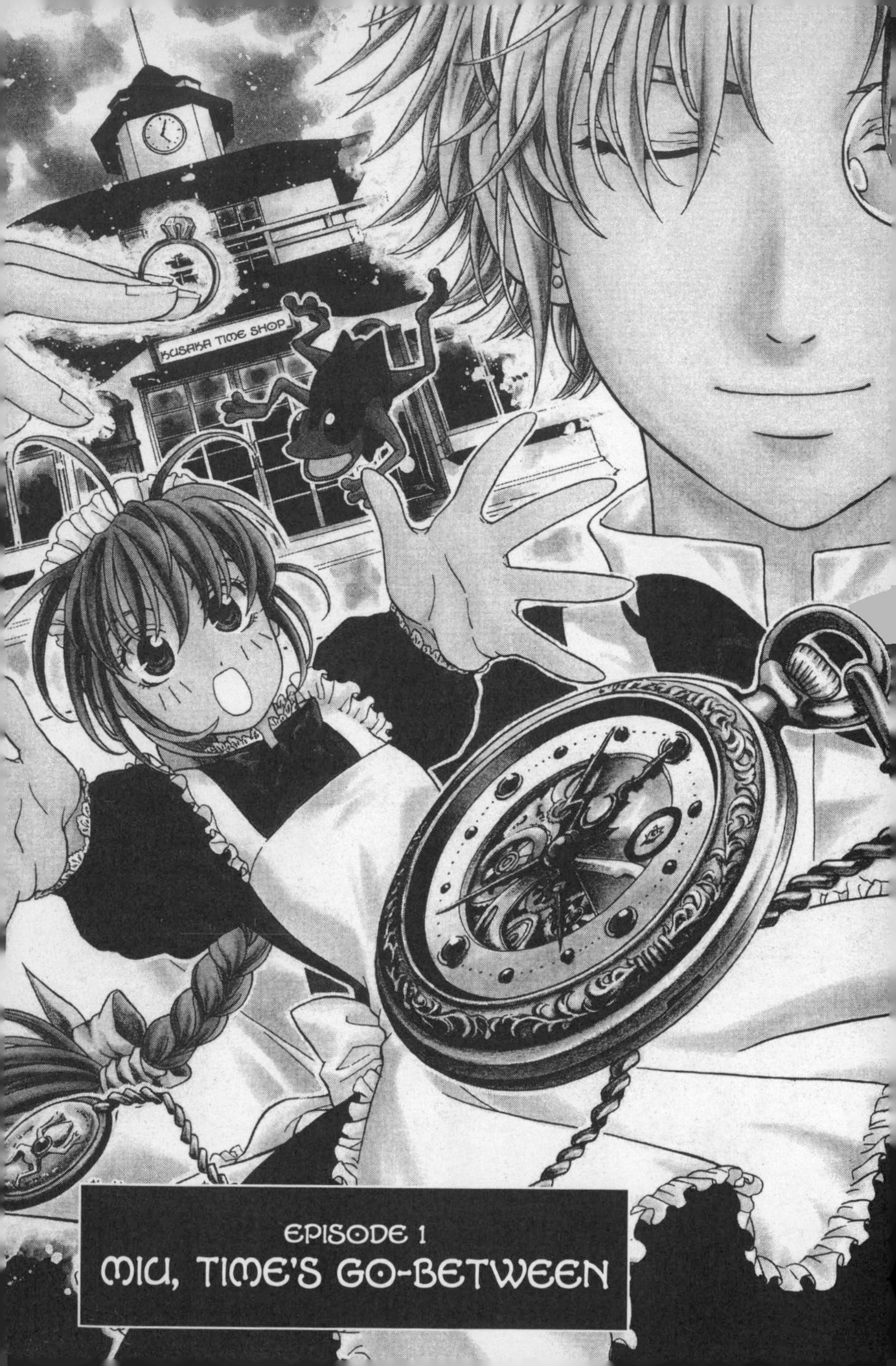
KUSAKA TIME SHOP

EPISODE 1

MIU, TIME'S GO-BETWEEN

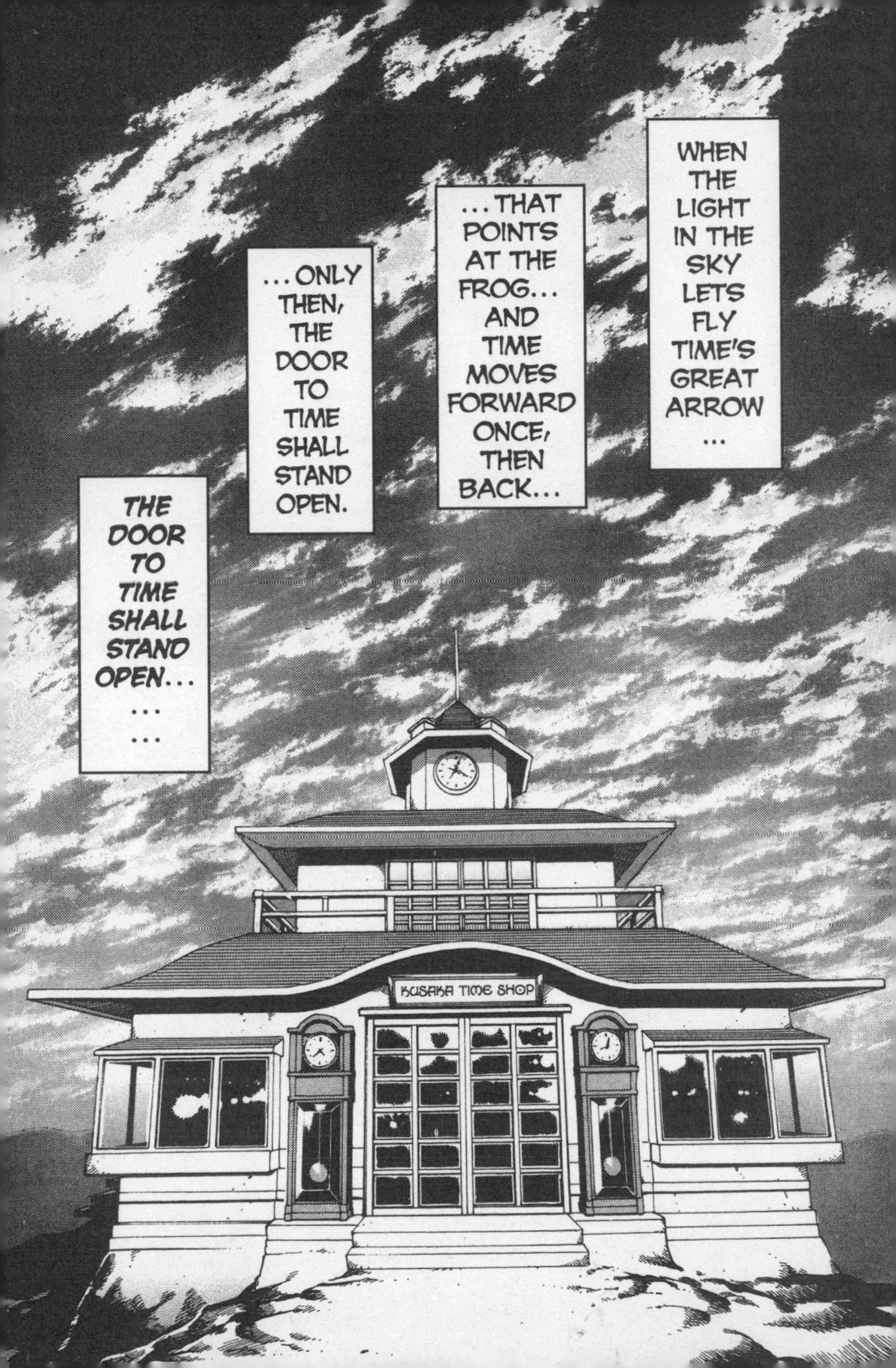
WHEN THE LIGHT IN THE SKY LETS FLY TIME'S GREAT ARROW ...
...THAT POINTS AT THE FROG... AND TIME MOVES FORWARD ONCE, THEN BACK...
...ONLY THEN, THE DOOR TO TIME SHALL STAND OPEN.
THE DOOR TO TIME SHALL STAND OPEN... ... ...
KUSAKA TIME SHOP

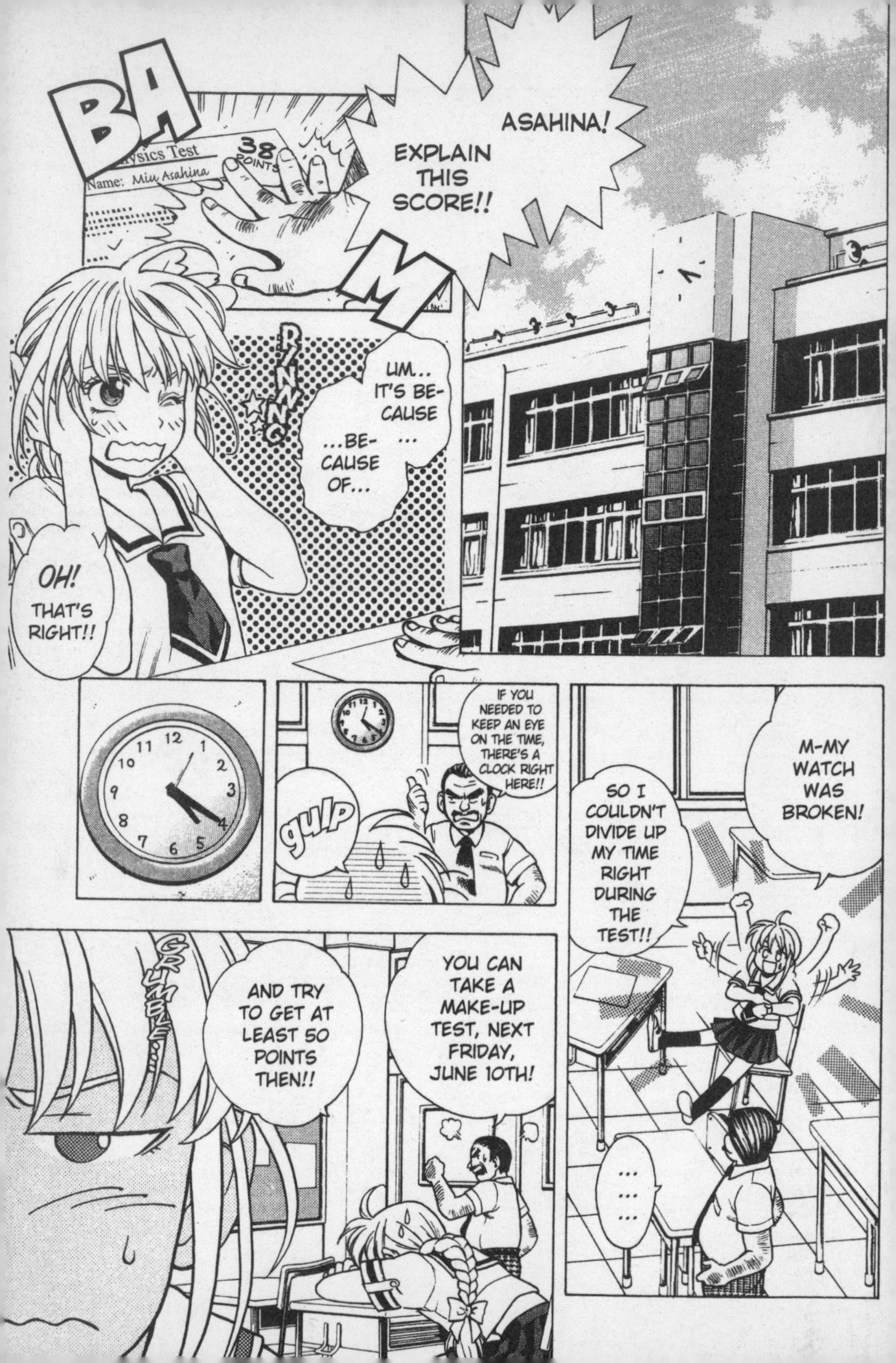
BAM
ASAHINA!
EXPLAIN THIS SCORE!!
38 POINTS
Name: Miu Asahina
PINNG
UM... IT'S BE-CAUSE...
...BE-CAUSE OF...
OH! THAT'S RIGHT!!
M-MY WATCH WAS BROKEN!
SO I COULDN'T DIVIDE UP MY TIME RIGHT DURING THE TEST!!
... ...
IF YOU NEEDED TO KEEP AN EYE ON THE TIME, THERE'S A CLOCK RIGHT HERE!!
gulp
YOU CAN TAKE A MAKE-UP TEST, NEXT FRIDAY, JUNE 10TH!
AND TRY TO GET AT LEAST 50 POINTS THEN!!
GRUMBLE

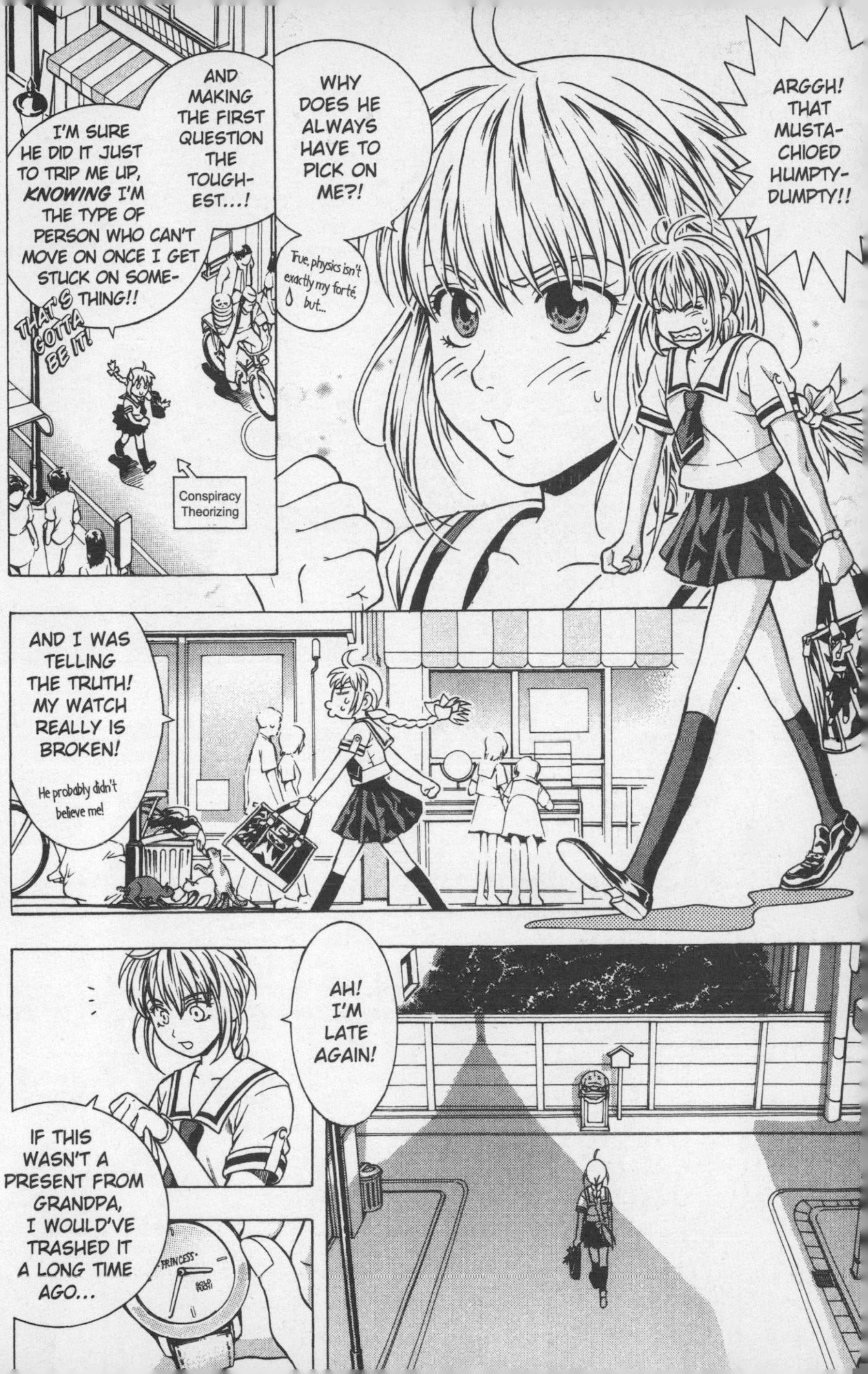
ARGGH! THAT MUSTACHIOED HUMPTY-DUMPTY!!
WHY DOES HE ALWAYS HAVE TO PICK ON ME?!
True, physics isn't exactly my forté, but...
AND MAKING THE FIRST QUESTION THE TOUGHEST...!
I'M SURE HE DID IT JUST TO TRIP ME UP, *KNOWING* I'M THE TYPE OF PERSON WHO CAN'T MOVE ON ONCE I GET STUCK ON SOMETHING!!
THAT'S GOTTA BE IT!
Conspiracy Theorizing
AND I WAS TELLING THE TRUTH! MY WATCH REALLY IS BROKEN!
He probably didn't believe me!
AH! I'M LATE AGAIN!
IF THIS WASN'T A PRESENT FROM GRANDPA, I WOULD'VE TRASHED IT A LONG TIME AGO...
PRINCESS

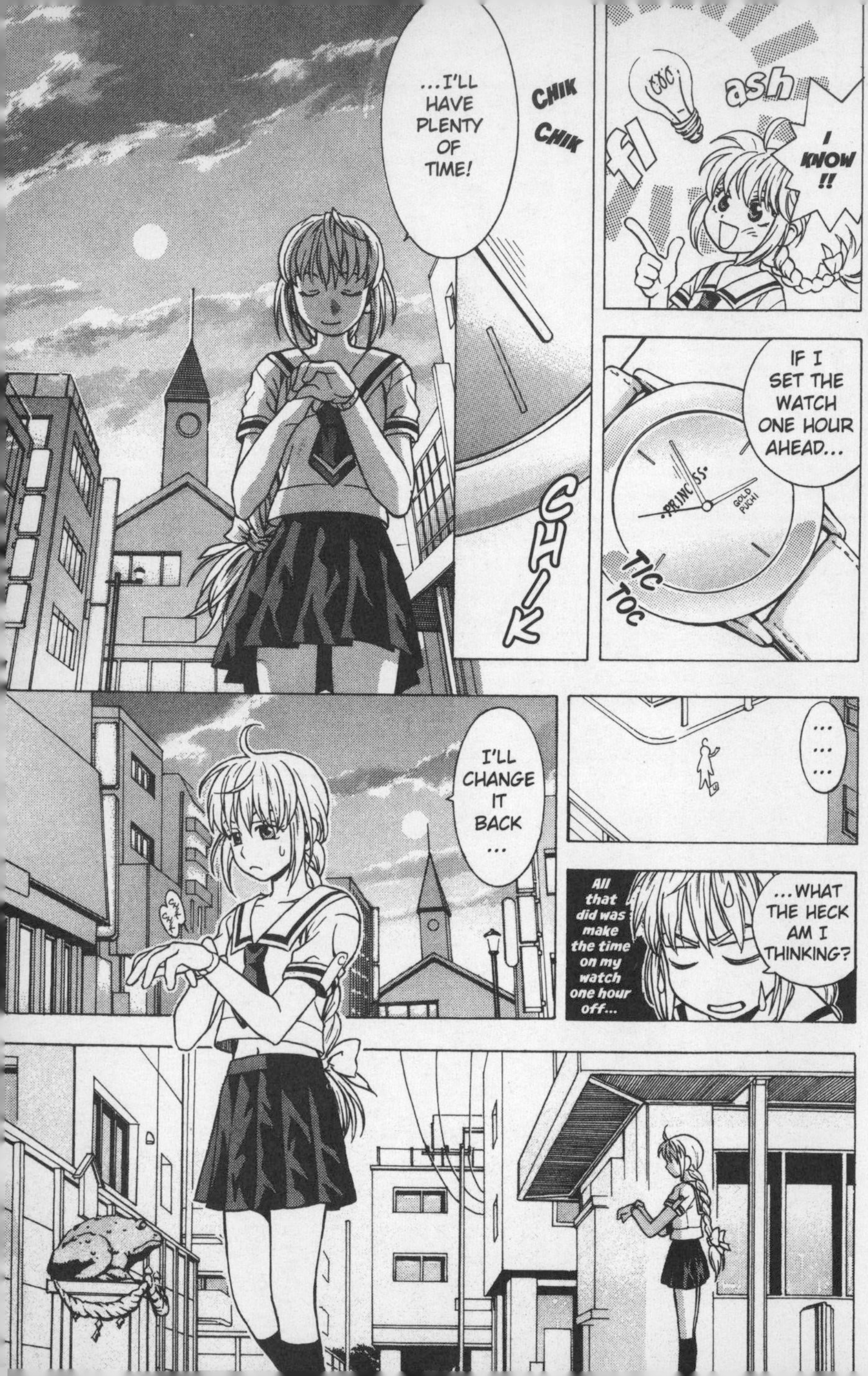
fl ash
I KNOW!!
IF I SET THE WATCH ONE HOUR AHEAD...
PRINCESS
GOLD PUCHI
TIC TOC
...I'LL HAVE PLENTY OF TIME!
CHIK
CHIK
CHIK
......
...WHAT THE HECK AM I THINKING?
All that did was make the time on my watch one hour off...
I'LL CHANGE IT BACK ...

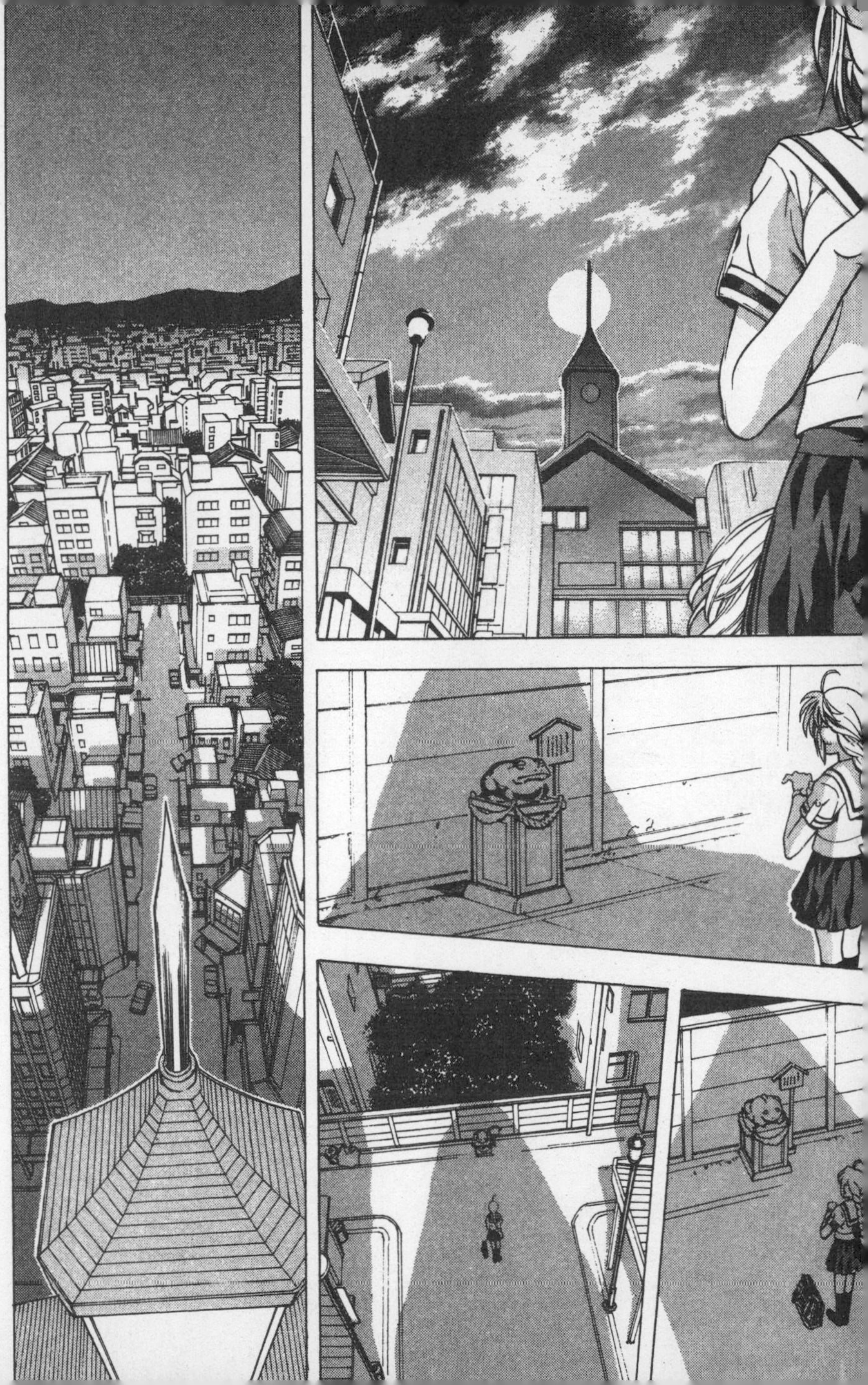

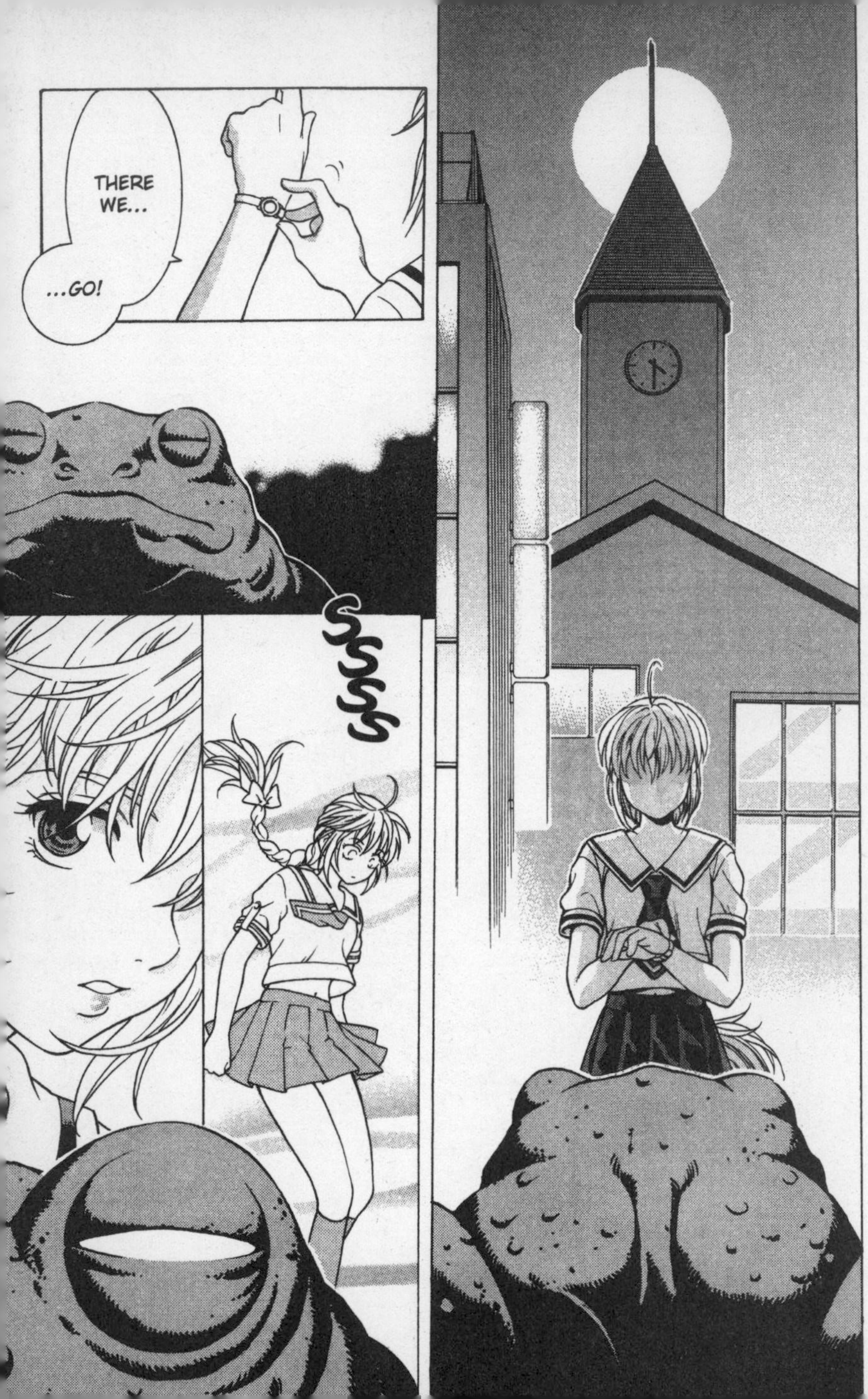
THERE WE...
...GO!
SSSS

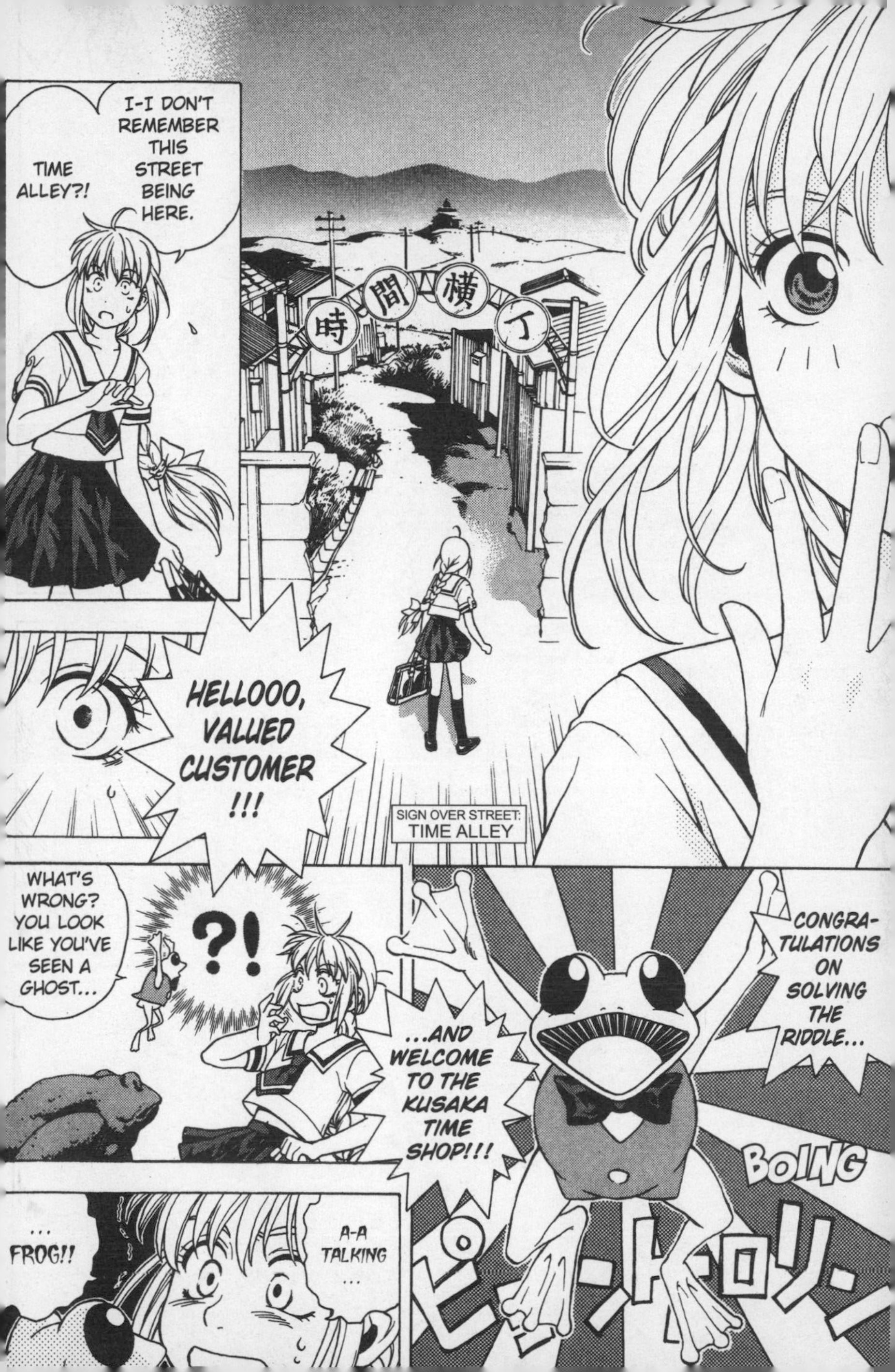

時間横丁
SIGN OVER STREET: TIME ALLEY
TIME ALLEY?! I-I DON'T REMEMBER THIS STREET BEING HERE.
HELLOOO, VALUED CUSTOMER!!!
CONGRATULATIONS ON SOLVING THE RIDDLE...
...AND WELCOME TO THE KUSAKA TIME SHOP!!!
BOING
?!
WHAT'S WRONG? YOU LOOK LIKE YOU'VE SEEN A GHOST...
A-A TALKING...
...FROG!!

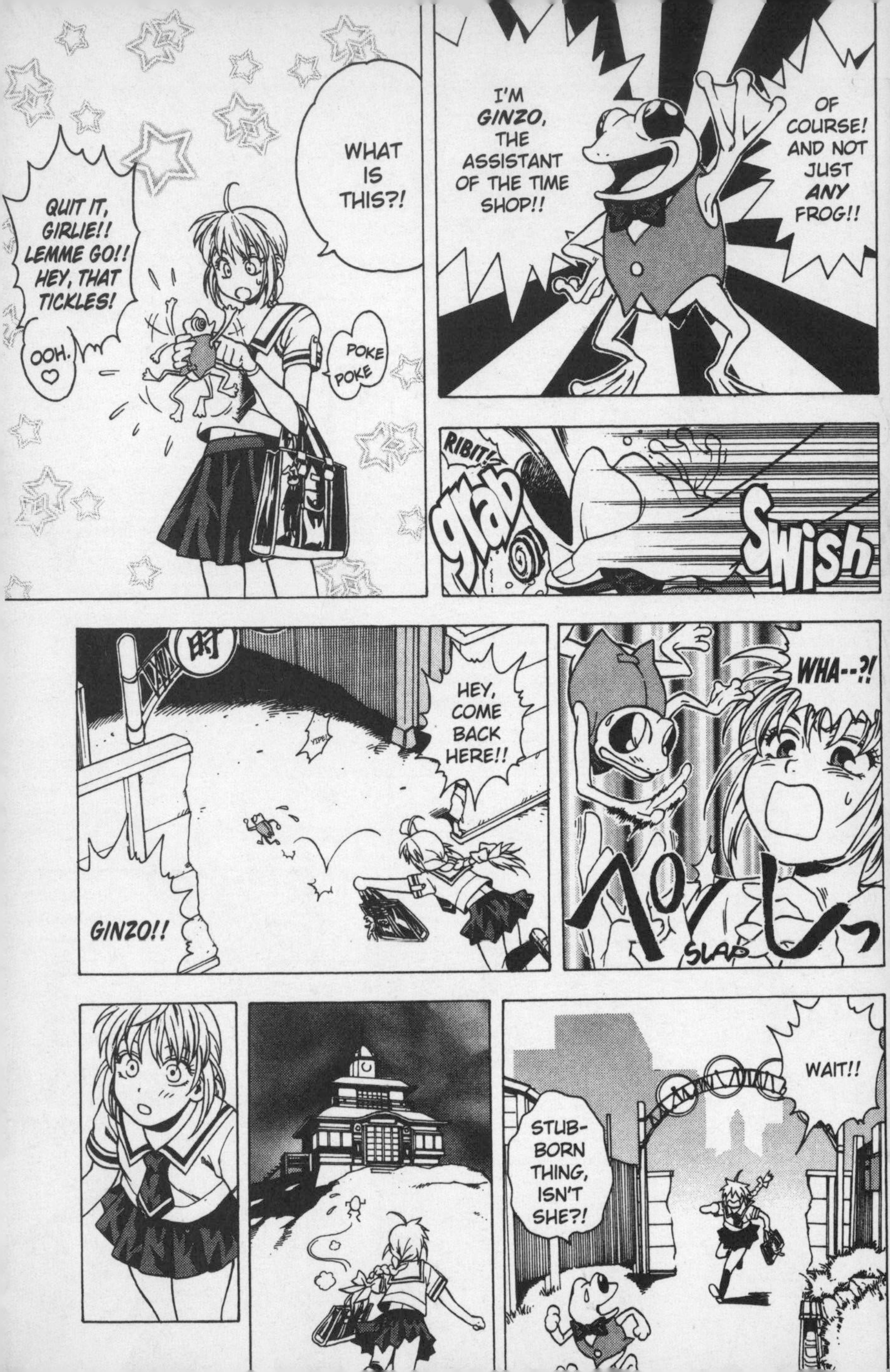
OF COURSE! AND NOT JUST ANY FROG!!
I'M GINZO, THE ASSISTANT OF THE TIME SHOP!!
RIBIT!
grab
Swish
WHAT IS THIS?!
POKE POKE
QUIT IT, GIRLIE!! LEMME GO!! HEY, THAT TICKLES!
OOH. ♡
WHA--?!
SLAP
HEY, COME BACK HERE!!
YIPE!
GINZO!!
WAIT!!
STUB-BORN THING, ISN'T SHE?!

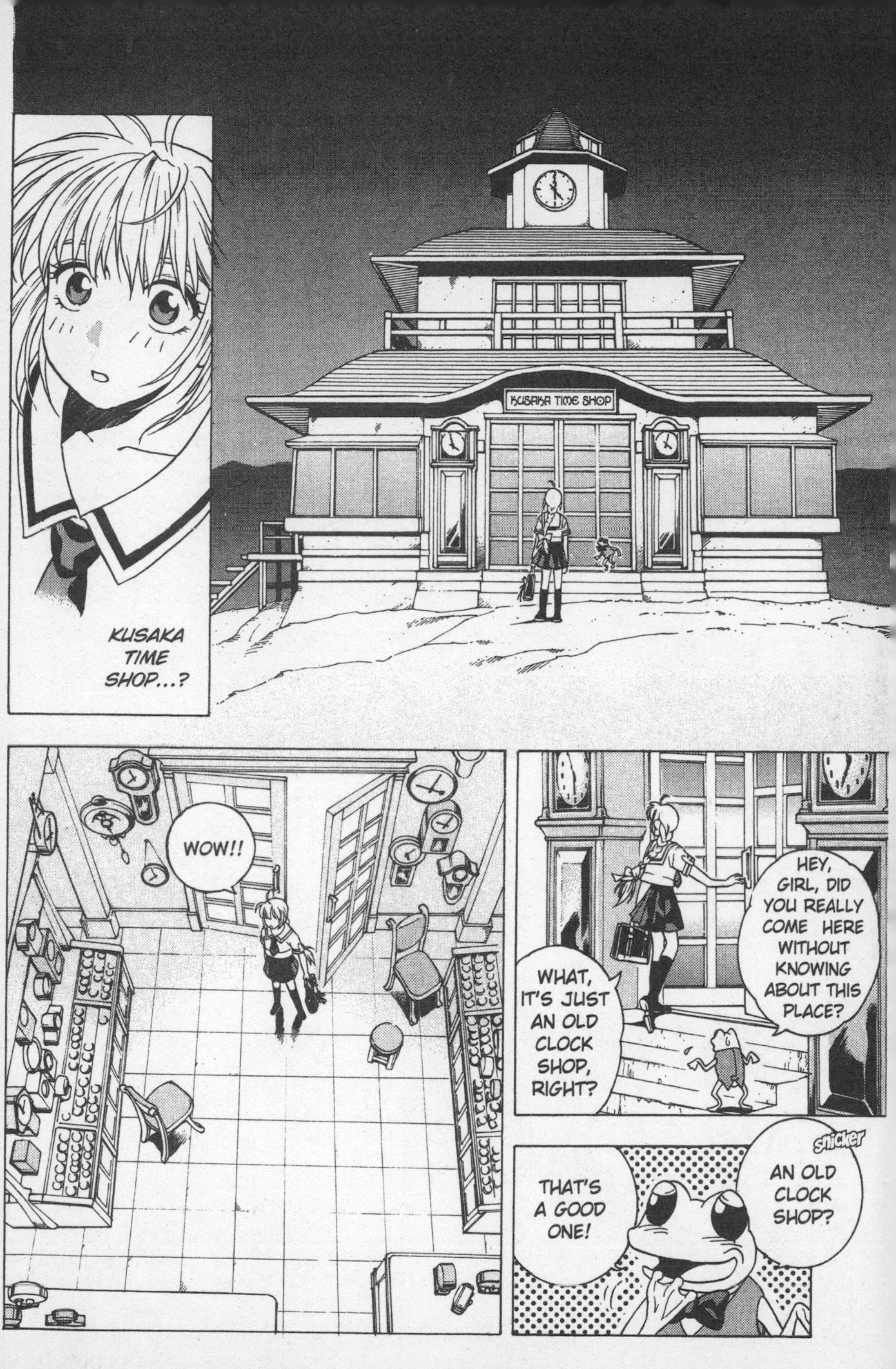
KUSAKA TIME SHOP
KUSAKA TIME SHOP...?
HEY, GIRL, DID YOU REALLY COME HERE WITHOUT KNOWING ABOUT THIS PLACE?
WHAT, IT'S JUST AN OLD CLOCK SHOP, RIGHT?
snicker
AN OLD CLOCK SHOP?
THAT'S A GOOD ONE!
WOW!!

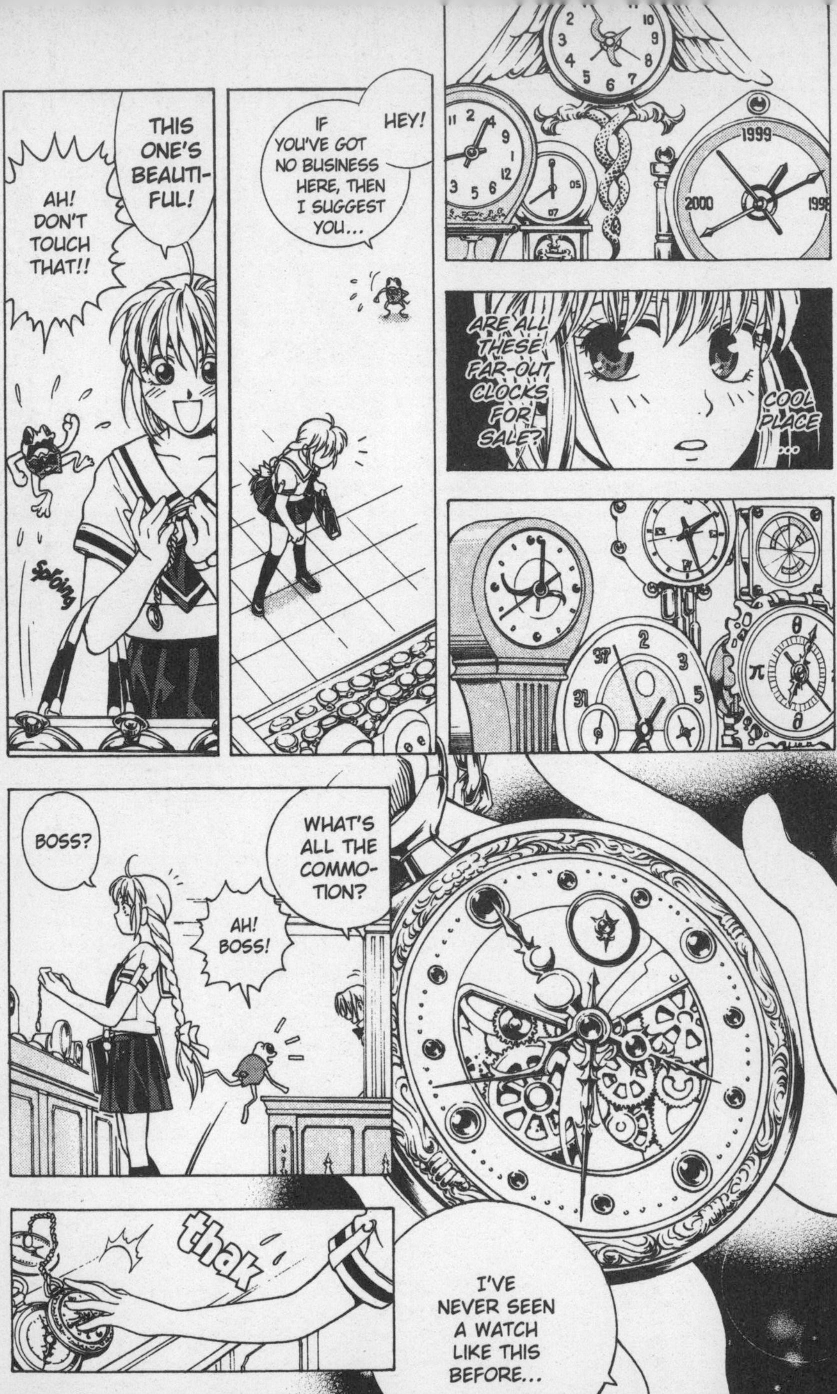
COOL PLACE...
ARE ALL THESE FAR-OUT CLOCKS FOR SALE?
HEY!
IF YOU'VE GOT NO BUSINESS HERE, THEN I SUGGEST YOU...
THIS ONE'S BEAUTI-FUL!
AH! DON'T TOUCH THAT!!
sproing
I'VE NEVER SEEN A WATCH LIKE THIS BEFORE...
WHAT'S ALL THE COMMO-TION?
AH! BOSS!
BOSS?
thak

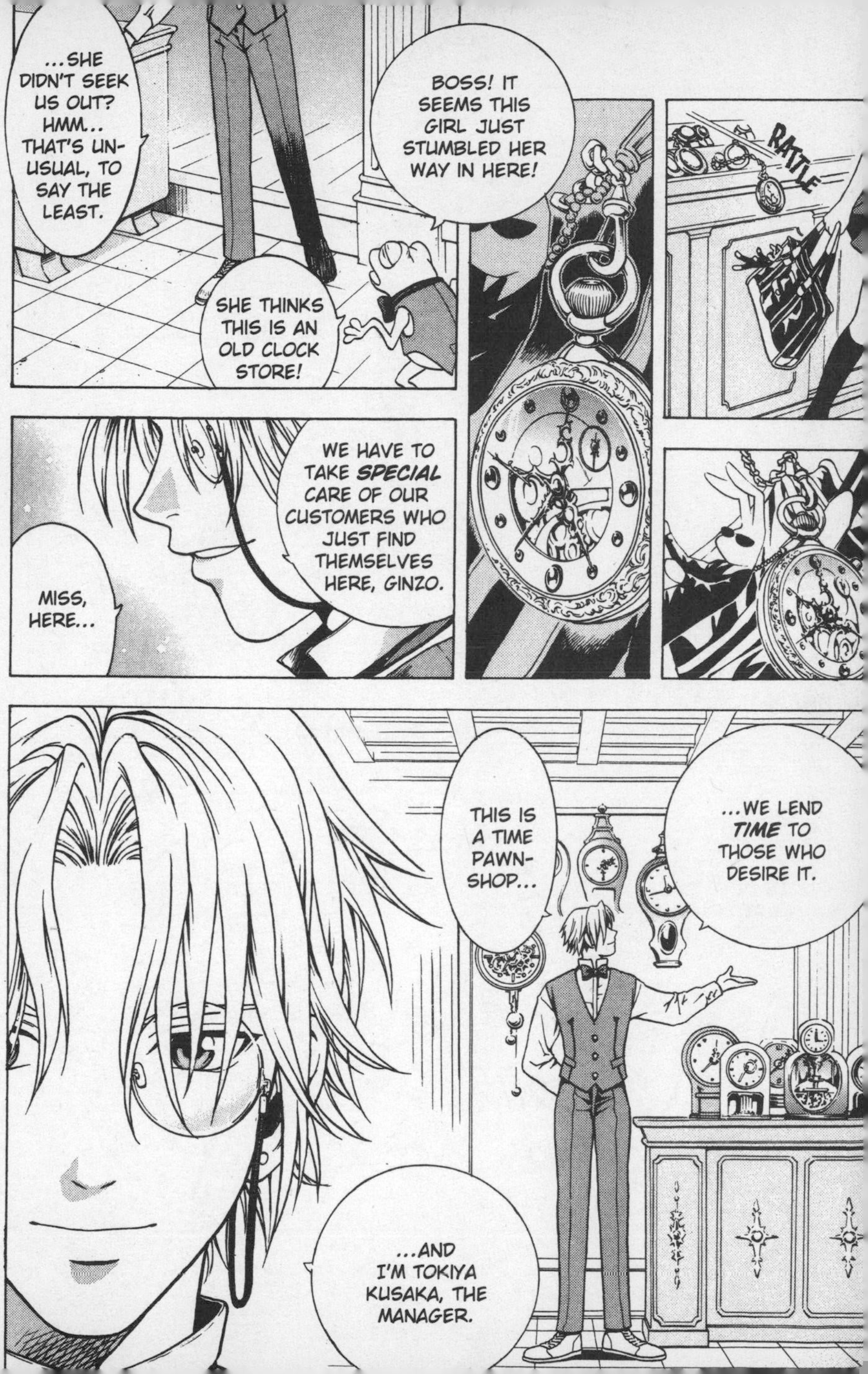
RATTLE
BOSS! IT SEEMS THIS GIRL JUST STUMBLED HER WAY IN HERE!
...SHE DIDN'T SEEK US OUT? HMM... THAT'S UN-USUAL, TO SAY THE LEAST.
SHE THINKS THIS IS AN OLD CLOCK STORE!
WE HAVE TO TAKE *SPECIAL* CARE OF OUR CUSTOMERS WHO JUST FIND THEMSELVES HERE, GINZO.
MISS, HERE...
...WE LEND *TIME* TO THOSE WHO DESIRE IT.
THIS IS A TIME PAWN-SHOP...
...AND I'M TOKIYA KUSAKA, THE MANAGER.

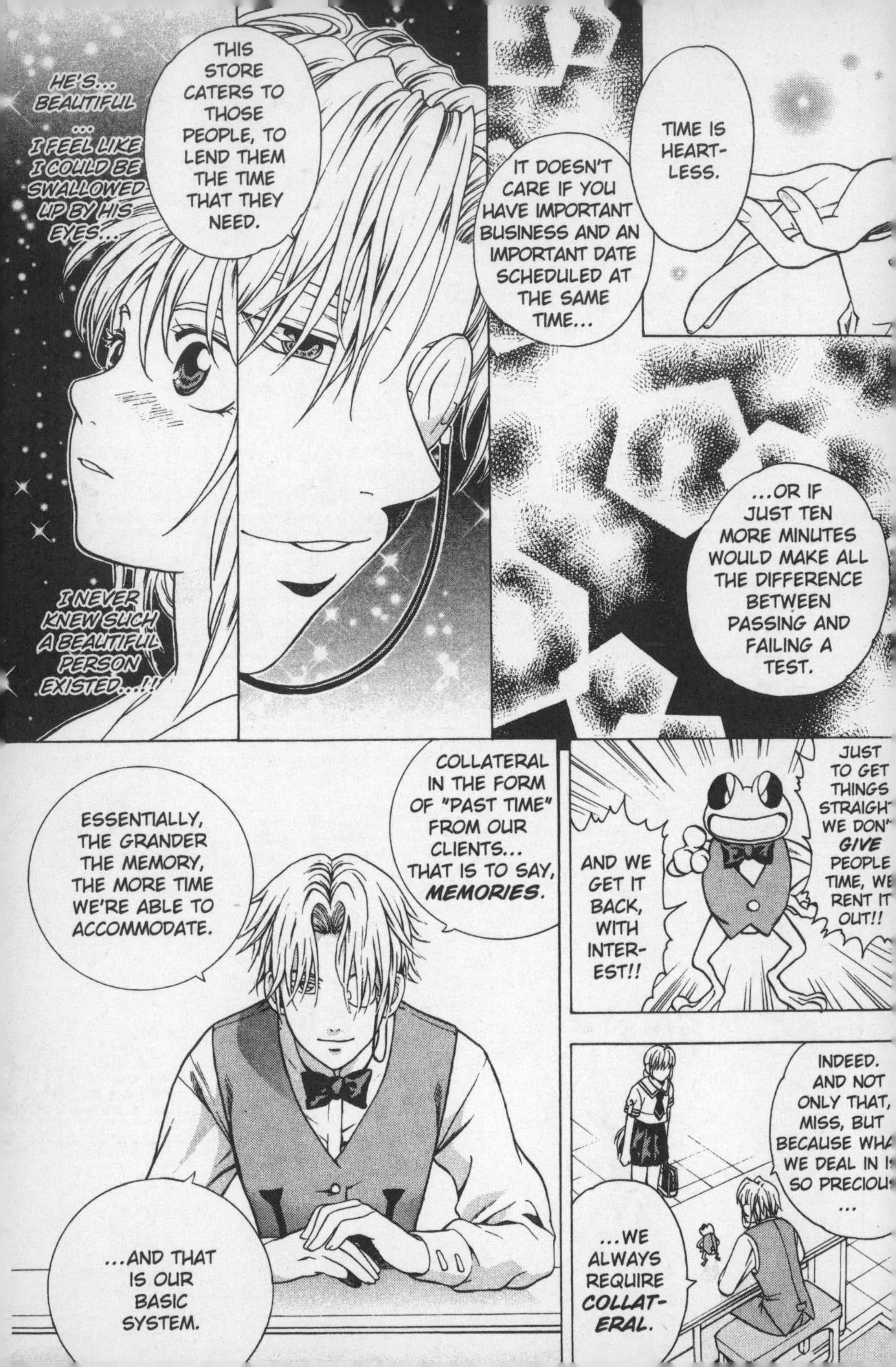
TIME IS HEART-LESS.
IT DOESN'T CARE IF YOU HAVE IMPORTANT BUSINESS AND AN IMPORTANT DATE SCHEDULED AT THE SAME TIME...
...OR IF JUST TEN MORE MINUTES WOULD MAKE ALL THE DIFFERENCE BETWEEN PASSING AND FAILING A TEST.
THIS STORE CATERS TO THOSE PEOPLE, TO LEND THEM THE TIME THAT THEY NEED.
HE'S... BEAUTIFUL ... I FEEL LIKE I COULD BE SWALLOWED UP BY HIS EYES...
I NEVER KNEW SUCH A BEAUTIFUL PERSON EXISTED...!!
JUST TO GET THINGS STRAIGH WE DON' GIVE PEOPLE TIME, WE RENT IT OUT!!
AND WE GET IT BACK, WITH INTER-EST!!
INDEED. AND NOT ONLY THAT, MISS, BUT BECAUSE WHA WE DEAL IN IS SO PRECIOU ...
...WE ALWAYS REQUIRE COLLAT-ERAL.
COLLATERAL IN THE FORM OF "PAST TIME" FROM OUR CLIENTS... THAT IS TO SAY, MEMORIES.
ESSENTIALLY, THE GRANDER THE MEMORY, THE MORE TIME WE'RE ABLE TO ACCOMMODATE.
...AND THAT IS OUR BASIC SYSTEM.

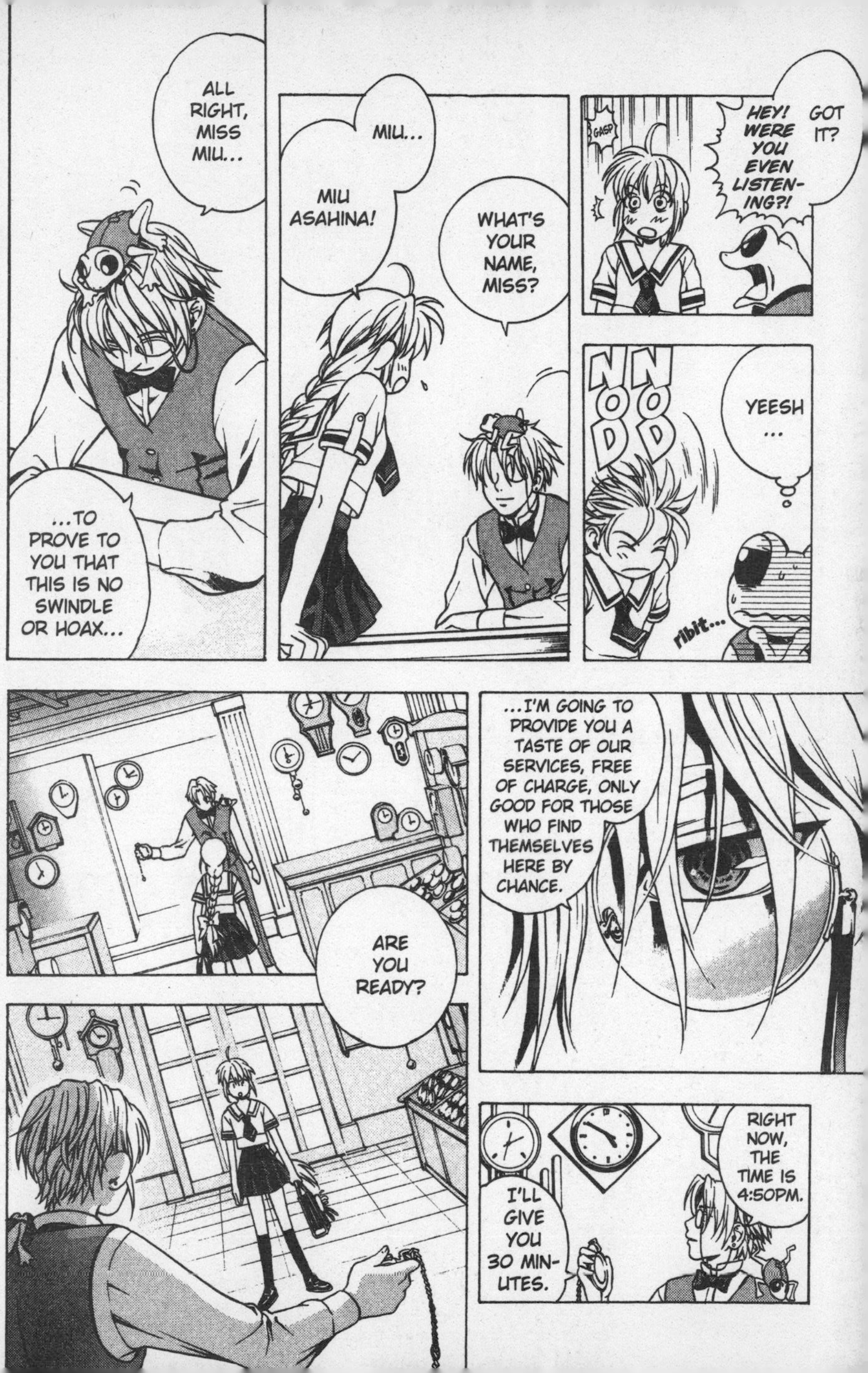
GOT IT?
HEY! WERE YOU EVEN LISTENING?!
GASP
YEESH ...
NOD NOD
ribit...
WHAT'S YOUR NAME, MISS?
MIU...
MIU ASAHINA!
ALL RIGHT, MISS MIU...
...TO PROVE TO YOU THAT THIS IS NO SWINDLE OR HOAX...
...I'M GOING TO PROVIDE YOU A TASTE OF OUR SERVICES, FREE OF CHARGE, ONLY GOOD FOR THOSE WHO FIND THEMSELVES HERE BY CHANCE.
ARE YOU READY?
RIGHT NOW, THE TIME IS 4:50PM.
I'LL GIVE YOU 30 MIN-UTES.

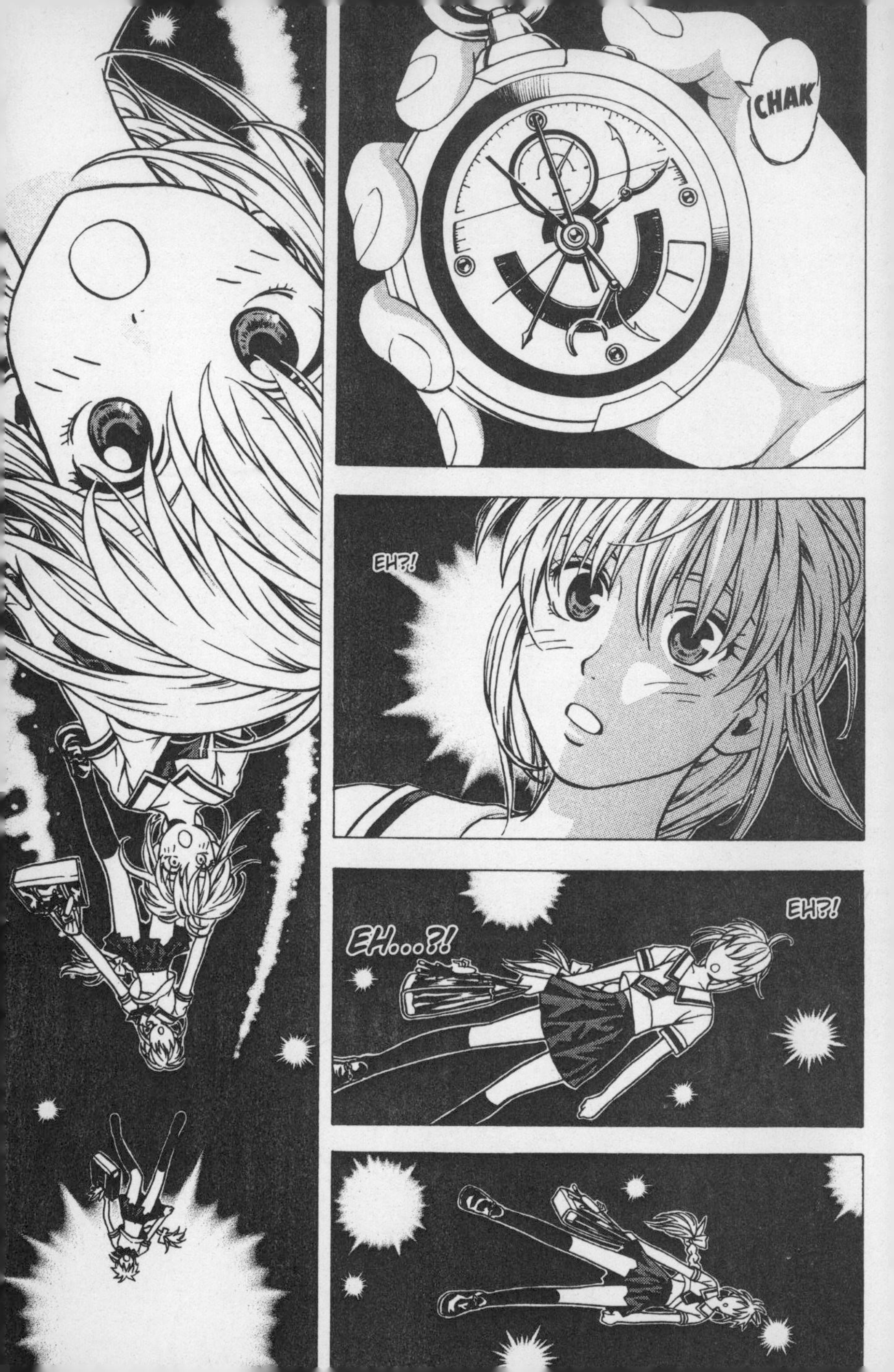
CHAK
EH?!
EH?!
EH...?!

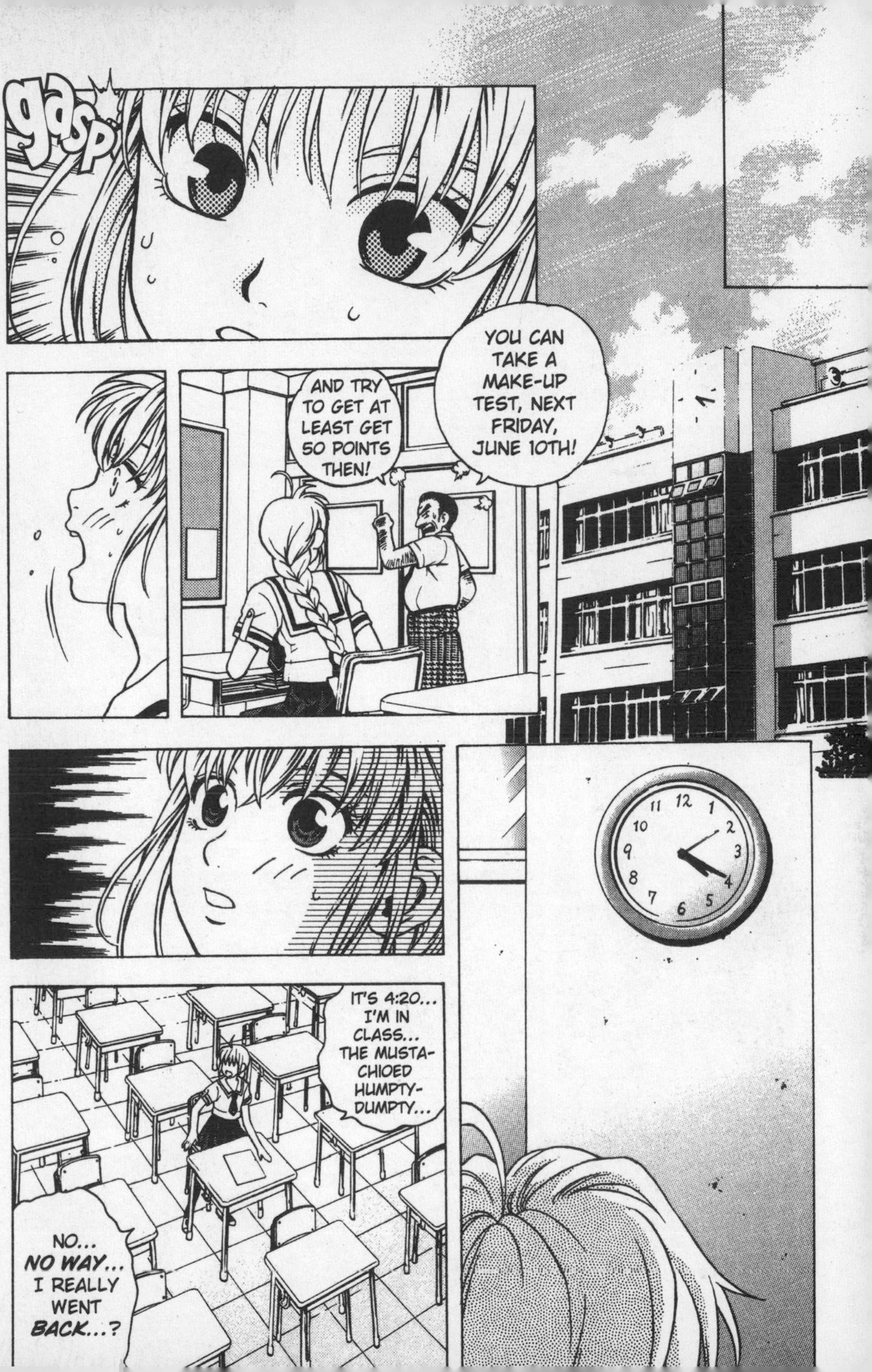
gasp
YOU CAN TAKE A MAKE-UP TEST, NEXT FRIDAY, JUNE 10TH!
AND TRY TO GET AT LEAST GET 50 POINTS THEN!
11 12 1 2 3 4 5 6 7 8 9 10
IT'S 4:20... I'M IN CLASS... THE MUSTA-CHIOED HUMPTY-DUMPTY...
NO... *NO WAY*... I REALLY WENT *BACK*...?

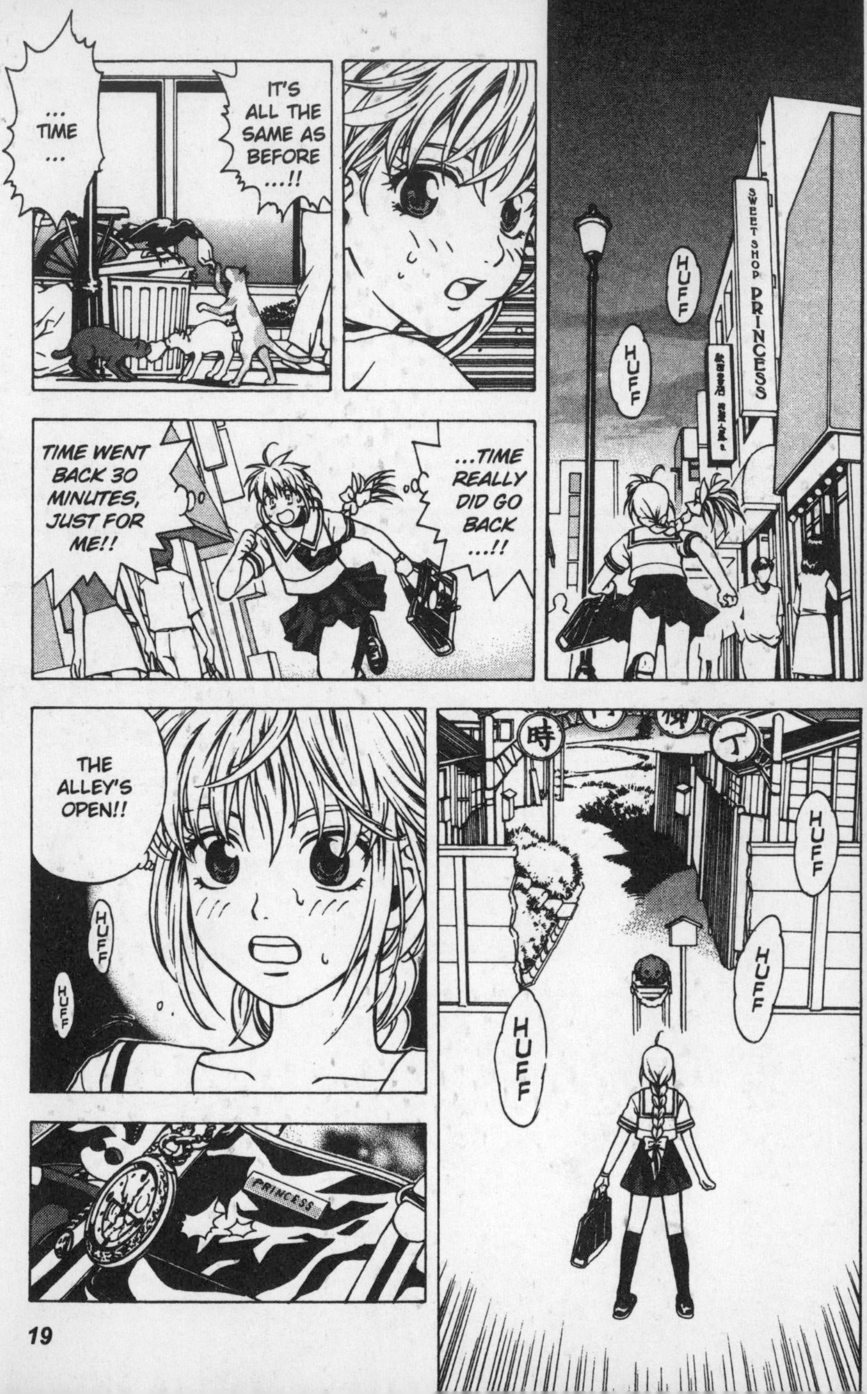

SWEET SHOP PRINCESS
HUFF
HUFF
IT'S ALL THE SAME AS BEFORE ...!!
... TIME ...
...TIME REALLY DID GO BACK ...!!
TIME WENT BACK 30 MINUTES, JUST FOR ME!!
HUFF
HUFF
HUFF
THE ALLEY'S OPEN!!
HUFF
HUFF
PRINCESS

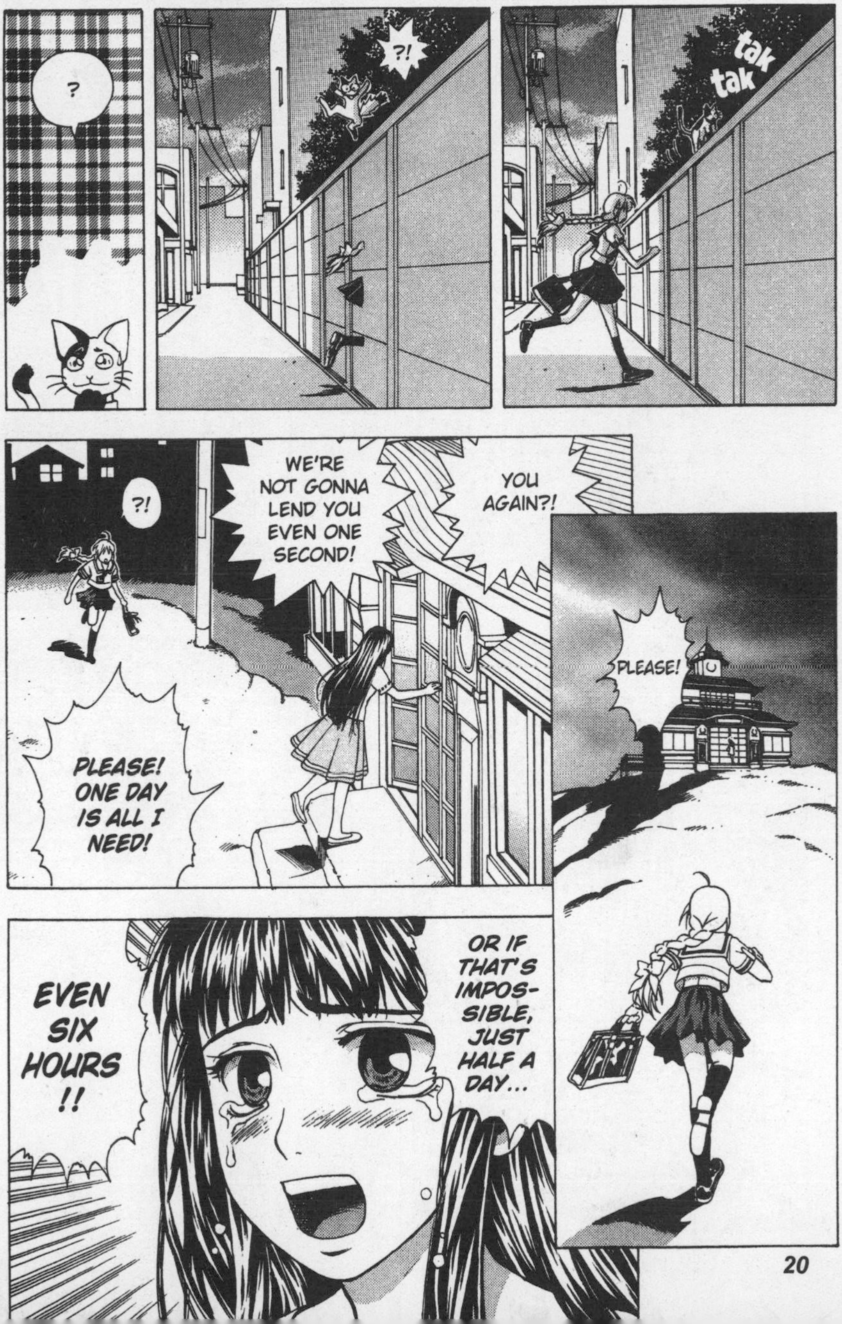
tak
tak
?!
?
PLEASE!
YOU AGAIN?!
WE'RE NOT GONNA LEND YOU EVEN ONE SECOND!
?!
PLEASE! ONE DAY IS ALL I NEED!
OR IF THAT'S IMPOS-SIBLE, JUST HALF A DAY...
EVEN SIX HOURS !!

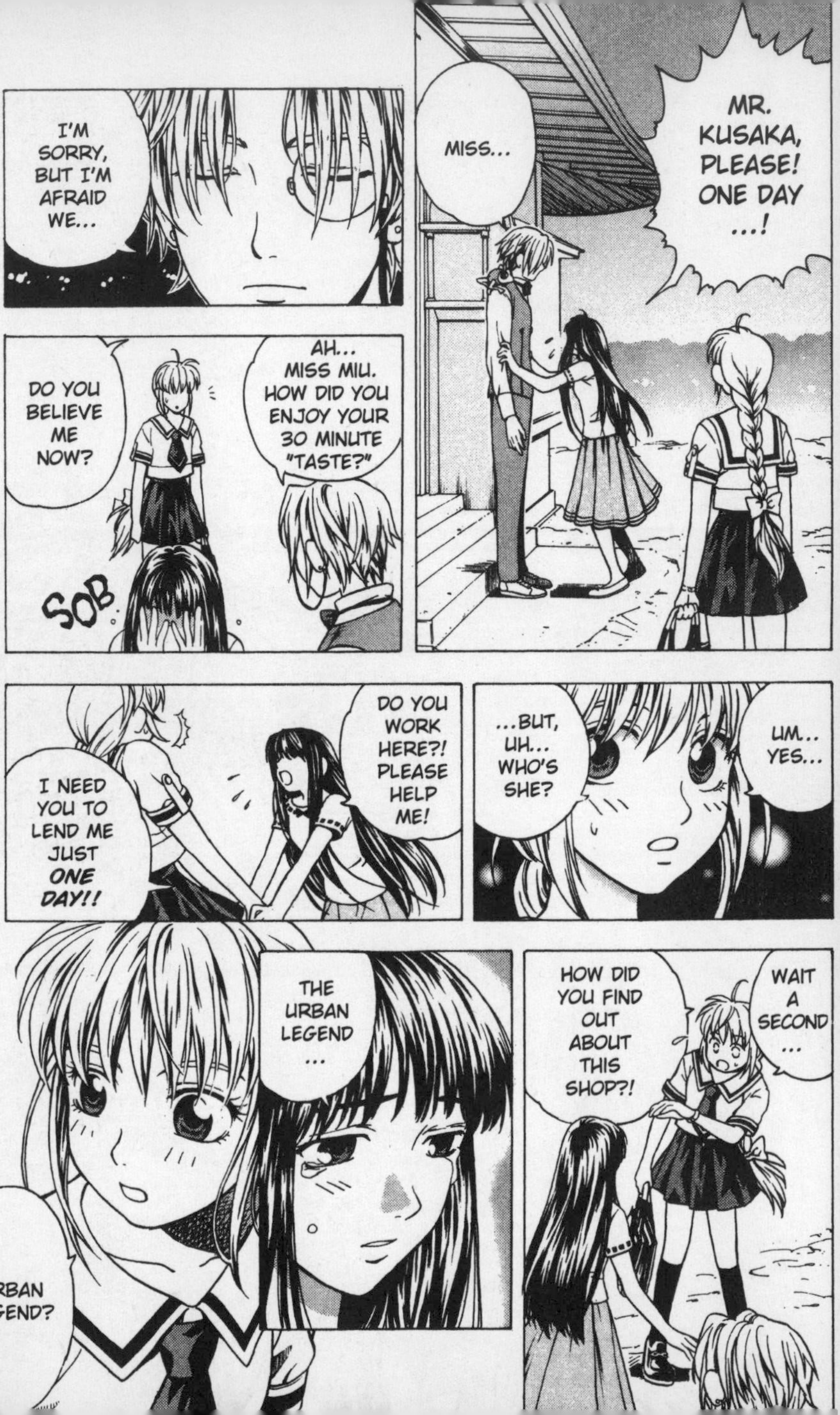
MR. KUSAKA, PLEASE! ONE DAY ...!
MISS...
I'M SORRY, BUT I'M AFRAID WE...
AH... MISS MIU. HOW DID YOU ENJOY YOUR 30 MINUTE "TASTE?"
DO YOU BELIEVE ME NOW?
SOB
UM... YES...
...BUT, UH... WHO'S SHE?
DO YOU WORK HERE?! PLEASE HELP ME!
I NEED YOU TO LEND ME JUST ONE DAY!!
WAIT A SECOND ...
HOW DID YOU FIND OUT ABOUT THIS SHOP?!
THE URBAN LEGEND ...
URBAN LEGEND?

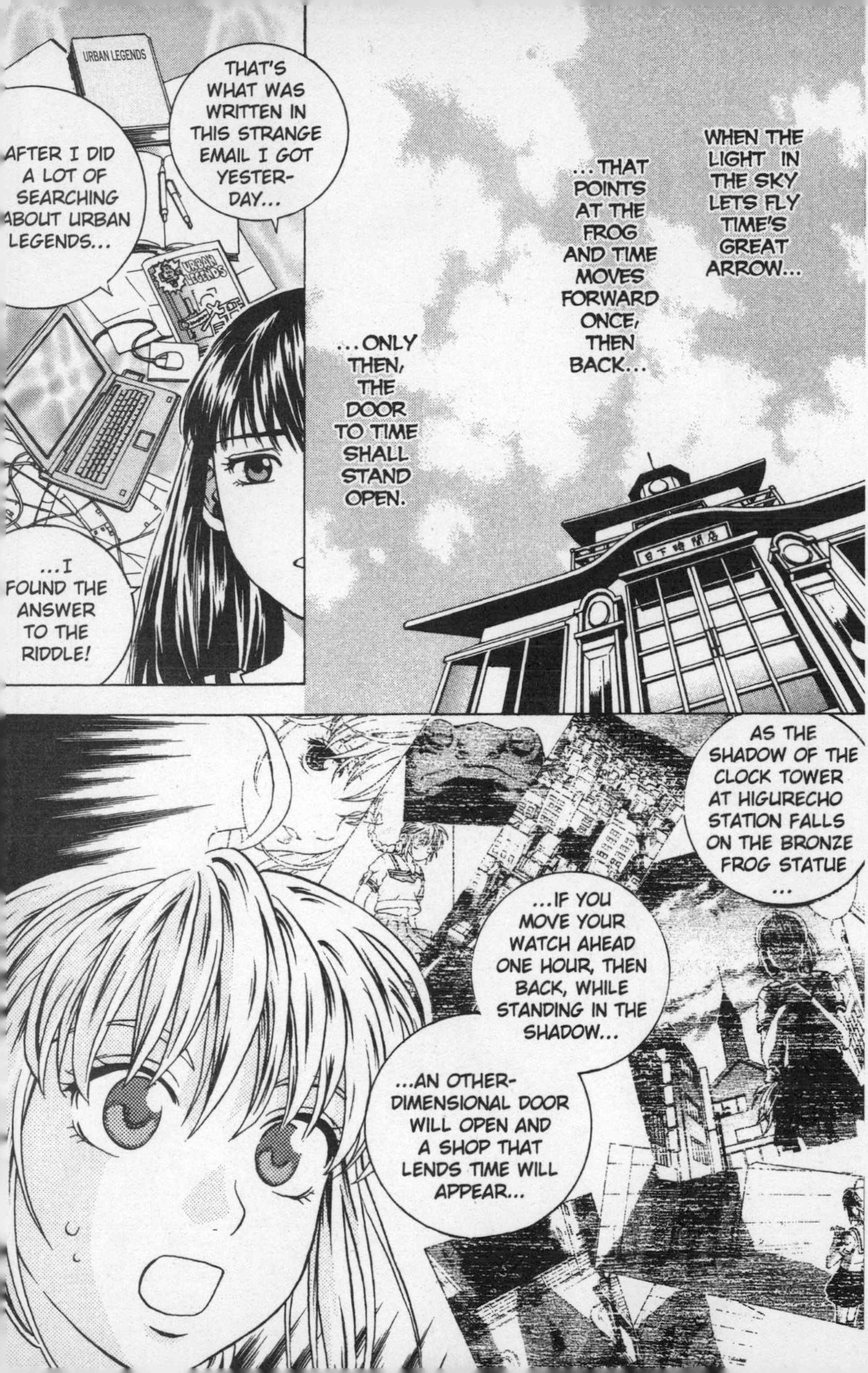
WHEN THE LIGHT IN THE SKY LETS FLY TIME'S GREAT ARROW...
...THAT POINTS AT THE FROG AND TIME MOVES FORWARD ONCE, THEN BACK...
...ONLY THEN, THE DOOR TO TIME SHALL STAND OPEN.
URBAN LEGENDS
THAT'S WHAT WAS WRITTEN IN THIS STRANGE EMAIL I GOT YESTER-DAY...
AFTER I DID A LOT OF SEARCHING ABOUT URBAN LEGENDS...
URBAN LEGENDS
...I FOUND THE ANSWER TO THE RIDDLE!
AS THE SHADOW OF THE CLOCK TOWER AT HIGURECHO STATION FALLS ON THE BRONZE FROG STATUE ...
...IF YOU MOVE YOUR WATCH AHEAD ONE HOUR, THEN BACK, WHILE STANDING IN THE SHADOW...
...AN OTHER-DIMENSIONAL DOOR WILL OPEN AND A SHOP THAT LENDS TIME WILL APPEAR...

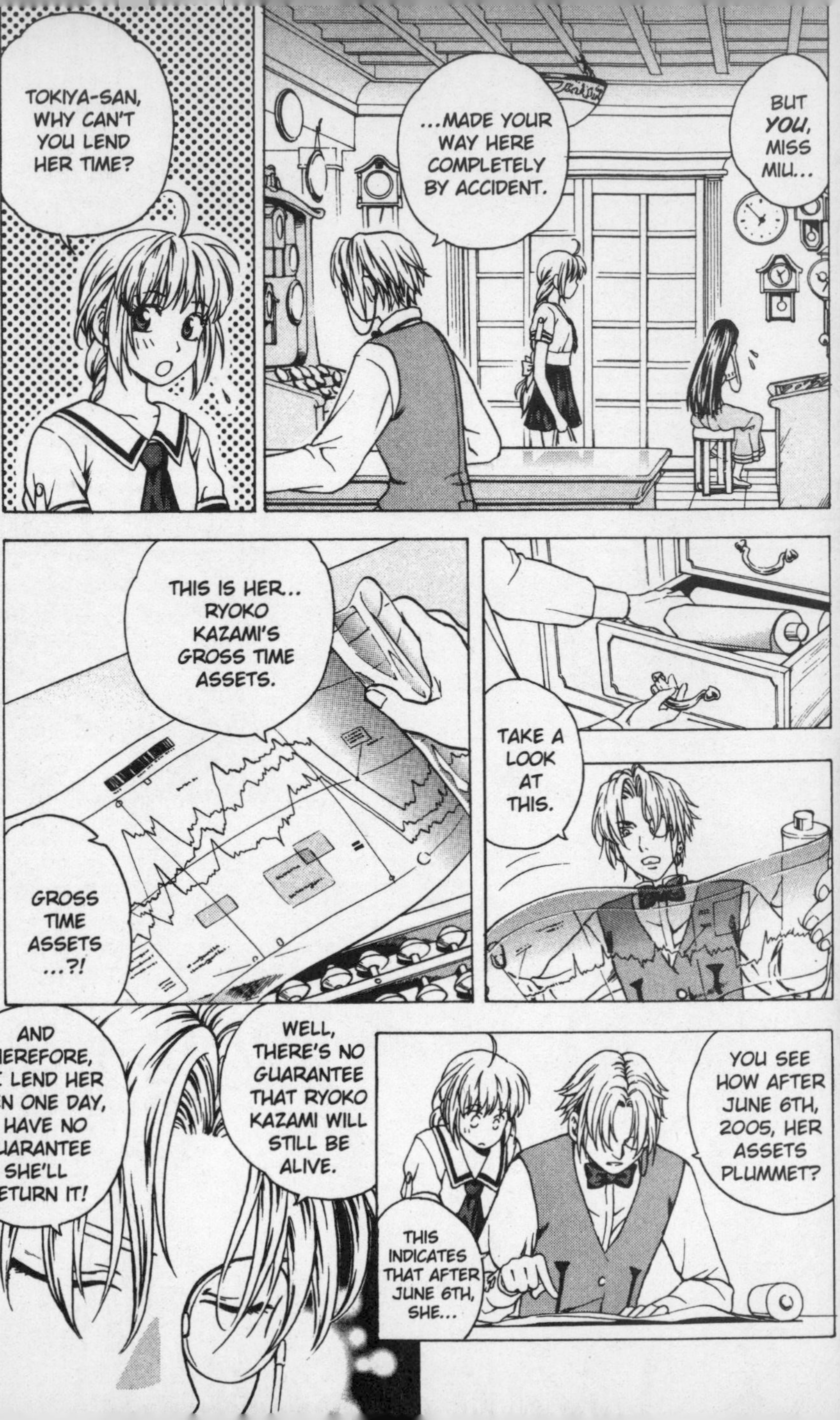
BUT *YOU*, MISS MIU...
...MADE YOUR WAY HERE COMPLETELY BY ACCIDENT.
TOKIYA-SAN, WHY CAN'T YOU LEND HER TIME?
TAKE A LOOK AT THIS.
THIS IS HER... RYOKO KAZAMI'S GROSS TIME ASSETS.
GROSS TIME ASSETS ...?!
YOU SEE HOW AFTER JUNE 6TH, 2005, HER ASSETS PLUMMET?
THIS INDICATES THAT AFTER JUNE 6TH, SHE...
WELL, THERE'S NO GUARANTEE THAT RYOKO KAZAMI WILL STILL BE ALIVE.
AND THEREFORE, IF I LEND HER EVEN ONE DAY, I HAVE NO GUARANTEE SHE'LL RETURN IT!

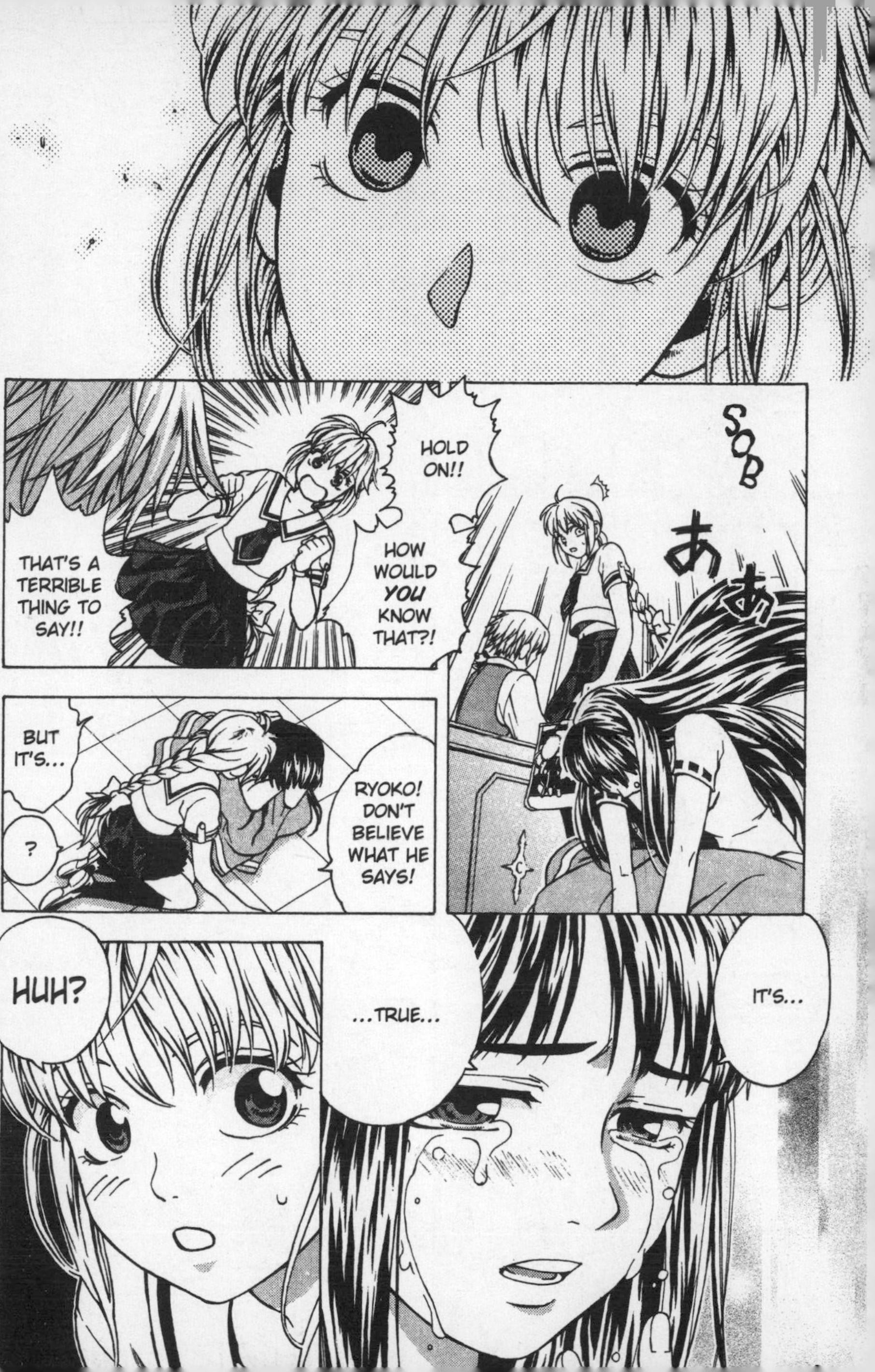
SOB
あぁ
HOLD ON!!
HOW WOULD *YOU* KNOW THAT?!
THAT'S A TERRIBLE THING TO SAY!!
RYOKO! DON'T BELIEVE WHAT HE SAYS!
BUT IT'S...
?
IT'S...
...TRUE...
HUH?

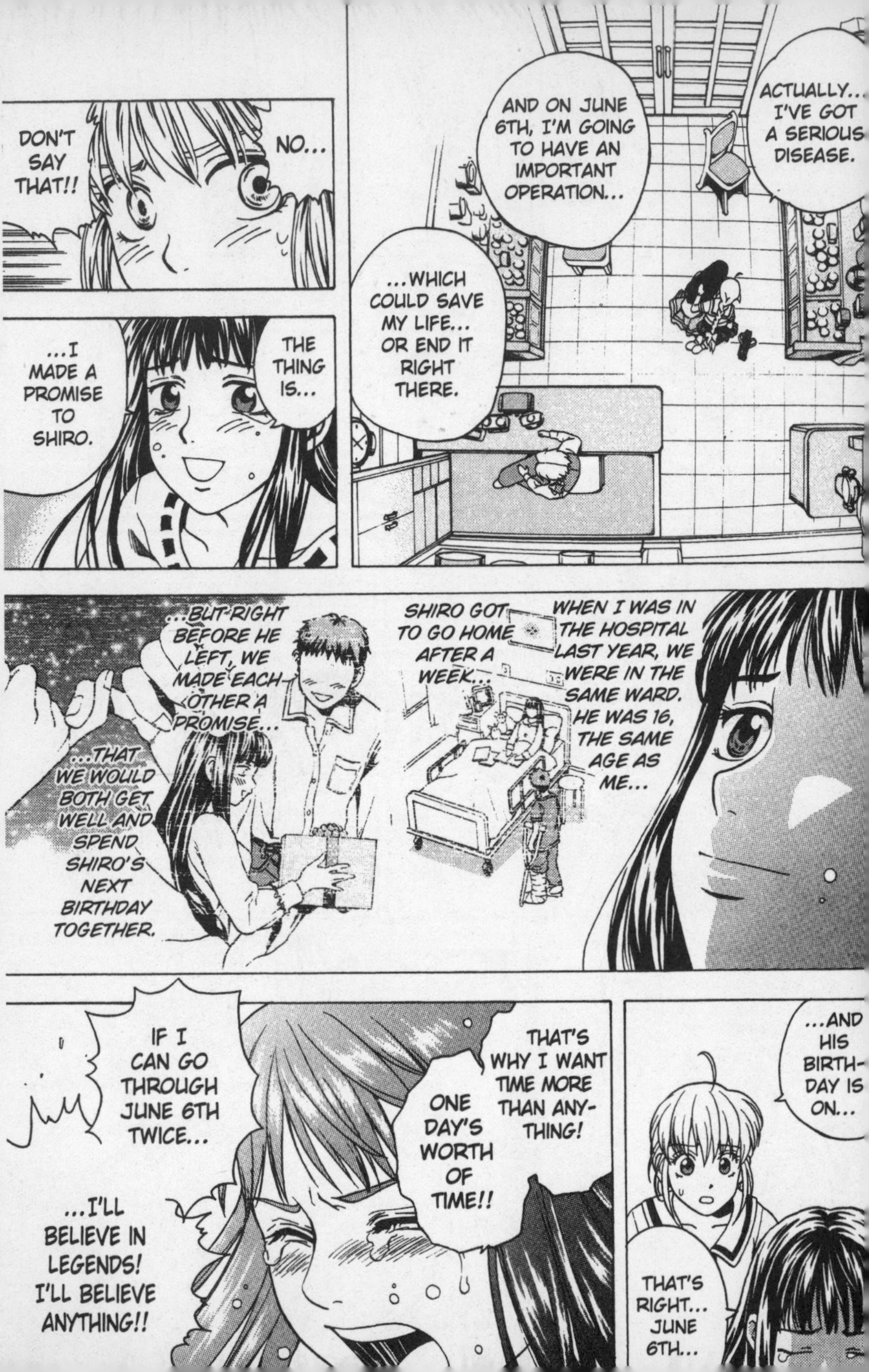
ACTUALLY... I'VE GOT A SERIOUS DISEASE.
AND ON JUNE 6TH, I'M GOING TO HAVE AN IMPORTANT OPERATION...
...WHICH COULD SAVE MY LIFE... OR END IT RIGHT THERE.
NO...
DON'T SAY THAT!!
THE THING IS...
...I MADE A PROMISE TO SHIRO.
WHEN I WAS IN THE HOSPITAL LAST YEAR, WE WERE IN THE SAME WARD. HE WAS 16, THE SAME AGE AS ME...
SHIRO GOT TO GO HOME AFTER A WEEK...
...BUT RIGHT BEFORE HE LEFT, WE MADE EACH OTHER A PROMISE...
...THAT WE WOULD BOTH GET WELL AND SPEND SHIRO'S NEXT BIRTHDAY TOGETHER.
...AND HIS BIRTH-DAY IS ON...
THAT'S RIGHT... JUNE 6TH...
THAT'S WHY I WANT TIME MORE THAN ANY-THING!
ONE DAY'S WORTH OF TIME!!
IF I CAN GO THROUGH JUNE 6TH TWICE...
...I'LL BELIEVE IN LEGENDS! I'LL BELIEVE ANYTHING!!

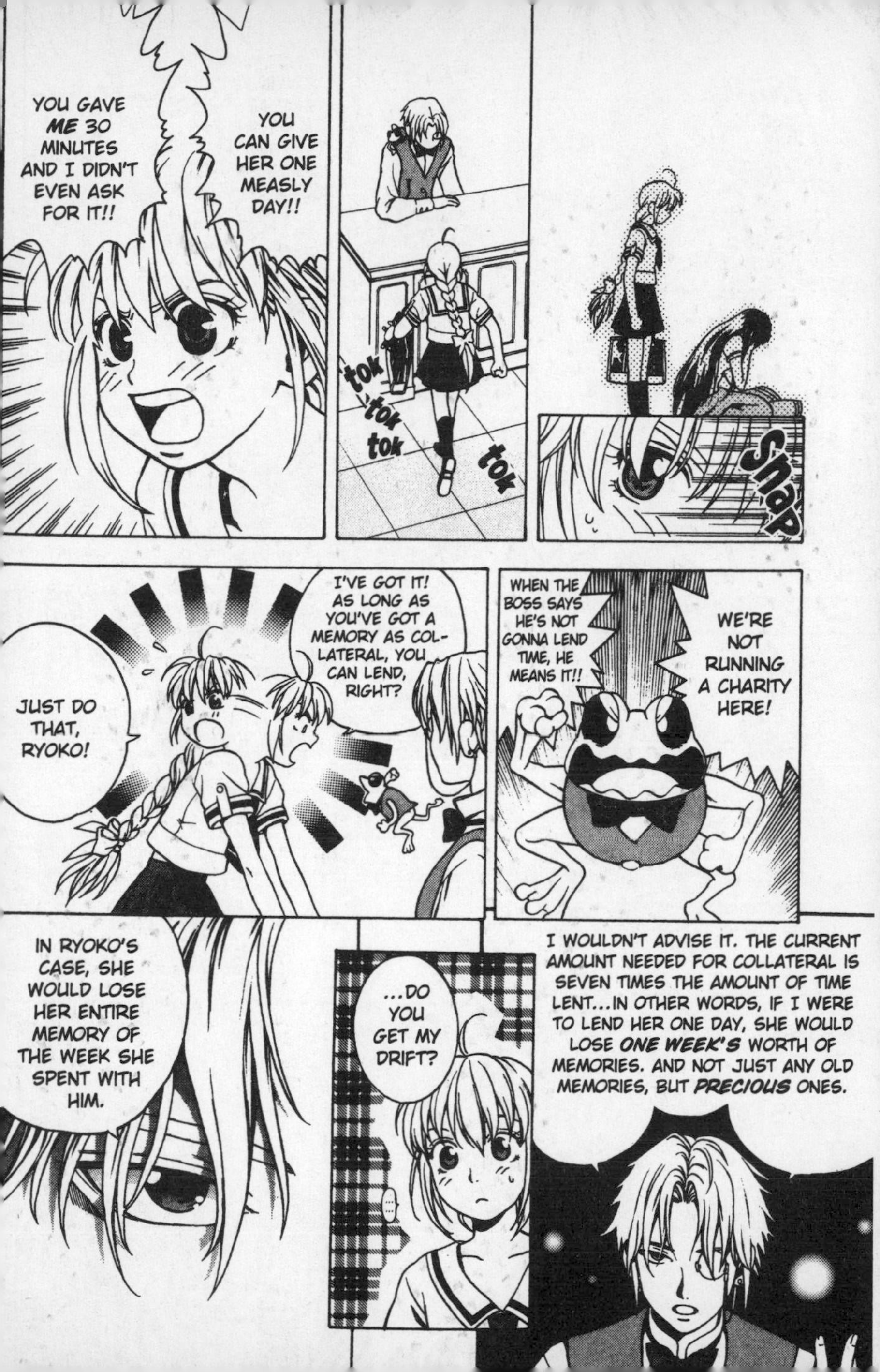
SNAP
TOK
TOK
TOK
TOK
YOU GAVE *ME* 30 MINUTES AND I DIDN'T EVEN ASK FOR IT!!
YOU CAN GIVE HER ONE MEASLY DAY!!
WE'RE NOT RUNNING A CHARITY HERE!
WHEN THE BOSS SAYS HE'S NOT GONNA LEND TIME, HE MEANS IT!!
I'VE GOT IT! AS LONG AS YOU'VE GOT A MEMORY AS COL-LATERAL, YOU CAN LEND, RIGHT?
JUST DO THAT, RYOKO!
I WOULDN'T ADVISE IT. THE CURRENT AMOUNT NEEDED FOR COLLATERAL IS SEVEN TIMES THE AMOUNT OF TIME LENT...IN OTHER WORDS, IF I WERE TO LEND HER ONE DAY, SHE WOULD LOSE *ONE WEEK'S* WORTH OF MEMORIES. AND NOT JUST ANY OLD MEMORIES, BUT *PRECIOUS* ONES.
...DO YOU GET MY DRIFT?
....
IN RYOKO'S CASE, SHE WOULD LOSE HER ENTIRE MEMORY OF THE WEEK SHE SPENT WITH HIM.

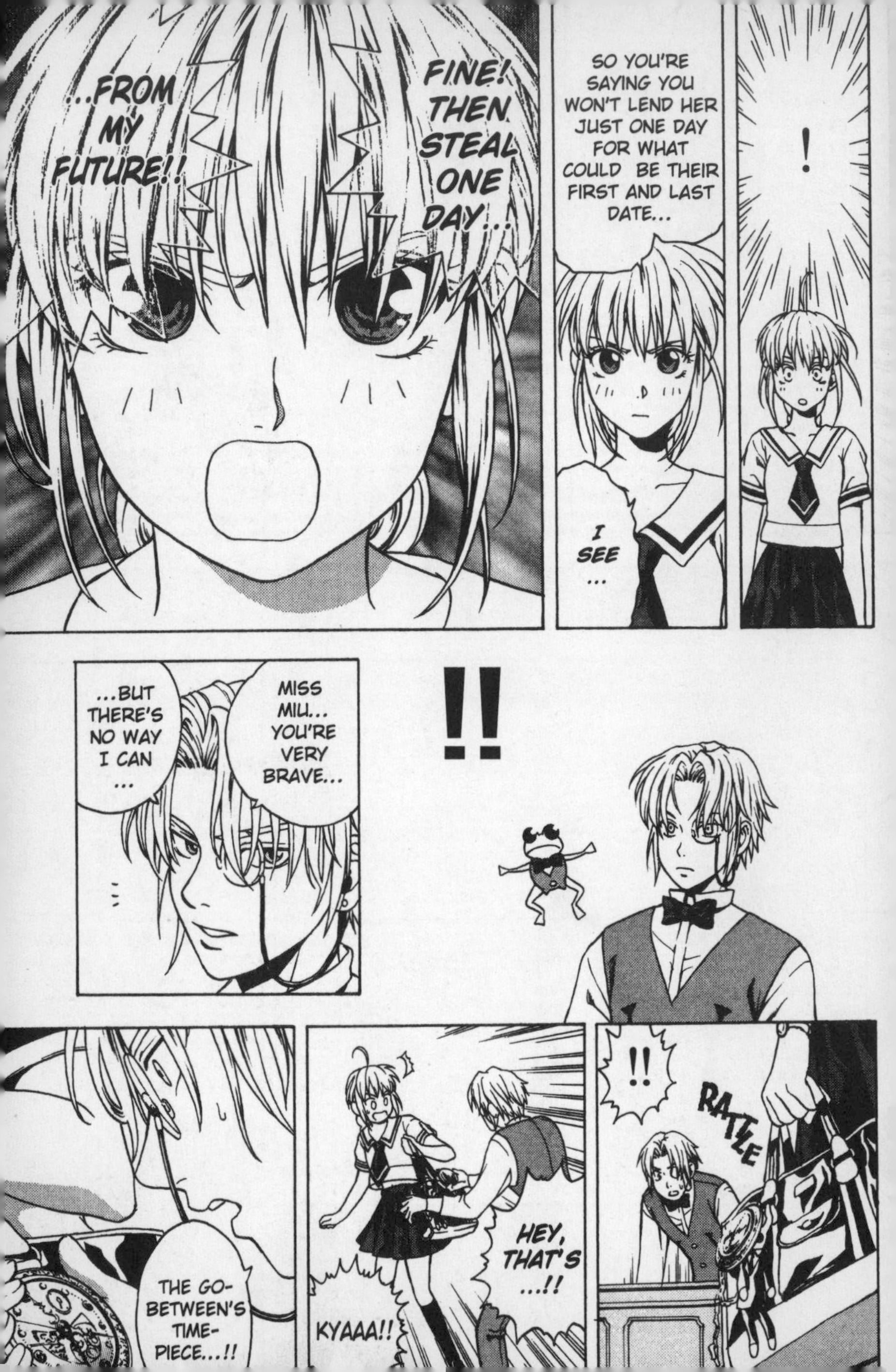
!
SO YOU'RE SAYING YOU WON'T LEND HER JUST ONE DAY FOR WHAT COULD BE THEIR FIRST AND LAST DATE...
I SEE ...
FINE! THEN STEAL ONE DAY...
...FROM MY FUTURE!!
!!
MISS MIU... YOU'RE VERY BRAVE...
...BUT THERE'S NO WAY I CAN ...
!!
RATTLE
HEY, THAT'S ...!!
KYAAA!!
THE GO-BETWEEN'S TIME-PIECE...!!

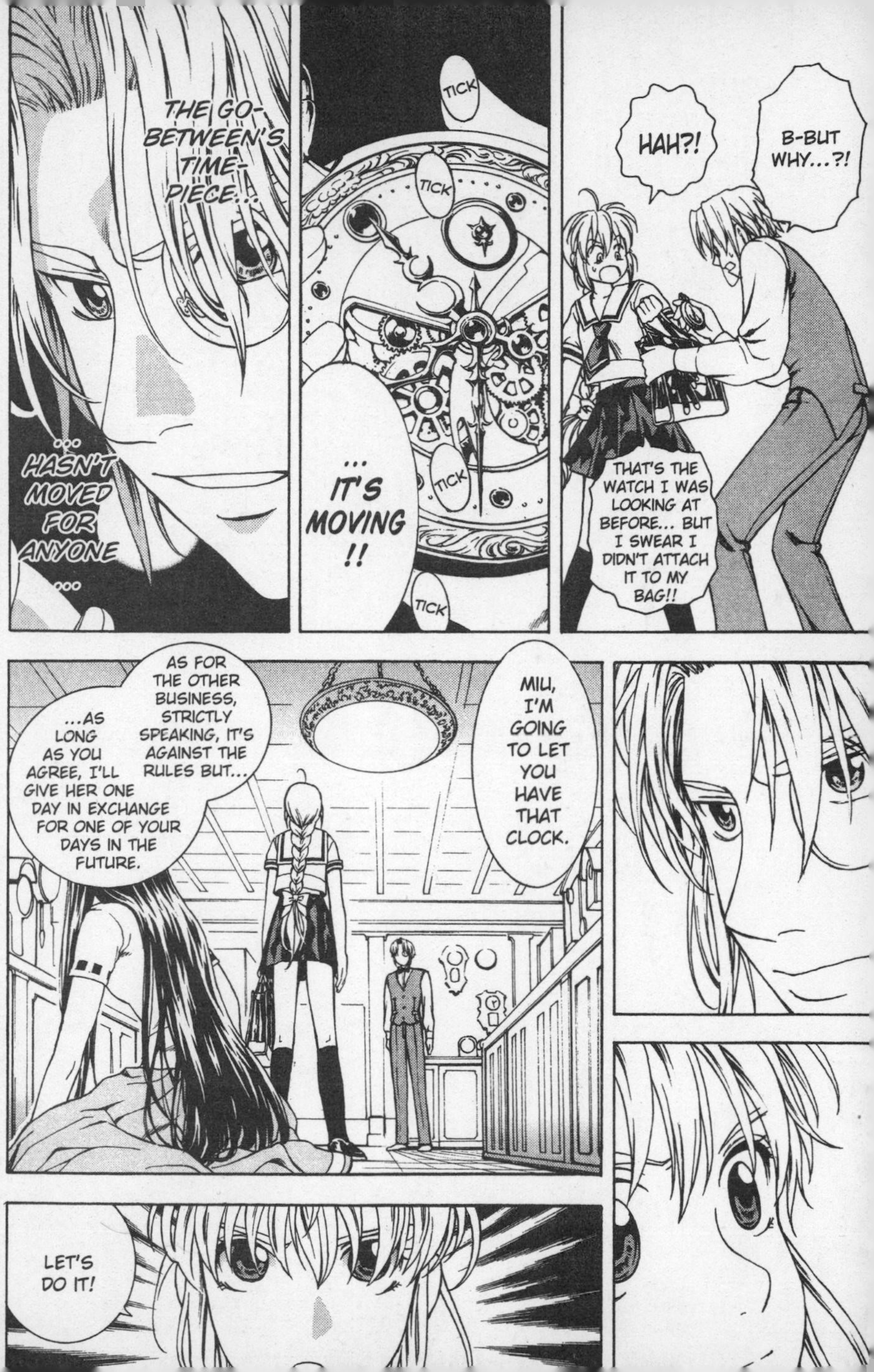
B-BUT WHY...?!
HAH?!
THAT'S THE WATCH I WAS LOOKING AT BEFORE... BUT I SWEAR I DIDN'T ATTACH IT TO MY BAG!!
TICK
TICK
... IT'S MOVING !!
TICK
TICK
THE GO-BETWEEN'S TIME-PIECE...
...HASN'T MOVED FOR ANYONE...
MIU, I'M GOING TO LET YOU HAVE THAT CLOCK.
AS FOR THE OTHER BUSINESS, STRICTLY SPEAKING, IT'S AGAINST THE RULES BUT...
...AS LONG AS YOU AGREE, I'LL GIVE HER ONE DAY IN EXCHANGE FOR ONE OF YOUR DAYS IN THE FUTURE.
LET'S DO IT!

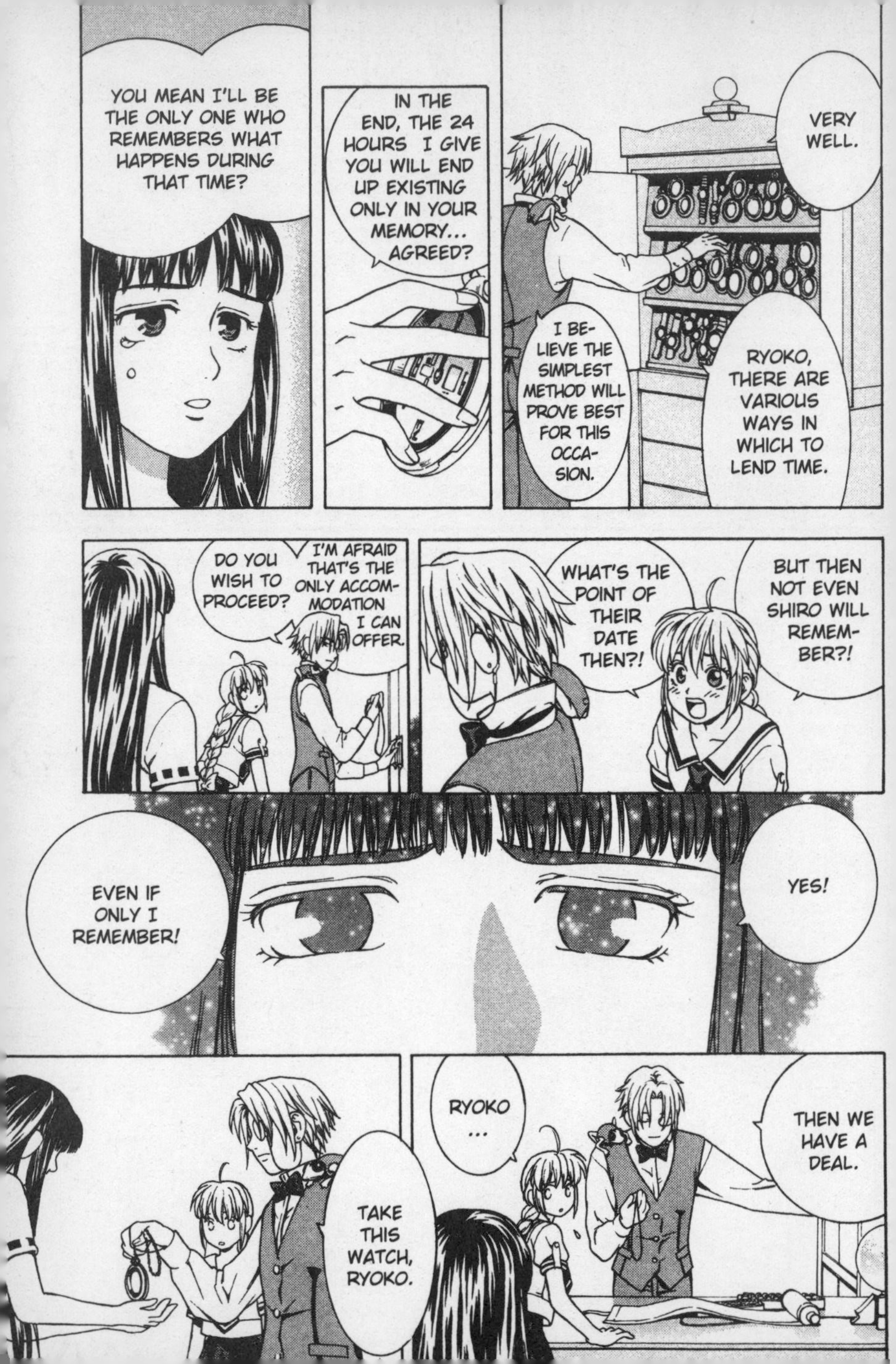
VERY WELL.
RYOKO, THERE ARE VARIOUS WAYS IN WHICH TO LEND TIME.
I BELIEVE THE SIMPLEST METHOD WILL PROVE BEST FOR THIS OCCASION.
IN THE END, THE 24 HOURS I GIVE YOU WILL END UP EXISTING ONLY IN YOUR MEMORY... AGREED?
YOU MEAN I'LL BE THE ONLY ONE WHO REMEMBERS WHAT HAPPENS DURING THAT TIME?
BUT THEN NOT EVEN SHIRO WILL REMEMBER?!
WHAT'S THE POINT OF THEIR DATE THEN?!
I'M AFRAID THAT'S THE ONLY ACCOMMODATION I CAN OFFER.
DO YOU WISH TO PROCEED?
YES!
EVEN IF ONLY I REMEMBER!
THEN WE HAVE A DEAL.
RYOKO ...
TAKE THIS WATCH, RYOKO.

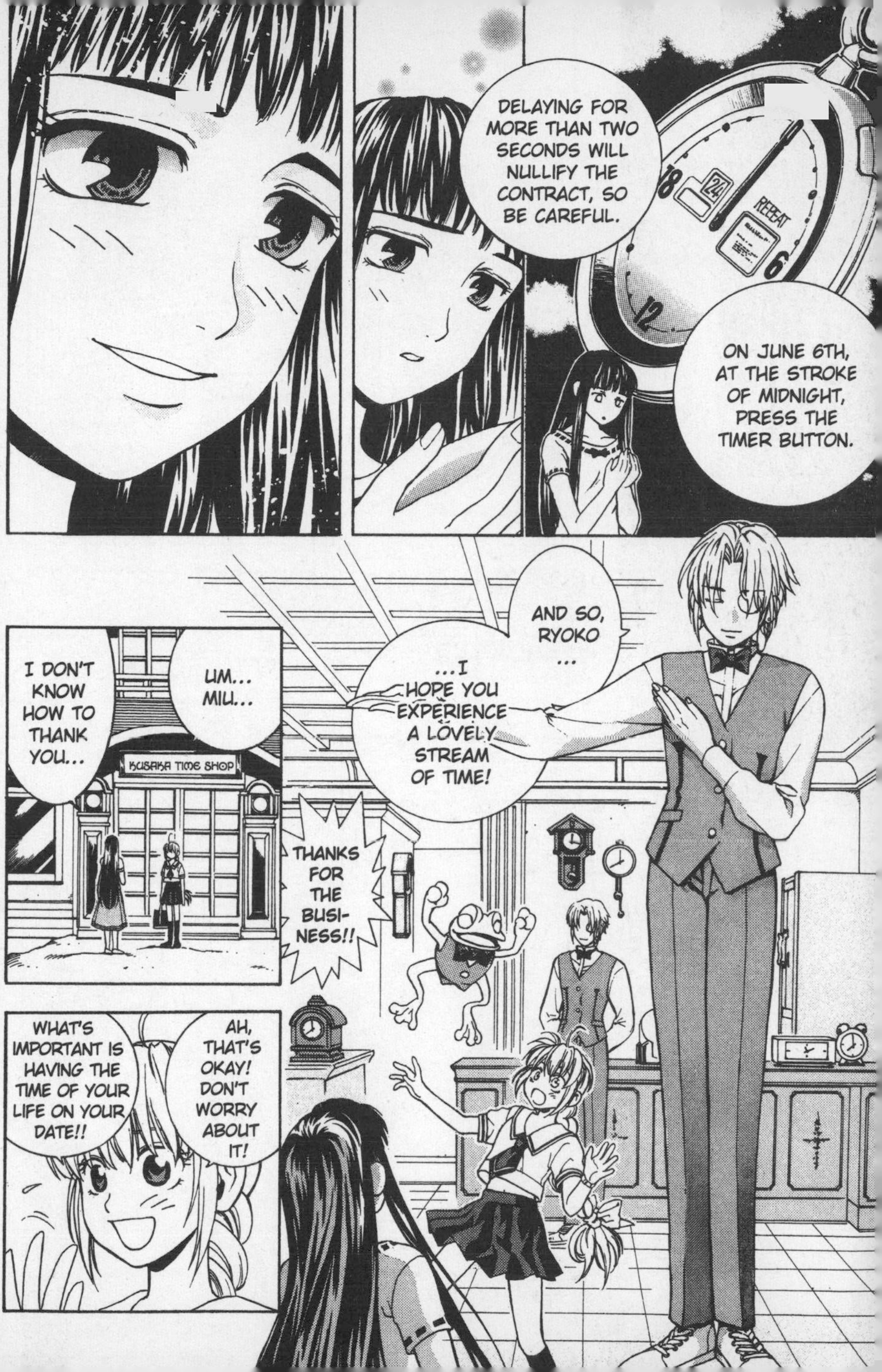
ON JUNE 6TH, AT THE STROKE OF MIDNIGHT, PRESS THE TIMER BUTTON.
DELAYING FOR MORE THAN TWO SECONDS WILL NULLIFY THE CONTRACT, SO BE CAREFUL.
AND SO, RYOKO...
...I HOPE YOU EXPERIENCE A LOVELY STREAM OF TIME!
THANKS FOR THE BUSINESS!!
UM... MIU...
I DON'T KNOW HOW TO THANK YOU...
KUSAKA TIME SHOP
AH, THAT'S OKAY! DON'T WORRY ABOUT IT!
WHAT'S IMPORTANT IS HAVING THE TIME OF YOUR LIFE ON YOUR DATE!!

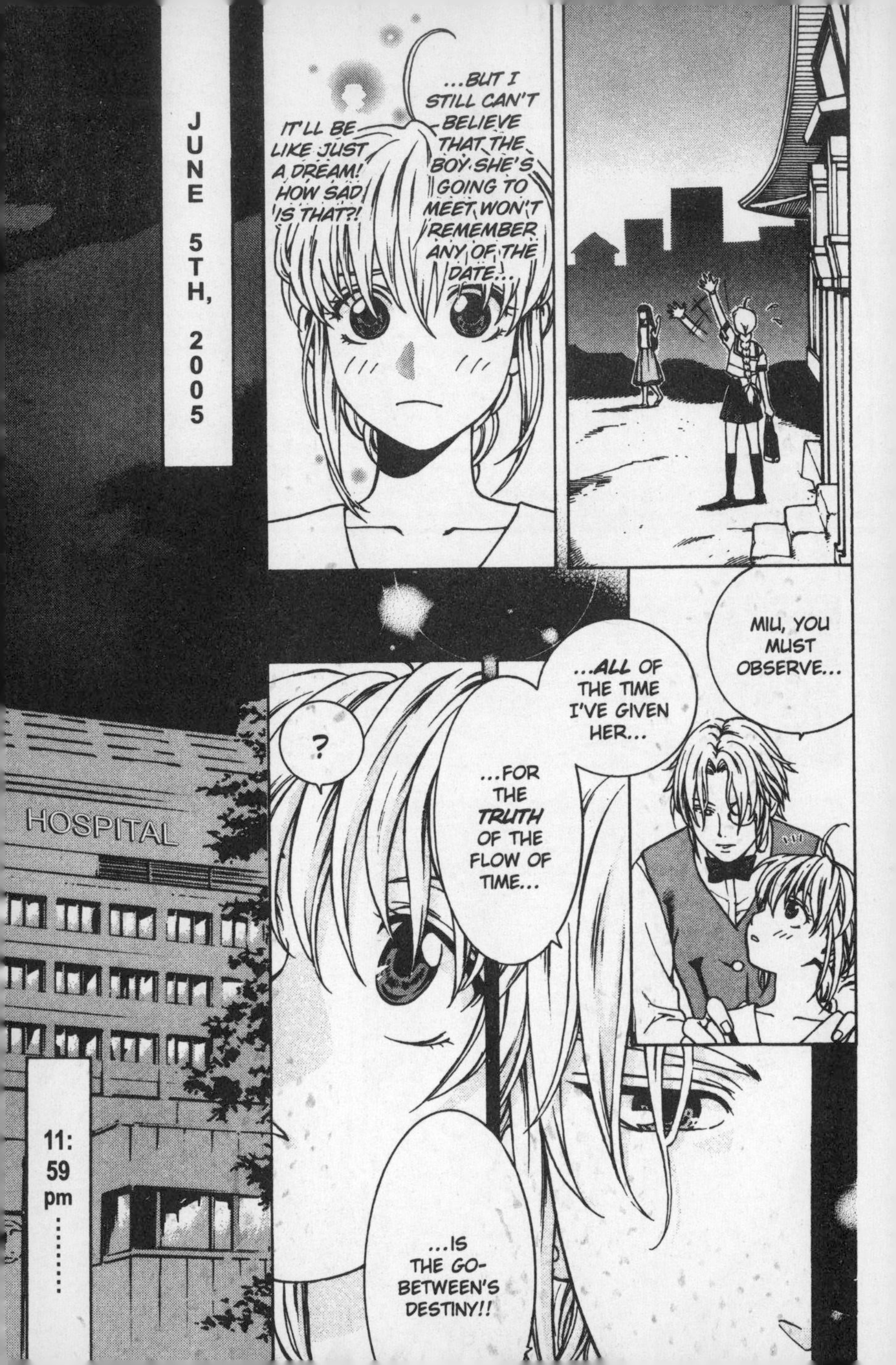

...BUT I STILL CAN'T BELIEVE THAT THE BOY SHE'S GOING TO MEET WON'T REMEMBER ANY OF THE DATE...
IT'LL BE LIKE JUST A DREAM! HOW SAD IS THAT?!
JUNE 5TH, 2005
MIU, YOU MUST OBSERVE...
...ALL OF THE TIME I'VE GIVEN HER...
...FOR THE TRUTH OF THE FLOW OF TIME...
?
...IS THE GO-BETWEEN'S DESTINY!!
HOSPITAL
11: 59 pm ....

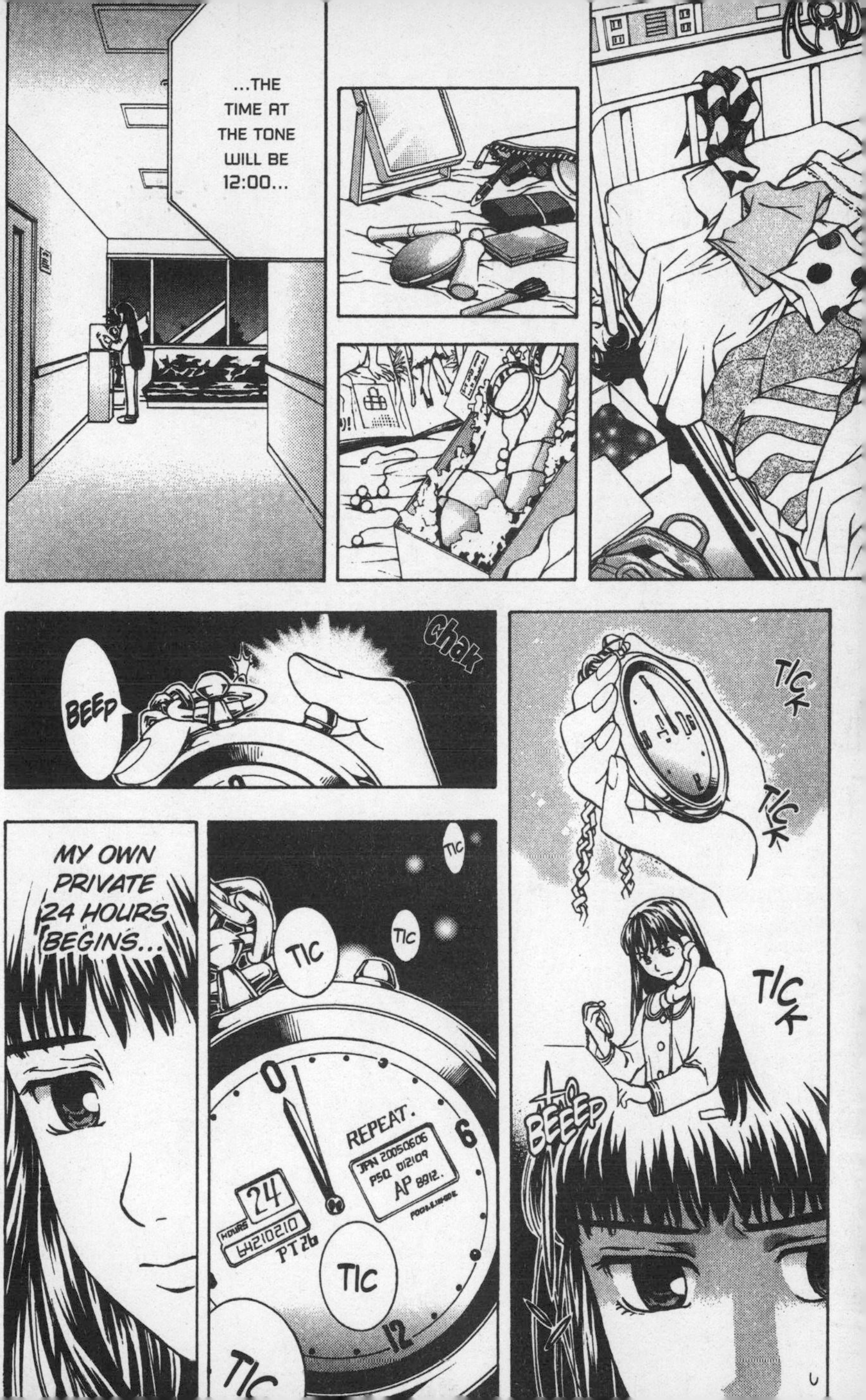
...THE TIME AT THE TONE WILL BE 12:00...
TICK
TICK
TICK
BEEEP
Chak
BEEP
TIC
TIC
TIC
REPEAT.
24
TIC
TIC
MY OWN PRIVATE 24 HOURS BEGINS...

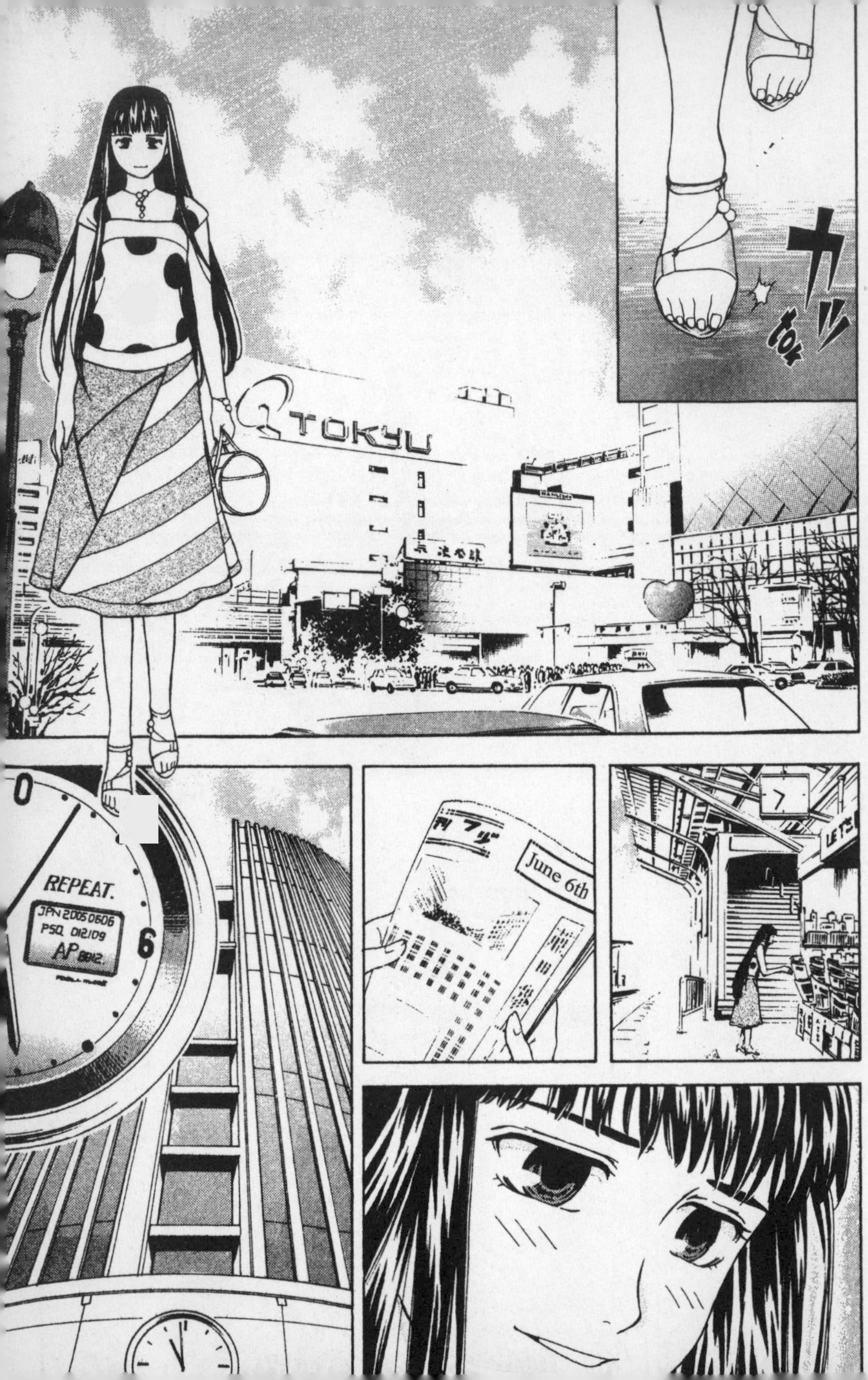
tok
TOKYU
June 6th
REPEAT.
JPN 20050606
PSQ 012109
AP 8812.

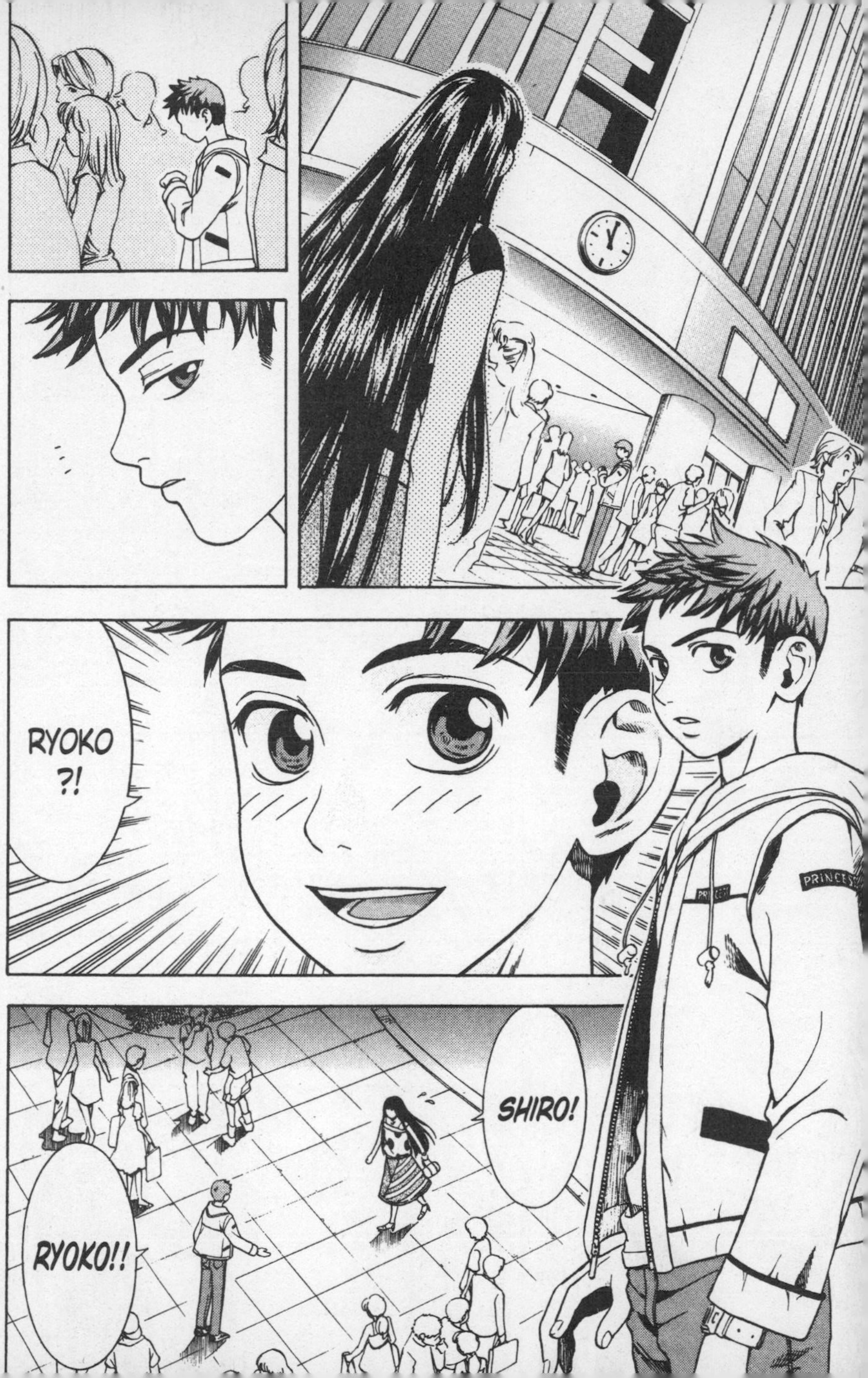
RYOKO ?!
SHIRO!
RYOKO!!

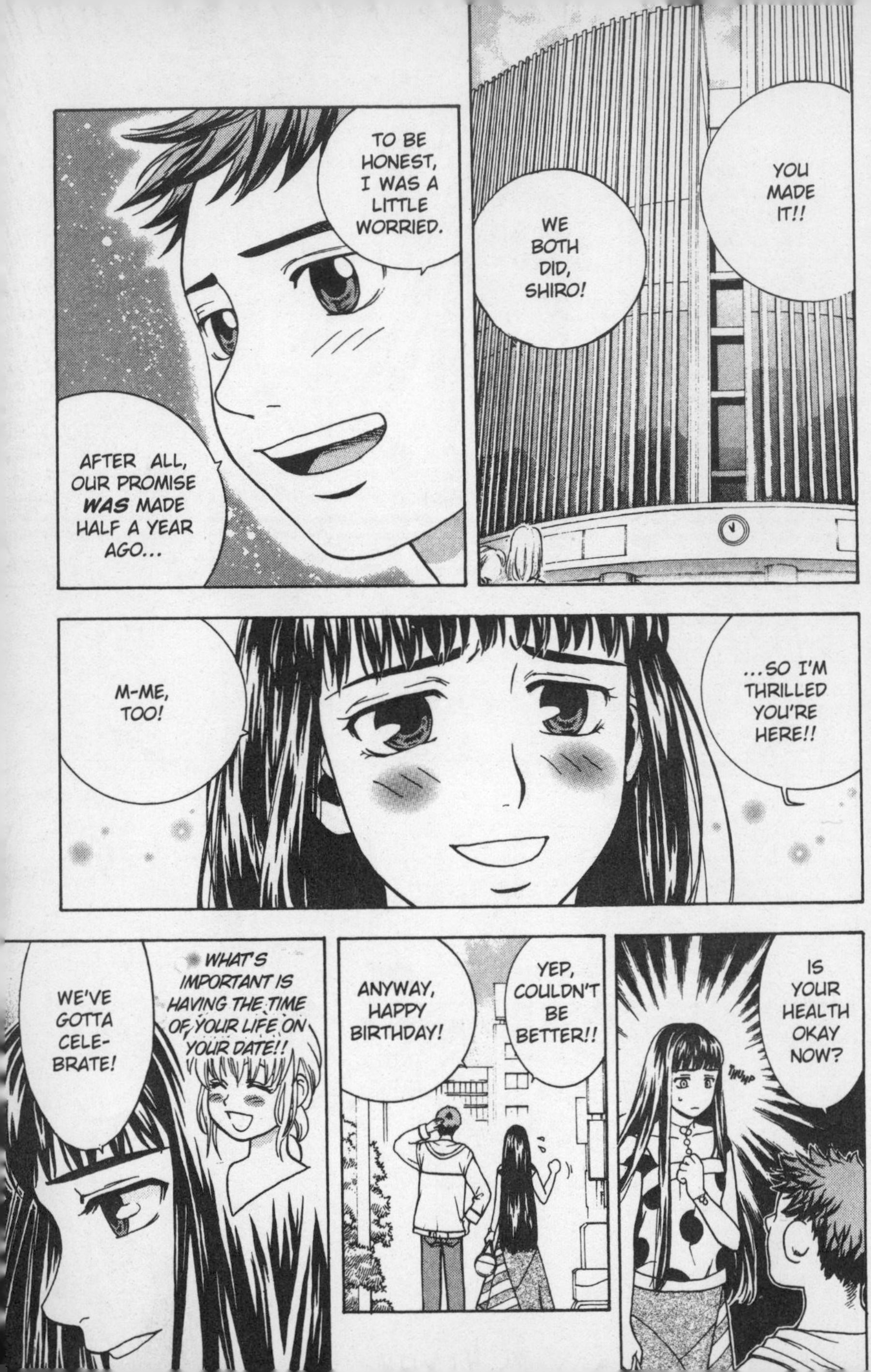
YOU MADE IT!!
WE BOTH DID, SHIRO!
TO BE HONEST, I WAS A LITTLE WORRIED.
AFTER ALL, OUR PROMISE WAS MADE HALF A YEAR AGO...
...SO I'M THRILLED YOU'RE HERE!!
M-ME, TOO!
IS YOUR HEALTH OKAY NOW?
THUMP
YEP, COULDN'T BE BETTER!!
ANYWAY, HAPPY BIRTHDAY!
WHAT'S IMPORTANT IS HAVING THE TIME OF YOUR LIFE ON YOUR DATE!!
WE'VE GOTTA CELE-BRATE!

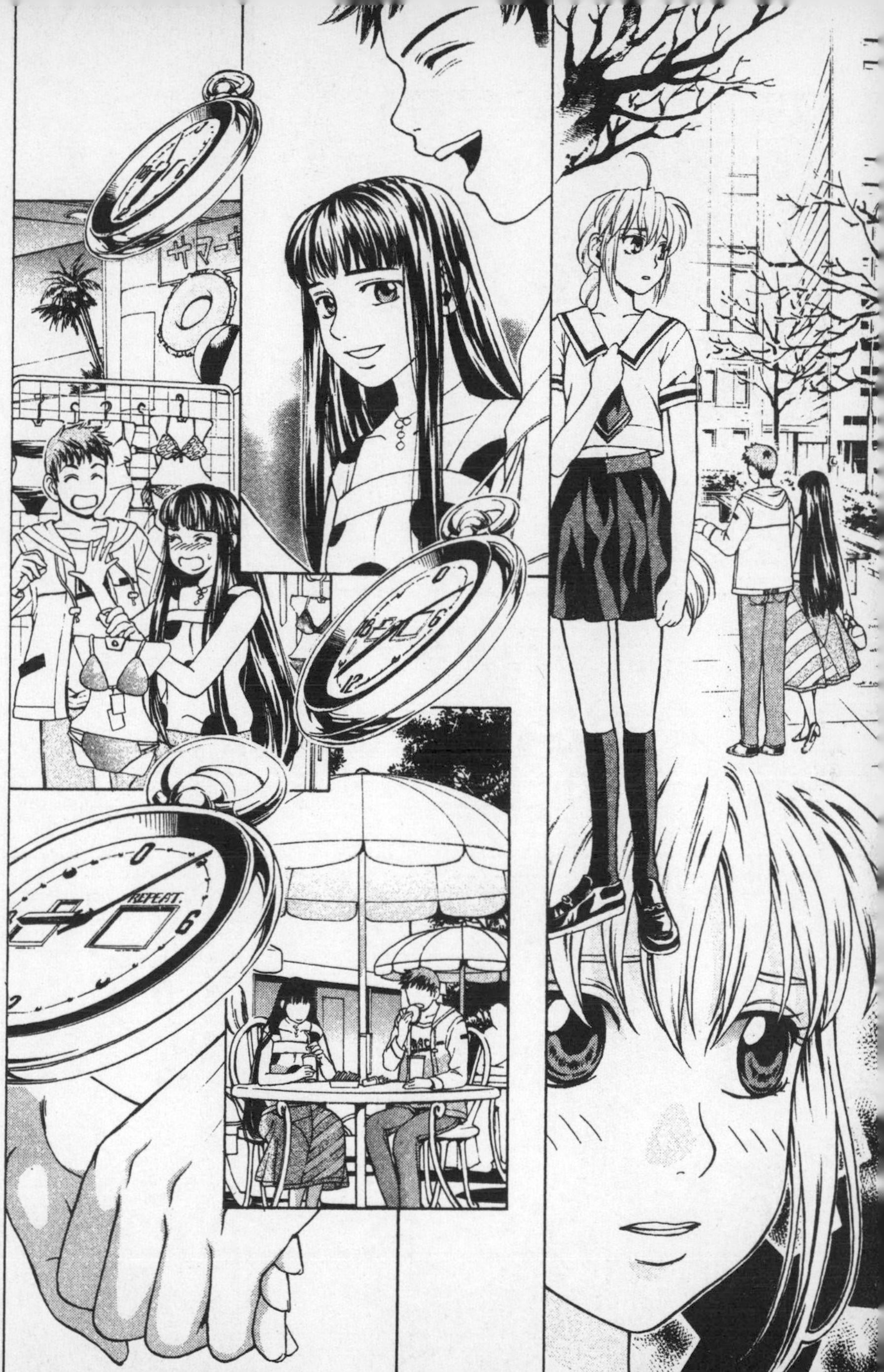
サマーセ
REPEAT.

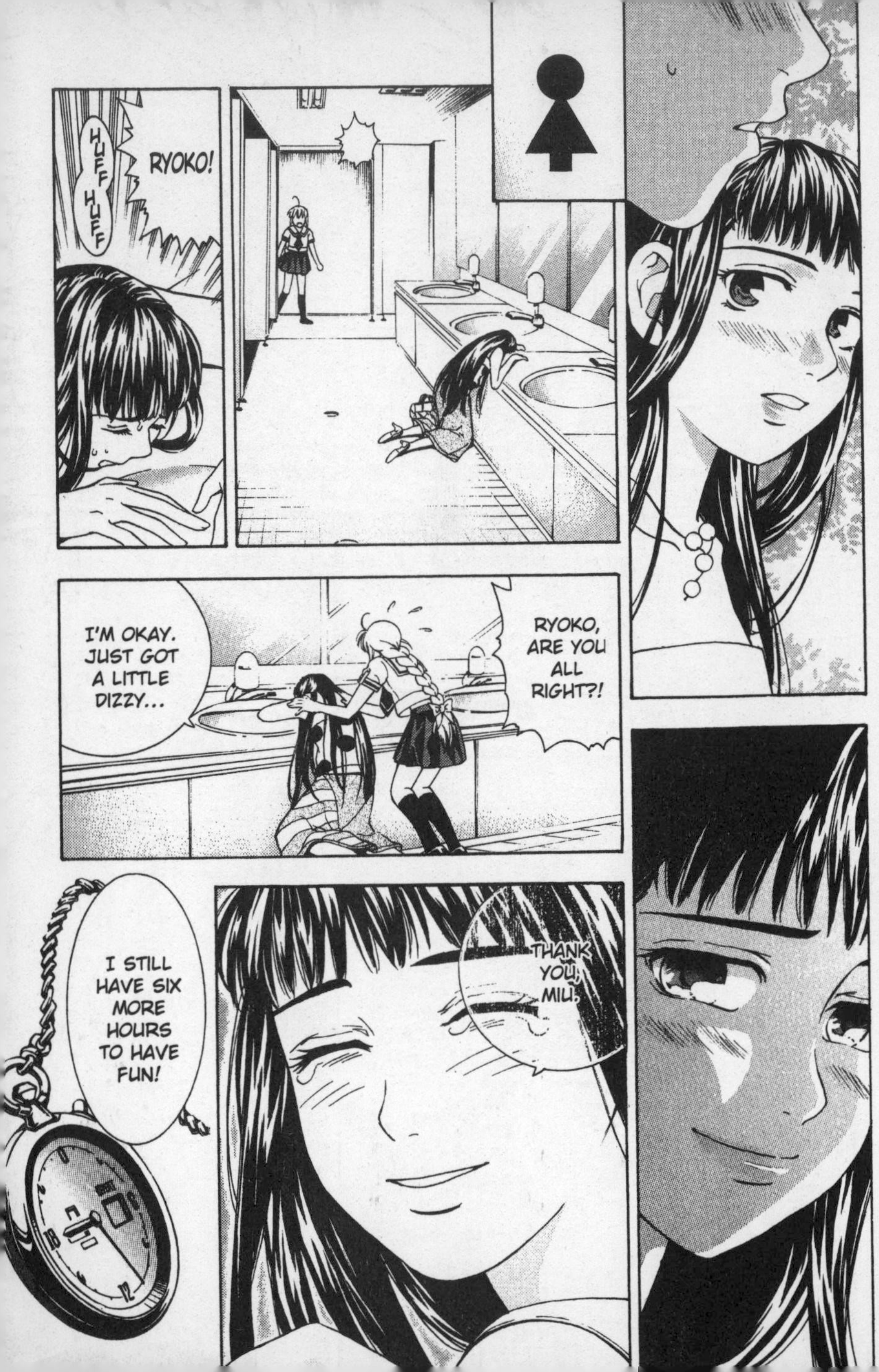
RYOKO!
HUFF HUFF
RYOKO, ARE YOU ALL RIGHT?!
I'M OKAY. JUST GOT A LITTLE DIZZY...
THANK YOU, MIU.
I STILL HAVE SIX MORE HOURS TO HAVE FUN!

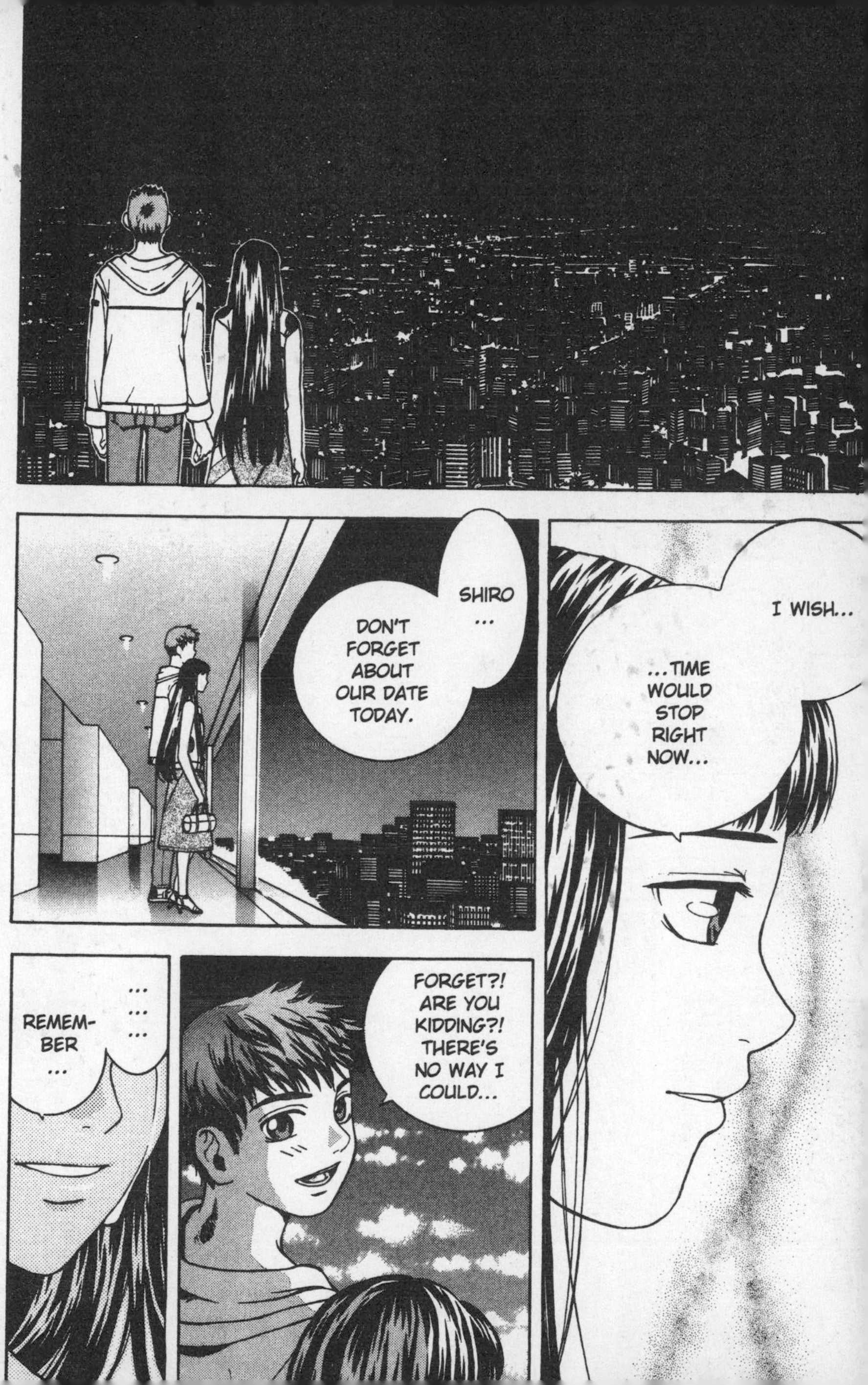
I WISH...
...TIME WOULD STOP RIGHT NOW...
SHIRO...
DON'T FORGET ABOUT OUR DATE TODAY.
FORGET?! ARE YOU KIDDING?! THERE'S NO WAY I COULD...
....
REMEMBER...

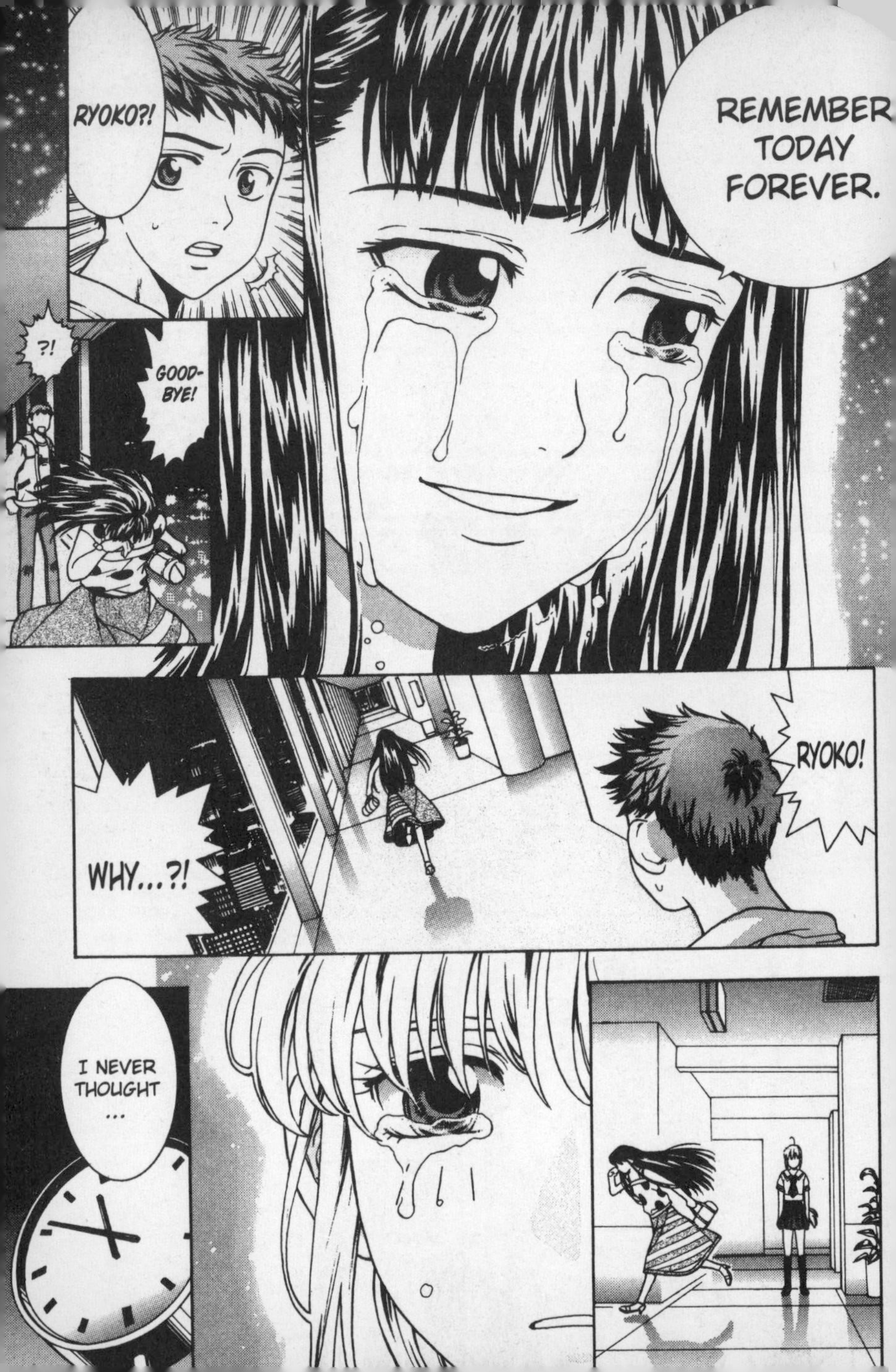

REMEMBER TODAY FOREVER.
RYOKO?!
GOOD-BYE!
?!
RYOKO!
WHY...?!
I NEVER THOUGHT ...

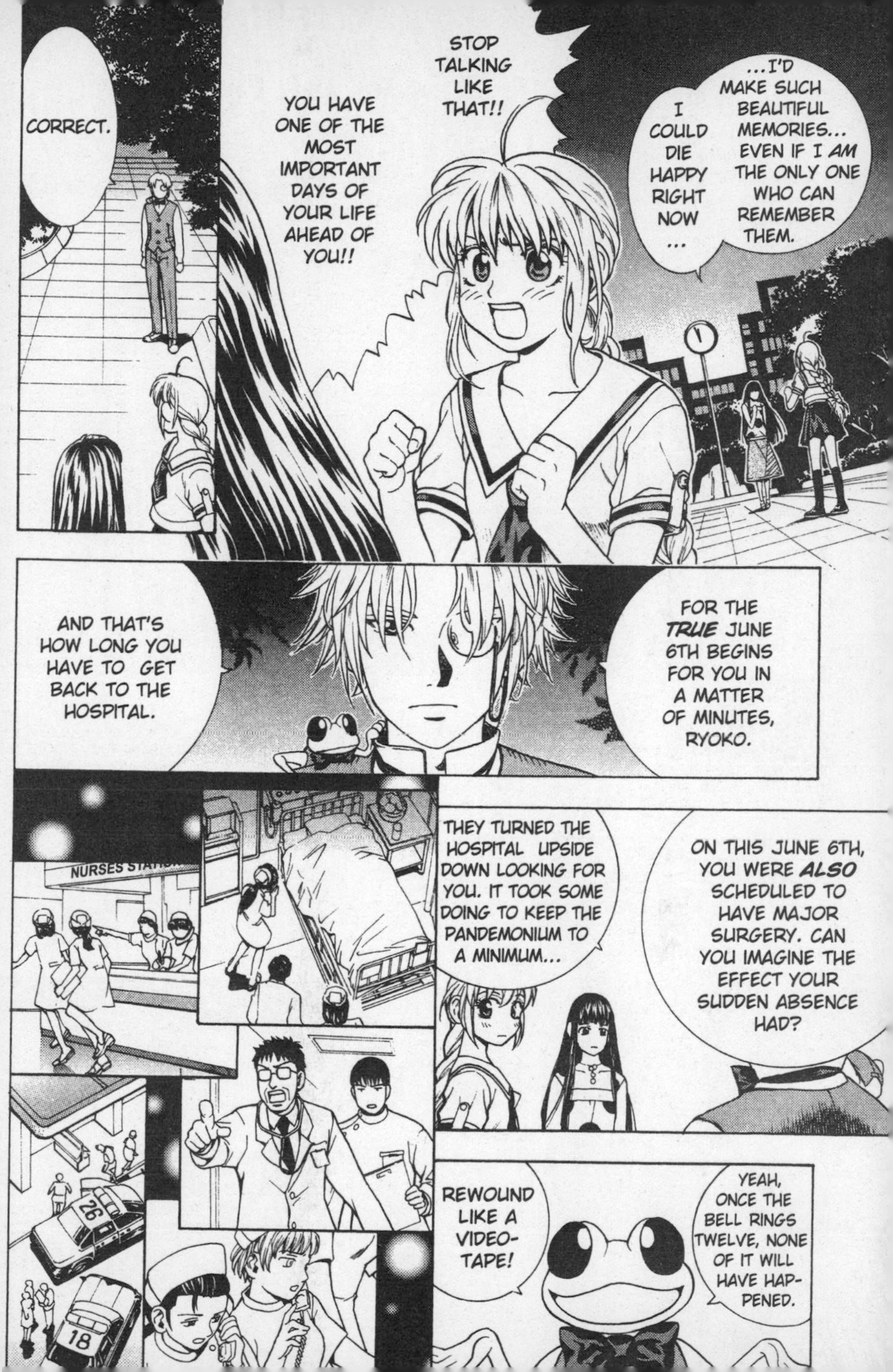
...I'D MAKE SUCH BEAUTIFUL MEMORIES... EVEN IF I *AM* THE ONLY ONE WHO CAN REMEMBER THEM.
I COULD DIE HAPPY RIGHT NOW ...
STOP TALKING LIKE THAT!!
YOU HAVE ONE OF THE MOST IMPORTANT DAYS OF YOUR LIFE AHEAD OF YOU!!
CORRECT.
FOR THE *TRUE* JUNE 6TH BEGINS FOR YOU IN A MATTER OF MINUTES, RYOKO.
AND THAT'S HOW LONG YOU HAVE TO GET BACK TO THE HOSPITAL.
ON THIS JUNE 6TH, YOU WERE *ALSO* SCHEDULED TO HAVE MAJOR SURGERY. CAN YOU IMAGINE THE EFFECT YOUR SUDDEN ABSENCE HAD?
THEY TURNED THE HOSPITAL UPSIDE DOWN LOOKING FOR YOU. IT TOOK SOME DOING TO KEEP THE PANDEMONIUM TO A MINIMUM...
YEAH, ONCE THE BELL RINGS TWELVE, NONE OF IT WILL HAVE HAP-PENED.
REWOUND LIKE A VIDEO-TAPE!

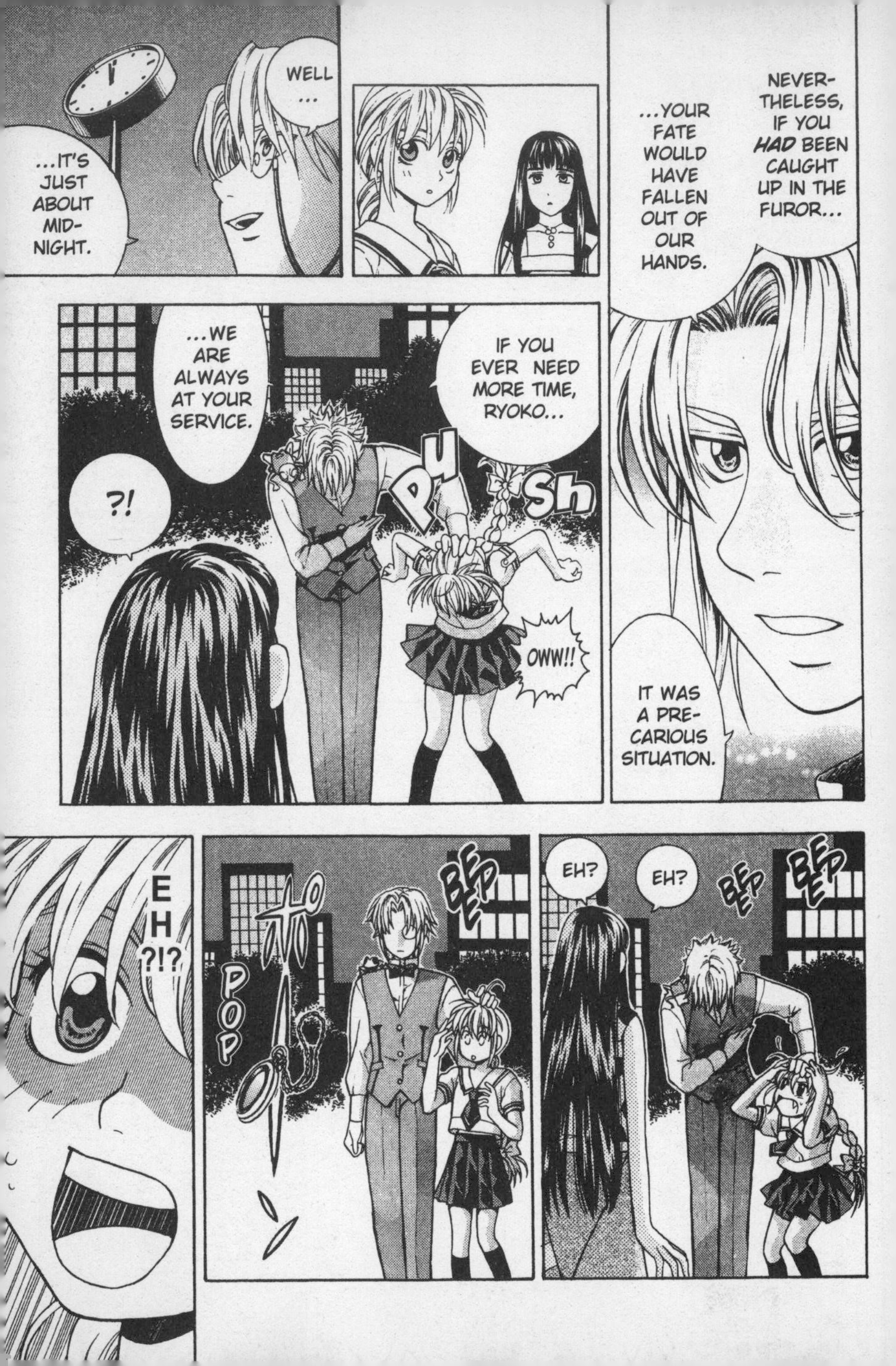
NEVER-THELESS, IF YOU *HAD* BEEN CAUGHT UP IN THE FUROR...
...YOUR FATE WOULD HAVE FALLEN OUT OF OUR HANDS.
IT WAS A PRECARIOUS SITUATION.
WELL ...
...IT'S JUST ABOUT MID-NIGHT.
IF YOU EVER NEED MORE TIME, RYOKO...
...WE ARE ALWAYS AT YOUR SERVICE.
PUSH
OWW!!
?!
EH?
EH?
BEEP
BEEP
BEEP
POP
EH?!?

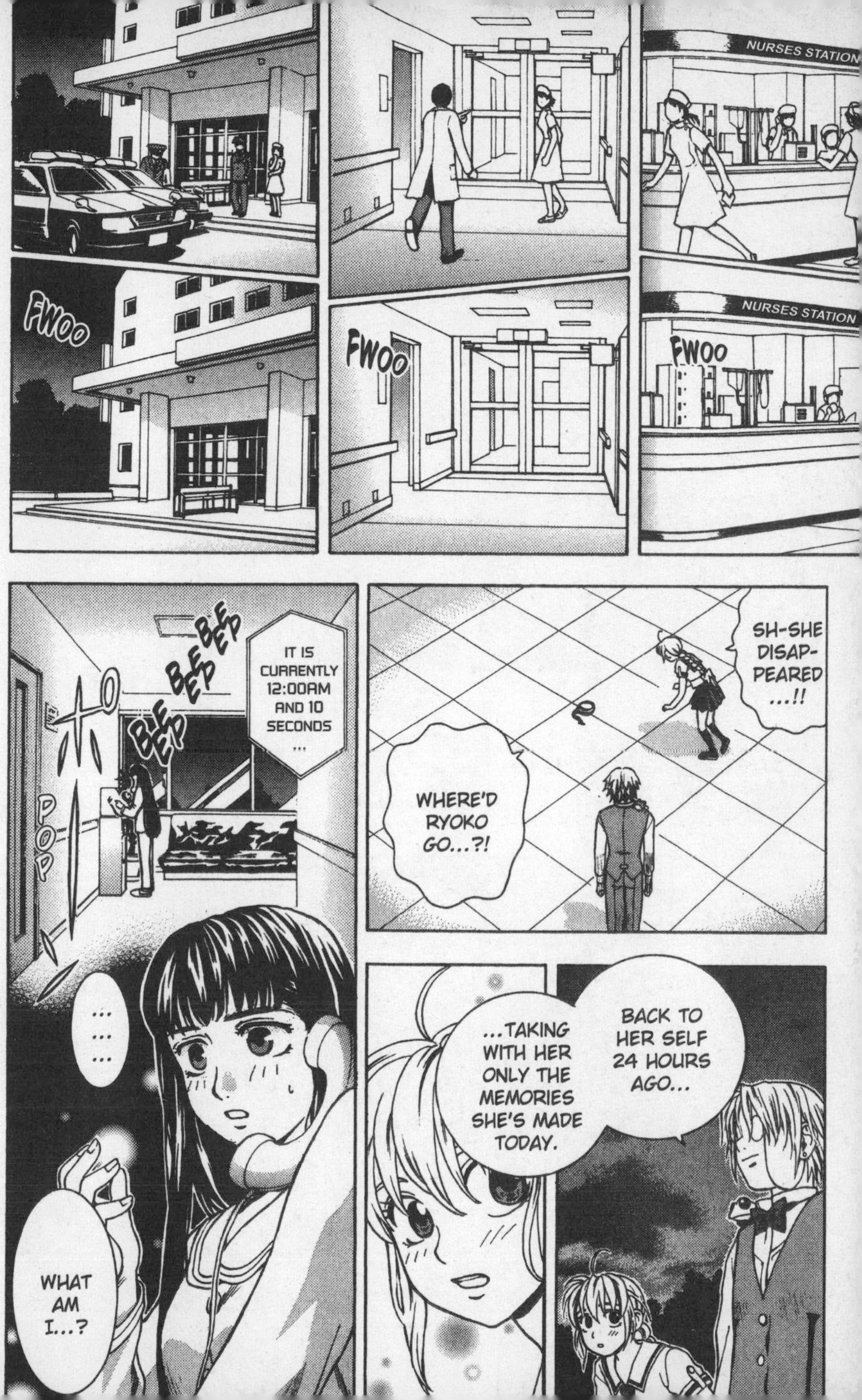
NURSES STATION
NURSES STATION
FWOO
FWOO
FWOO
SH-SHE DISAPPEARED...!!
WHERE'D RYOKO GO...?!
BACK TO HER SELF 24 HOURS AGO...
...TAKING WITH HER ONLY THE MEMORIES SHE'S MADE TODAY.
BEEP BEEP BEEP
IT IS CURRENTLY 12:00AM AND 10 SECONDS ...
POP
...
...
...
WHAT AM I...?

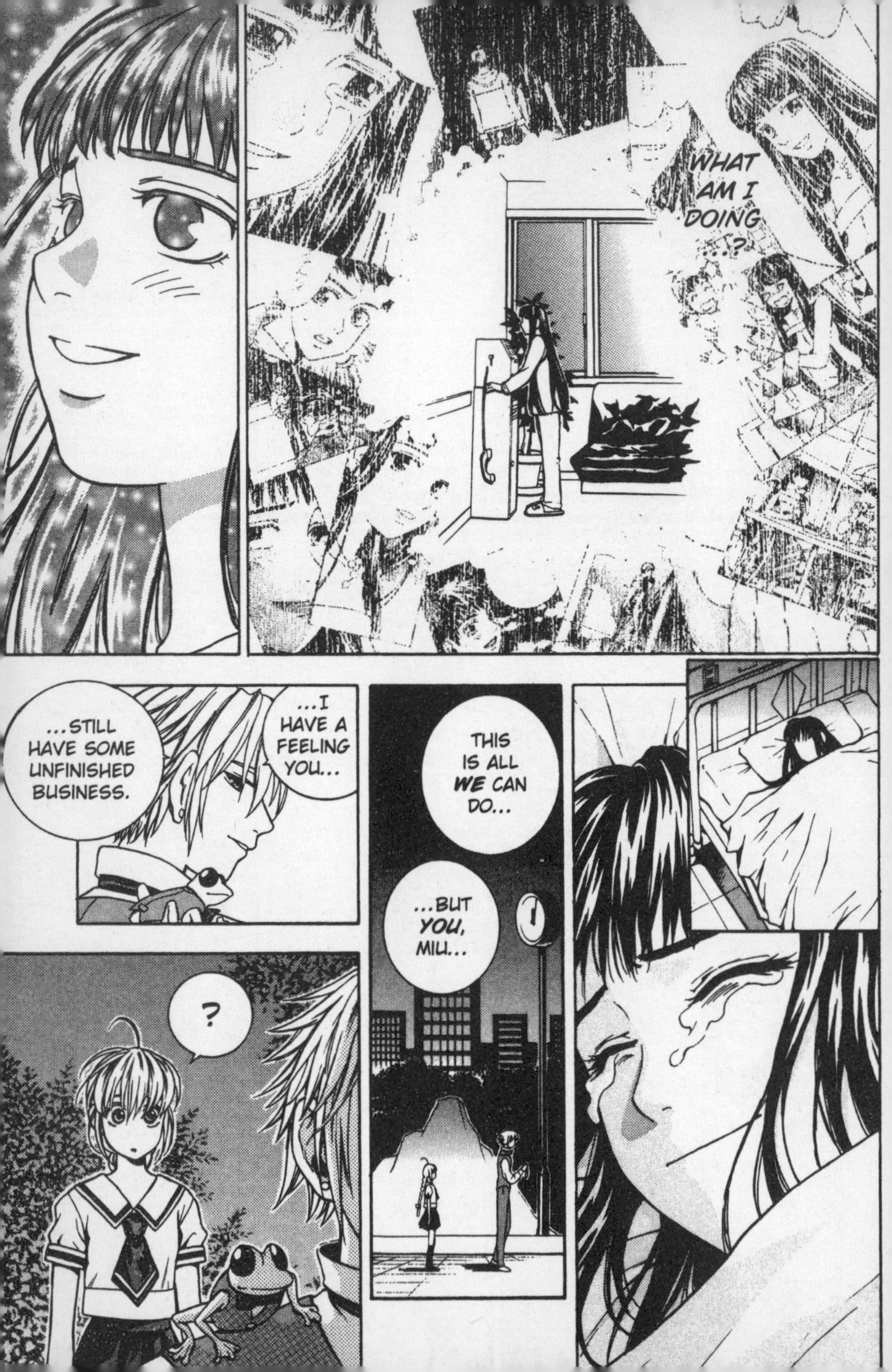
WHAT AM I DOING ...?
THIS IS ALL WE CAN DO...
...BUT YOU, MIU...
...I HAVE A FEELING YOU...
...STILL HAVE SOME UNFINISHED BUSINESS.
?

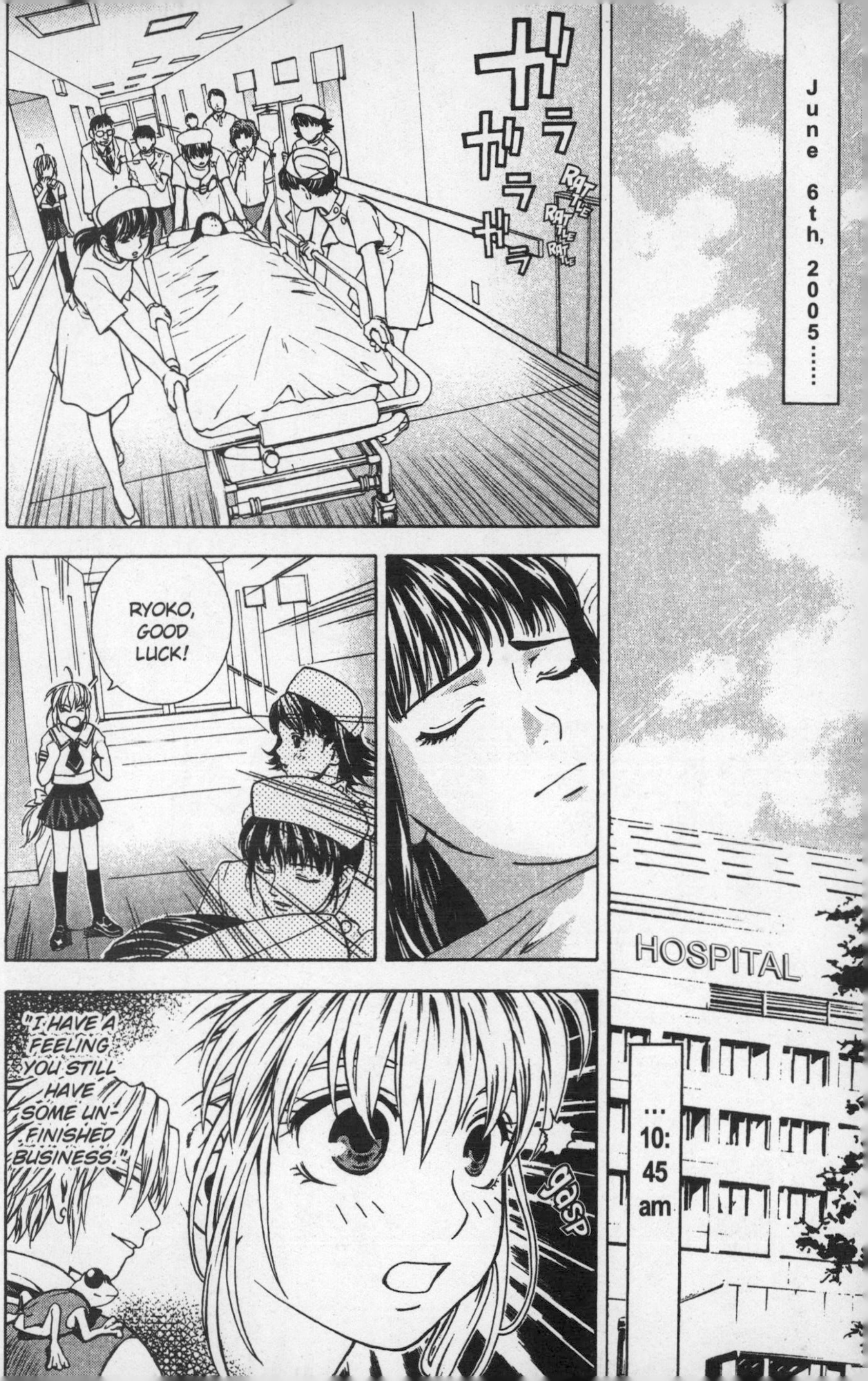

June 6th, 2005......
HOSPITAL
... 10: 45 am
ガラ
ガラ
ガラ
RATTLE RATTLE RATTLE
RYOKO, GOOD LUCK!
"I HAVE A FEELING YOU STILL HAVE SOME UN-FINISHED BUSINESS."
gasp

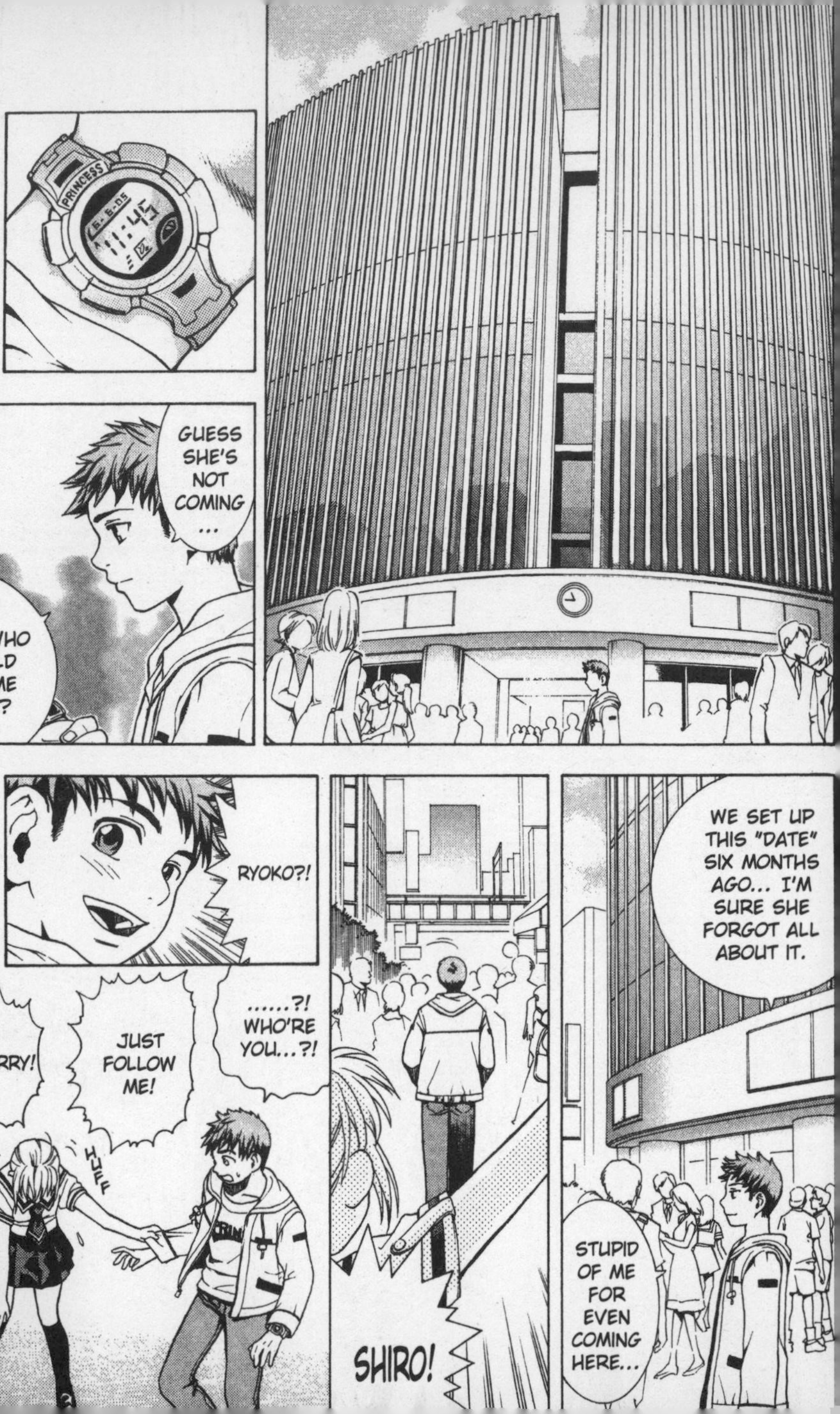
PRINCESS
GUESS SHE'S NOT COMING ...
AND WHO COULD BLAME HER?
WE SET UP THIS "DATE" SIX MONTHS AGO... I'M SURE SHE FORGOT ALL ABOUT IT.
STUPID OF ME FOR EVEN COMING HERE...
SHIRO!
RYOKO?!
......?! WHO'RE YOU...?!
JUST FOLLOW ME!
HURRY!
HUFF
HUFF

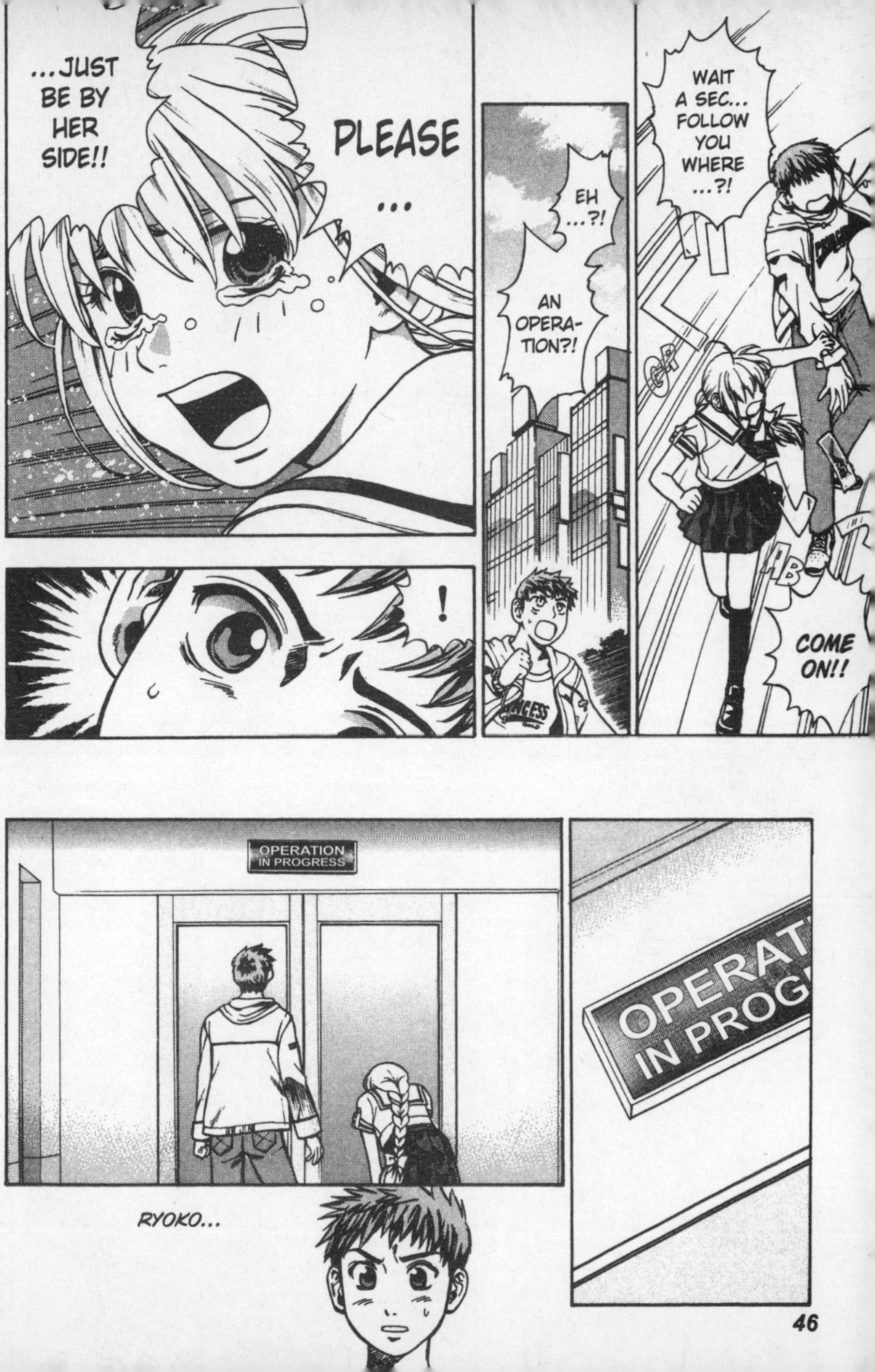
WAIT A SEC... FOLLOW YOU WHERE ...?!
COME ON!!
EH ...?!
AN OPERATION?!
...JUST BE BY HER SIDE!!
PLEASE
...
!
OPERAT
IN PROG
OPERATION IN PROGRESS
RYOKO...

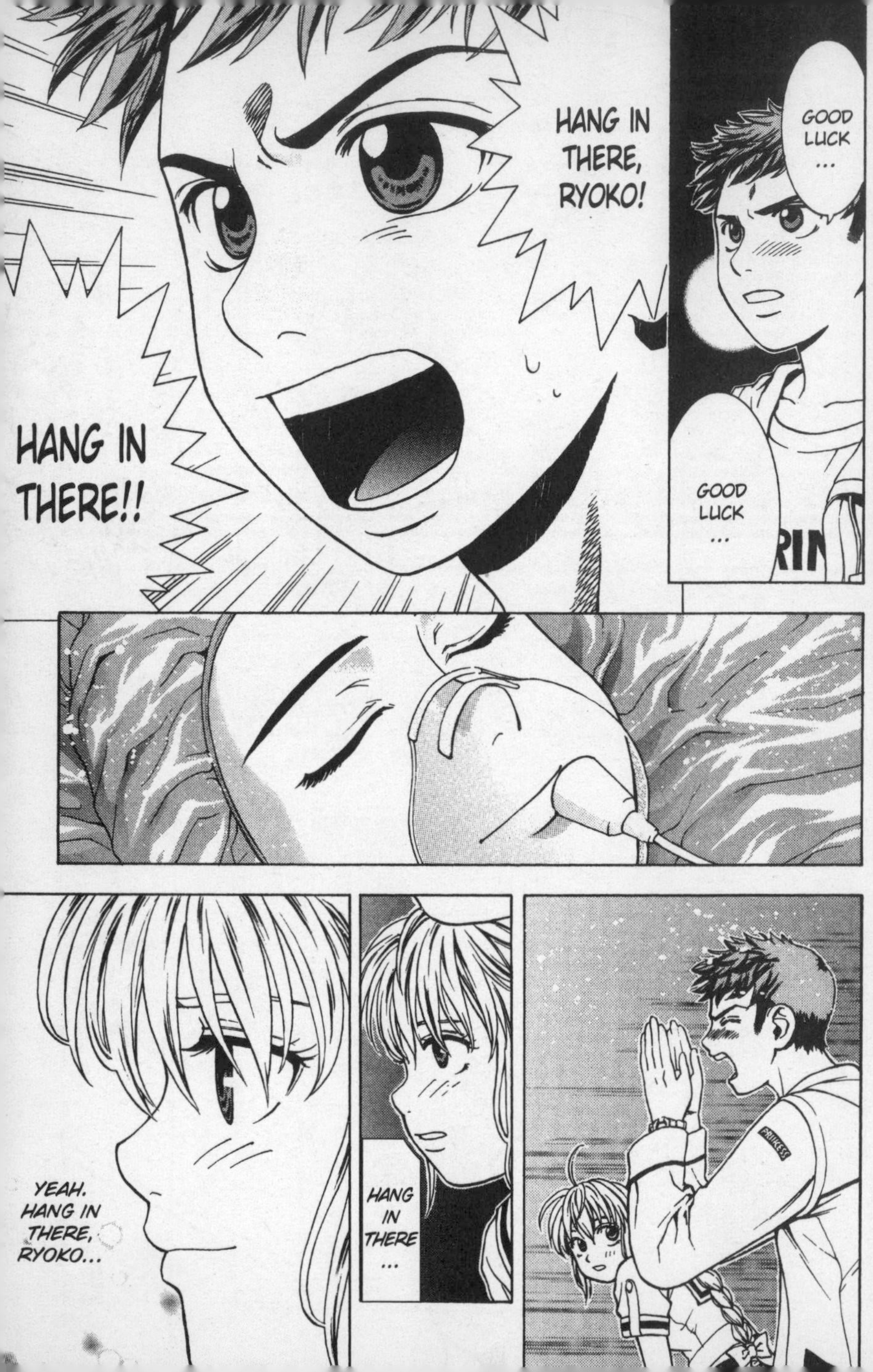
GOOD LUCK ...
GOOD LUCK ...
HANG IN THERE, RYOKO!
HANG IN THERE!!
HANG IN THERE ...
YEAH. HANG IN THERE, RYOKO...

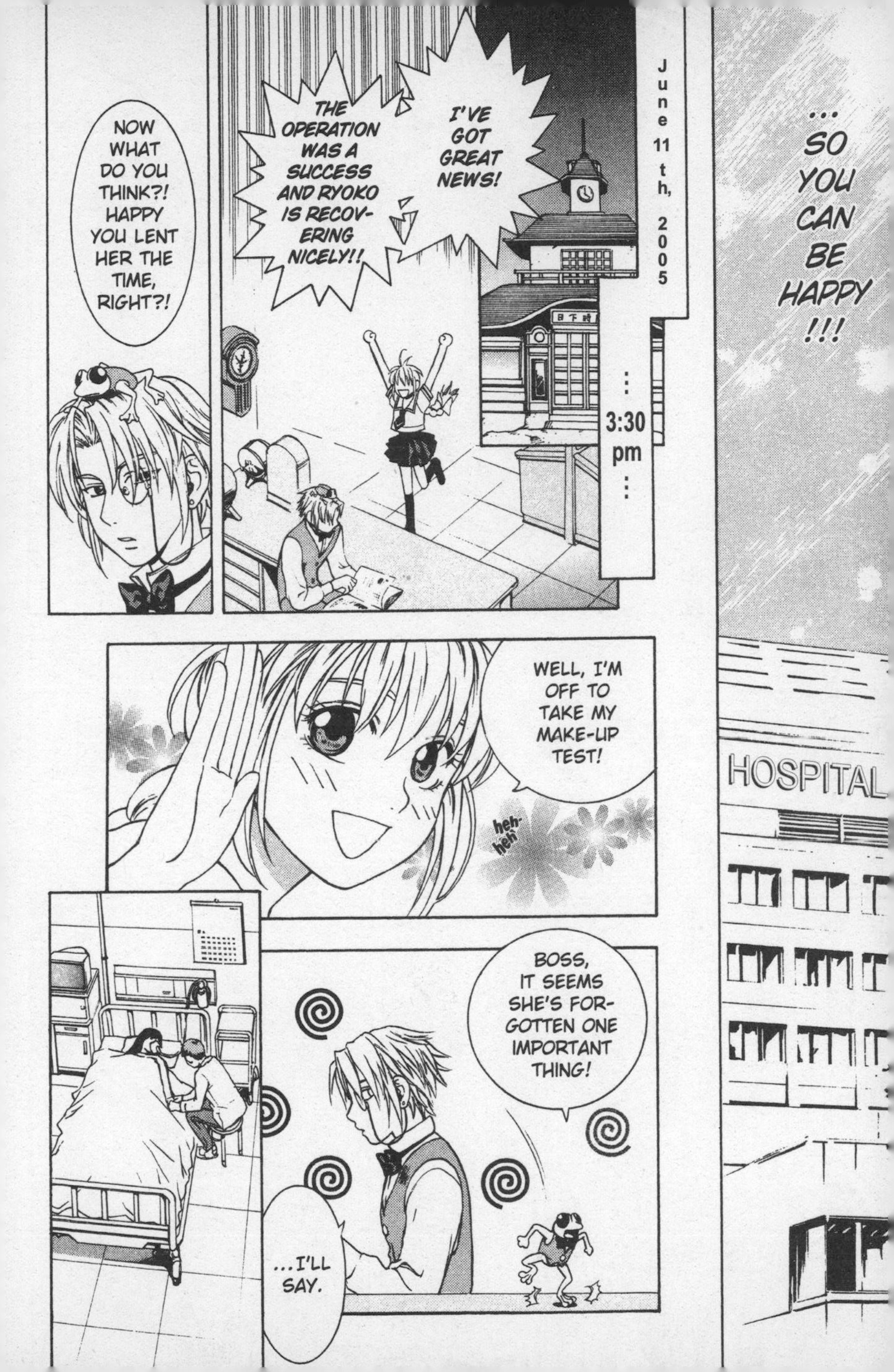

...SO YOU CAN BE HAPPY!!!
HOSPITAL
June 11th, 2005 ...3:30 pm...
I'VE GOT GREAT NEWS!
THE OPERATION WAS A SUCCESS AND RYOKO IS RECOVERING NICELY!!
NOW WHAT DO YOU THINK?! HAPPY YOU LENT HER THE TIME, RIGHT?!
WELL, I'M OFF TO TAKE MY MAKE-UP TEST!
heh-heh
BOSS, IT SEEMS SHE'S FORGOTTEN ONE IMPORTANT THING!
...I'LL SAY.

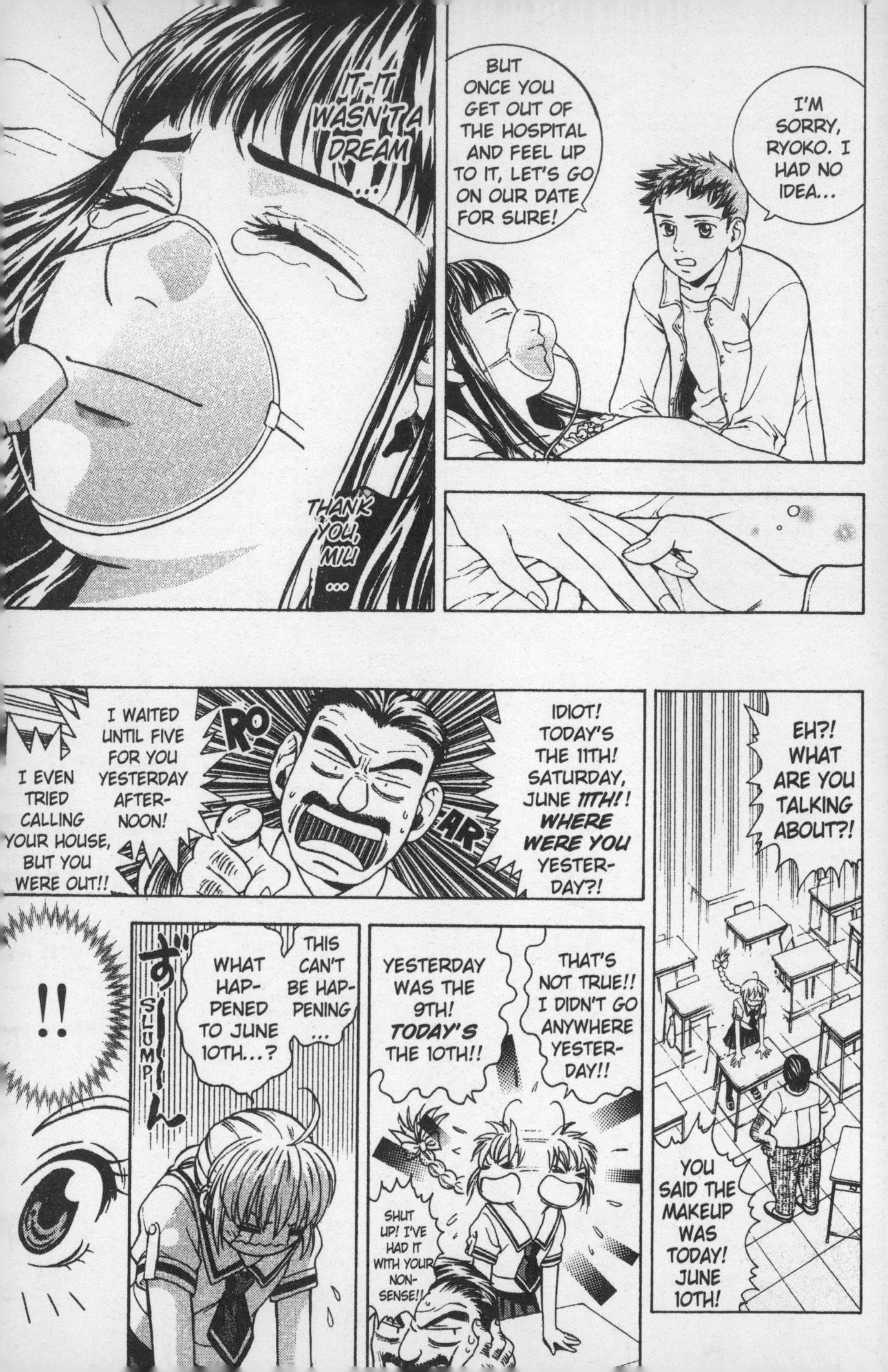
I'M SORRY, RYOKO. I HAD NO IDEA...
BUT ONCE YOU GET OUT OF THE HOSPITAL AND FEEL UP TO IT, LET'S GO ON OUR DATE FOR SURE!
IT-IT WASN'T A DREAM...!
THANK YOU, MIU...
EH?! WHAT ARE YOU TALKING ABOUT?!
YOU SAID THE MAKEUP WAS TODAY! JUNE 10TH!
IDIOT! TODAY'S THE 11TH! SATURDAY, JUNE 11TH!! WHERE WERE YOU YESTERDAY?!
ROAR
I WAITED UNTIL FIVE FOR YOU YESTERDAY AFTERNOON!
I EVEN TRIED CALLING YOUR HOUSE, BUT YOU WERE OUT!!
THAT'S NOT TRUE!! I DIDN'T GO ANYWHERE YESTERDAY!!
YESTERDAY WAS THE 9TH! TODAY'S THE 10TH!!
SHUT UP! I'VE HAD IT WITH YOUR NONSENSE!!
THIS CAN'T BE HAPPENING...
WHAT HAPPENED TO JUNE 10TH...?
ず
SLUMP
ん
!!

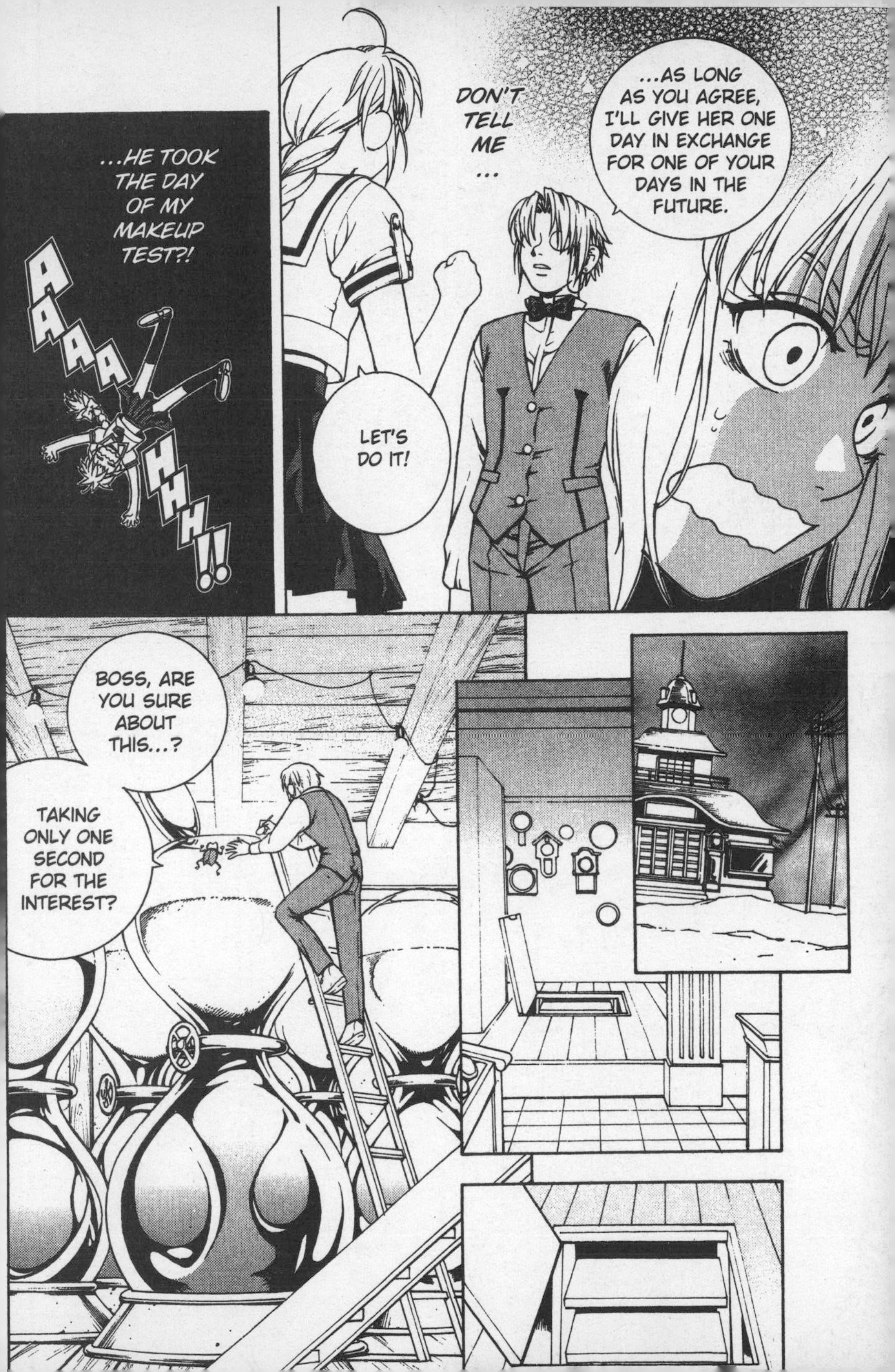
...AS LONG AS YOU AGREE, I'LL GIVE HER ONE DAY IN EXCHANGE FOR ONE OF YOUR DAYS IN THE FUTURE.
DON'T TELL ME ...
LET'S DO IT!
...HE TOOK THE DAY OF MY MAKEUP TEST?!
AAAAHHHH!!
BOSS, ARE YOU SURE ABOUT THIS...?
TAKING ONLY ONE SECOND FOR THE INTEREST?

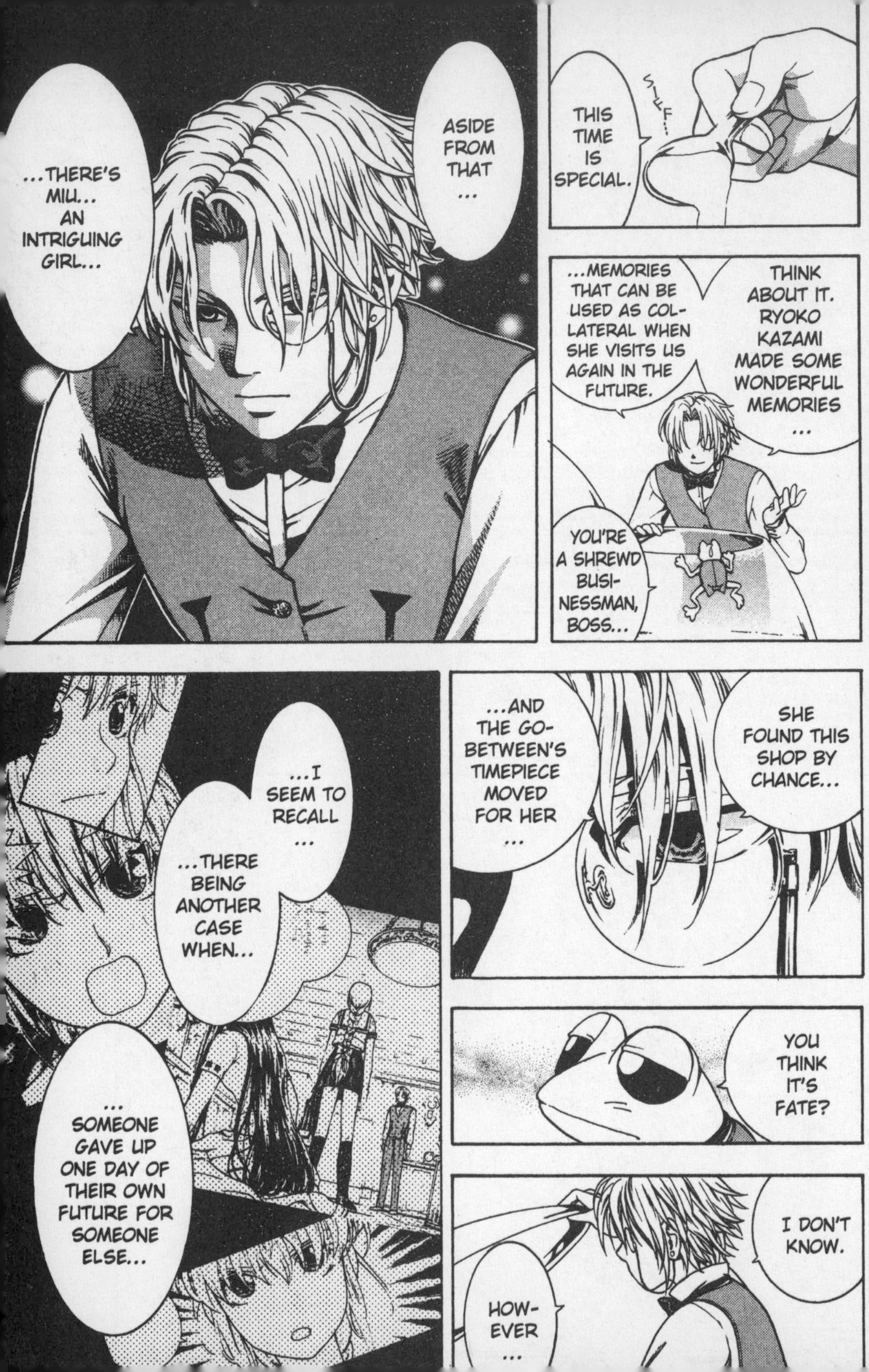
SIFF...
THIS TIME IS SPECIAL.
THINK ABOUT IT. RYOKO KAZAMI MADE SOME WONDERFUL MEMORIES ...
...MEMORIES THAT CAN BE USED AS COL-LATERAL WHEN SHE VISITS US AGAIN IN THE FUTURE.
YOU'RE A SHREWD BUSI-NESSMAN, BOSS...
ASIDE FROM THAT ...
...THERE'S MIU... AN INTRIGUING GIRL...
SHE FOUND THIS SHOP BY CHANCE...
...AND THE GO-BETWEEN'S TIMEPIECE MOVED FOR HER ...
YOU THINK IT'S FATE?
I DON'T KNOW.
HOW-EVER ...
...I SEEM TO RECALL ...
...THERE BEING ANOTHER CASE WHEN...
... SOMEONE GAVE UP ONE DAY OF THEIR OWN FUTURE FOR SOMEONE ELSE...

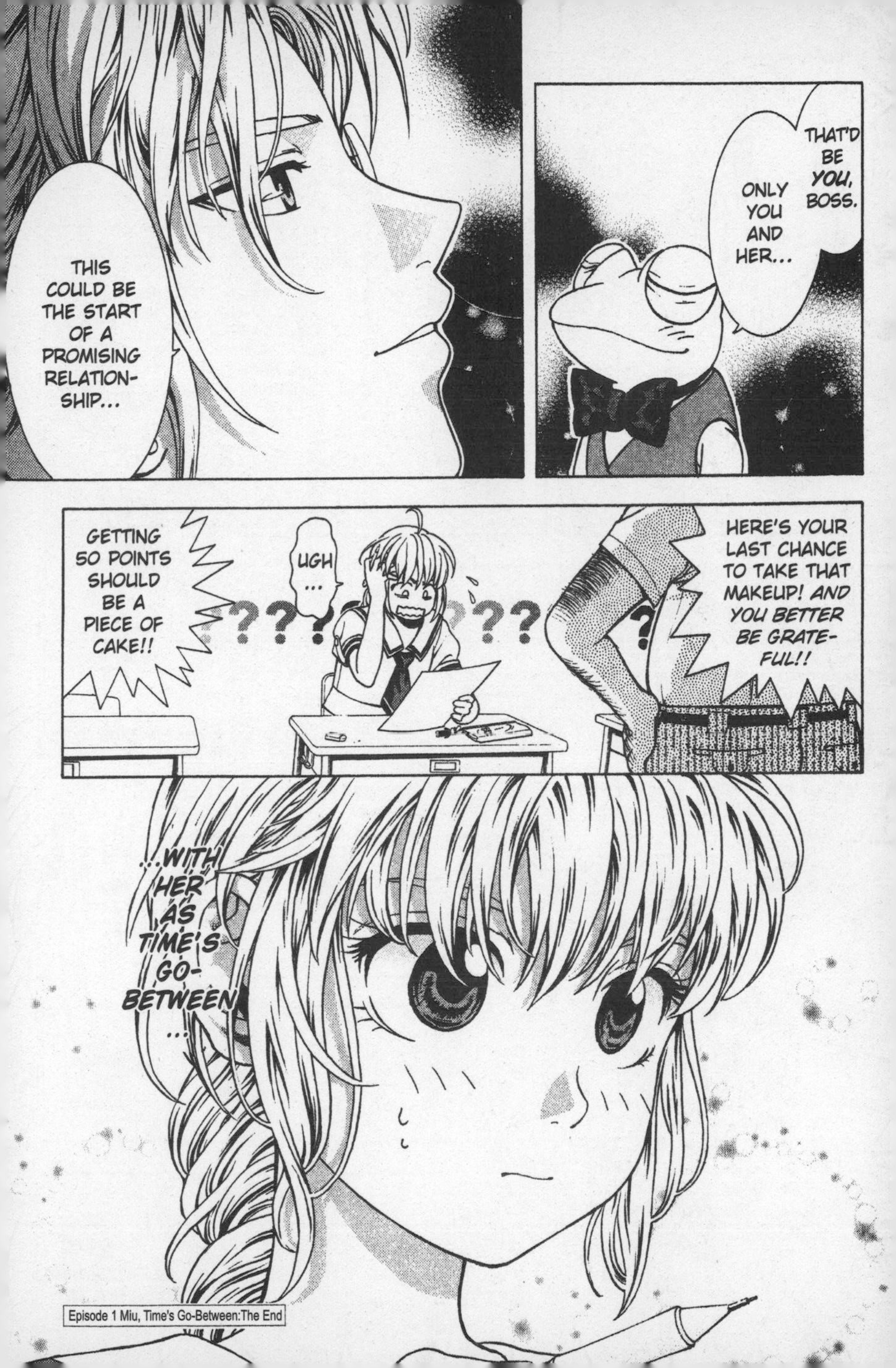
THAT'D BE *YOU*, BOSS.
ONLY YOU AND HER...
THIS COULD BE THE START OF A PROMISING RELATION-SHIP...
HERE'S YOUR LAST CHANCE TO TAKE THAT MAKEUP! *AND YOU BETTER BE GRATE-FUL!!*
???
UGH ...
???
GETTING 50 POINTS SHOULD BE A PIECE OF CAKE!!
...WITH HER AS TIME'S GO-BETWEEN...
Episode 1 Miu, Time's Go-Between: The End

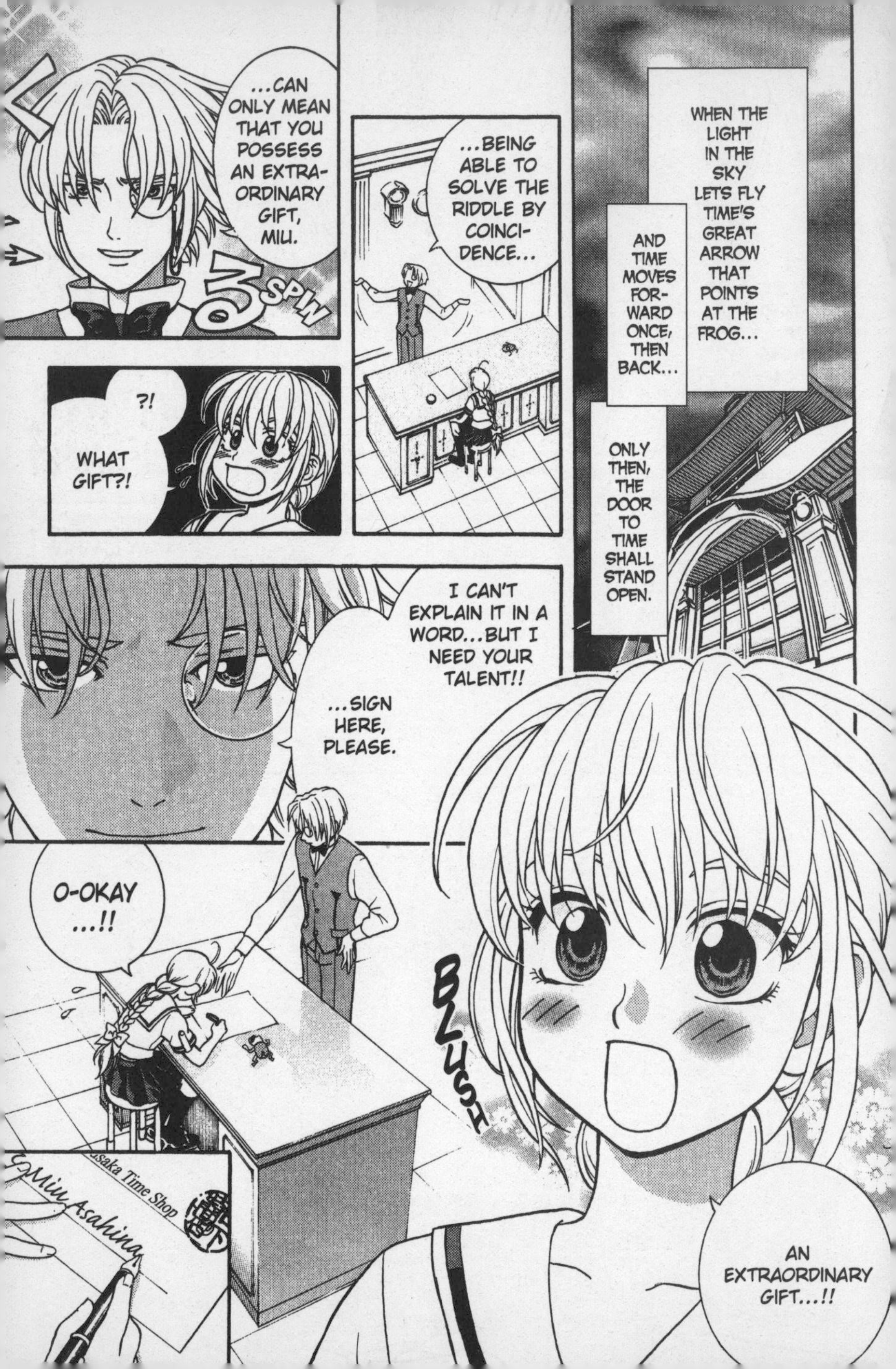
WHEN THE LIGHT IN THE SKY LETS FLY TIME'S GREAT ARROW THAT POINTS AT THE FROG...
AND TIME MOVES FOR-WARD ONCE, THEN BACK...
ONLY THEN, THE DOOR TO TIME SHALL STAND OPEN.
...BEING ABLE TO SOLVE THE RIDDLE BY COINCI-DENCE...
...CAN ONLY MEAN THAT YOU POSSESS AN EXTRA-ORDINARY GIFT, MIU.
SPIN
?!
WHAT GIFT?!
BLUSH
AN EXTRAORDINARY GIFT...!!
I CAN'T EXPLAIN IT IN A WORD...BUT I NEED YOUR TALENT!!
...SIGN HERE, PLEASE.
O-OKAY ...!!
Asaka Time Shop
Miu Asahina

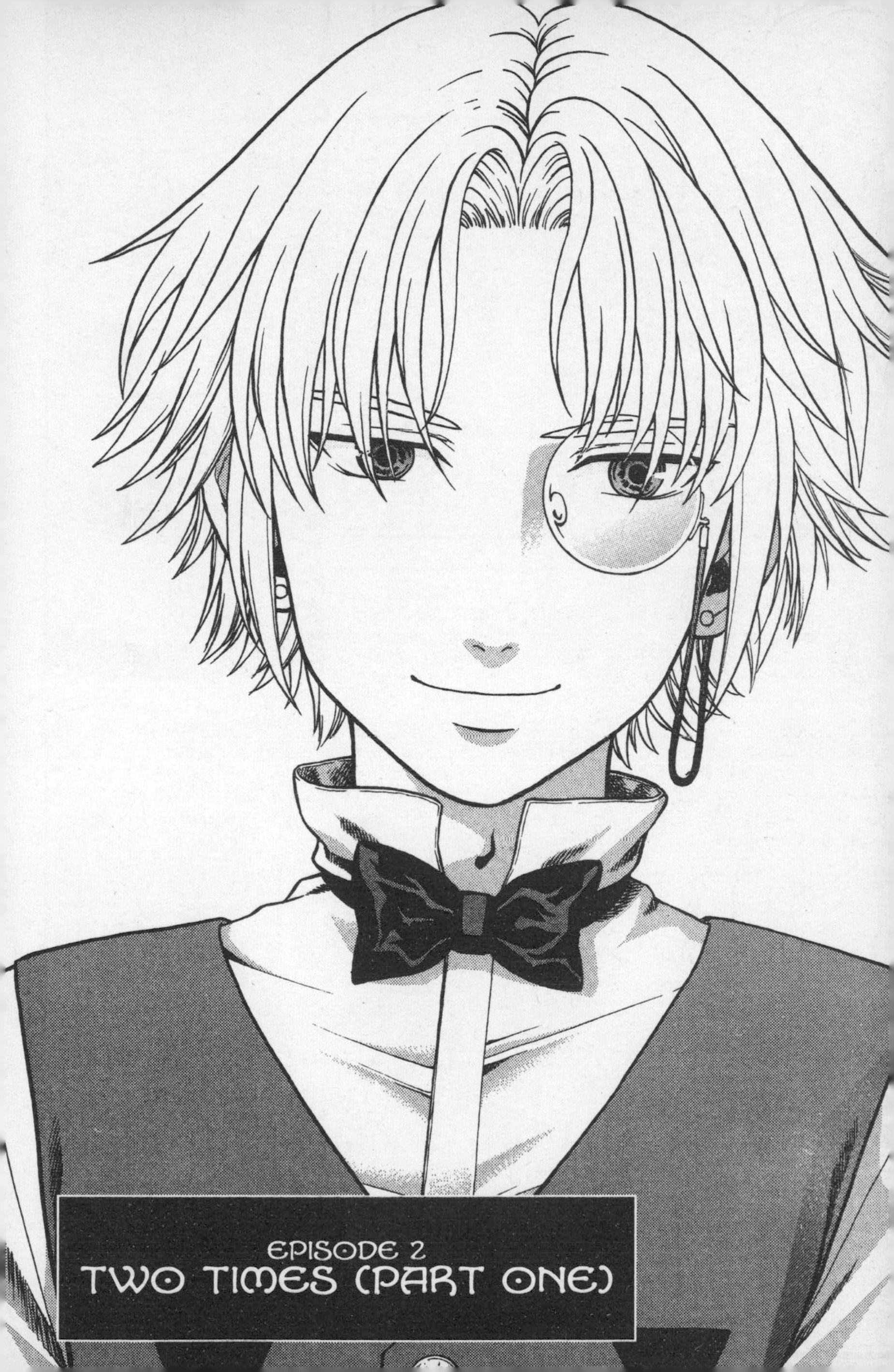
EPISODE 2
TWO TIMES (PART ONE)

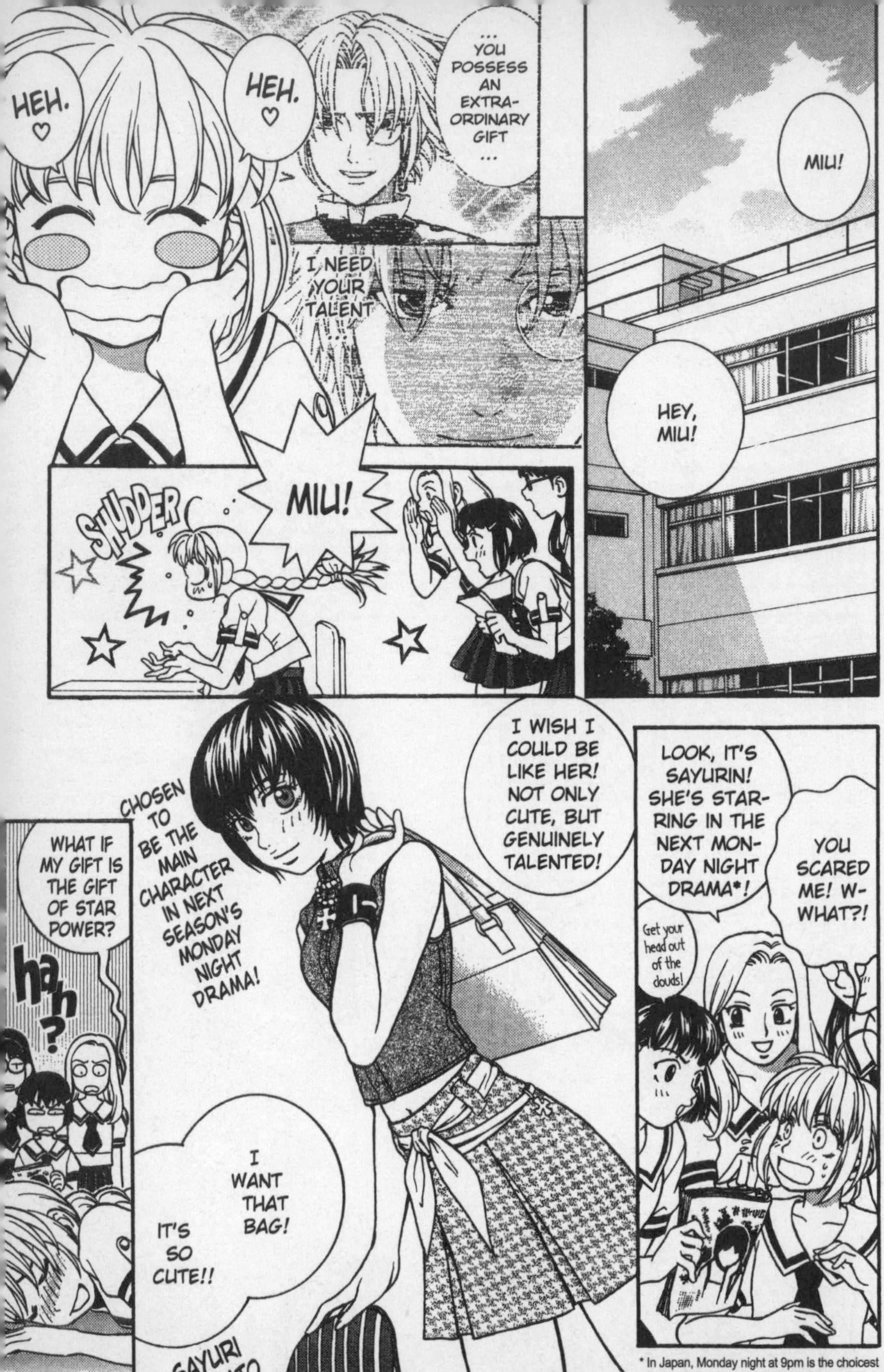
MIU!
HEY, MIU!
... YOU POSSESS AN EXTRA-ORDINARY GIFT ...
HEH. ♥
HEH. ♥
I NEED YOUR TALENT ...
MIU!
SHUDDER
LOOK, IT'S SAYURIN! SHE'S STAR-RING IN THE NEXT MON-DAY NIGHT DRAMA*!
YOU SCARED ME! W-WHAT?!
Get your head out of the clouds!
I WISH I COULD BE LIKE HER! NOT ONLY CUTE, BUT GENUINELY TALENTED!
CHOSEN TO BE THE MAIN CHARACTER IN NEXT SEASON'S MONDAY NIGHT DRAMA!
I WANT THAT BAG!
IT'S SO CUTE!!
SAYURI KITASATO
WHAT IF MY GIFT IS THE GIFT OF STAR POWER?
hah?

* In Japan, Monday night at 9pm is the choicest prime time spot, especially for dramas.

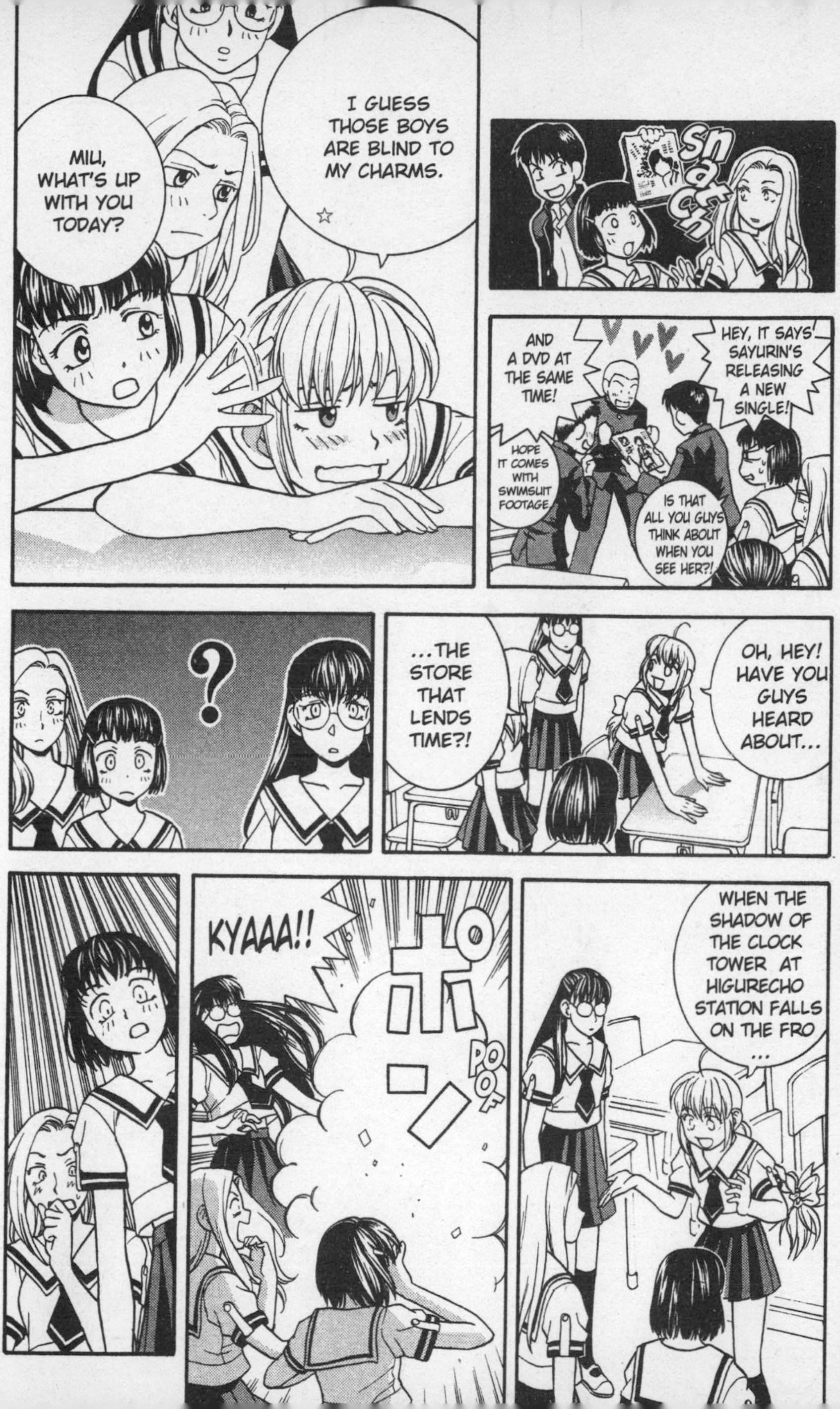
snatch
HEY, IT SAYS SAYURIN'S RELEASING A NEW SINGLE!
AND A DVD AT THE SAME TIME!
HOPE IT COMES WITH SWIMSUIT FOOTAGE
IS THAT ALL YOU GUYS THINK ABOUT WHEN YOU SEE HER?!
I GUESS THOSE BOYS ARE BLIND TO MY CHARMS. ☆
MIU, WHAT'S UP WITH YOU TODAY?
OH, HEY! HAVE YOU GUYS HEARD ABOUT...
...THE STORE THAT LENDS TIME?!
?
WHEN THE SHADOW OF THE CLOCK TOWER AT HIGURECHO STATION FALLS ON THE FRO...
POOF
KYAAA!!

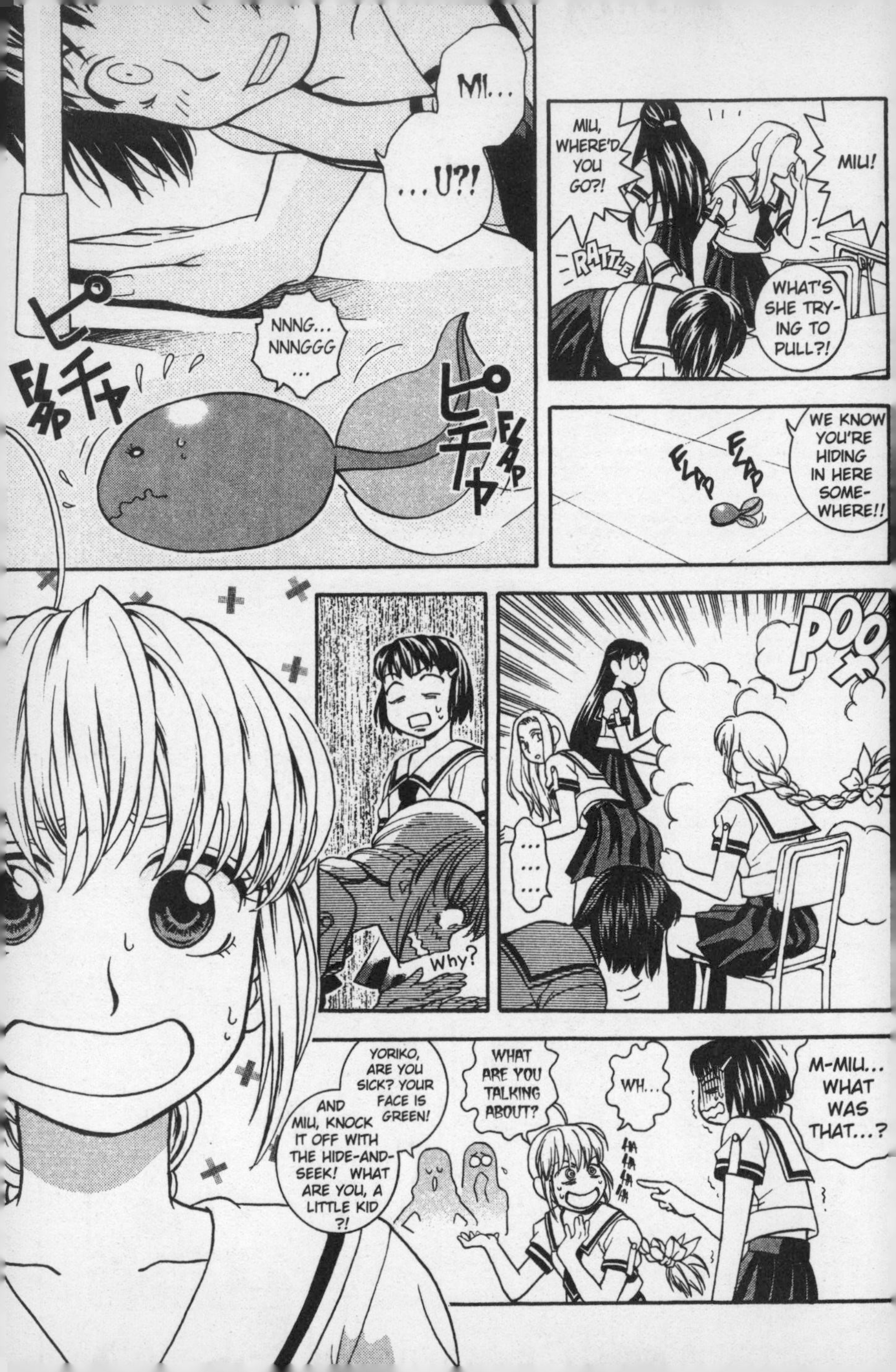
MIU!
MIU, WHERE'D YOU GO?!
RATTLE
WHAT'S SHE TRYING TO PULL?!
WE KNOW YOU'RE HIDING IN HERE SOME-WHERE!!
FLAP
FLAP
MI...
...U?!
NNNG... NNNGGG ...
ピチャ
FLAP
ピチャ
FLAP
POOF
......
Why?
M-MIU... WHAT WAS THAT...?
WH...
WHAT ARE YOU TALKING ABOUT?
YORIKO, ARE YOU SICK? YOUR FACE IS GREEN!
AND MIU, KNOCK IT OFF WITH THE HIDE-AND-SEEK! WHAT ARE YOU, A LITTLE KID ?!

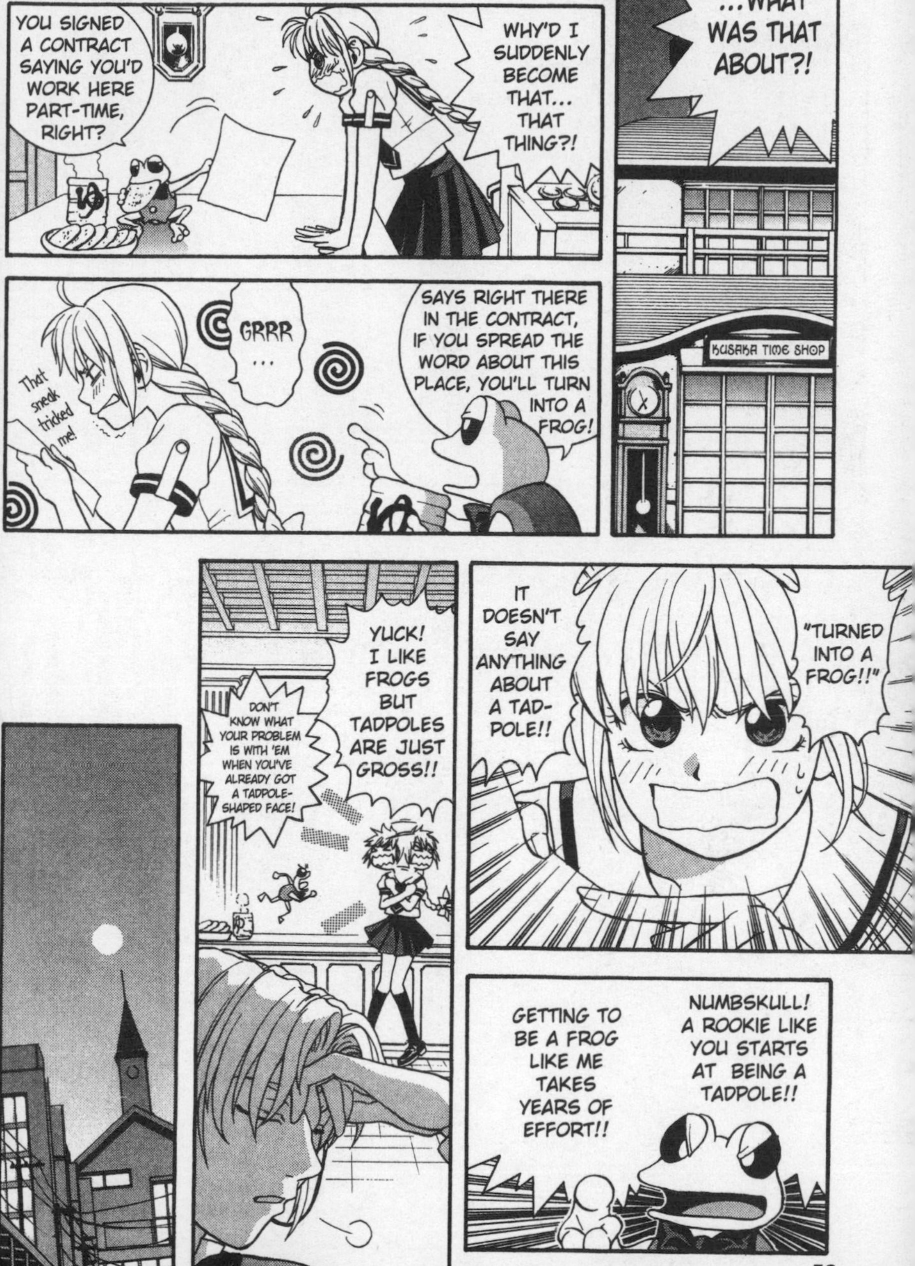
...WHAT WAS THAT ABOUT?!
KUSAKA TIME SHOP
WHY'D I SUDDENLY BECOME THAT... THAT THING?!
YOU SIGNED A CONTRACT SAYING YOU'D WORK HERE PART-TIME, RIGHT?
SAYS RIGHT THERE IN THE CONTRACT, IF YOU SPREAD THE WORD ABOUT THIS PLACE, YOU'LL TURN INTO A FROG!
GRRR ...
That sneak tricked me!
"TURNED INTO A FROG!!"
IT DOESN'T SAY ANYTHING ABOUT A TAD-POLE!!
NUMBSKULL! A ROOKIE LIKE YOU STARTS AT BEING A TADPOLE!!
GETTING TO BE A FROG LIKE ME TAKES YEARS OF EFFORT!!
YUCK! I LIKE FROGS BUT TADPOLES ARE JUST GROSS!!
DON'T KNOW WHAT YOUR PROBLEM IS WITH 'EM WHEN YOU'VE ALREADY GOT A TADPOLE-SHAPED FACE!

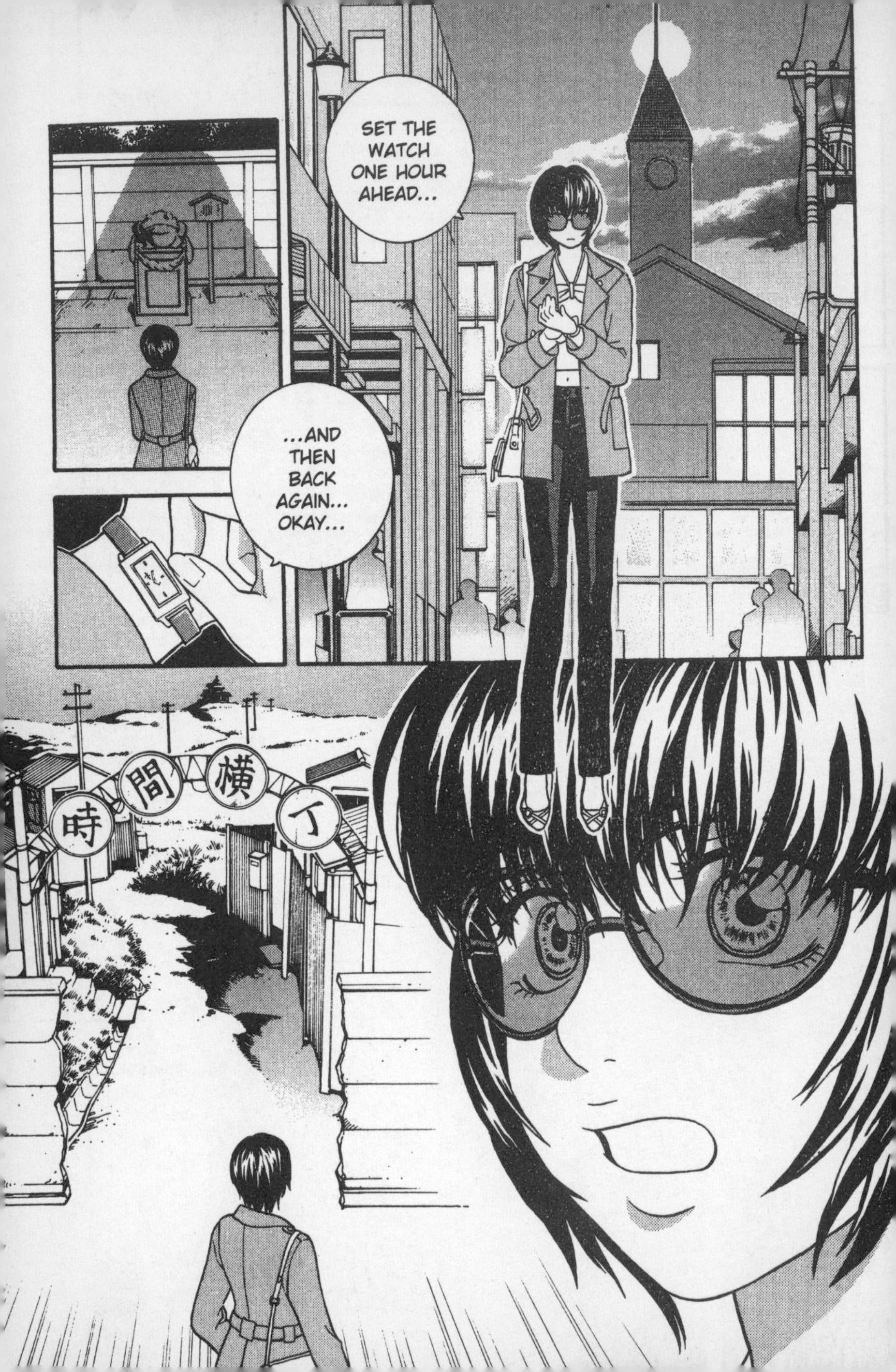
SET THE WATCH ONE HOUR AHEAD...
...AND THEN BACK AGAIN... OKAY...
時間横丁

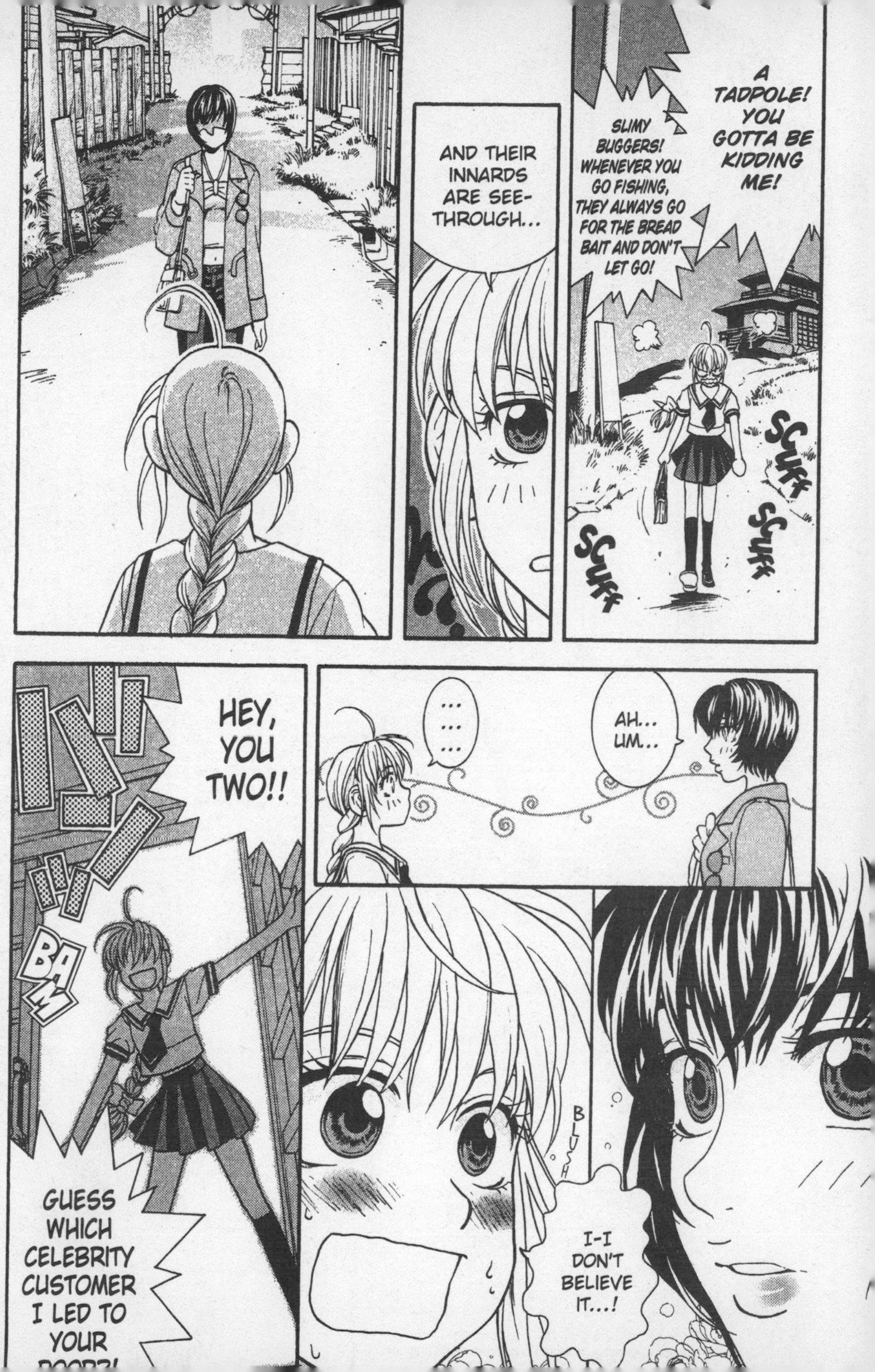
A TADPOLE! YOU GOTTA BE KIDDING ME!
SLIMY BUGGERS! WHENEVER YOU GO FISHING, THEY ALWAYS GO FOR THE BREAD BAIT AND DON'T LET GO!
SCUFF
SCUFF
SCUFF
AND THEIR INNARDS ARE SEE-THROUGH...
AH... UM...
... ...
BLUSH
I-I DON'T BELIEVE IT...!
HEY, YOU TWO!!
BAM
GUESS WHICH CELEBRITY CUSTOMER I LED TO YOUR

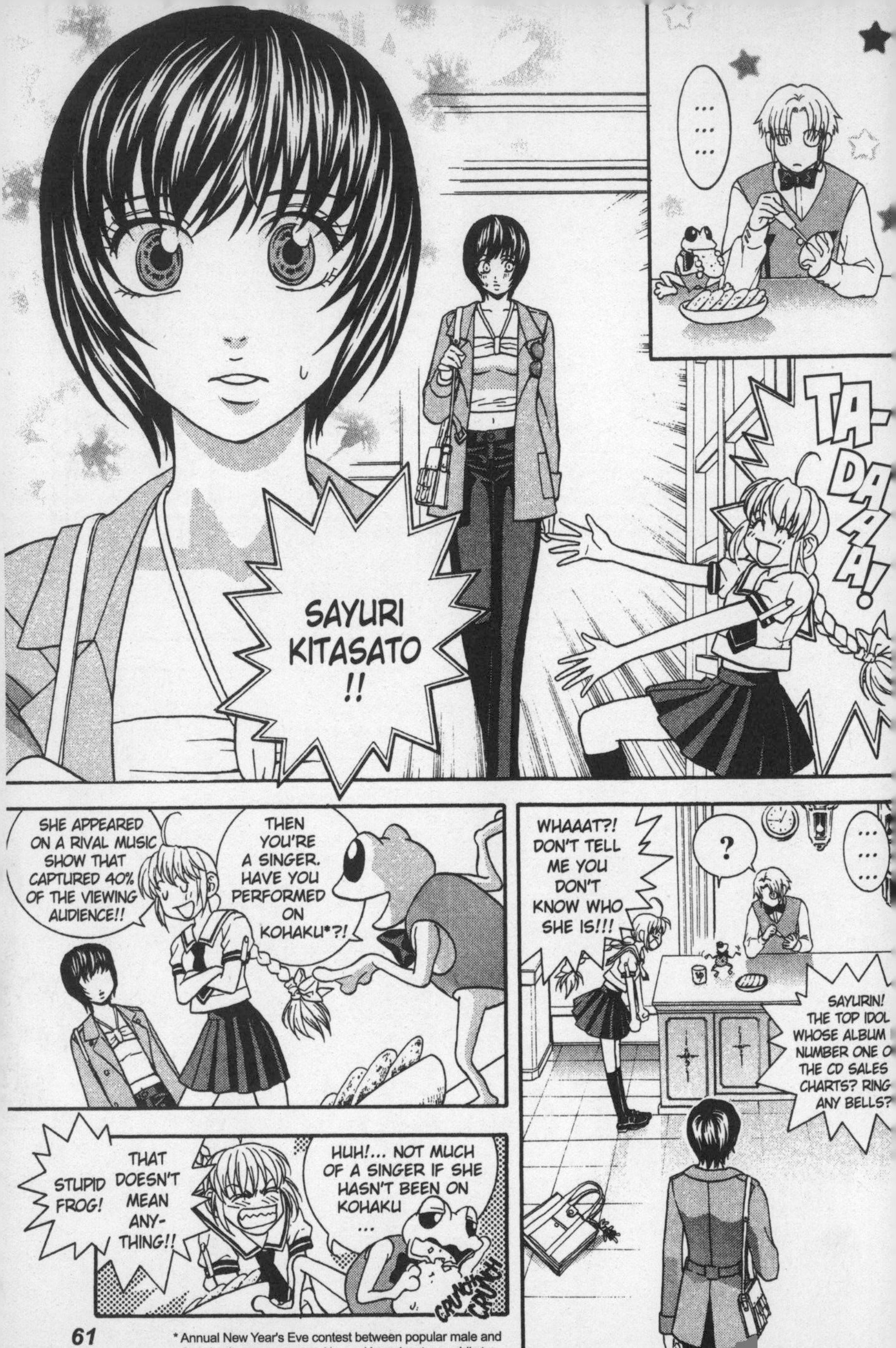
......
TA-DAAAA!
SAYURI KITASATO !!
......
?
WHAAAT?! DON'T TELL ME YOU DON'T KNOW WHO SHE IS!!!
SAYURIN! THE TOP IDOL WHOSE ALBUM NUMBER ONE O THE CD SALES CHARTS? RING ANY BELLS?
THEN YOU'RE A SINGER. HAVE YOU PERFORMED ON KOHAKU*?!
SHE APPEARED ON A RIVAL MUSIC SHOW THAT CAPTURED 40% OF THE VIEWING AUDIENCE!!
HUH!... NOT MUCH OF A SINGER IF SHE HASN'T BEEN ON KOHAKU ...
THAT DOESN'T MEAN ANY-THING!!
STUPID FROG!
CRUNCH CRUNCH

* Annual New Year's Eve contest between popular male and female singers, sponsored by and broadcast on public tv.

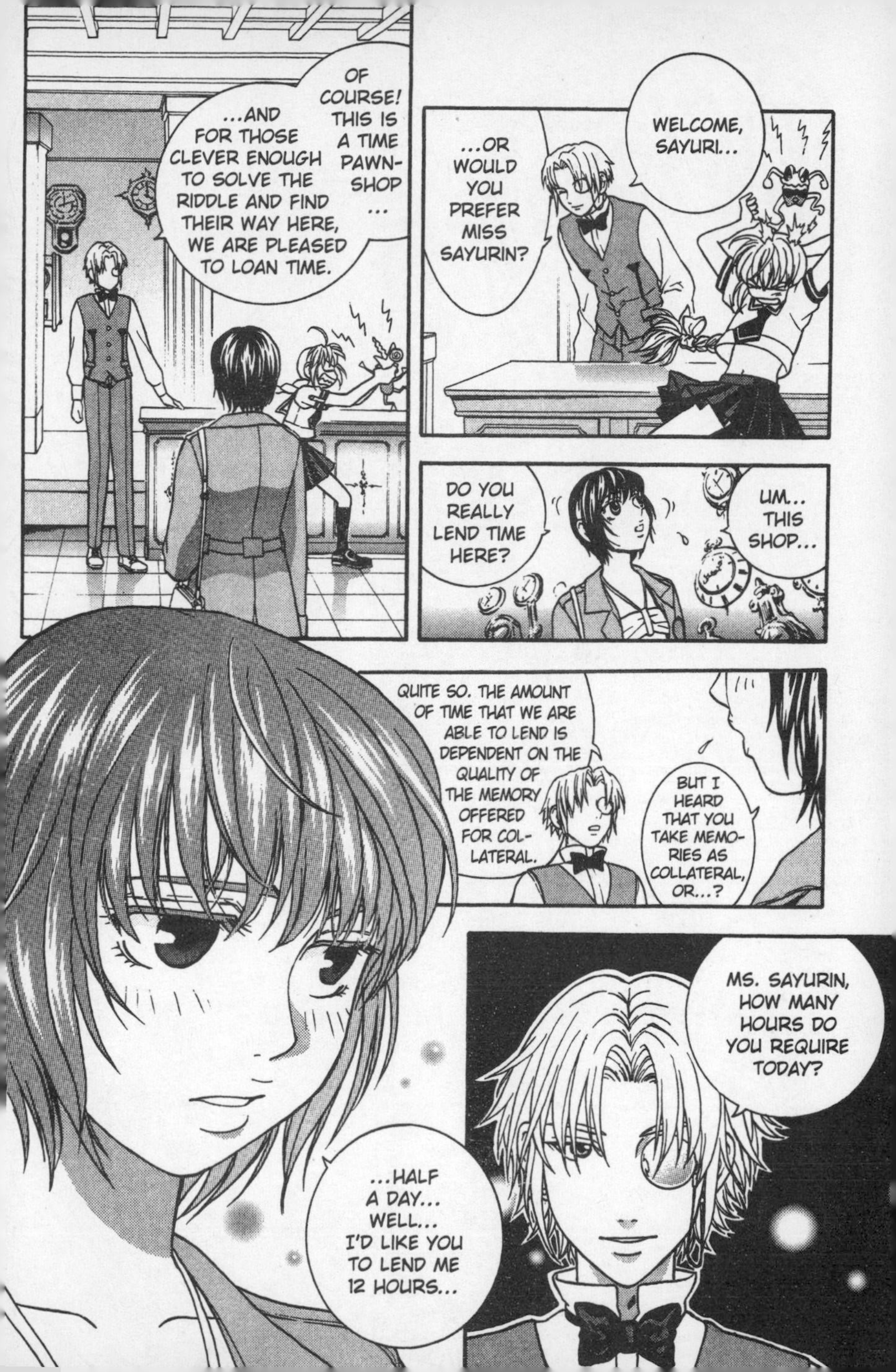
WELCOME, SAYURI...
...OR WOULD YOU PREFER MISS SAYURIN?
UM... THIS SHOP...
DO YOU REALLY LEND TIME HERE?
OF COURSE! THIS IS A TIME PAWNSHOP...
...AND FOR THOSE CLEVER ENOUGH TO SOLVE THE RIDDLE AND FIND THEIR WAY HERE, WE ARE PLEASED TO LOAN TIME.
BUT I HEARD THAT YOU TAKE MEMORIES AS COLLATERAL, OR...?
QUITE SO. THE AMOUNT OF TIME THAT WE ARE ABLE TO LEND IS DEPENDENT ON THE QUALITY OF THE MEMORY OFFERED FOR COLLATERAL.
MS. SAYURIN, HOW MANY HOURS DO YOU REQUIRE TODAY?
...HALF A DAY... WELL... I'D LIKE YOU TO LEND ME 12 HOURS...

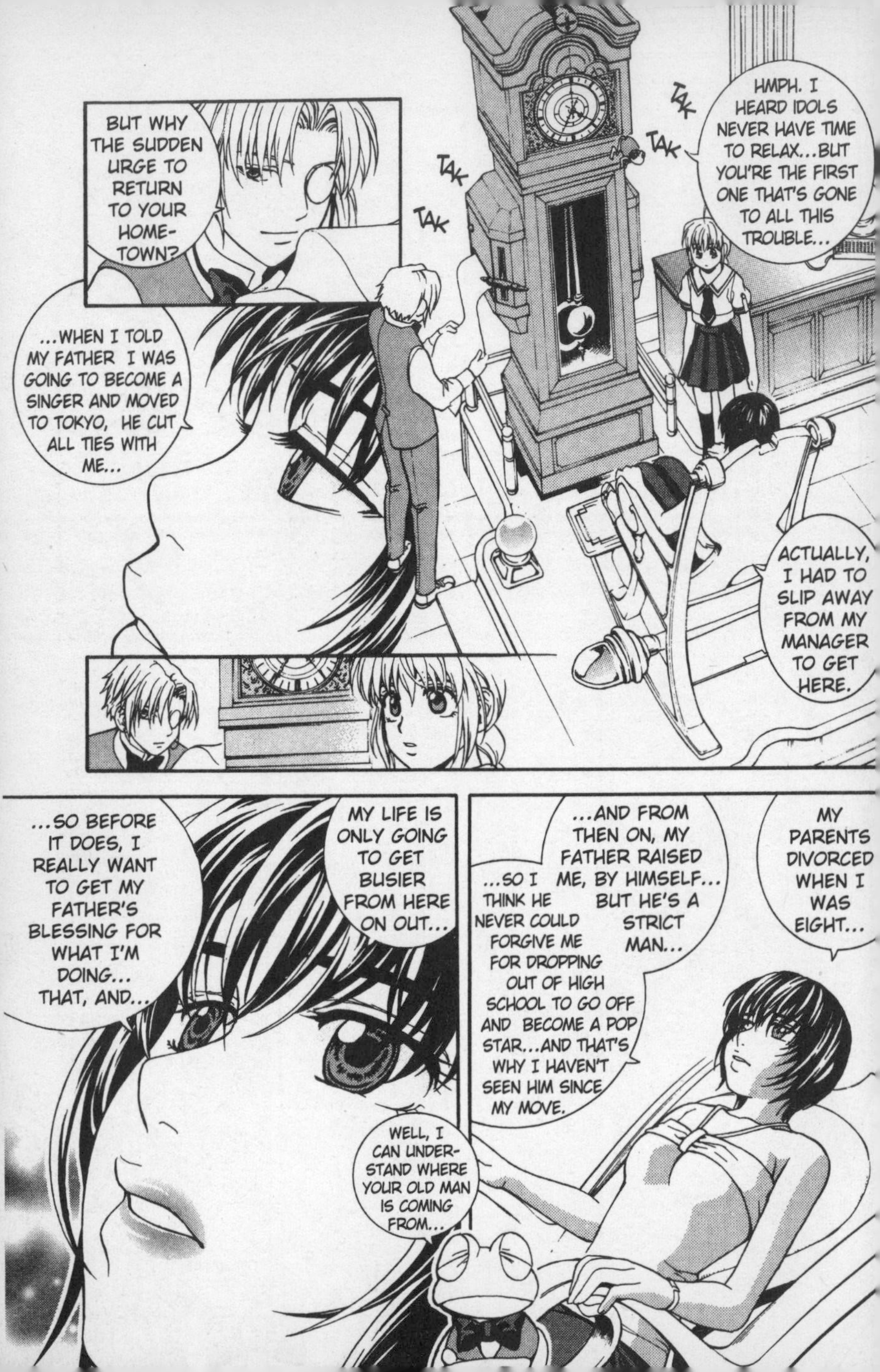
TAK
TAK
TAK
TAK
HMPH. I HEARD IDOLS NEVER HAVE TIME TO RELAX...BUT YOU'RE THE FIRST ONE THAT'S GONE TO ALL THIS TROUBLE...
ACTUALLY, I HAD TO SLIP AWAY FROM MY MANAGER TO GET HERE.
BUT WHY THE SUDDEN URGE TO RETURN TO YOUR HOME-TOWN?
...WHEN I TOLD MY FATHER I WAS GOING TO BECOME A SINGER AND MOVED TO TOKYO, HE CUT ALL TIES WITH ME...
MY PARENTS DIVORCED WHEN I WAS EIGHT...
...AND FROM THEN ON, MY FATHER RAISED ME, BY HIMSELF... BUT HE'S A STRICT MAN...
...SO I THINK HE NEVER COULD FORGIVE ME FOR DROPPING OUT OF HIGH SCHOOL TO GO OFF AND BECOME A POP STAR...AND THAT'S WHY I HAVEN'T SEEN HIM SINCE MY MOVE.
WELL, I CAN UNDER-STAND WHERE YOUR OLD MAN IS COMING FROM...
MY LIFE IS ONLY GOING TO GET BUSIER FROM HERE ON OUT...
...SO BEFORE IT DOES, I REALLY WANT TO GET MY FATHER'S BLESSING FOR WHAT I'M DOING... THAT, AND...

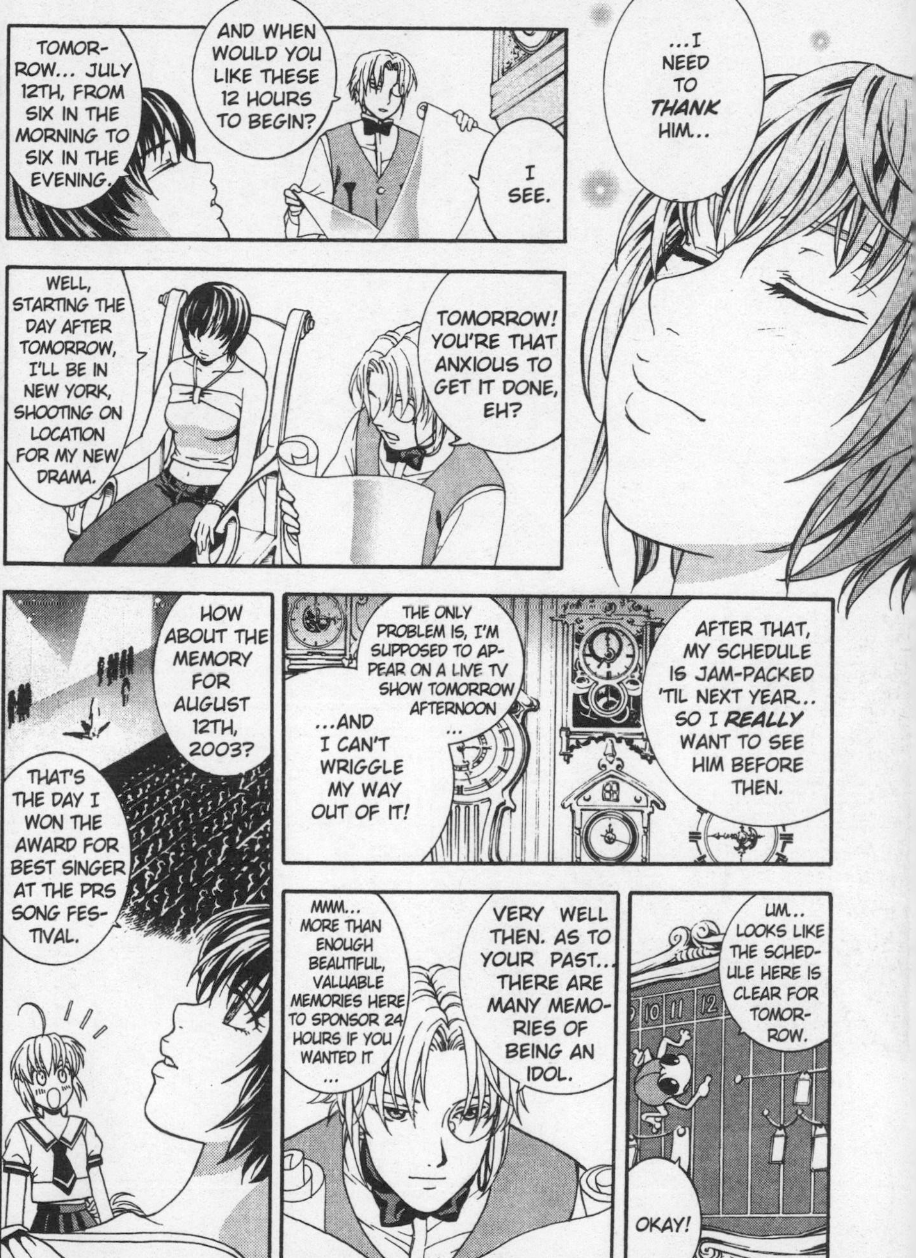
...I NEED TO *THANK* HIM...
AND WHEN WOULD YOU LIKE THESE 12 HOURS TO BEGIN?
TOMOR-ROW... JULY 12TH, FROM SIX IN THE MORNING TO SIX IN THE EVENING.
I SEE.
TOMORROW! YOU'RE THAT ANXIOUS TO GET IT DONE, EH?
WELL, STARTING THE DAY AFTER TOMORROW, I'LL BE IN NEW YORK, SHOOTING ON LOCATION FOR MY NEW DRAMA.
AFTER THAT, MY SCHEDULE IS JAM-PACKED 'TIL NEXT YEAR... SO I *REALLY* WANT TO SEE HIM BEFORE THEN.
THE ONLY PROBLEM IS, I'M SUPPOSED TO AP-PEAR ON A LIVE TV SHOW TOMORROW AFTERNOON ...
...AND I CAN'T WRIGGLE MY WAY OUT OF IT!
UM... LOOKS LIKE THE SCHED-ULE HERE IS CLEAR FOR TOMOR-ROW.
OKAY!
VERY WELL THEN. AS TO YOUR PAST... THERE ARE MANY MEMO-RIES OF BEING AN IDOL.
MMM... MORE THAN ENOUGH BEAUTIFUL, VALUABLE MEMORIES HERE TO SPONSOR 24 HOURS IF YOU WANTED IT ...
HOW ABOUT THE MEMORY FOR AUGUST 12TH, 2003?
THAT'S THE DAY I WON THE AWARD FOR BEST SINGER AT THE PRS SONG FES-TIVAL.

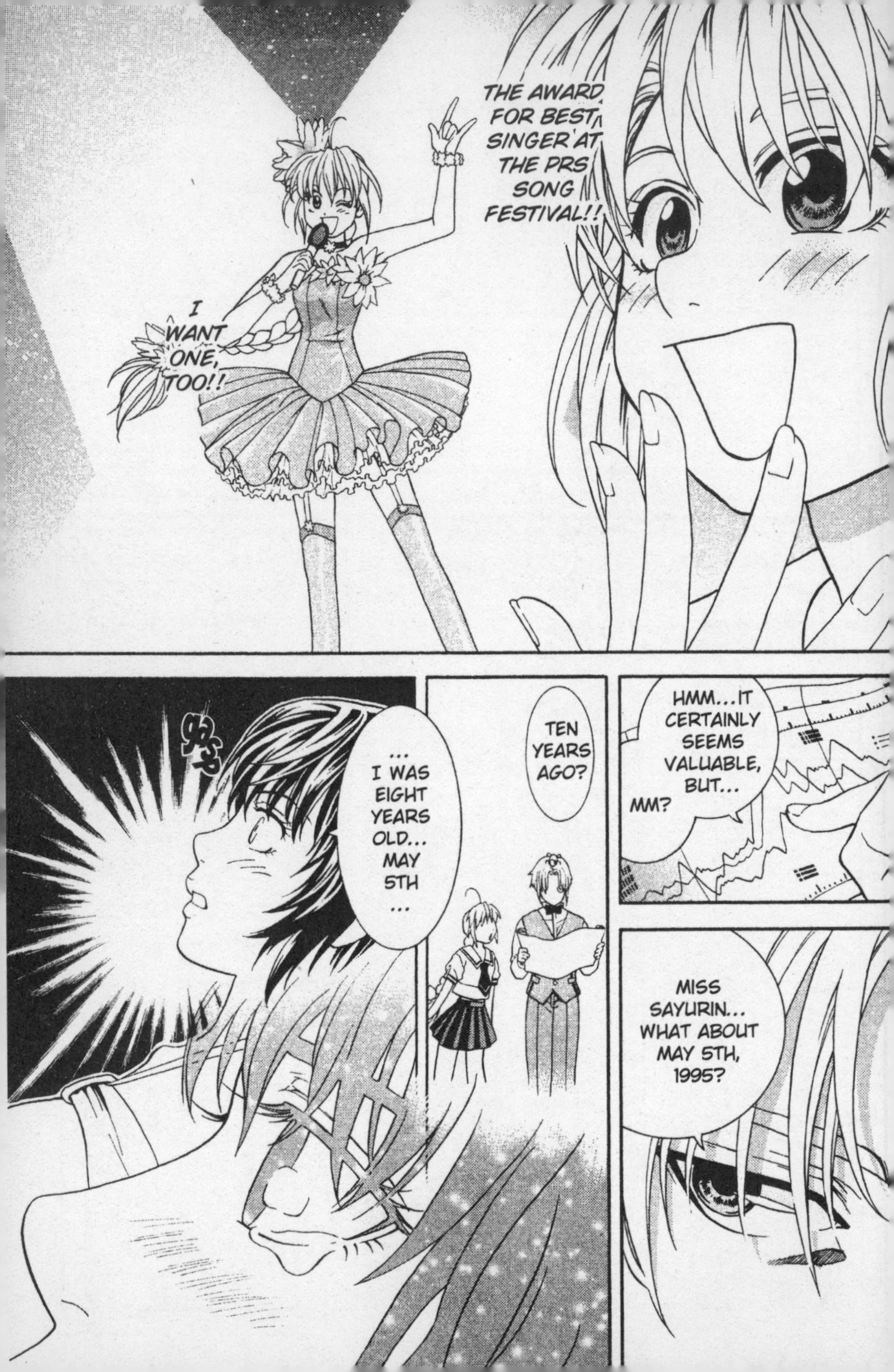
THE AWARD FOR BEST SINGER AT THE PRS SONG FESTIVAL!!
I WANT ONE, TOO!!
HMM...IT CERTAINLY SEEMS VALUABLE, BUT...
MM?
MISS SAYURIN... WHAT ABOUT MAY 5TH, 1995?
TEN YEARS AGO?
... I WAS EIGHT YEARS OLD... MAY 5TH ...
gasp

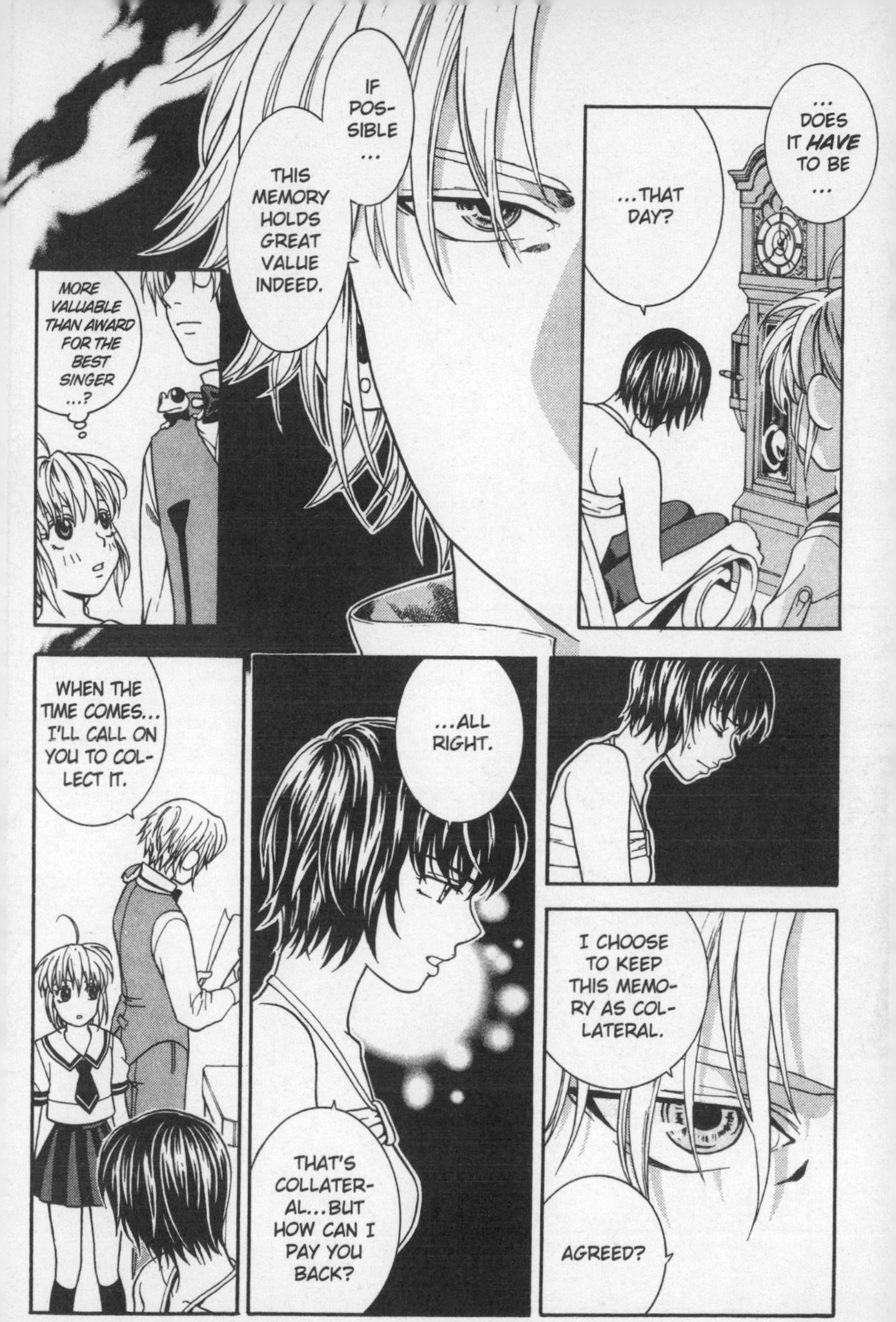
...DOES IT HAVE TO BE ...
...THAT DAY?
IF POSSIBLE ...
THIS MEMORY HOLDS GREAT VALUE INDEED.
MORE VALUABLE THAN AWARD FOR THE BEST SINGER ...?
I CHOOSE TO KEEP THIS MEMORY AS COLLATERAL.
AGREED?
...ALL RIGHT.
THAT'S COLLATERAL...BUT HOW CAN I PAY YOU BACK?
WHEN THE TIME COMES... I'LL CALL ON YOU TO COLLECT IT.

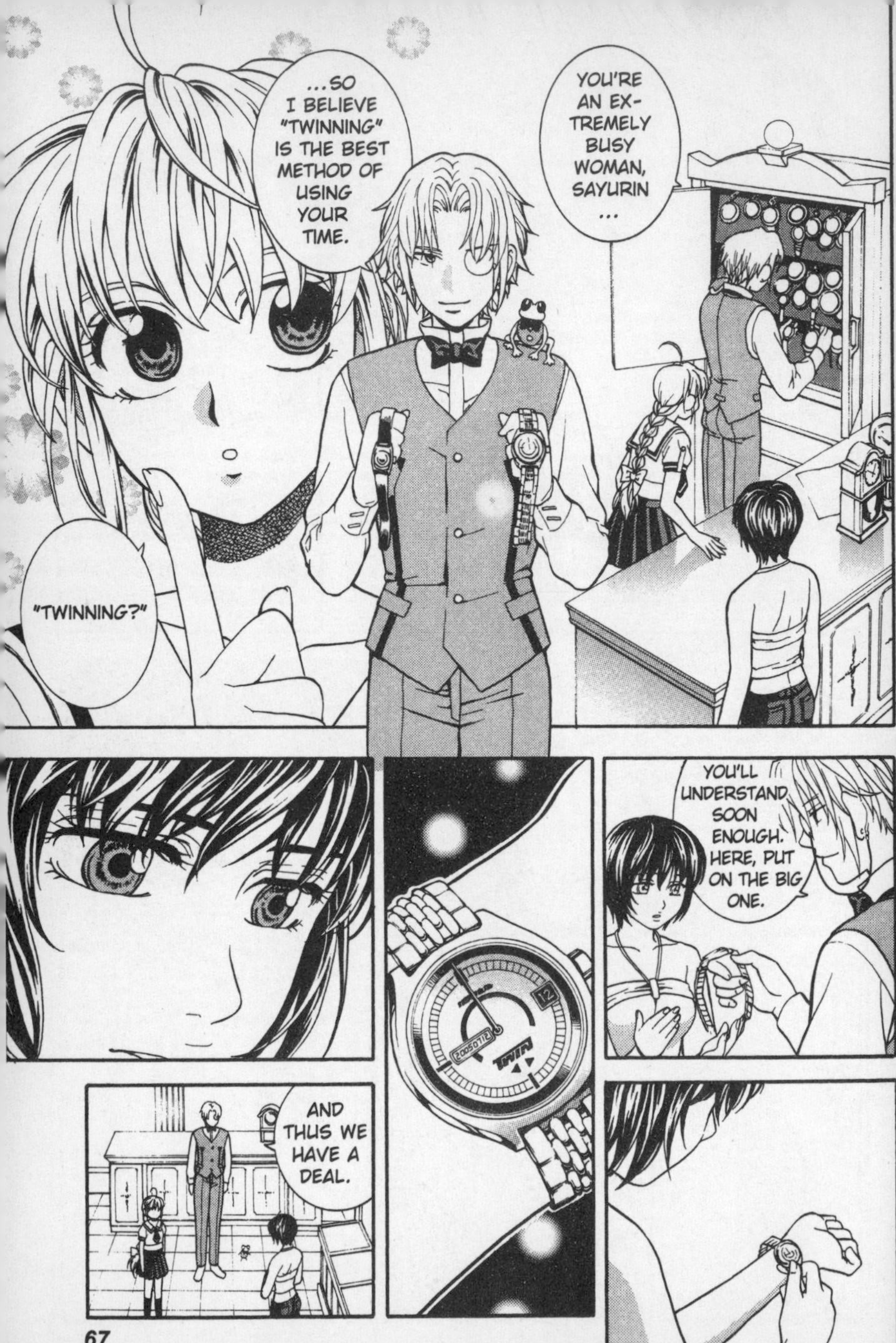
YOU'RE AN EX-TREMELY BUSY WOMAN, SAYURIN ...
...SO I BELIEVE "TWINNING" IS THE BEST METHOD OF USING YOUR TIME.
"TWINNING?"
YOU'LL UNDERSTAND SOON ENOUGH. HERE, PUT ON THE BIG ONE.
AND THUS WE HAVE A DEAL.

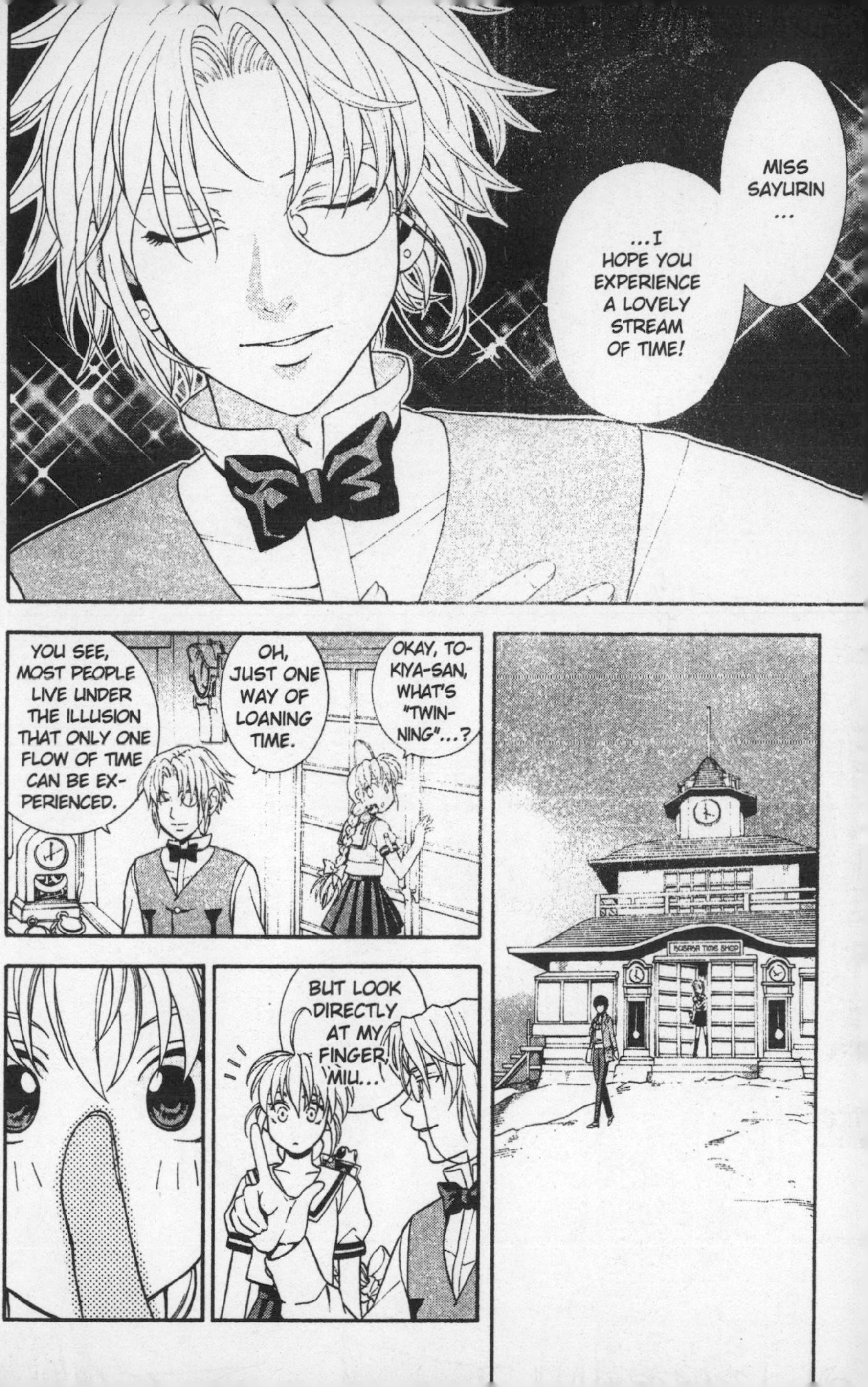
MISS SAYURIN ...
...I HOPE YOU EXPERIENCE A LOVELY STREAM OF TIME!
OKAY, TO-KIYA-SAN, WHAT'S "TWIN-NING"...?
OH, JUST ONE WAY OF LOANING TIME.
YOU SEE, MOST PEOPLE LIVE UNDER THE ILLUSION THAT ONLY ONE FLOW OF TIME CAN BE EX-PERIENCED.
BUT LOOK DIRECTLY AT MY FINGER, MIU...

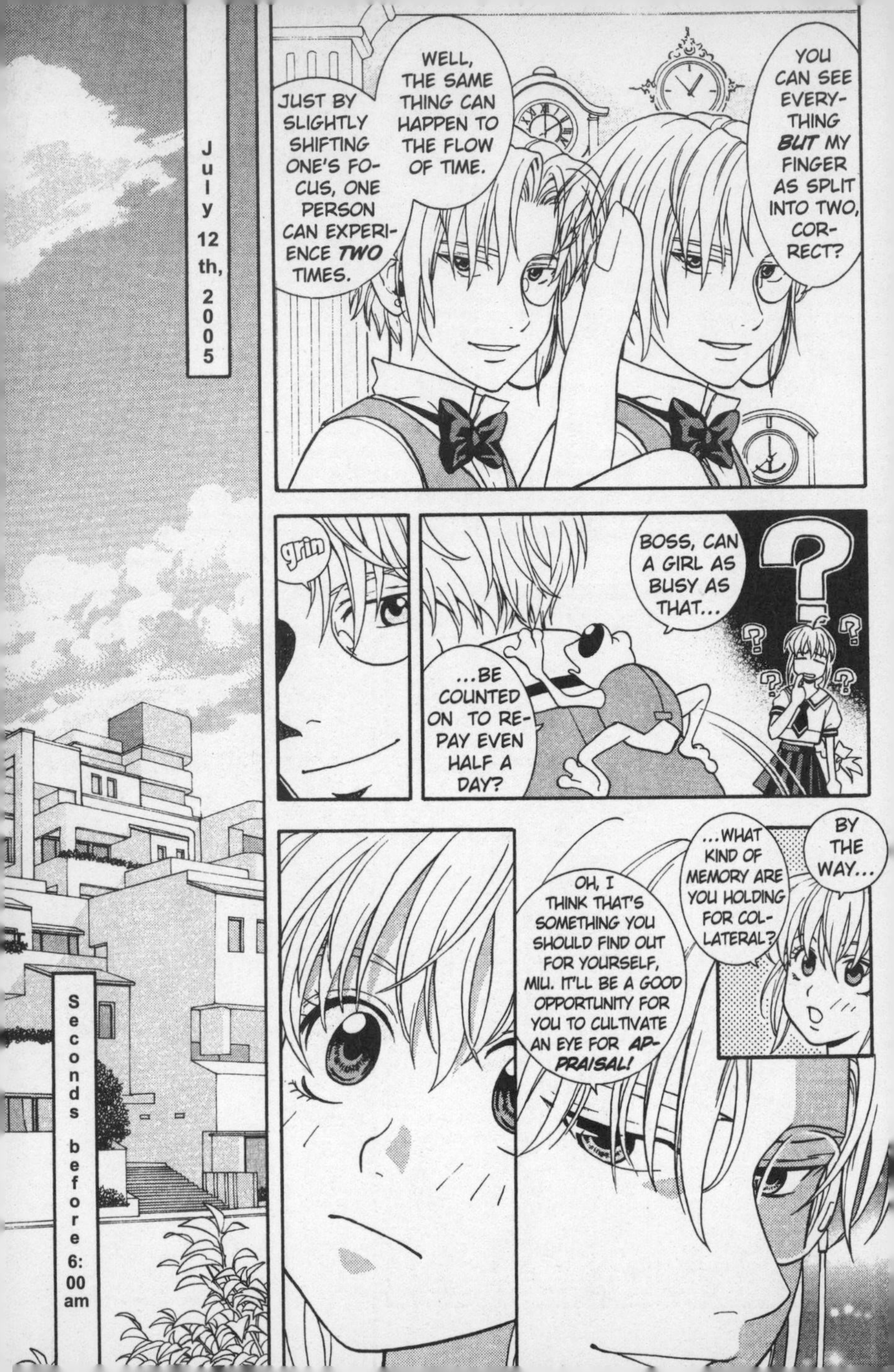
YOU CAN SEE EVERY-THING BUT MY FINGER AS SPLIT INTO TWO, COR-RECT?
WELL, THE SAME THING CAN HAPPEN TO THE FLOW OF TIME.
JUST BY SLIGHTLY SHIFTING ONE'S FO-CUS, ONE PERSON CAN EXPERI-ENCE TWO TIMES.
BOSS, CAN A GIRL AS BUSY AS THAT...
...BE COUNTED ON TO RE-PAY EVEN HALF A DAY?
grin
BY THE WAY...
...WHAT KIND OF MEMORY ARE YOU HOLDING FOR COL-LATERAL?
OH, I THINK THAT'S SOMETHING YOU SHOULD FIND OUT FOR YOURSELF, MIU. IT'LL BE A GOOD OPPORTUNITY FOR YOU TO CULTIVATE AN EYE FOR AP-PRAISAL!
July 12th, 2005
Seconds before 6:00 am

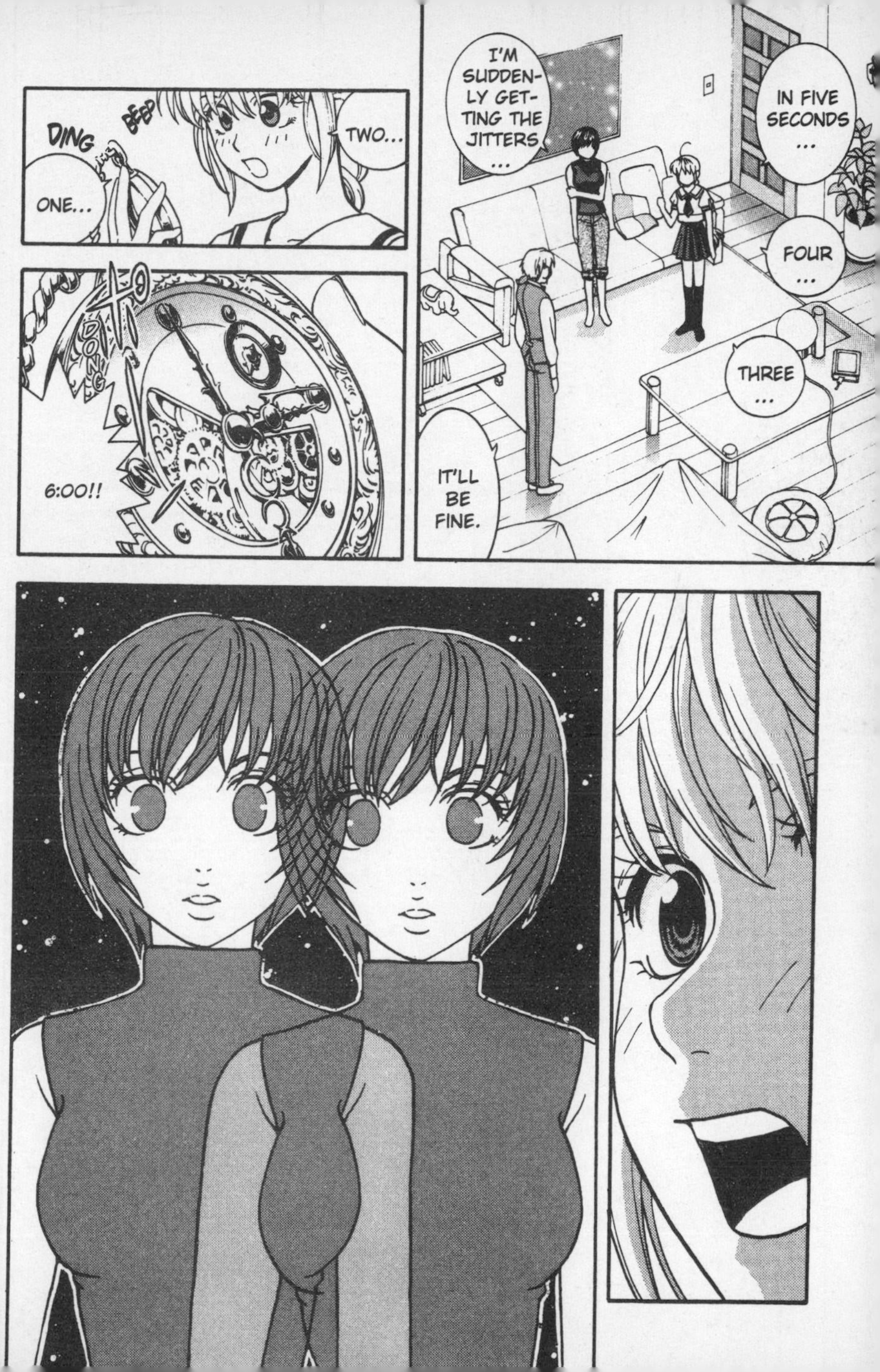
IN FIVE SECONDS ...
FOUR ...
THREE ...
I'M SUDDEN-LY GET-TING THE JITTERS ...
IT'LL BE FINE.
TWO...
BEEP
DING
ONE...
DONG
6:00!!

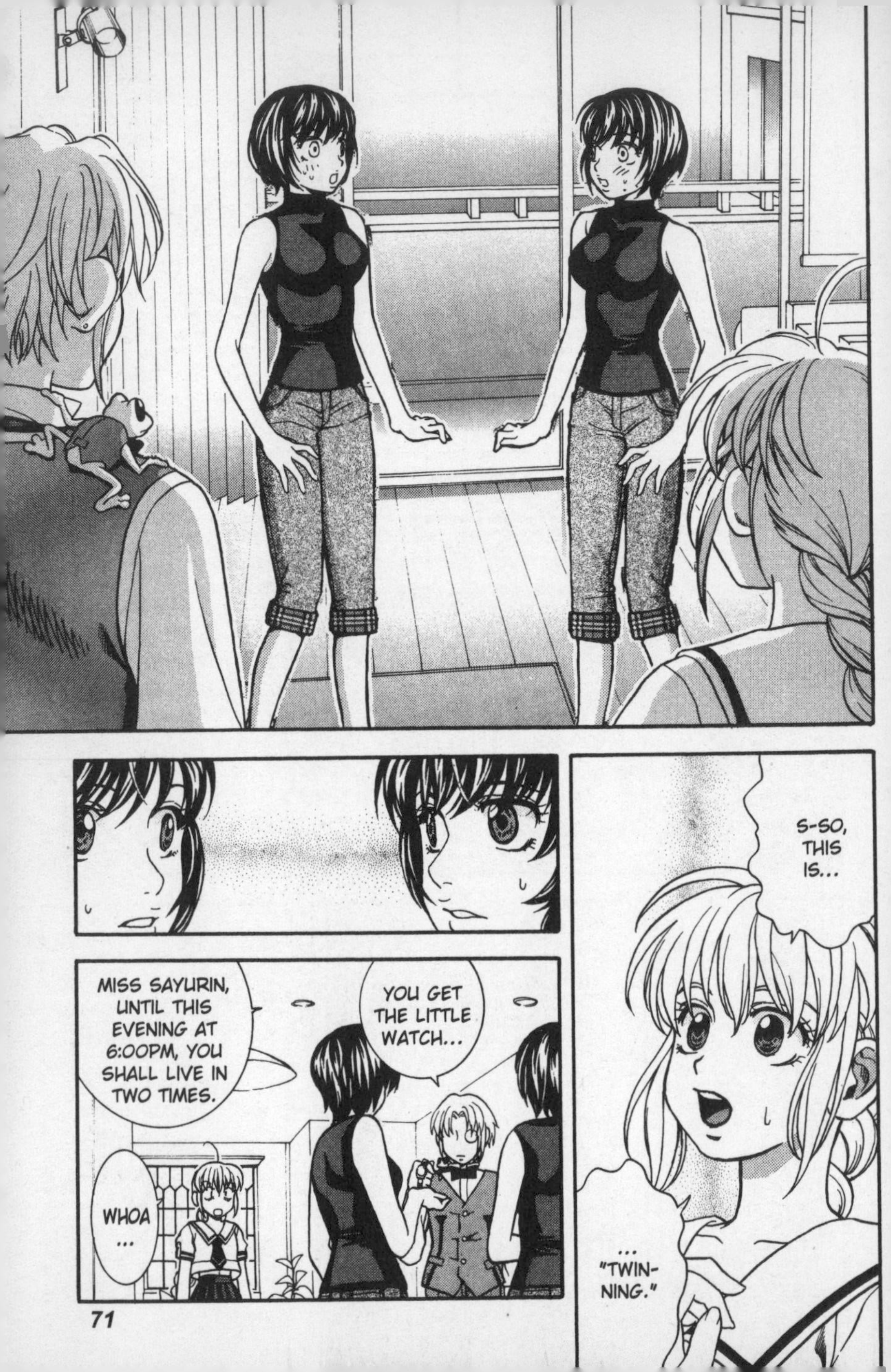
S-SO, THIS IS...
... "TWIN-NING."
YOU GET THE LITTLE WATCH...
MISS SAYURIN, UNTIL THIS EVENING AT 6:00PM, YOU SHALL LIVE IN TWO TIMES.
WHOA ...

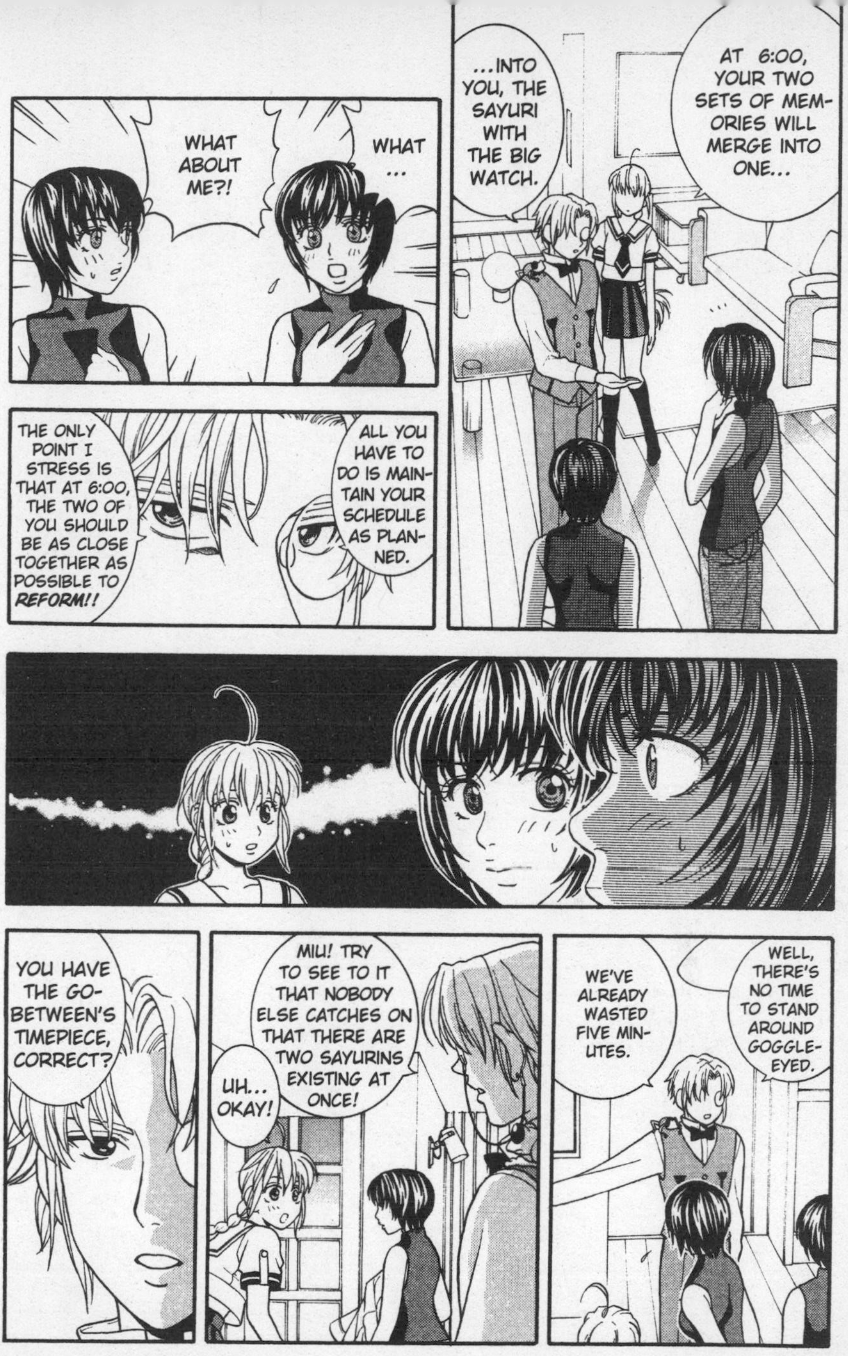
AT 6:00, YOUR TWO SETS OF MEMORIES WILL MERGE INTO ONE...
...INTO YOU, THE SAYURI WITH THE BIG WATCH.
...
WHAT ...
WHAT ABOUT ME?!
ALL YOU HAVE TO DO IS MAINTAIN YOUR SCHEDULE AS PLANNED.
THE ONLY POINT I STRESS IS THAT AT 6:00, THE TWO OF YOU SHOULD BE AS CLOSE TOGETHER AS POSSIBLE TO *REFORM!!*
WELL, THERE'S NO TIME TO STAND AROUND GOGGLE-EYED.
WE'VE ALREADY WASTED FIVE MINUTES.
MIU! TRY TO SEE TO IT THAT NOBODY ELSE CATCHES ON THAT THERE ARE TWO SAYURINS EXISTING AT ONCE!
UH... OKAY!
YOU HAVE THE GO-BETWEEN'S TIMEPIECE, CORRECT?

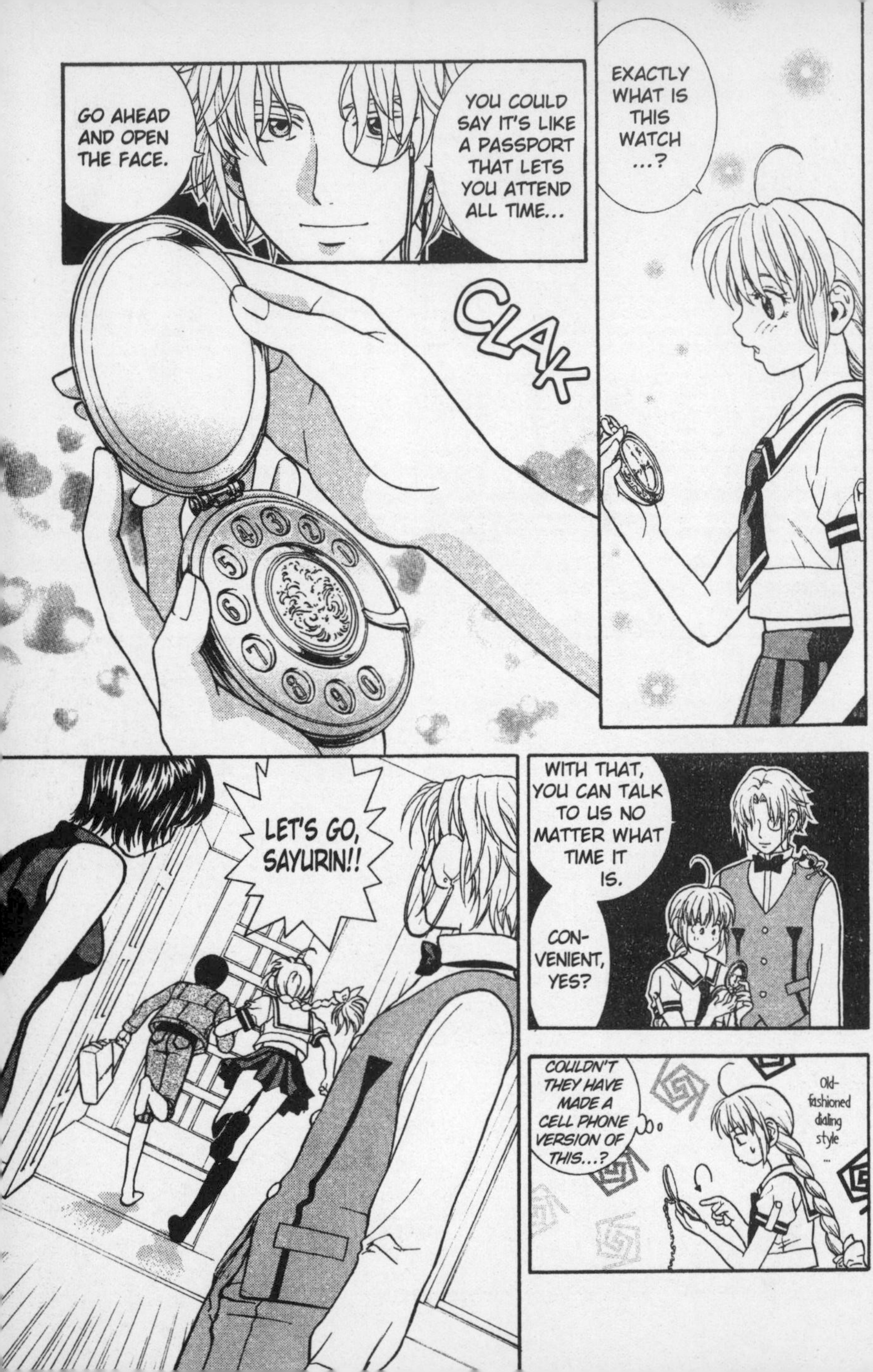
EXACTLY WHAT IS THIS WATCH ...?
YOU COULD SAY IT'S LIKE A PASSPORT THAT LETS YOU ATTEND ALL TIME...
GO AHEAD AND OPEN THE FACE.
CLAK
WITH THAT, YOU CAN TALK TO US NO MATTER WHAT TIME IT IS.
CON-VENIENT, YES?
COULDN'T THEY HAVE MADE A CELL PHONE VERSION OF THIS...?
Old-fashioned dialing style ...
LET'S GO, SAYURIN!!

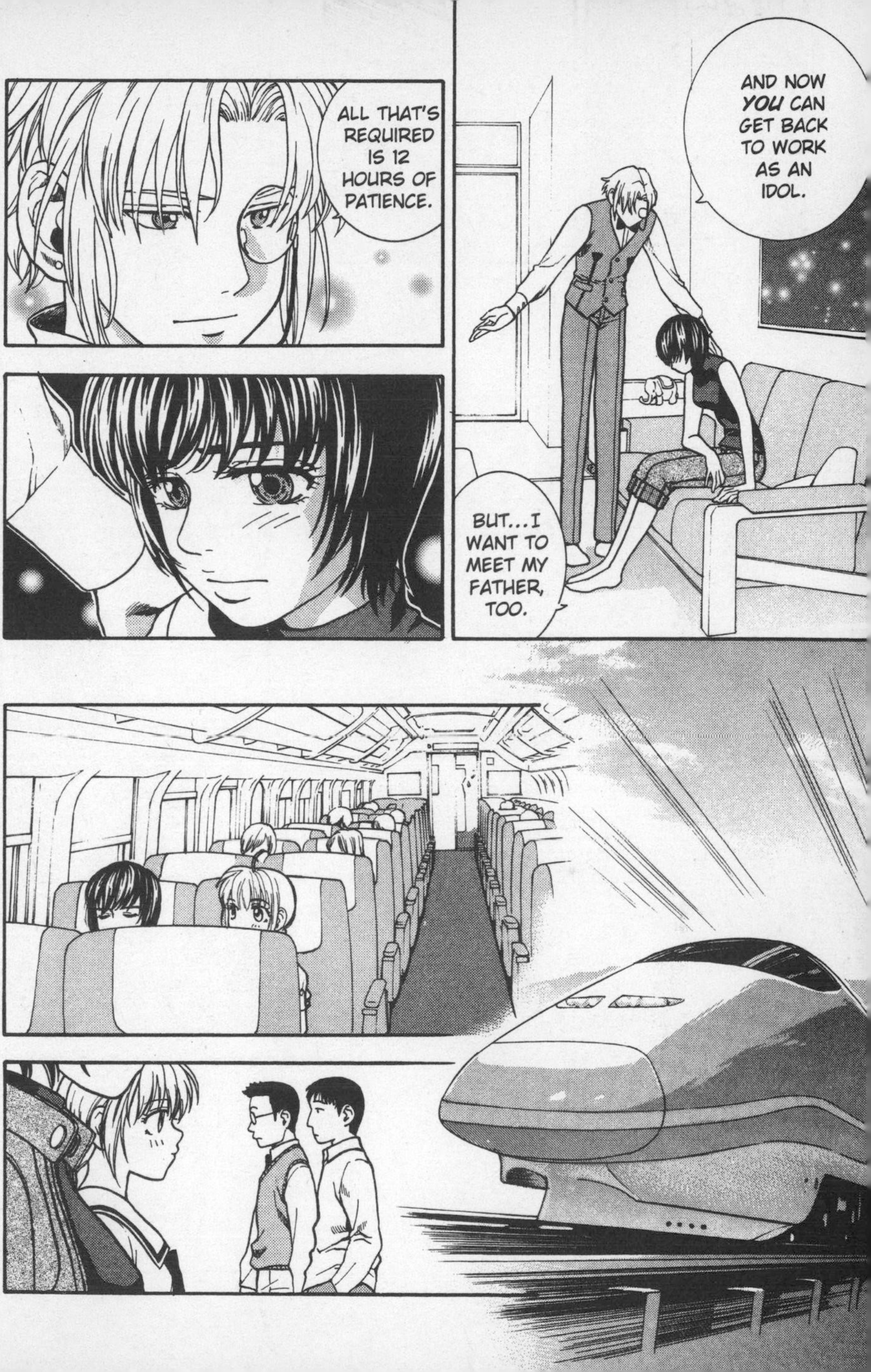
AND NOW *YOU* CAN GET BACK TO WORK AS AN IDOL.
BUT...I WANT TO MEET MY FATHER, TOO.
ALL THAT'S REQUIRED IS 12 HOURS OF PATIENCE.

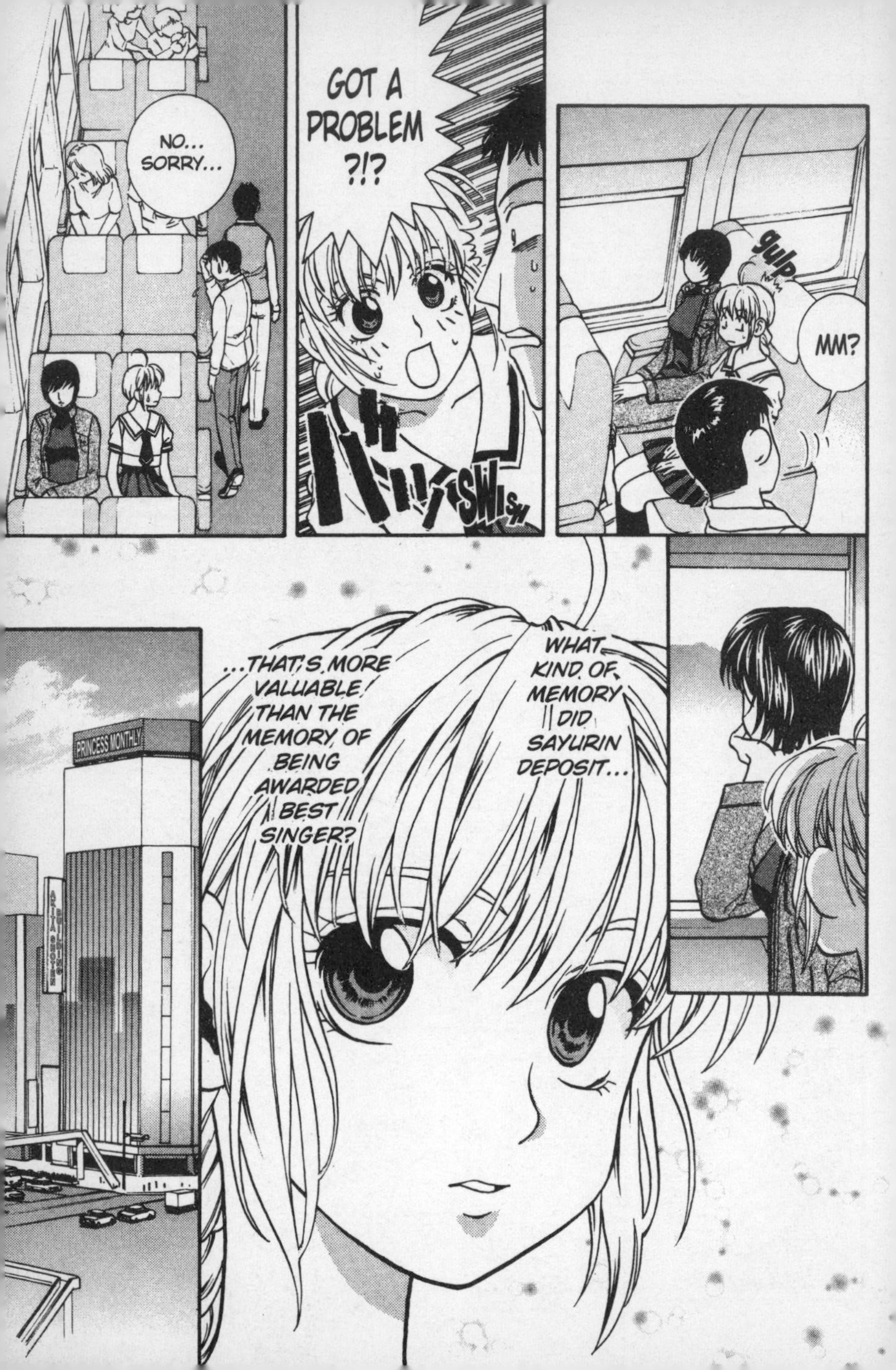
gulp
MM?
GOT A PROBLEM ?!?
SWISH
NO... SORRY...
WHAT KIND OF MEMORY DID SAYURIN DEPOSIT...
...THAT'S MORE VALUABLE THAN THE MEMORY OF BEING AWARDED BEST SINGER?
PRINCESS MONTHLY
AKITA SHOTEN BUILDING

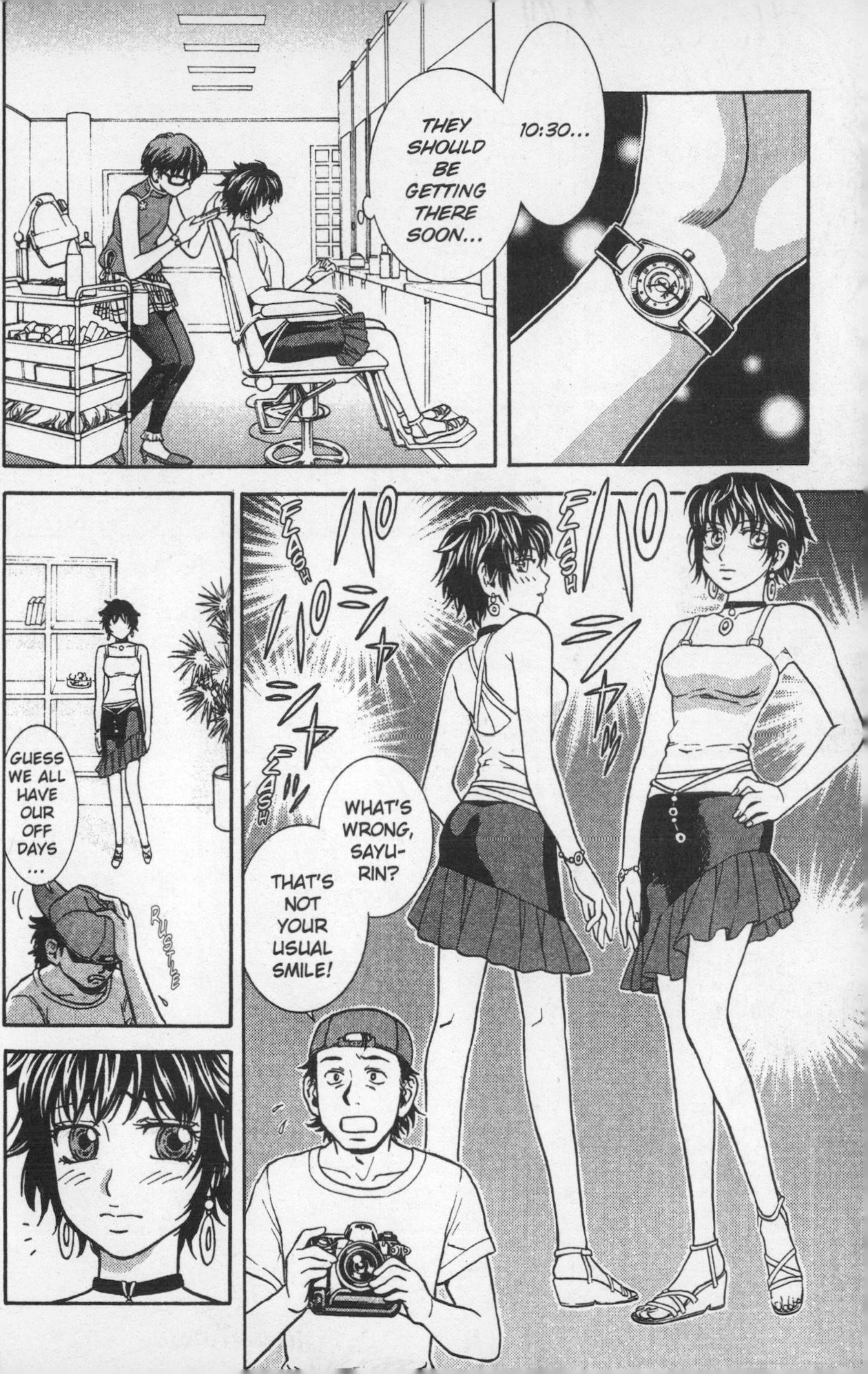
10:30...
THEY SHOULD BE GETTING THERE SOON...
FLASH
FLASH
FLASH
WHAT'S WRONG, SAYU-RIN?
THAT'S NOT YOUR USUAL SMILE!
GUESS WE ALL HAVE OUR OFF DAYS...
RUSTLE

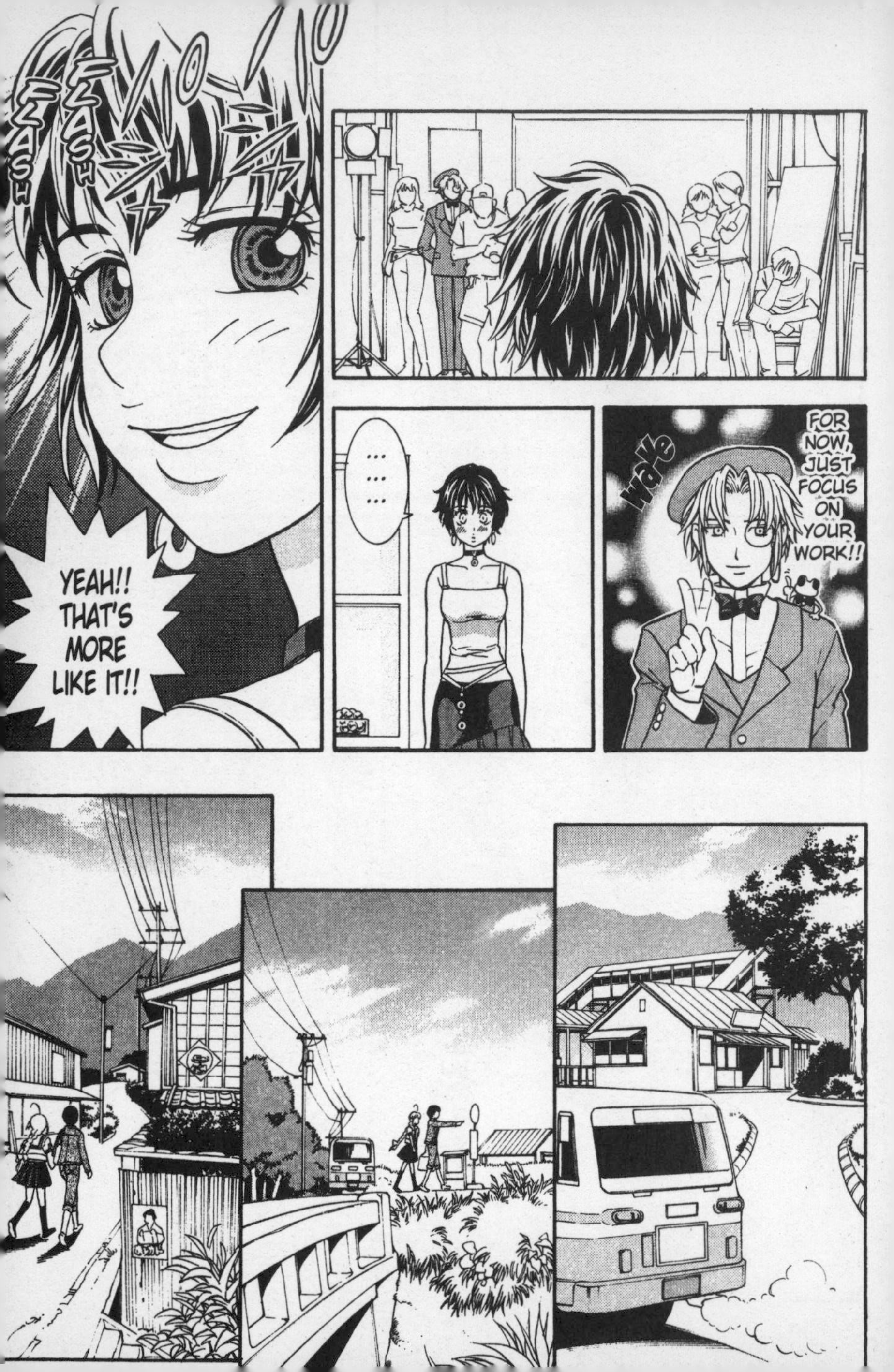
wave
FOR NOW, JUST FOCUS ON YOUR WORK!!
...
...
...
FLASH
FLASH
YEAH!! THAT'S MORE LIKE IT!!

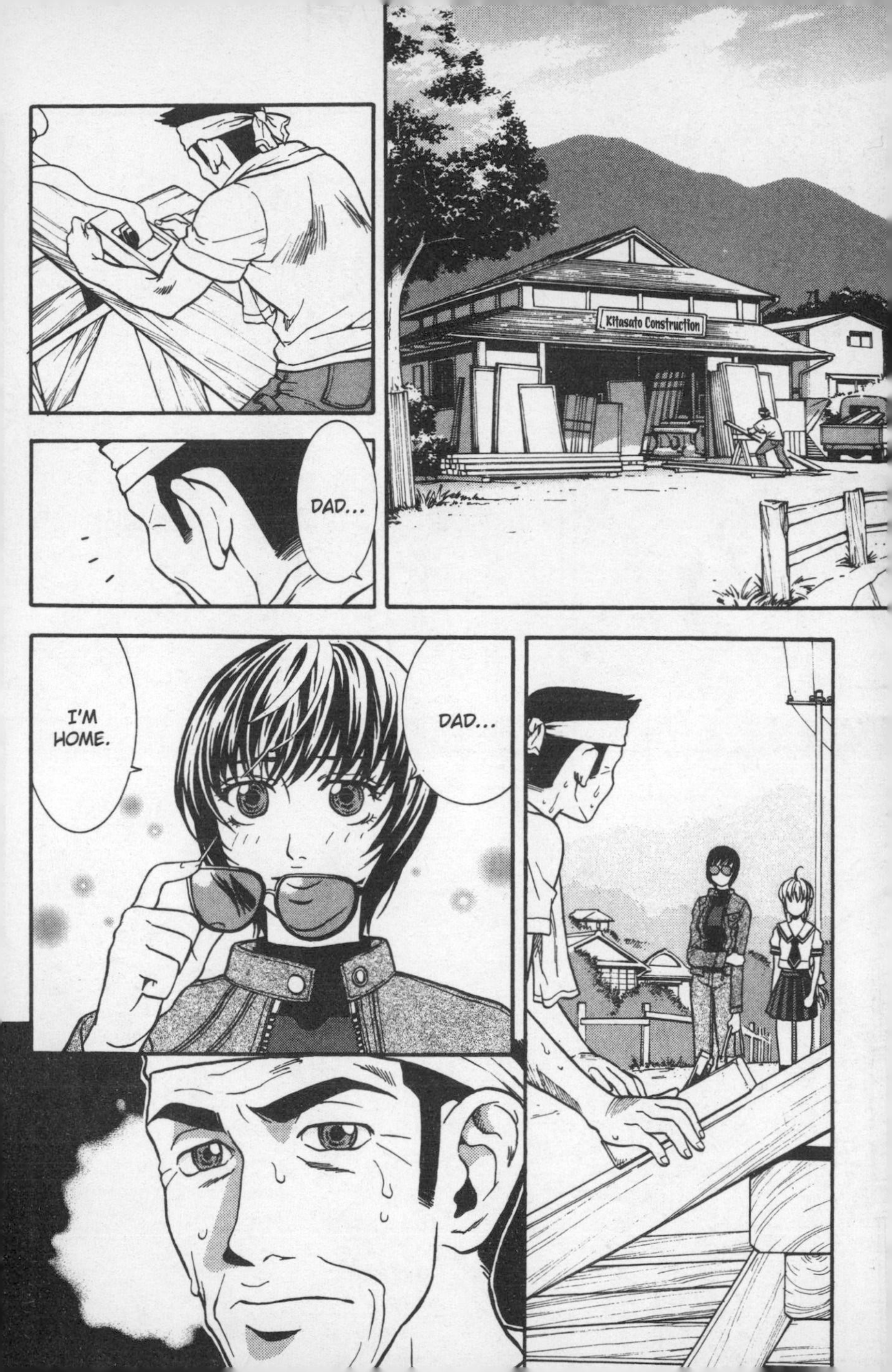
Kitasato Construction
DAD...
DAD...
I'M HOME.

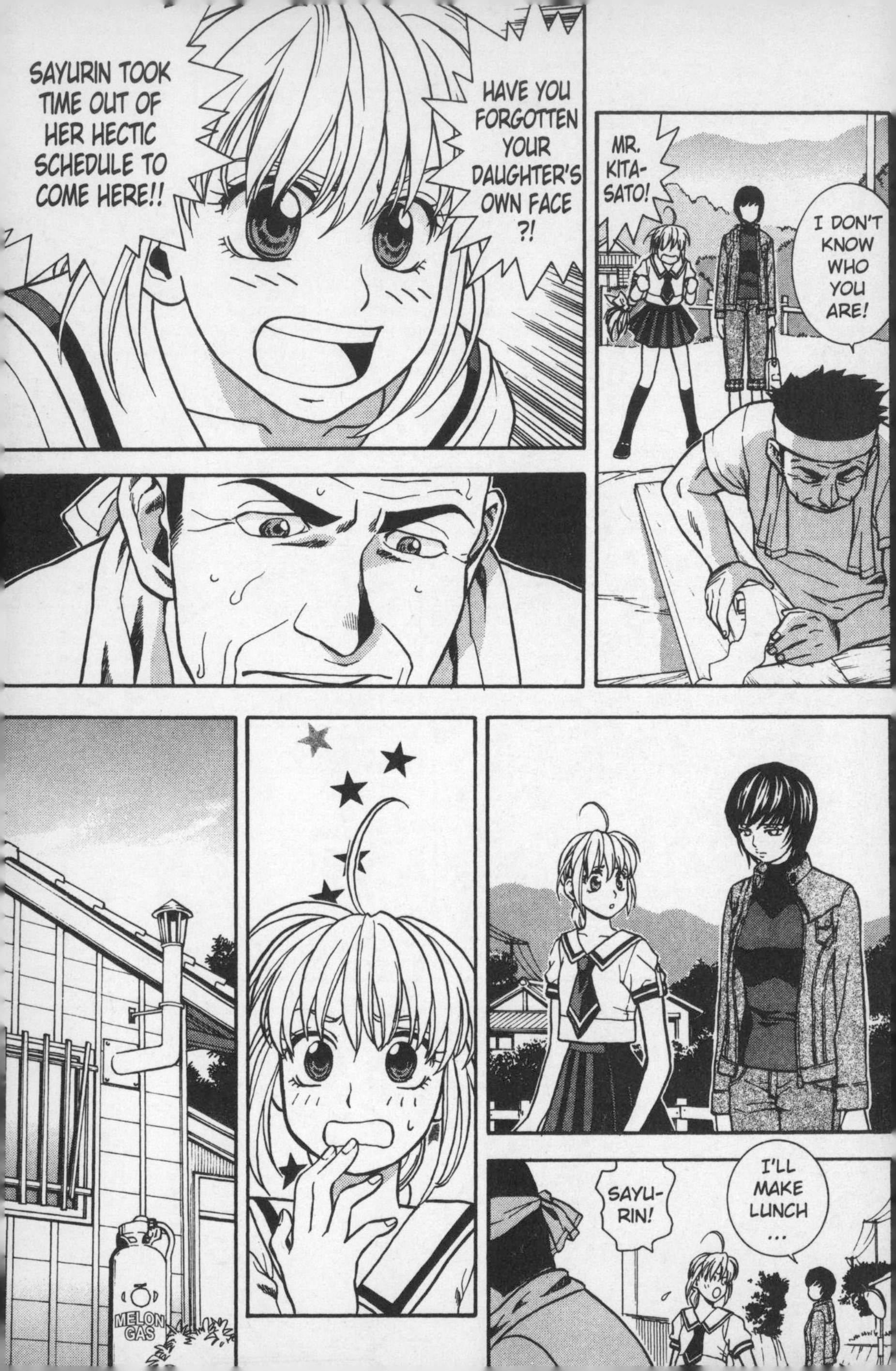
MR. KITA-SATO!
I DON'T KNOW WHO YOU ARE!
HAVE YOU FORGOTTEN YOUR DAUGHTER'S OWN FACE ?!
SAYURIN TOOK TIME OUT OF HER HECTIC SCHEDULE TO COME HERE!!
I'LL MAKE LUNCH ...
SAYU-RIN!
MELON GAS

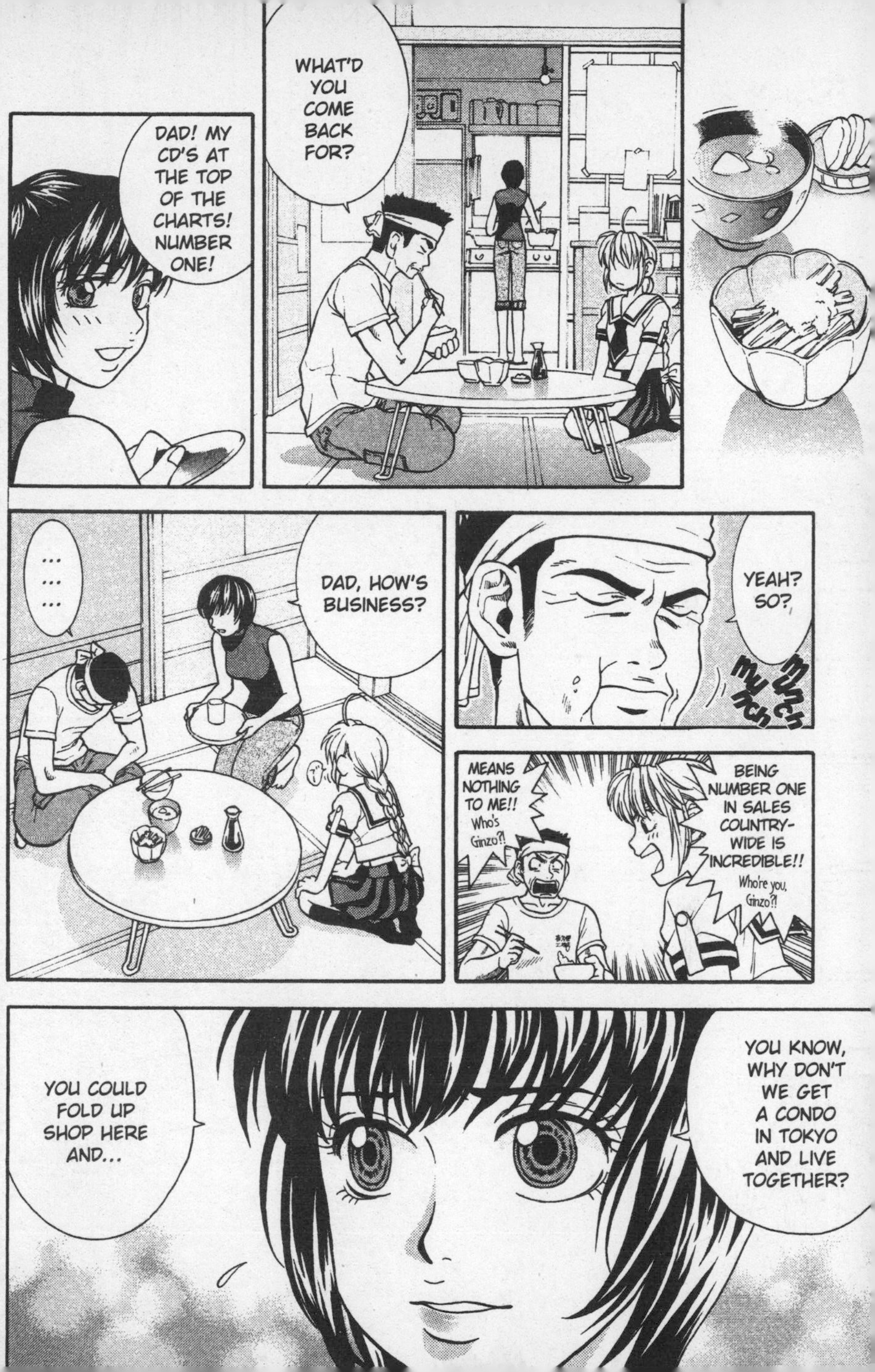
WHAT'D YOU COME BACK FOR?
DAD! MY CD'S AT THE TOP OF THE CHARTS! NUMBER ONE!
YEAH? SO?
MUNCH MUNCH
BEING NUMBER ONE IN SALES COUNTRY-WIDE IS INCREDIBLE!!
Who're you, Ginzo?!
MEANS NOTHING TO ME!!
Who's Ginzo?!
DAD, HOW'S BUSINESS?
... ...
YOU KNOW, WHY DON'T WE GET A CONDO IN TOKYO AND LIVE TOGETHER?
YOU COULD FOLD UP SHOP HERE AND...

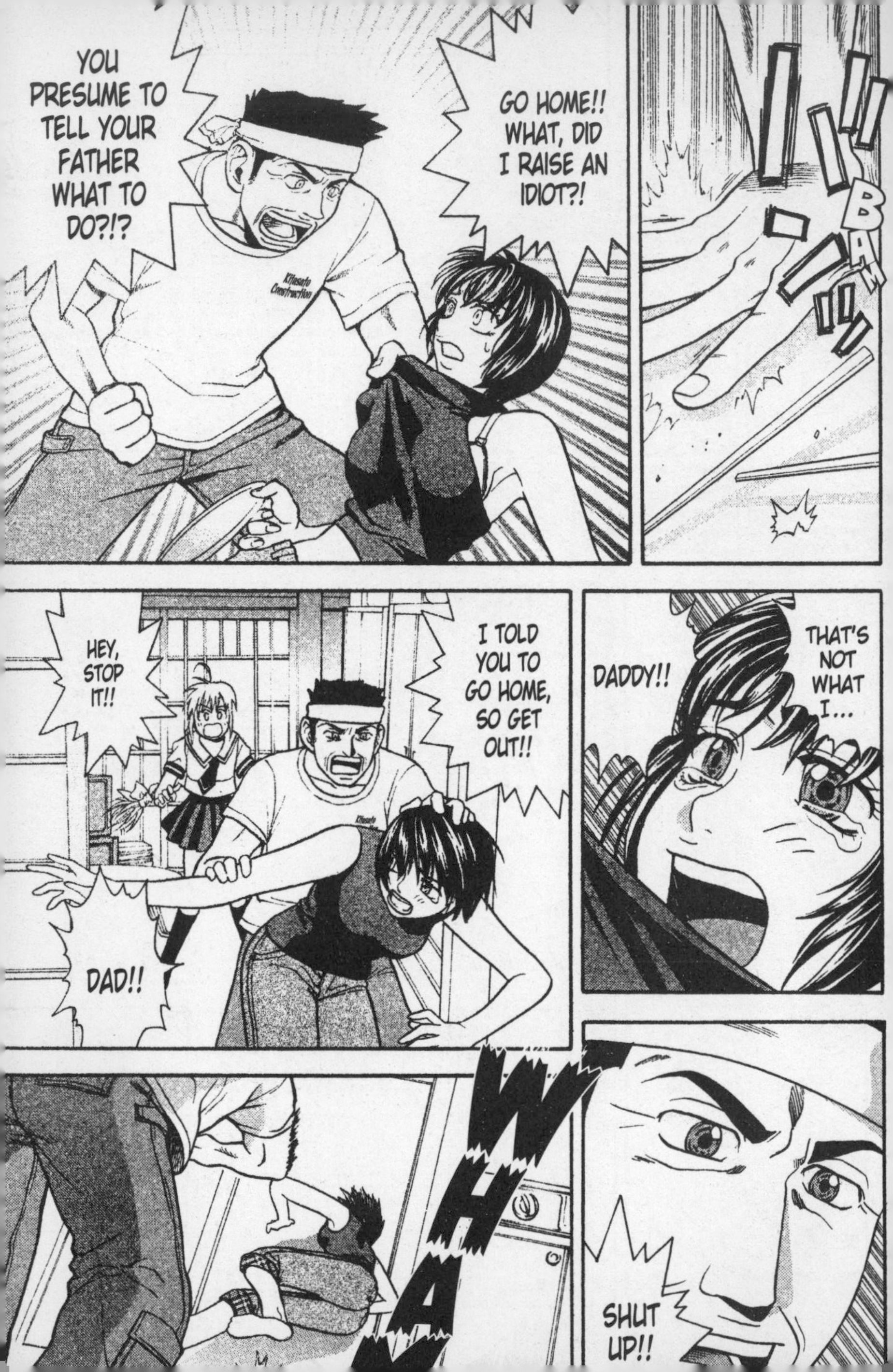
BAM
GO HOME!! WHAT, DID I RAISE AN IDIOT?!
YOU PRESUME TO TELL YOUR FATHER WHAT TO DO?!?
Kitasato Construction
THAT'S NOT WHAT I...
DADDY!!
I TOLD YOU TO GO HOME, SO GET OUT!!
HEY, STOP IT!!
DAD!!
SHUT UP!!
WHAM

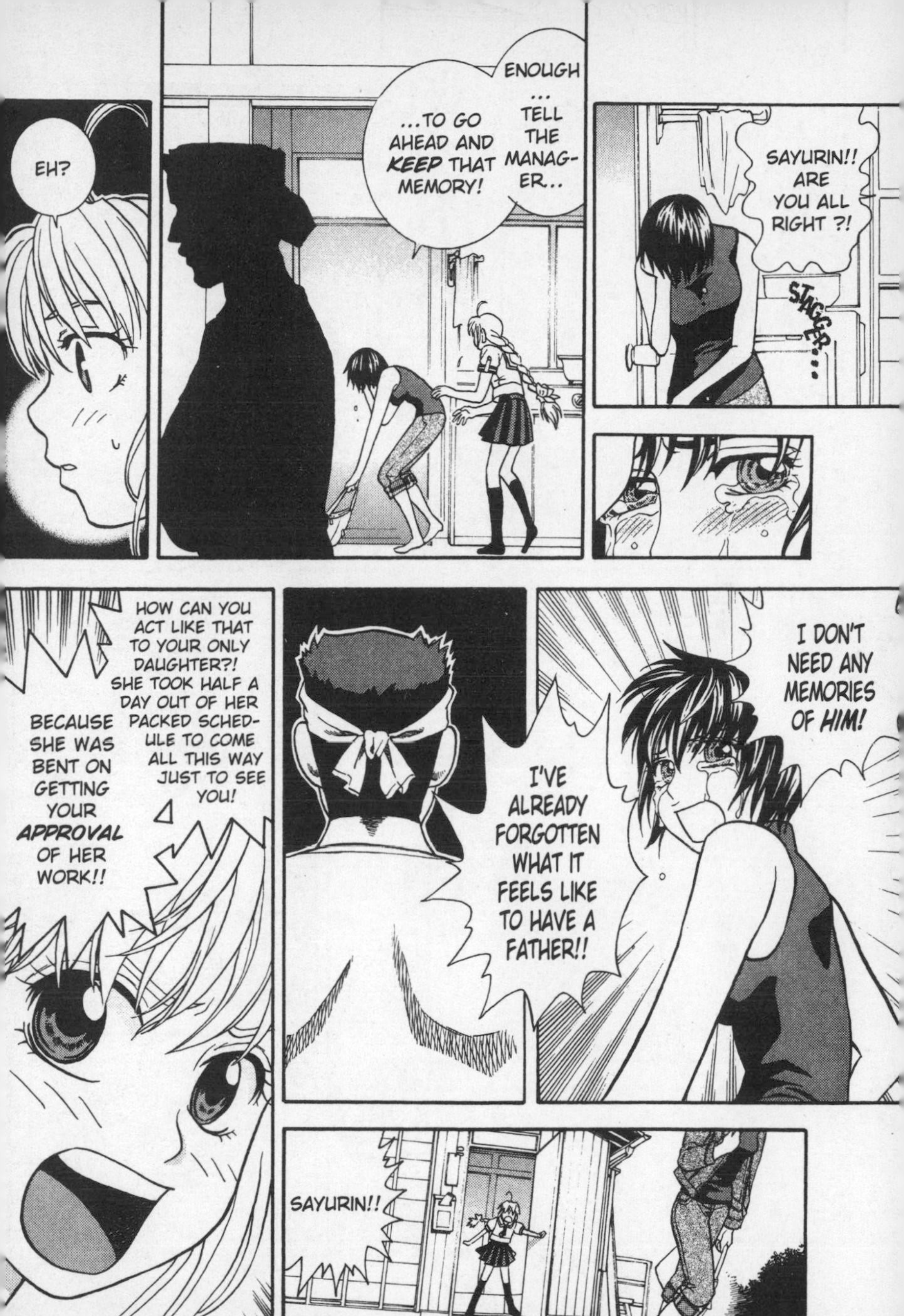
SAYURIN!! ARE YOU ALL RIGHT ?!
STAGGER...
ENOUGH ... TELL THE MANAGER...
...TO GO AHEAD AND KEEP THAT MEMORY!
EH?
I DON'T NEED ANY MEMORIES OF HIM!
I'VE ALREADY FORGOTTEN WHAT IT FEELS LIKE TO HAVE A FATHER!!
SAYURIN!!
HOW CAN YOU ACT LIKE THAT TO YOUR ONLY DAUGHTER?! SHE TOOK HALF A DAY OUT OF HER PACKED SCHEDULE TO COME ALL THIS WAY JUST TO SEE YOU!
BECAUSE SHE WAS BENT ON GETTING YOUR APPROVAL OF HER WORK!!

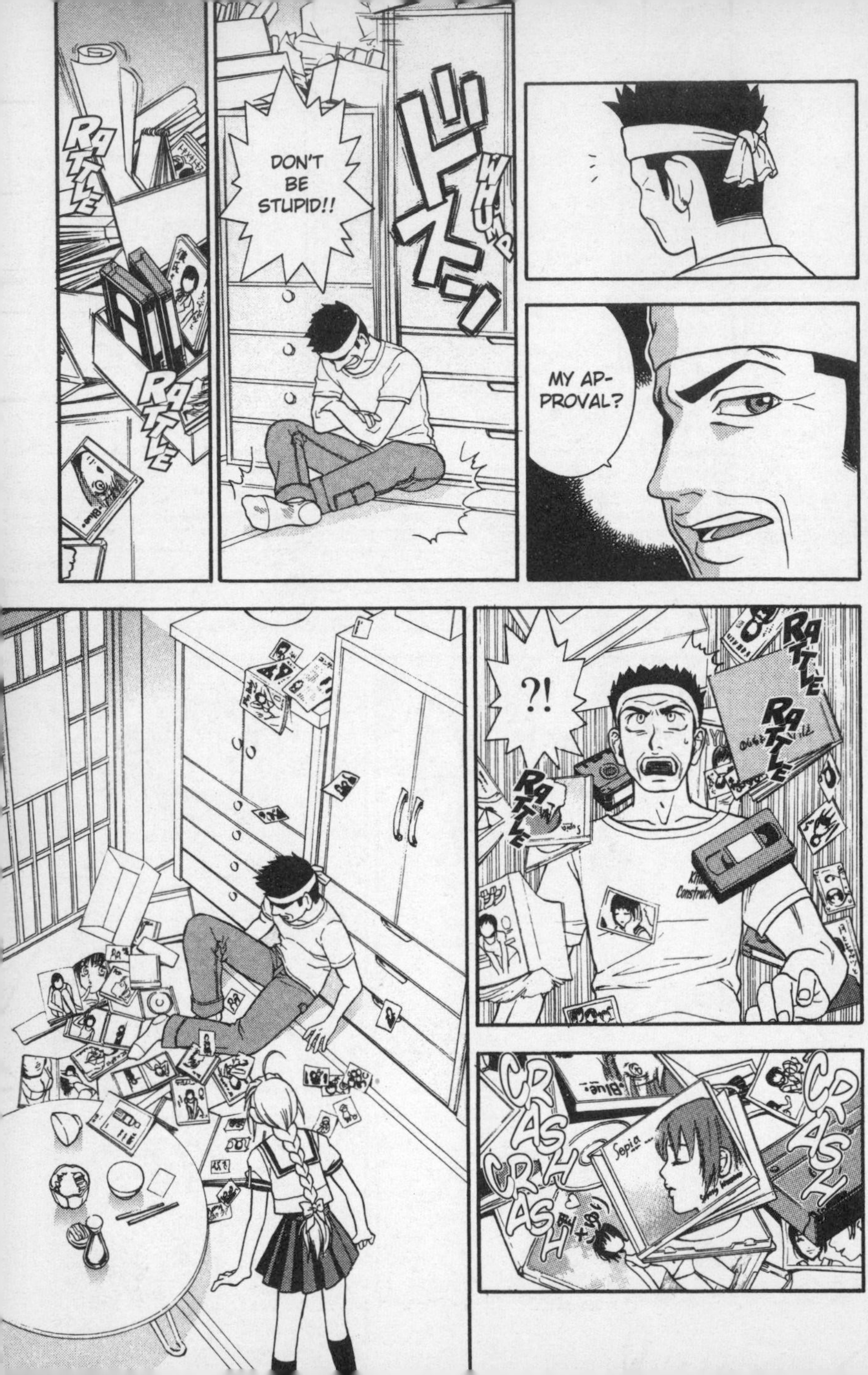
MY AP-PROVAL?
DON'T BE STUPID!!
WHUMP
RATTLE
RATTLE
?!
RATTLE
RATTLE
RATTLE
CRASH
CRASH
CRASH
Sepia

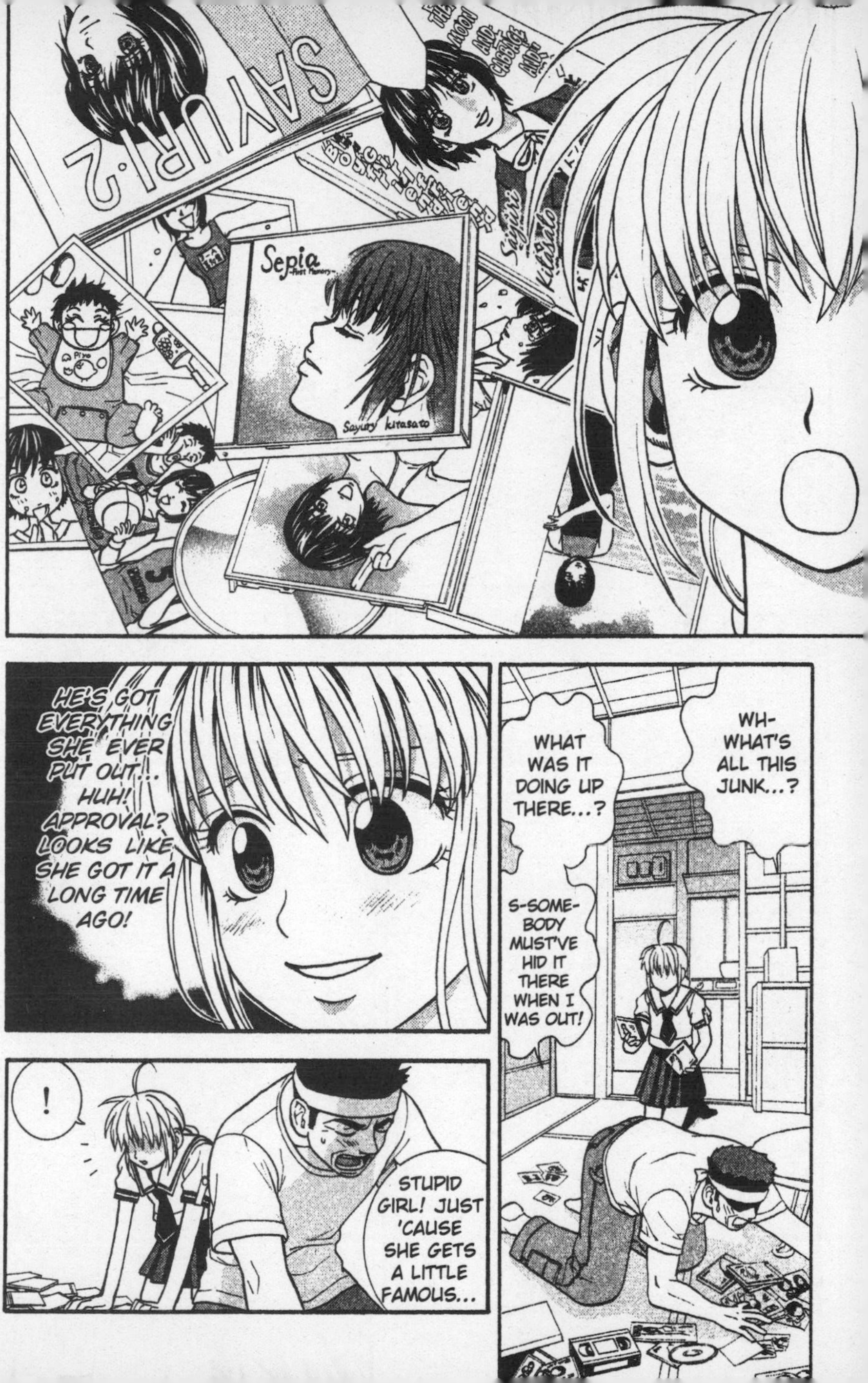
SAYURI 2
Sepia
Sayuri kitasato
WH- WHAT'S ALL THIS JUNK...?
WHAT WAS IT DOING UP THERE...?
S-SOMEBODY MUST'VE HID IT THERE WHEN I WAS OUT!
HE'S GOT EVERYTHING SHE EVER PUT OUT... HUH! APPROVAL? LOOKS LIKE SHE GOT IT A LONG TIME AGO!
!
STUPID GIRL! JUST 'CAUSE SHE GETS A LITTLE FAMOUS...

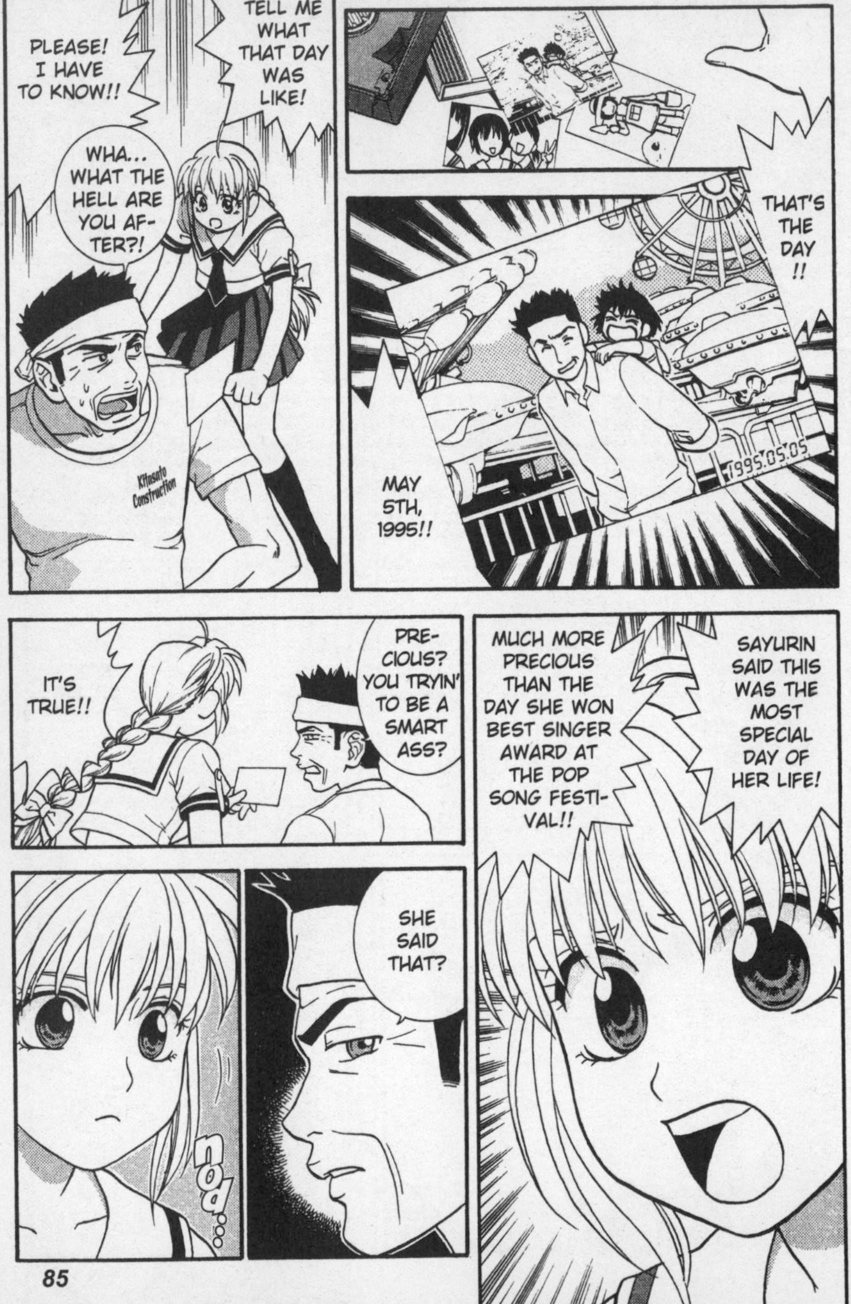
THAT'S THE DAY!!
MAY 5TH, 1995!!
1995.05.05
MR. KITASATO TELL ME WHAT THAT DAY WAS LIKE!
PLEASE! I HAVE TO KNOW!!
WHA... WHAT THE HELL ARE YOU AFTER?!
Kitasato Construction
SAYURIN SAID THIS WAS THE MOST SPECIAL DAY OF HER LIFE!
MUCH MORE PRECIOUS THAN THE DAY SHE WON BEST SINGER AWARD AT THE POP SONG FESTIVAL!!
PRE-CIOUS? YOU TRYIN' TO BE A SMART ASS?
IT'S TRUE!!
SHE SAID THAT?
nod...

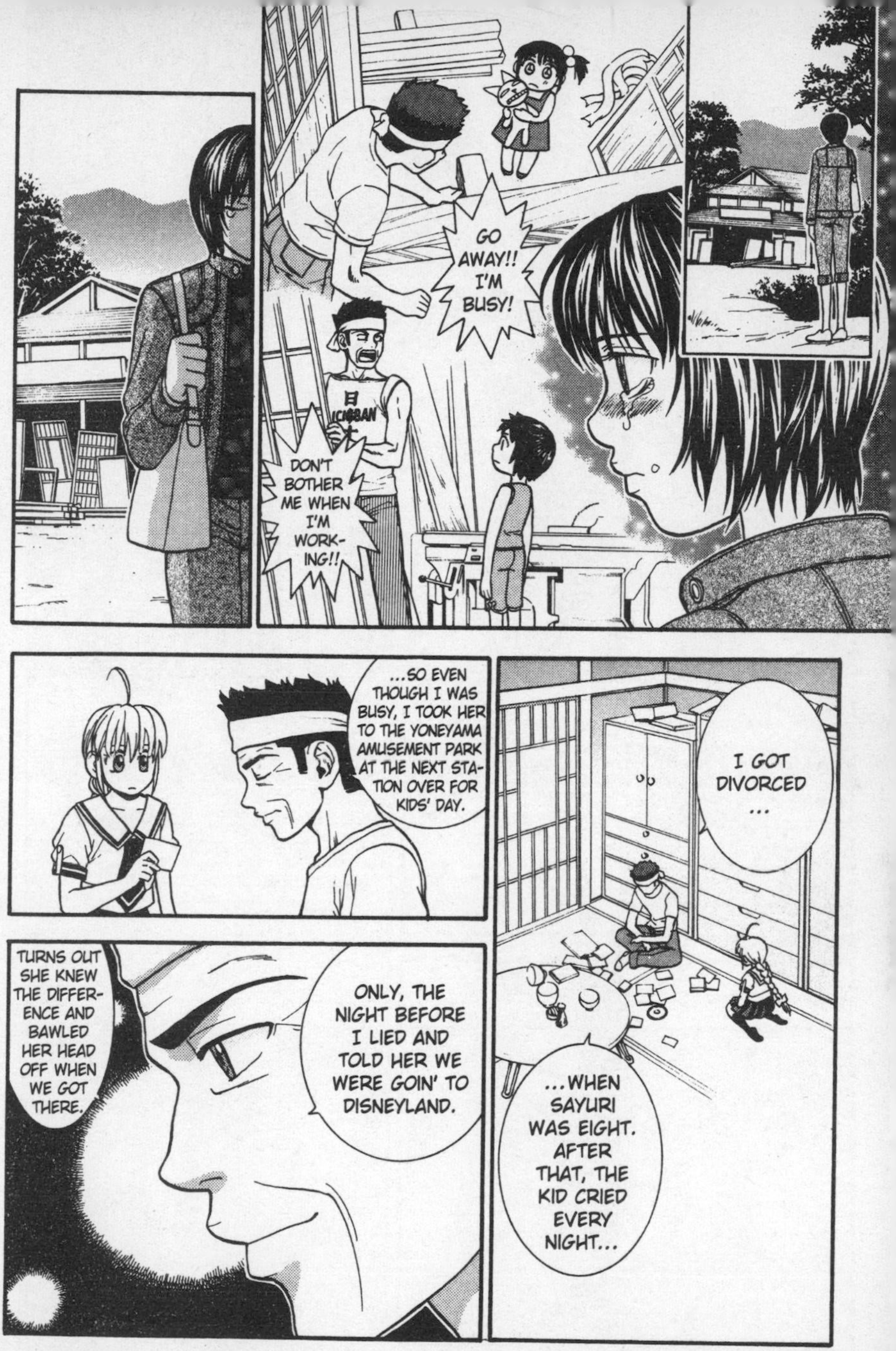
GO AWAY!! I'M BUSY!
DON'T BOTHER ME WHEN I'M WORK-ING!!
I GOT DIVORCED ...
...WHEN SAYURI WAS EIGHT. AFTER THAT, THE KID CRIED EVERY NIGHT...
...SO EVEN THOUGH I WAS BUSY, I TOOK HER TO THE YONEYAMA AMUSEMENT PARK AT THE NEXT STA-TION OVER FOR KIDS' DAY.
ONLY, THE NIGHT BEFORE I LIED AND TOLD HER WE WERE GOIN' TO DISNEYLAND.
TURNS OUT SHE KNEW THE DIFFER-ENCE AND BAWLED HER HEAD OFF WHEN WE GOT THERE.

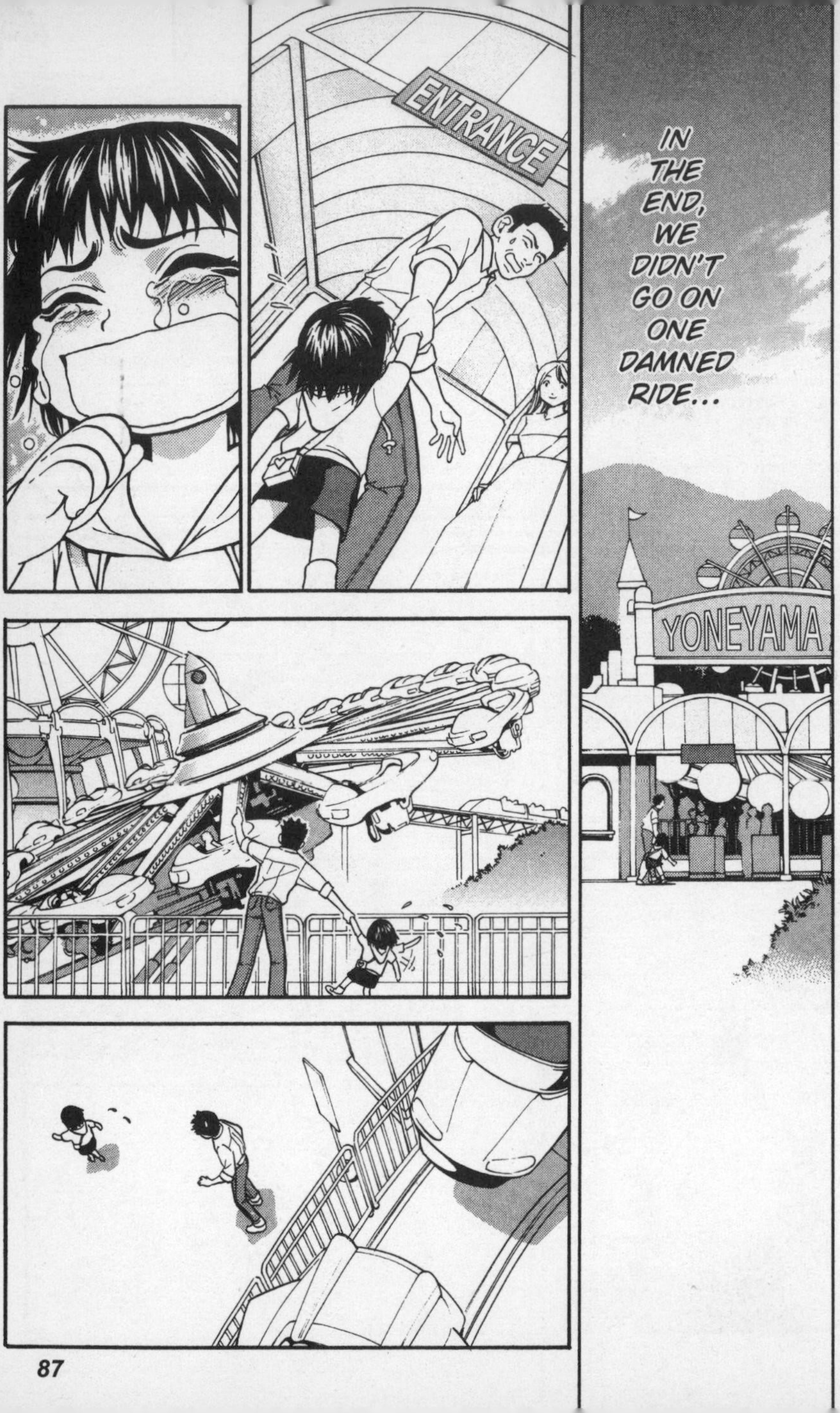
IN THE END, WE DIDN'T GO ON ONE DAMNED RIDE...
YONEYAMA
ENTRANCE

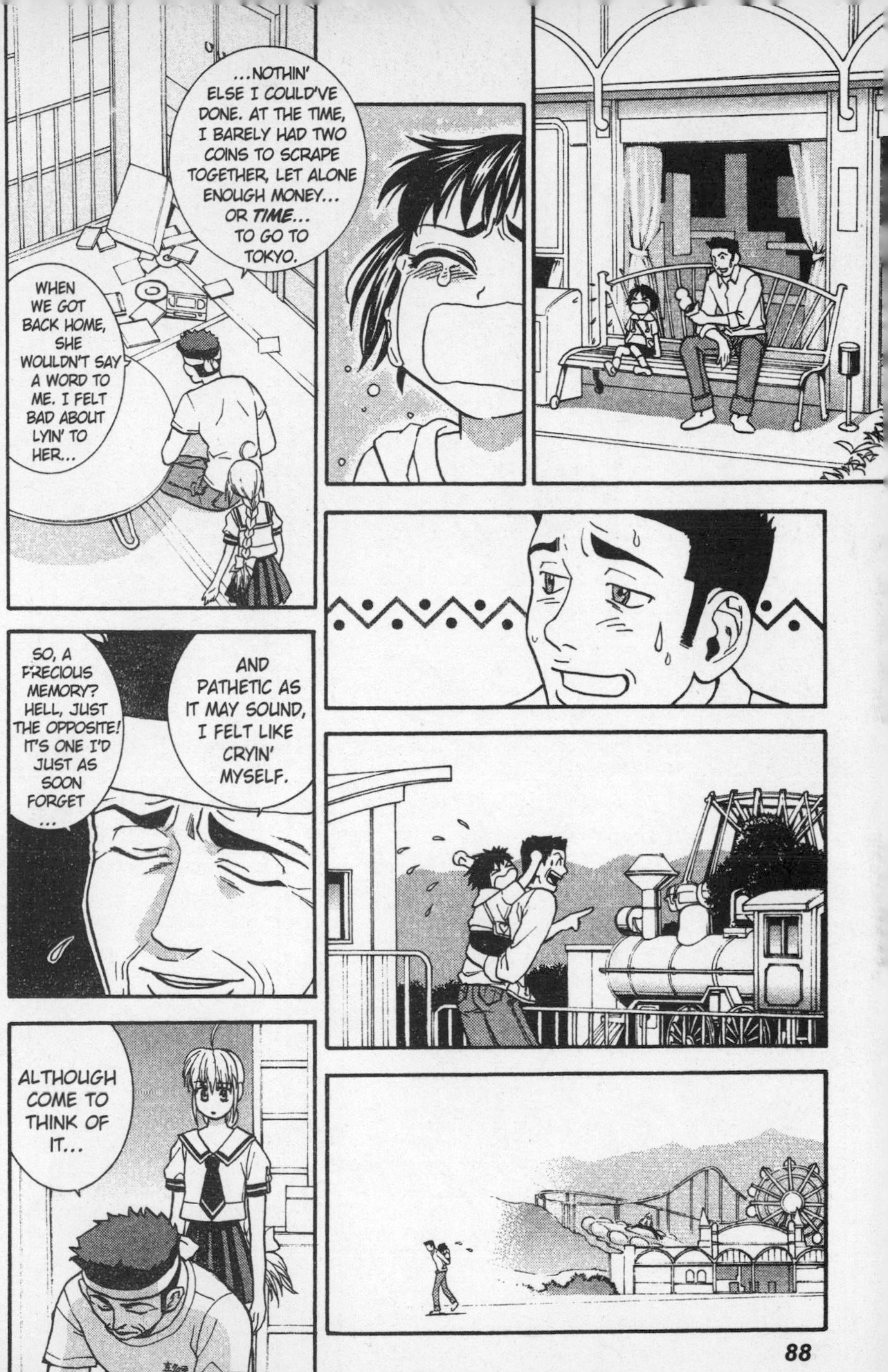
...NOTHIN' ELSE I COULD'VE DONE. AT THE TIME, I BARELY HAD TWO COINS TO SCRAPE TOGETHER, LET ALONE ENOUGH MONEY... OR *TIME*... TO GO TO TOKYO.
WHEN WE GOT BACK HOME, SHE WOULDN'T SAY A WORD TO ME. I FELT BAD ABOUT LYIN' TO HER...
AND PATHETIC AS IT MAY SOUND, I FELT LIKE CRYIN' MYSELF.
SO, A PRECIOUS MEMORY? HELL, JUST THE OPPOSITE! IT'S ONE I'D JUST AS SOON FORGET...
ALTHOUGH COME TO THINK OF IT...

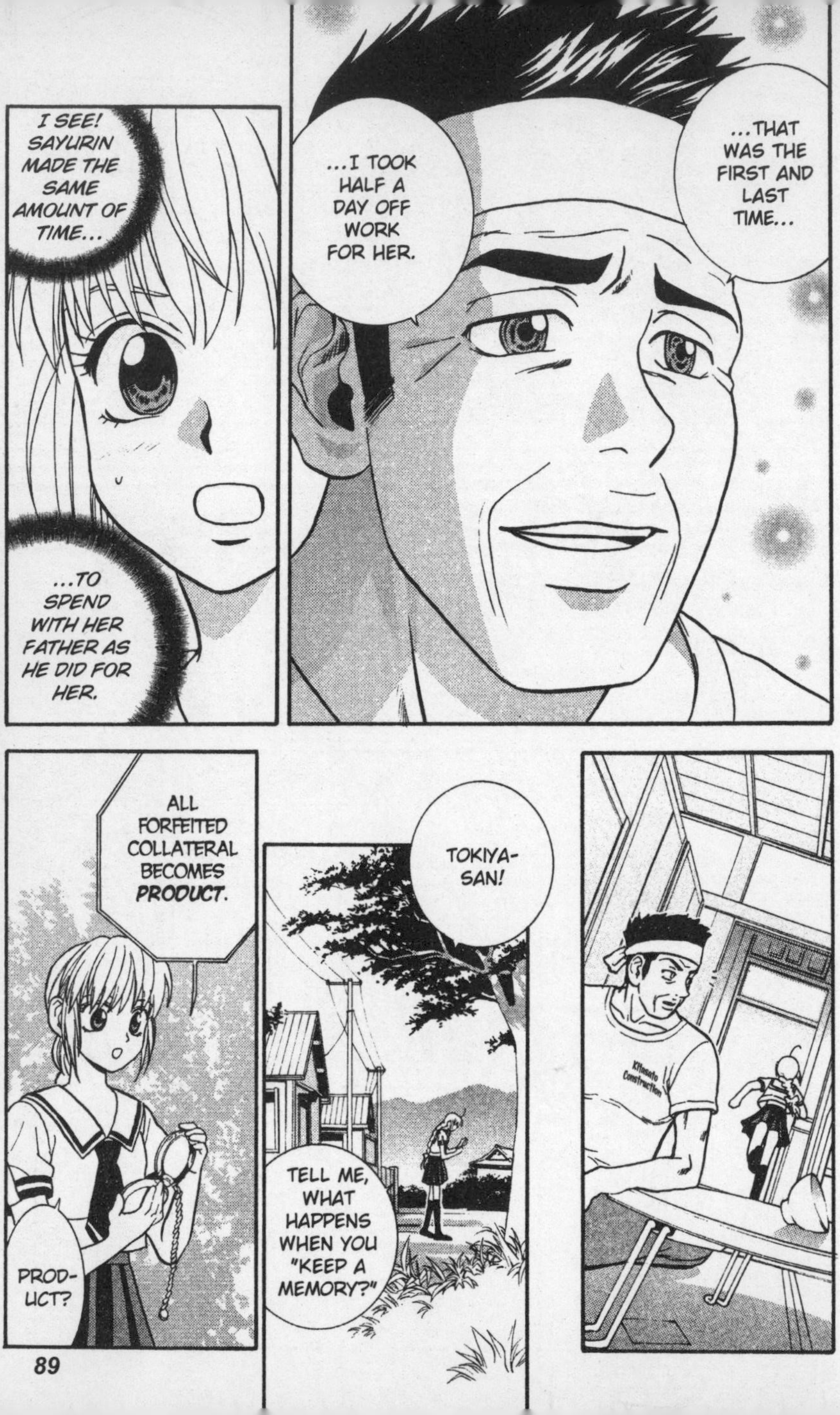
...THAT WAS THE FIRST AND LAST TIME...
...I TOOK HALF A DAY OFF WORK FOR HER.
I SEE! SAYURIN MADE THE SAME AMOUNT OF TIME...
...TO SPEND WITH HER FATHER AS HE DID FOR HER.
TOKIYA-SAN!
TELL ME, WHAT HAPPENS WHEN YOU "KEEP A MEMORY?"
ALL FORFEITED COLLATERAL BECOMES **PRODUCT**.
PROD-UCT?

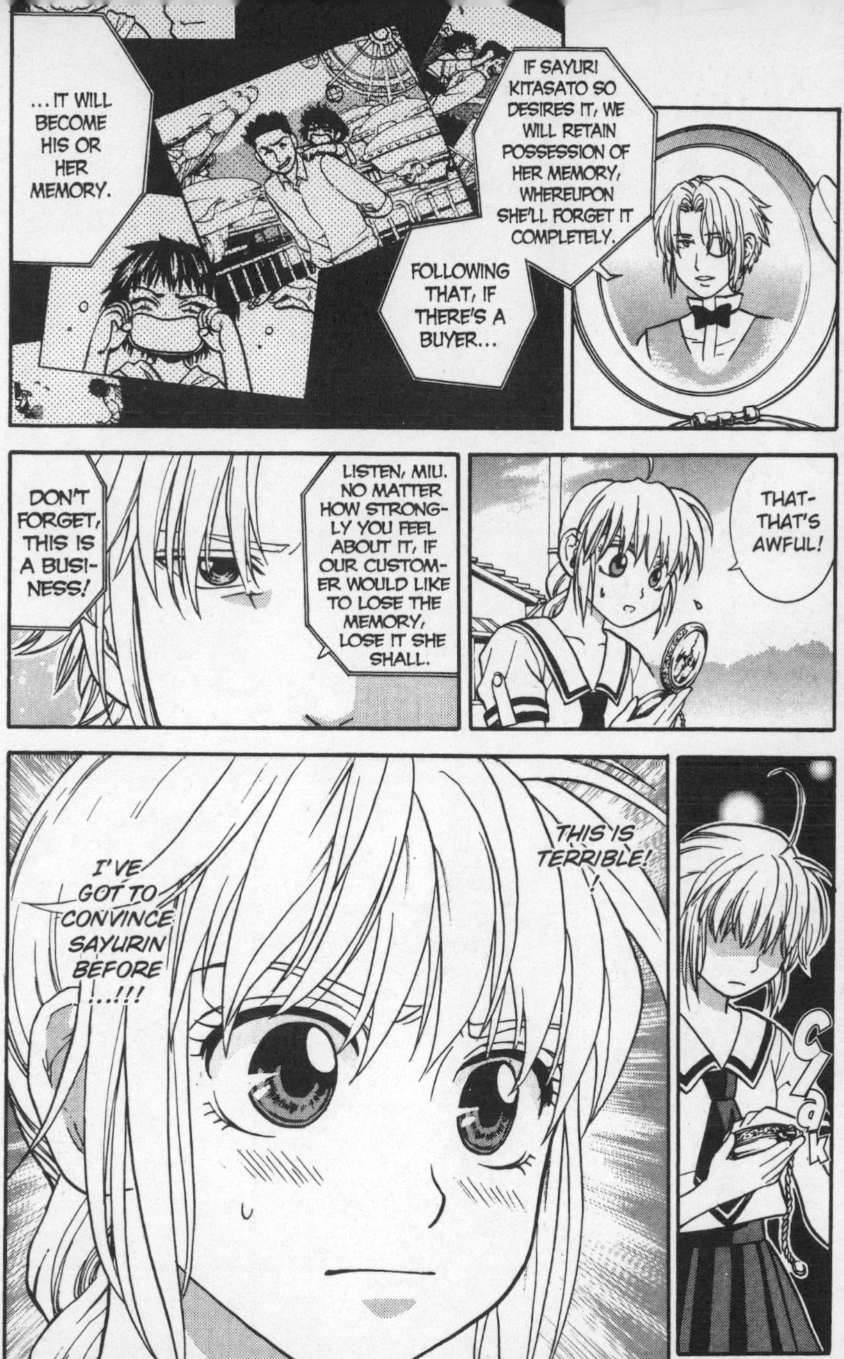
IF SAYURI KITASATO SO DESIRES IT, WE WILL RETAIN POSSESSION OF HER MEMORY, WHEREUPON SHE'LL FORGET IT COMPLETELY.
FOLLOWING THAT, IF THERE'S A BUYER...
...IT WILL BECOME HIS OR HER MEMORY.
THAT-THAT'S AWFUL!
LISTEN, MIU. NO MATTER HOW STRONGLY YOU FEEL ABOUT IT, IF OUR CUSTOMER WOULD LIKE TO LOSE THE MEMORY, LOSE IT SHE SHALL.
DON'T FORGET, THIS IS A BUSINESS!
Clak
THIS IS TERRIBLE!!
I'VE GOT TO CONVINCE SAYURIN BEFORE...!!!
Episode 2 Two Times (Part One): The End

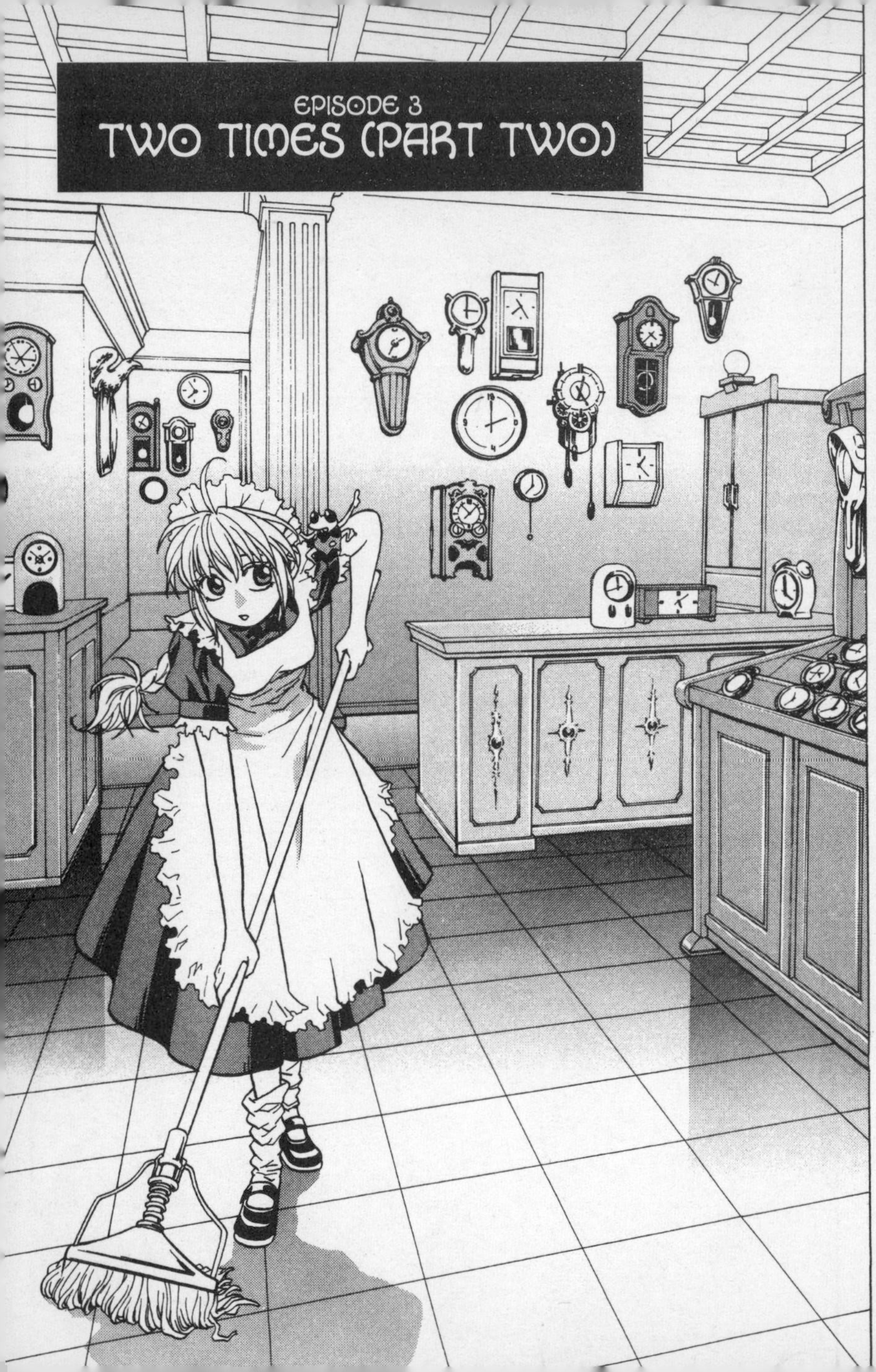
EPISODE 3
TWO TIMES (PART TWO)

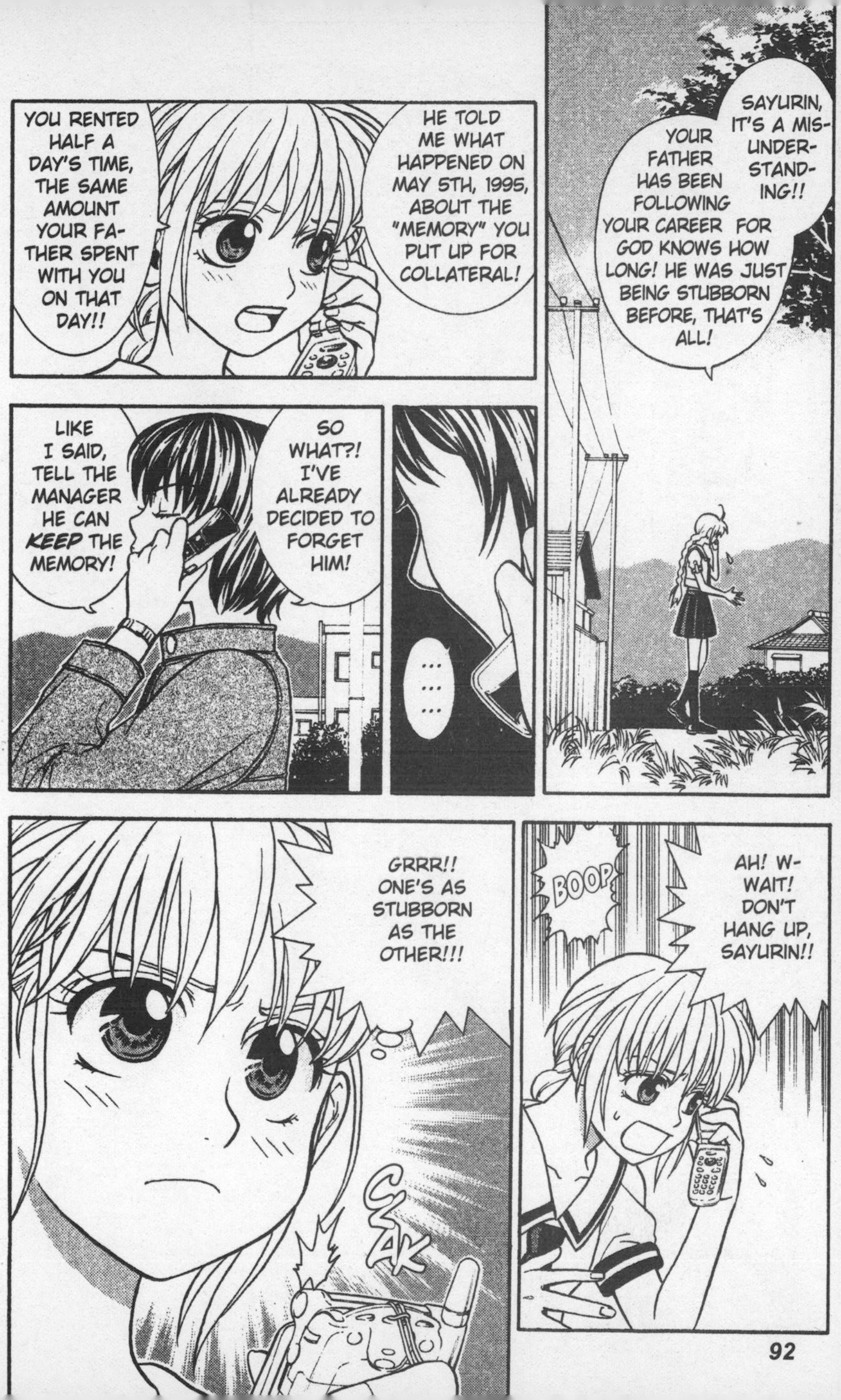

SAYURIN, IT'S A MIS-UNDER-STAND-ING!!
YOUR FATHER HAS BEEN FOLLOWING YOUR CAREER FOR GOD KNOWS HOW LONG! HE WAS JUST BEING STUBBORN BEFORE, THAT'S ALL!
HE TOLD ME WHAT HAPPENED ON MAY 5TH, 1995, ABOUT THE "MEMORY" YOU PUT UP FOR COLLATERAL!
YOU RENTED HALF A DAY'S TIME, THE SAME AMOUNT YOUR FA-THER SPENT WITH YOU ON THAT DAY!!
... ...
SO WHAT?! I'VE ALREADY DECIDED TO FORGET HIM!
LIKE I SAID, TELL THE MANAGER HE CAN KEEP THE MEMORY!
AH! W-WAIT! DON'T HANG UP, SAYURIN!!
BOOP
GRRR!! ONE'S AS STUBBORN AS THE OTHER!!!
CLAK

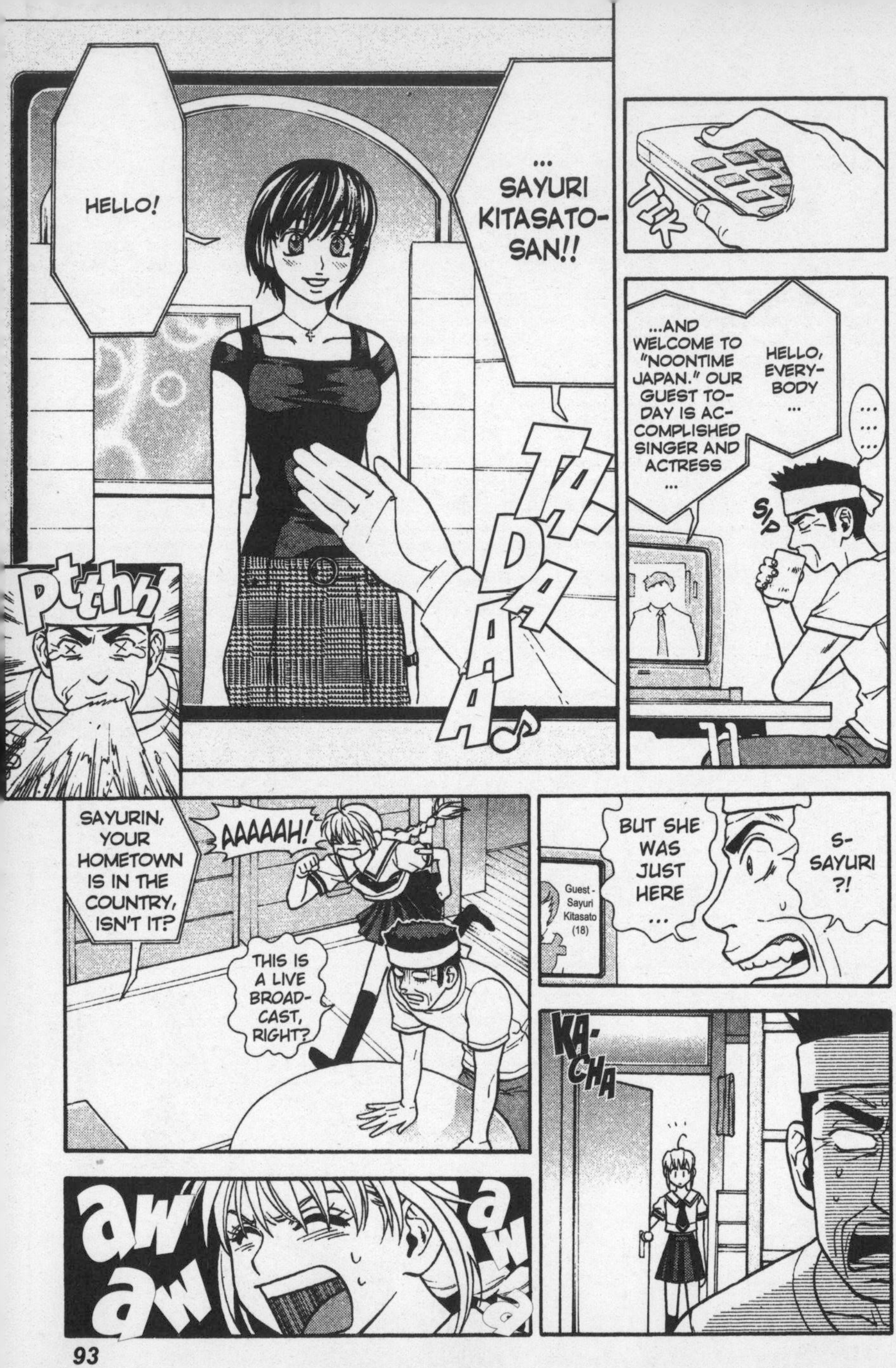
TIK
HELLO, EVERYBODY ...
...AND WELCOME TO "NOONTIME JAPAN." OUR GUEST TODAY IS ACCOMPLISHED SINGER AND ACTRESS ...
....
SIP
... SAYURI KITASATO-SAN!!
TA-DAAAA
HELLO!
ptthh
S-SAYURI?!
BUT SHE WAS JUST HERE ...
Guest - Sayuri Kitasato (18)
KA-CHA
SAYURIN, YOUR HOMETOWN IS IN THE COUNTRY, ISN'T IT?
AAAAAH!
THIS IS A LIVE BROADCAST, RIGHT?
aw aw
aw aw aw

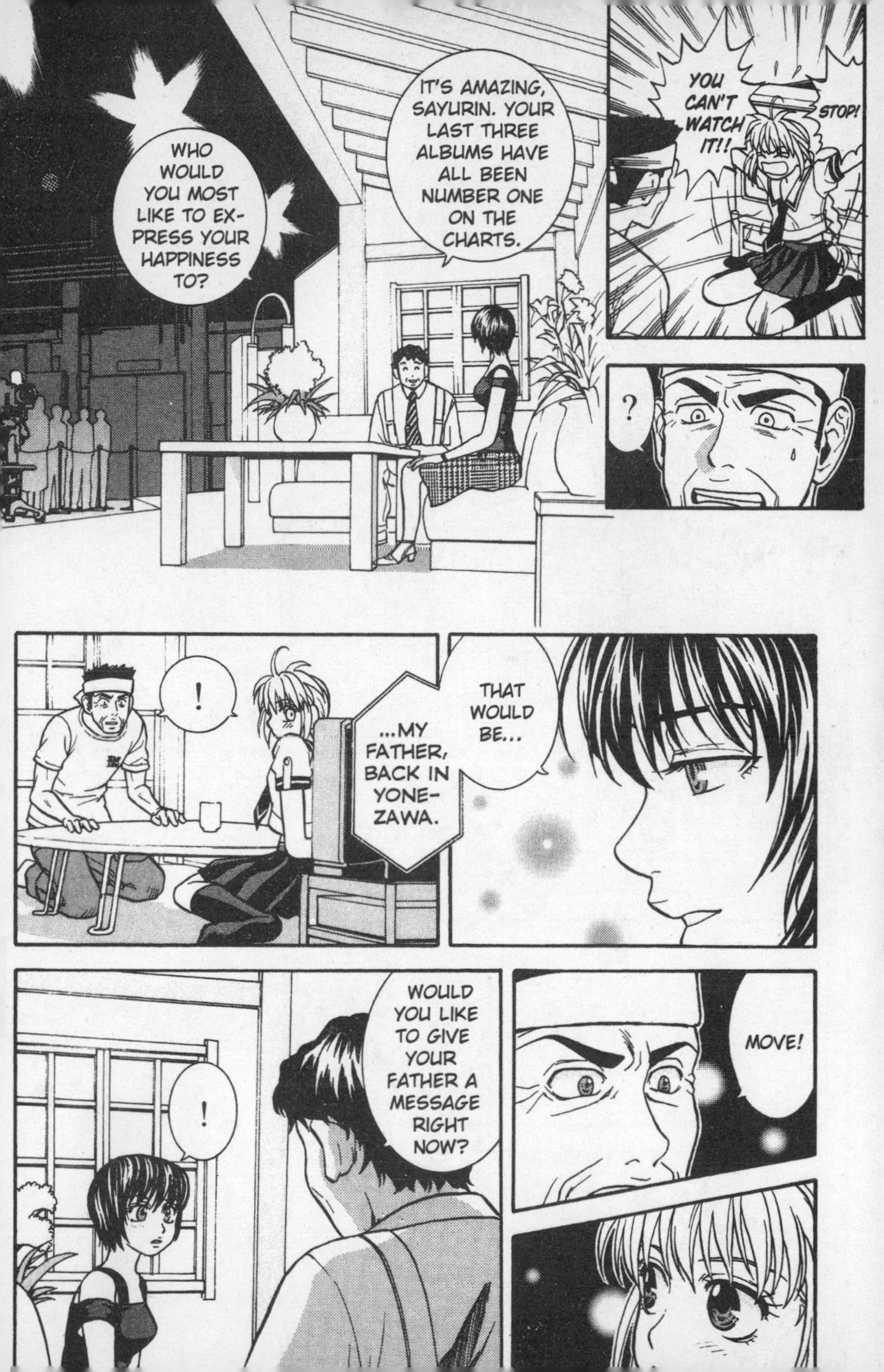
STOP!
YOU CAN'T WATCH IT!!
?
IT'S AMAZING, SAYURIN. YOUR LAST THREE ALBUMS HAVE ALL BEEN NUMBER ONE ON THE CHARTS.
WHO WOULD YOU MOST LIKE TO EX-PRESS YOUR HAPPINESS TO?
THAT WOULD BE...
...MY FATHER, BACK IN YONE-ZAWA.
!
MOVE!
WOULD YOU LIKE TO GIVE YOUR FATHER A MESSAGE RIGHT NOW?
!

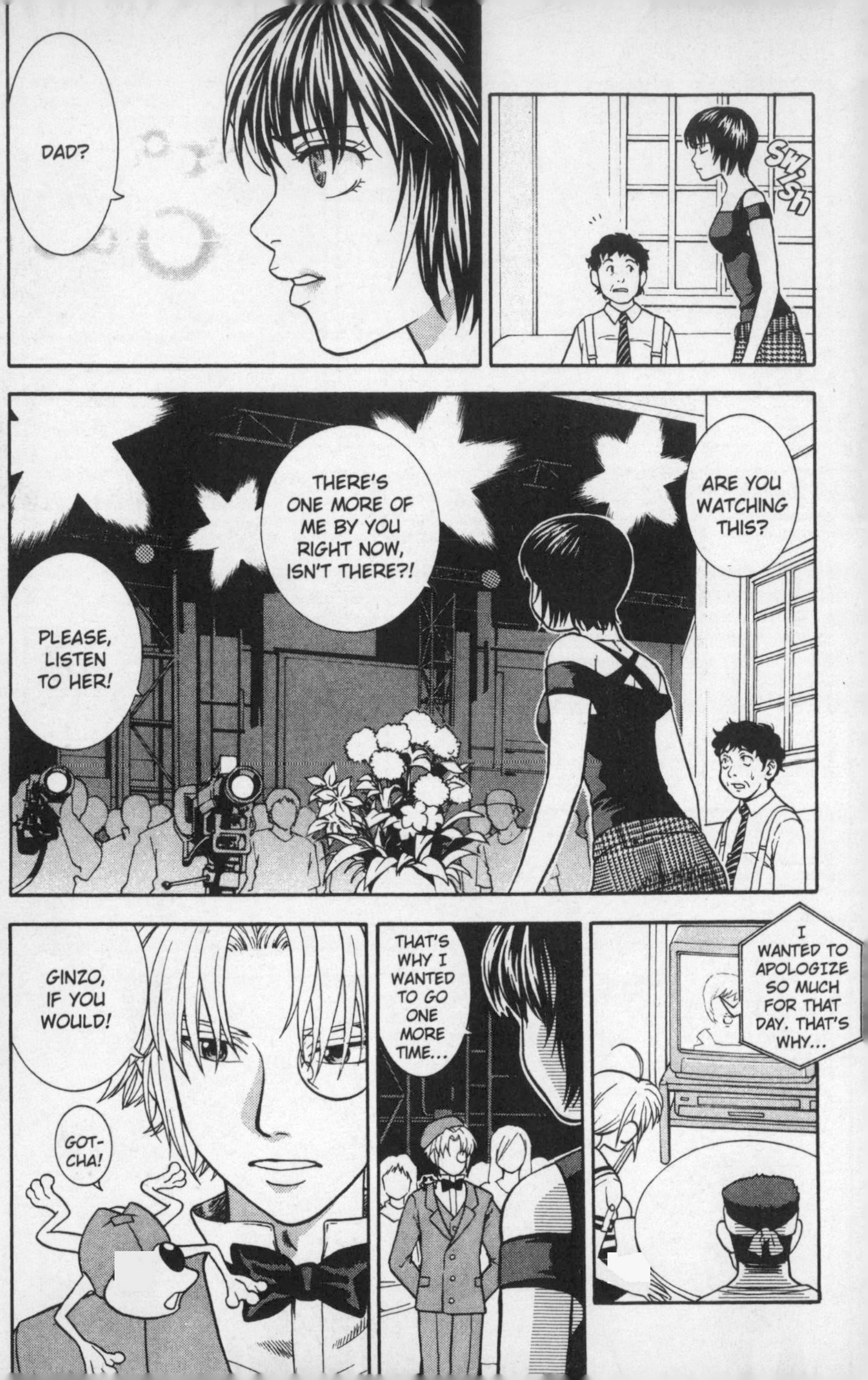
SWISH
DAD?
ARE YOU WATCHING THIS?
THERE'S ONE MORE OF ME BY YOU RIGHT NOW, ISN'T THERE?!
PLEASE, LISTEN TO HER!
I WANTED TO APOLOGIZE SO MUCH FOR THAT DAY. THAT'S WHY...
THAT'S WHY I WANTED TO GO ONE MORE TIME...
GINZO, IF YOU WOULD!
GOT-CHA!

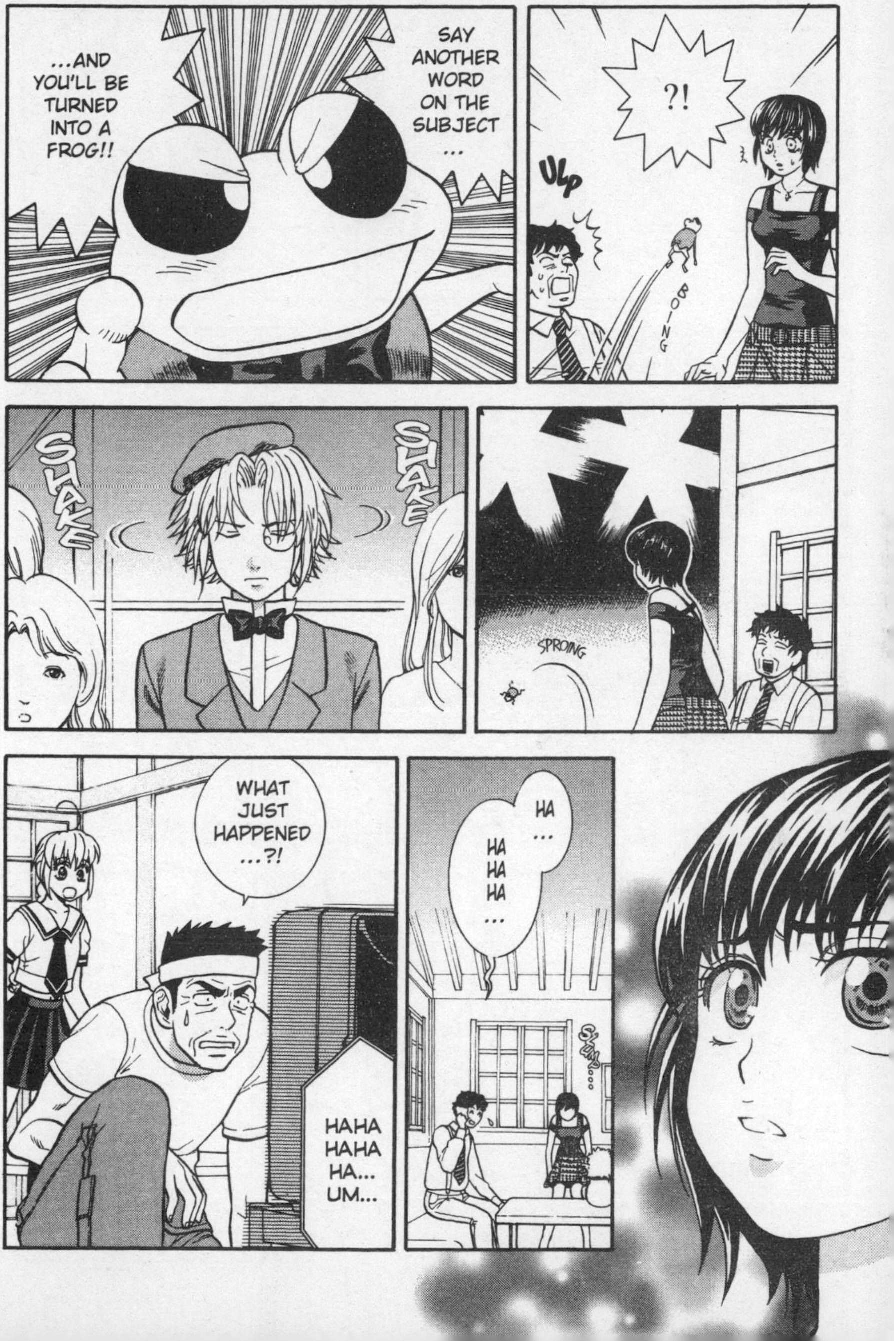
?!
ULP
BOING
SAY ANOTHER WORD ON THE SUBJECT ...
...AND YOU'LL BE TURNED INTO A FROG!!
SPROING
SHAKE
SHAKE
HA ...
HA HA HA ...
SLUMP...
WHAT JUST HAPPENED ...?!
HAHA HAHA HA... UM...

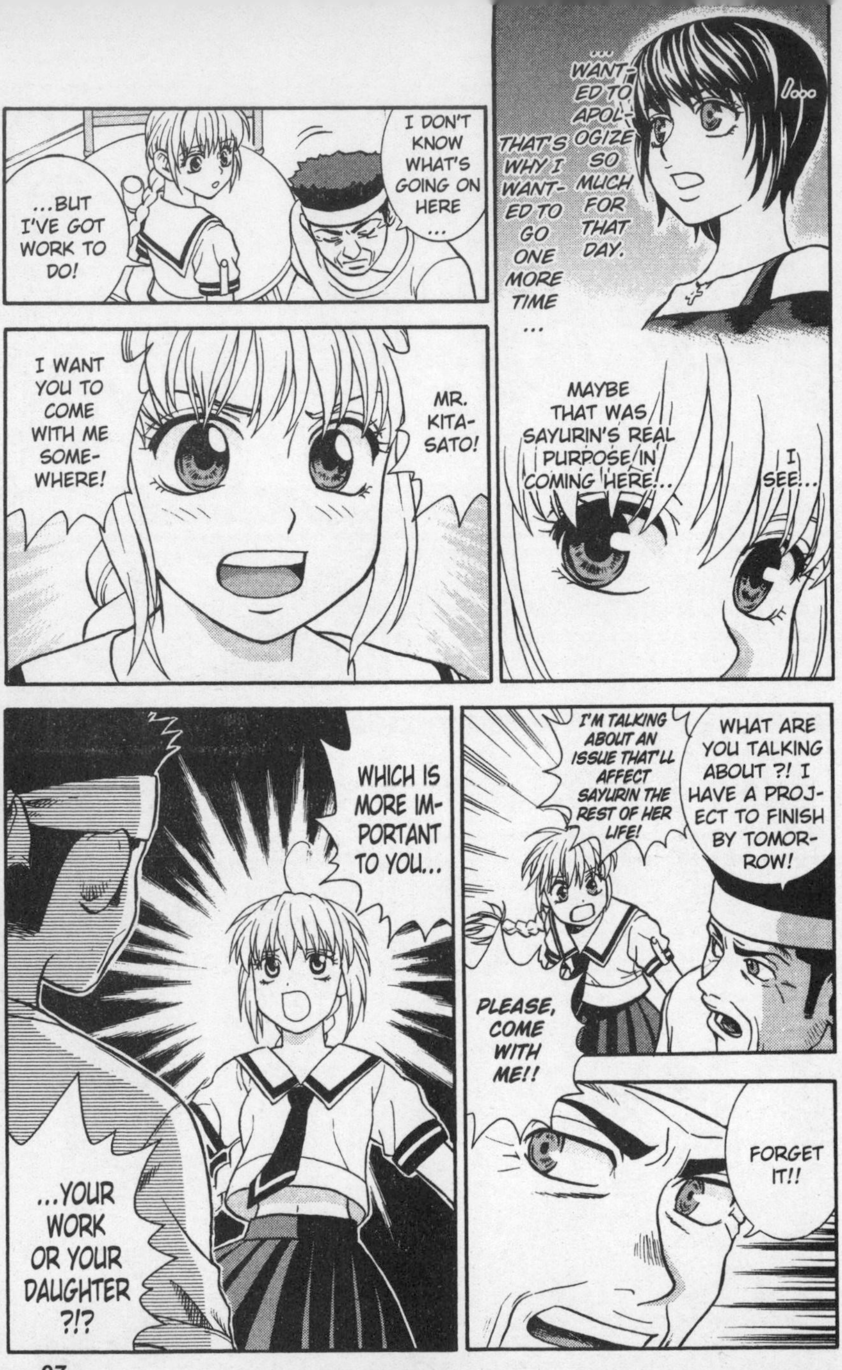

...WANTED TO APOLOGIZE SO MUCH FOR THAT DAY.
THAT'S WHY I WANTED TO GO ONE MORE TIME ...
I SEE...
MAYBE THAT WAS SAYURIN'S REAL PURPOSE IN COMING HERE...
I DON'T KNOW WHAT'S GOING ON HERE ...
...BUT I'VE GOT WORK TO DO!
MR. KITASATO!
I WANT YOU TO COME WITH ME SOMEWHERE!
WHAT ARE YOU TALKING ABOUT?! I HAVE A PROJECT TO FINISH BY TOMORROW!
I'M TALKING ABOUT AN ISSUE THAT'LL AFFECT SAYURIN THE REST OF HER LIFE!
PLEASE, COME WITH ME!!
FORGET IT!!
WHICH IS MORE IMPORTANT TO YOU...
...YOUR WORK OR YOUR DAUGHTER?!?

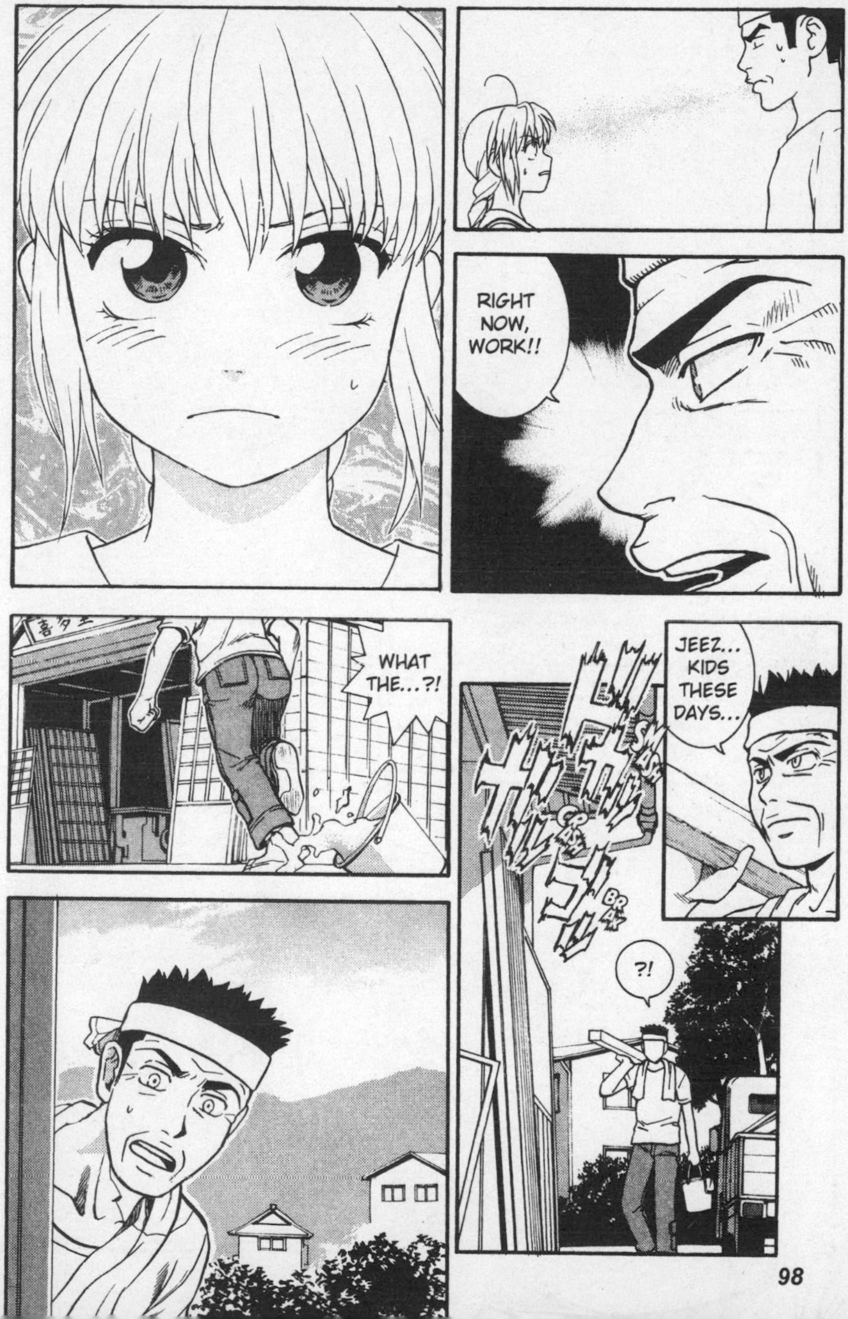
RIGHT NOW, WORK!!
JEEZ... KIDS THESE DAYS...
SMASH
CRASH
BRAK
?!
WHAT THE...?!

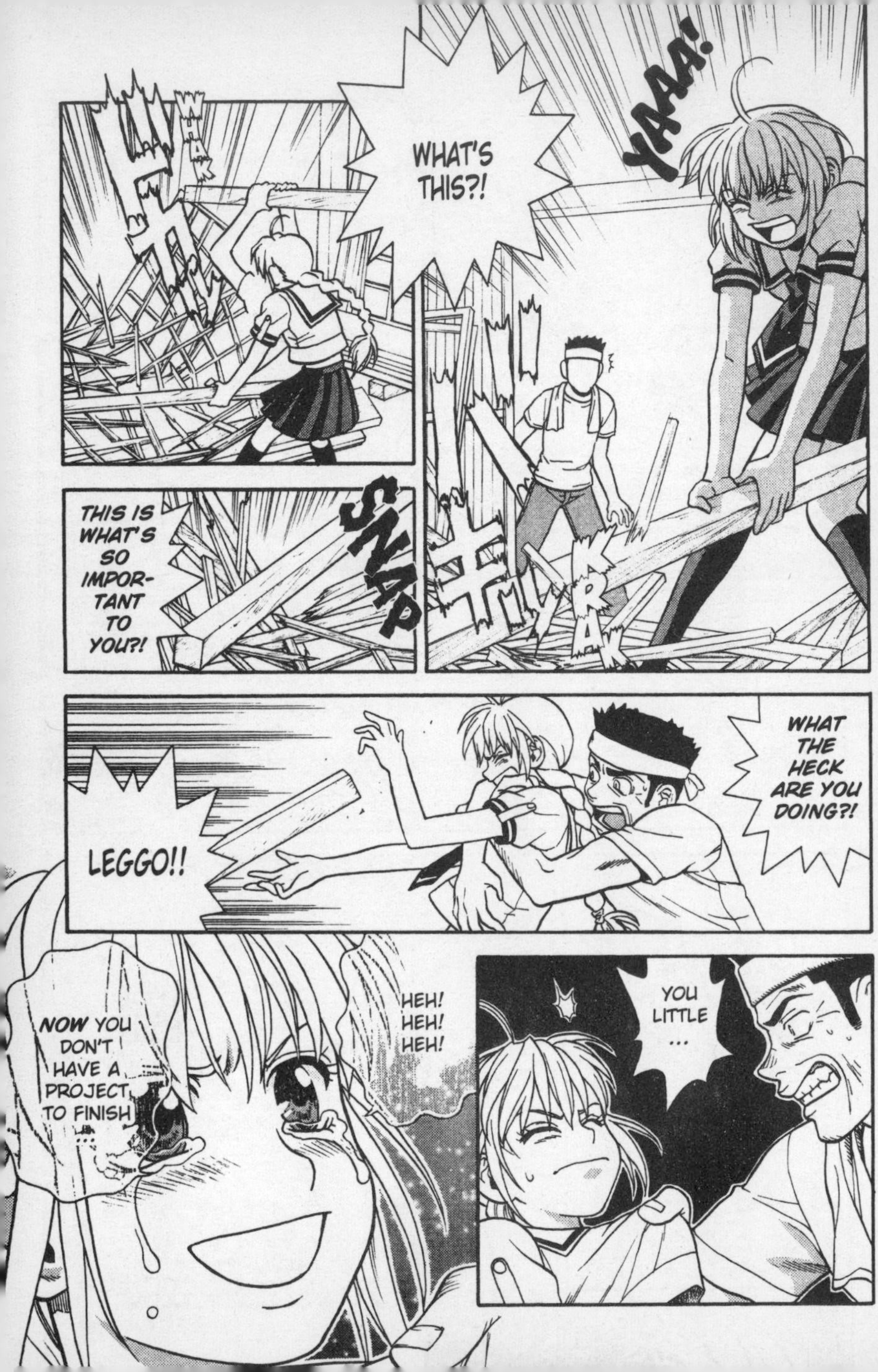
YAAA!
KRAK
WHAT'S THIS?!
WHAK
THIS IS WHAT'S SO IMPORTANT TO YOU?!
SNAP
WHAT THE HECK ARE YOU DOING?!
LEGGO!!
YOU LITTLE ...
HEH! HEH! HEH!
NOW YOU DON'T HAVE A PROJECT TO FINISH ...

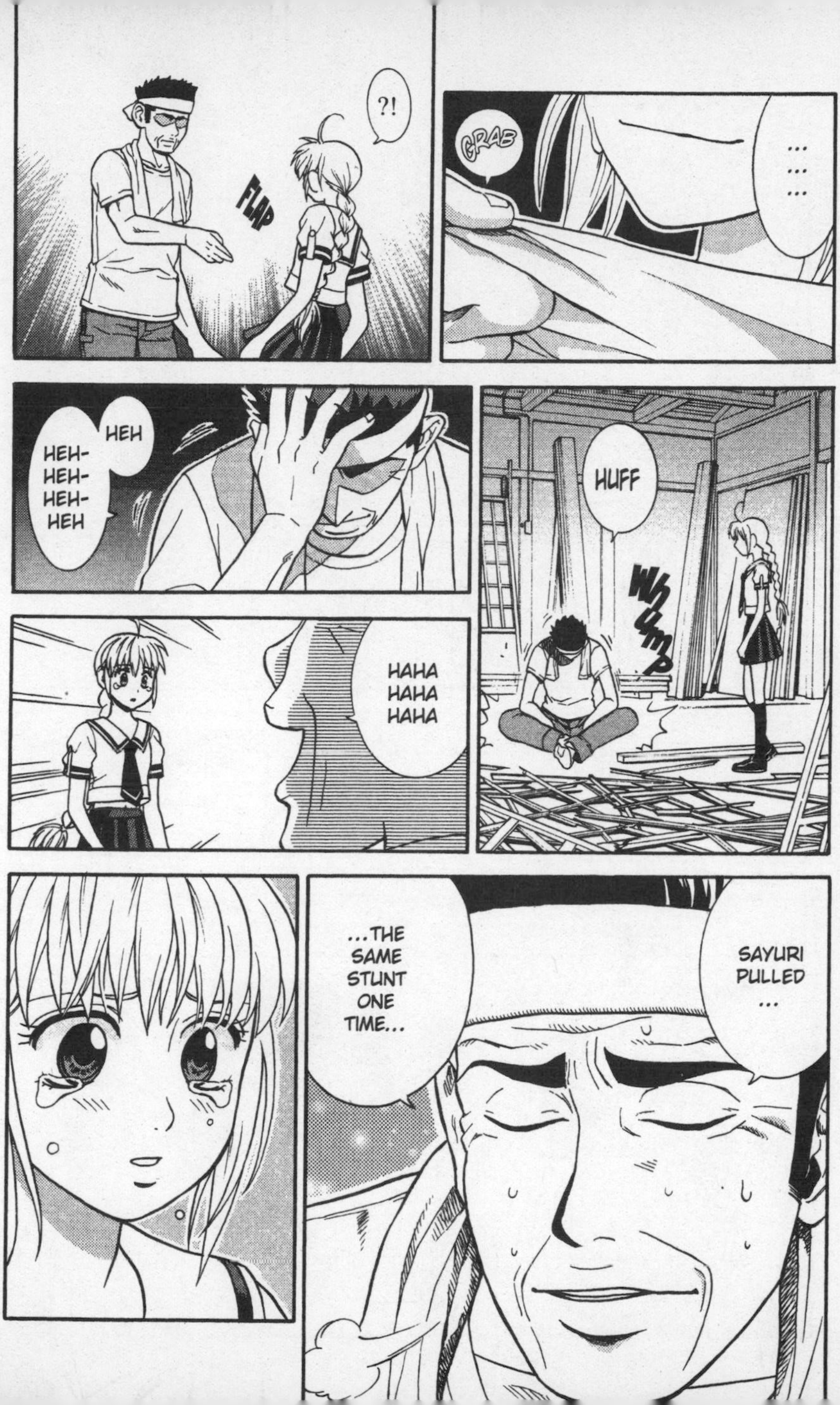
GRAB
...
...
...
?!
FLAP
HUFF
WHUMP
HEH
HEH-HEH-HEH-HEH
HAHA HAHA HAHA
SAYURI PULLED ...
...THE SAME STUNT ONE TIME...

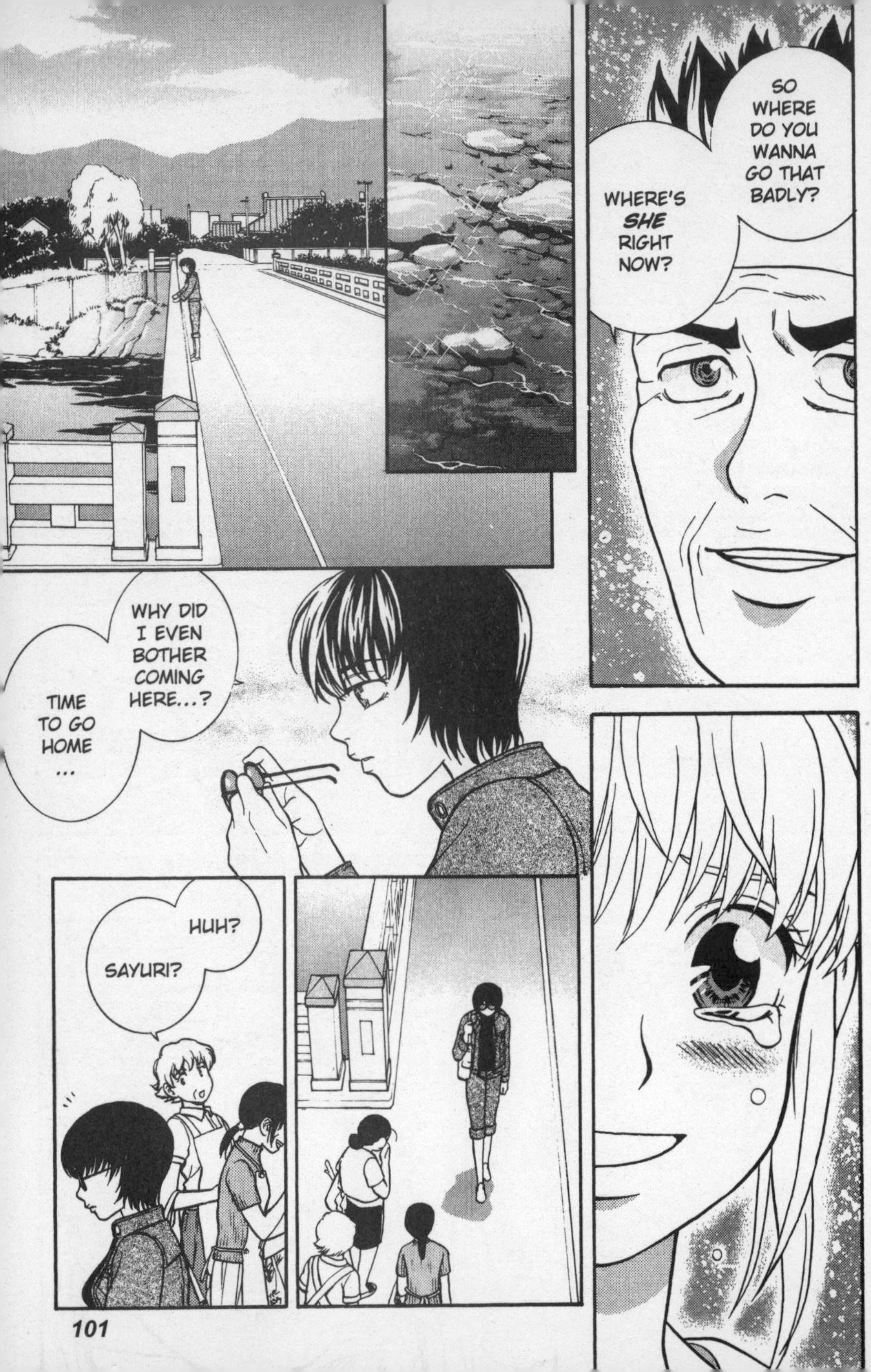
SO WHERE DO YOU WANNA GO THAT BADLY?
WHERE'S *SHE* RIGHT NOW?
WHY DID I EVEN BOTHER COMING HERE...?
TIME TO GO HOME ...
HUH?
SAYURI?

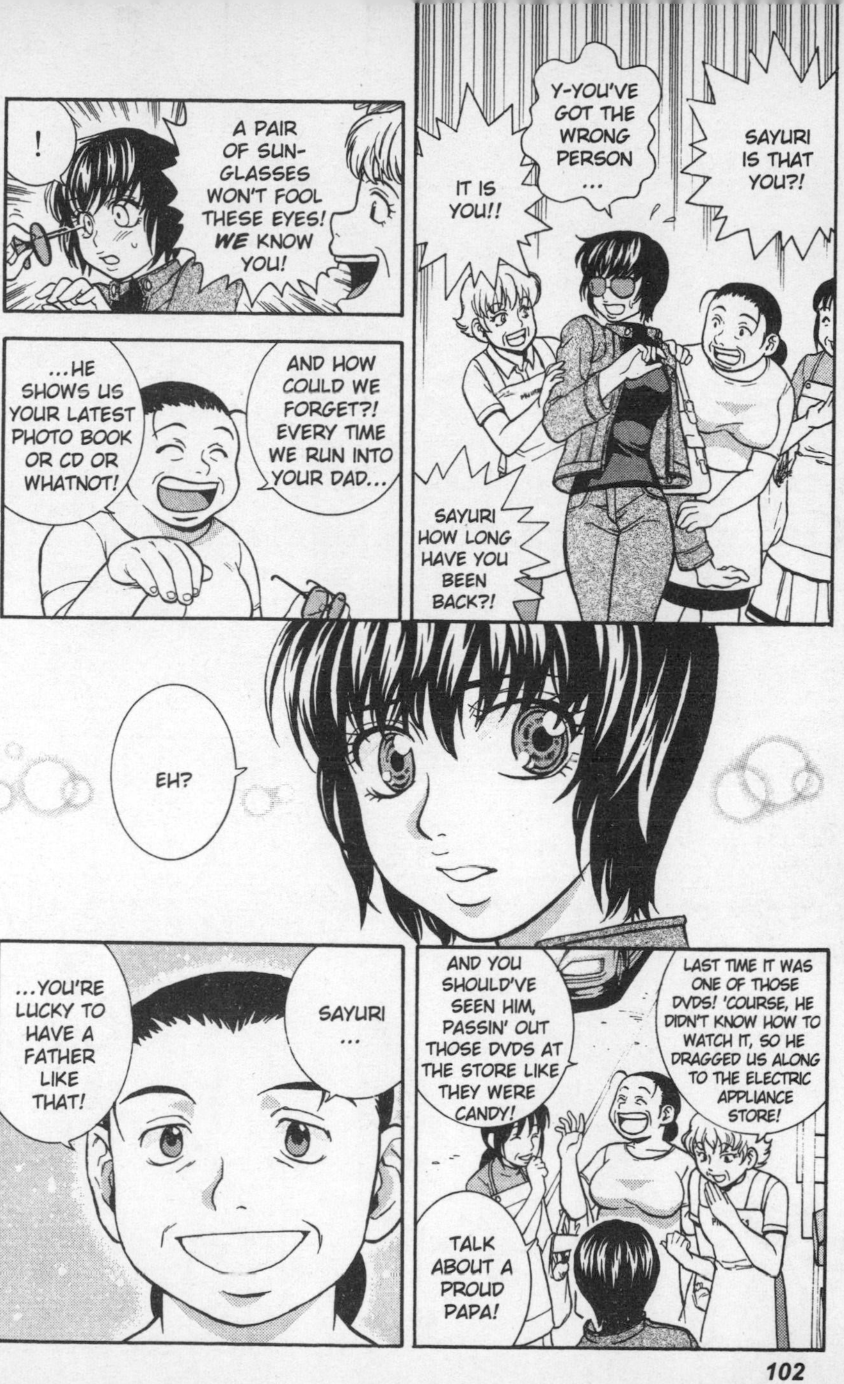
SAYURI IS THAT YOU?!
Y-YOU'VE GOT THE WRONG PERSON ...
IT IS YOU!!
SAYURI HOW LONG HAVE YOU BEEN BACK?!
!
A PAIR OF SUN-GLASSES WON'T FOOL THESE EYES! *WE* KNOW YOU!
AND HOW COULD WE FORGET?! EVERY TIME WE RUN INTO YOUR DAD...
...HE SHOWS US YOUR LATEST PHOTO BOOK OR CD OR WHATNOT!
EH?
LAST TIME IT WAS ONE OF THOSE DVDS! 'COURSE, HE DIDN'T KNOW HOW TO WATCH IT, SO HE DRAGGED US ALONG TO THE ELECTRIC APPLIANCE STORE!
AND YOU SHOULD'VE SEEN HIM, PASSIN' OUT THOSE DVDS AT THE STORE LIKE THEY WERE CANDY!
TALK ABOUT A PROUD PAPA!
SAYURI ...
...YOU'RE LUCKY TO HAVE A FATHER LIKE THAT!

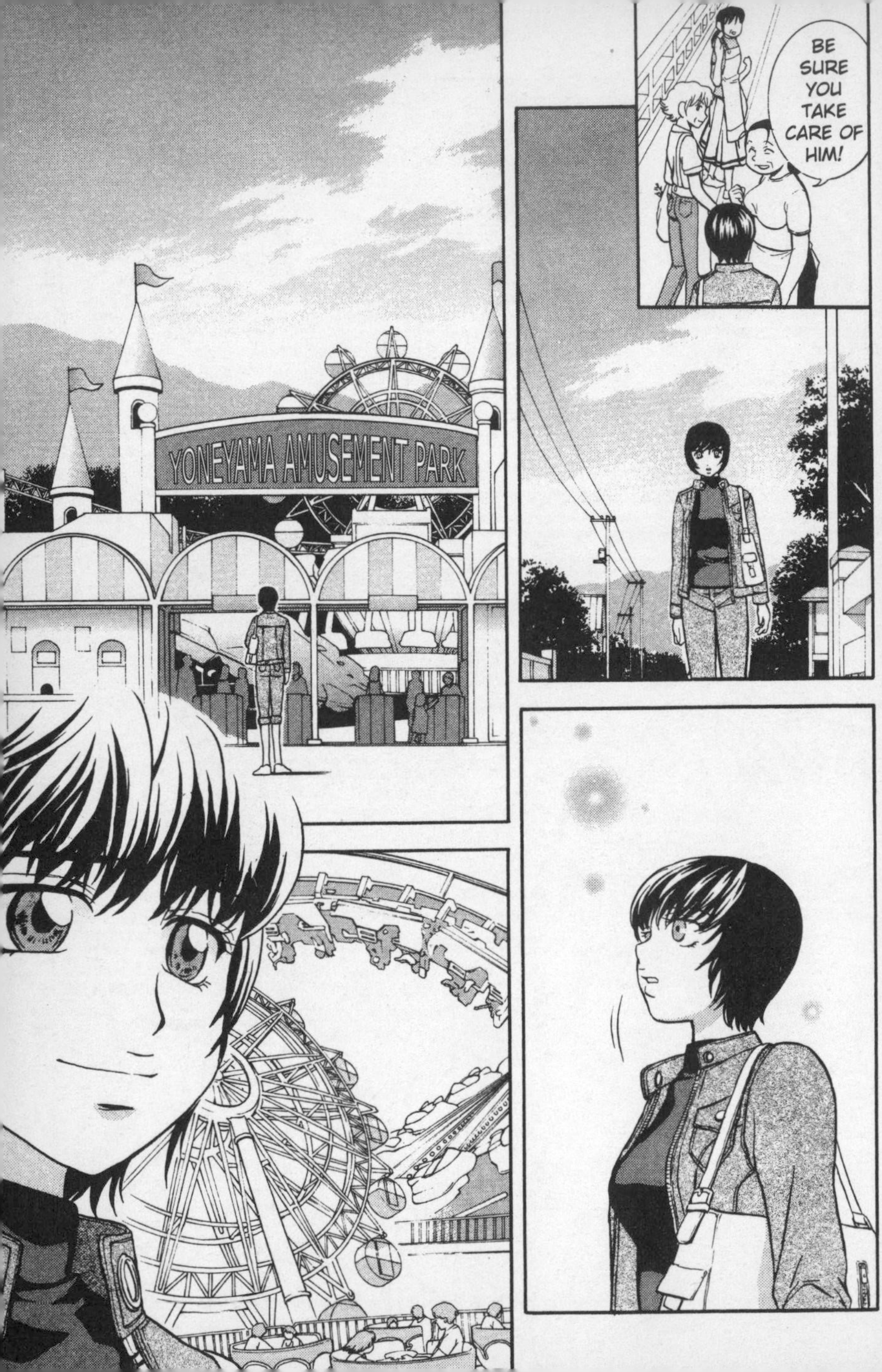
BE SURE YOU TAKE CARE OF HIM!
YONEYAMA AMUSEMENT PARK

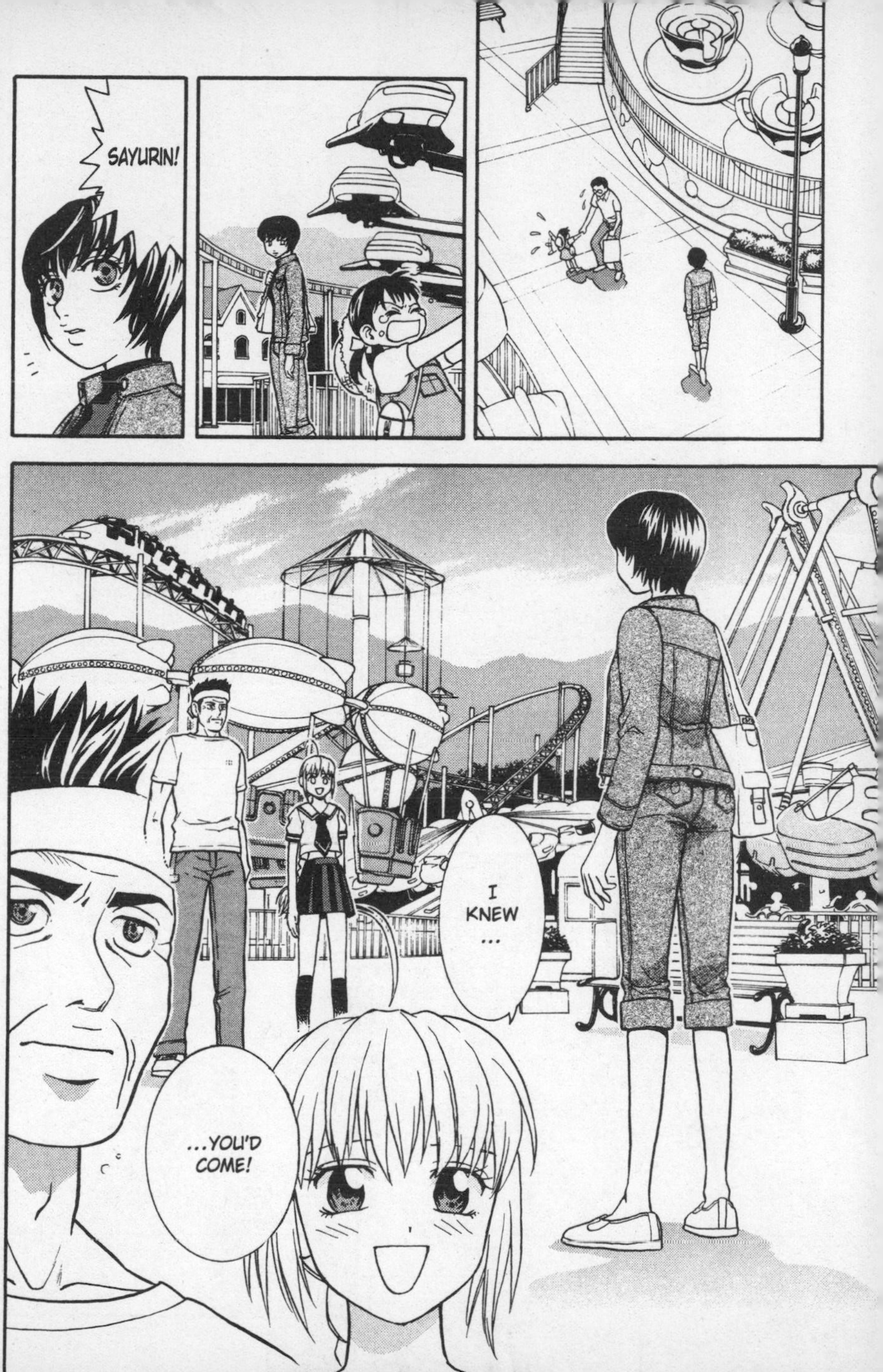
SAYURIN!
I KNEW ...
...YOU'D COME!

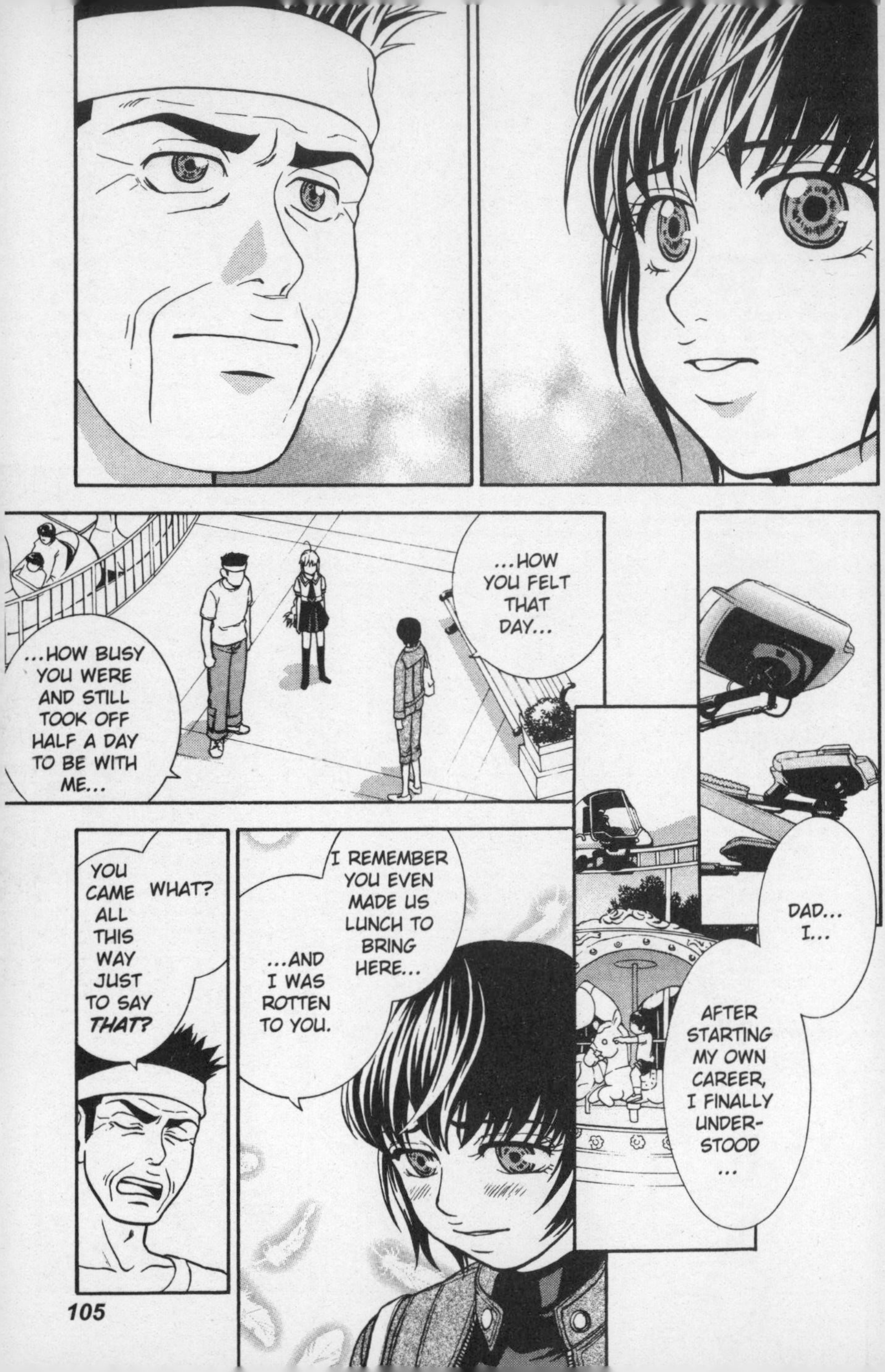
DAD... I...
AFTER STARTING MY OWN CAREER, I FINALLY UNDER-STOOD ...
...HOW YOU FELT THAT DAY...
...HOW BUSY YOU WERE AND STILL TOOK OFF HALF A DAY TO BE WITH ME...
I REMEMBER YOU EVEN MADE US LUNCH TO BRING HERE...
...AND I WAS ROTTEN TO YOU.
WHAT?
YOU CAME ALL THIS WAY JUST TO SAY *THAT?*

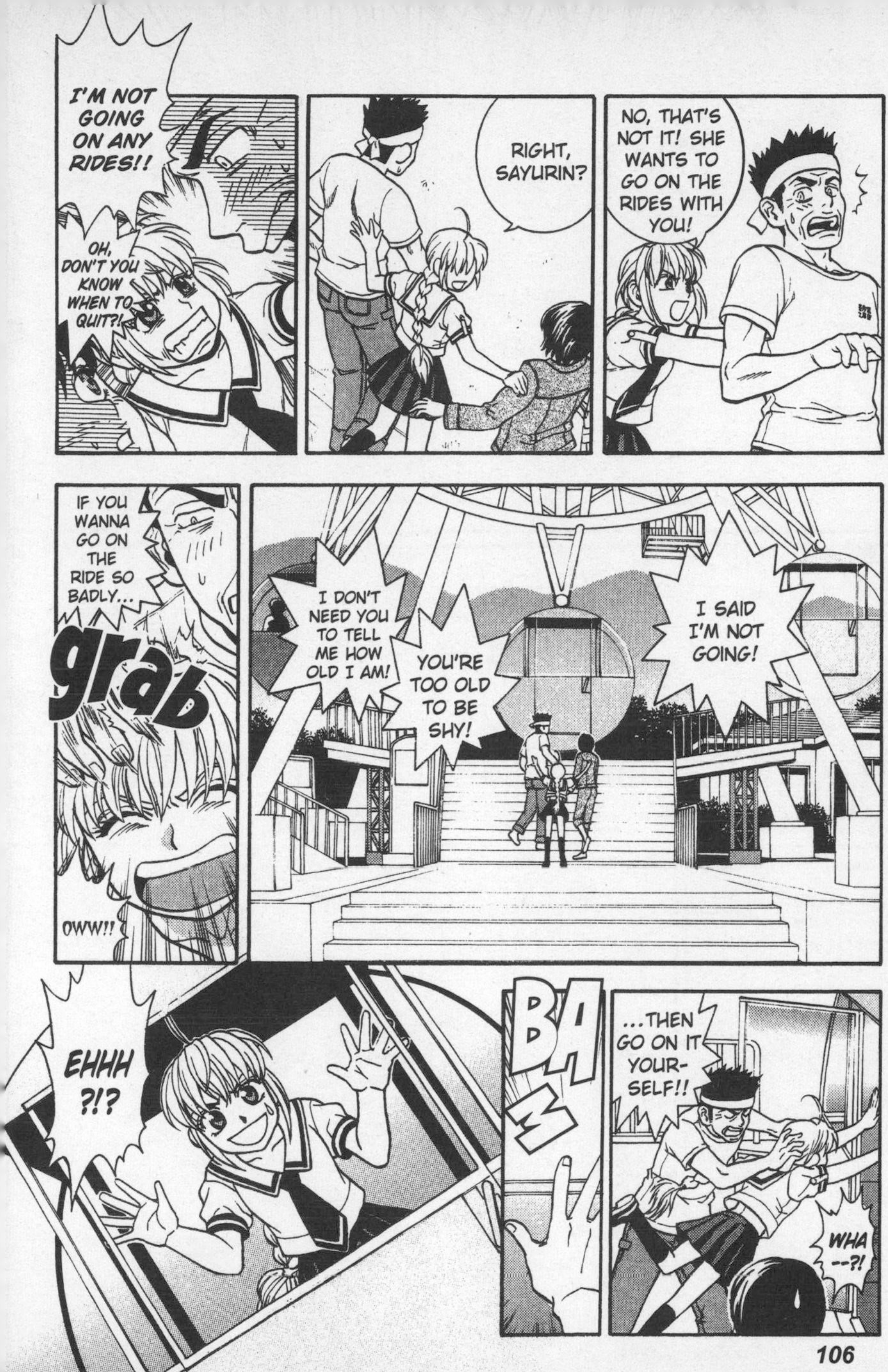
NO, THAT'S NOT IT! SHE WANTS TO GO ON THE RIDES WITH YOU!
RIGHT, SAYURIN?
I'M NOT GOING ON ANY RIDES!!
OH, DON'T YOU KNOW WHEN TO QUIT?!
I SAID I'M NOT GOING!
YOU'RE TOO OLD TO BE SHY!
I DON'T NEED YOU TO TELL ME HOW OLD I AM!
IF YOU WANNA GO ON THE RIDE SO BADLY...
grab
OWW!!
...THEN GO ON IT YOURSELF!!
WHA--?!
BAM
EHHH ?!?

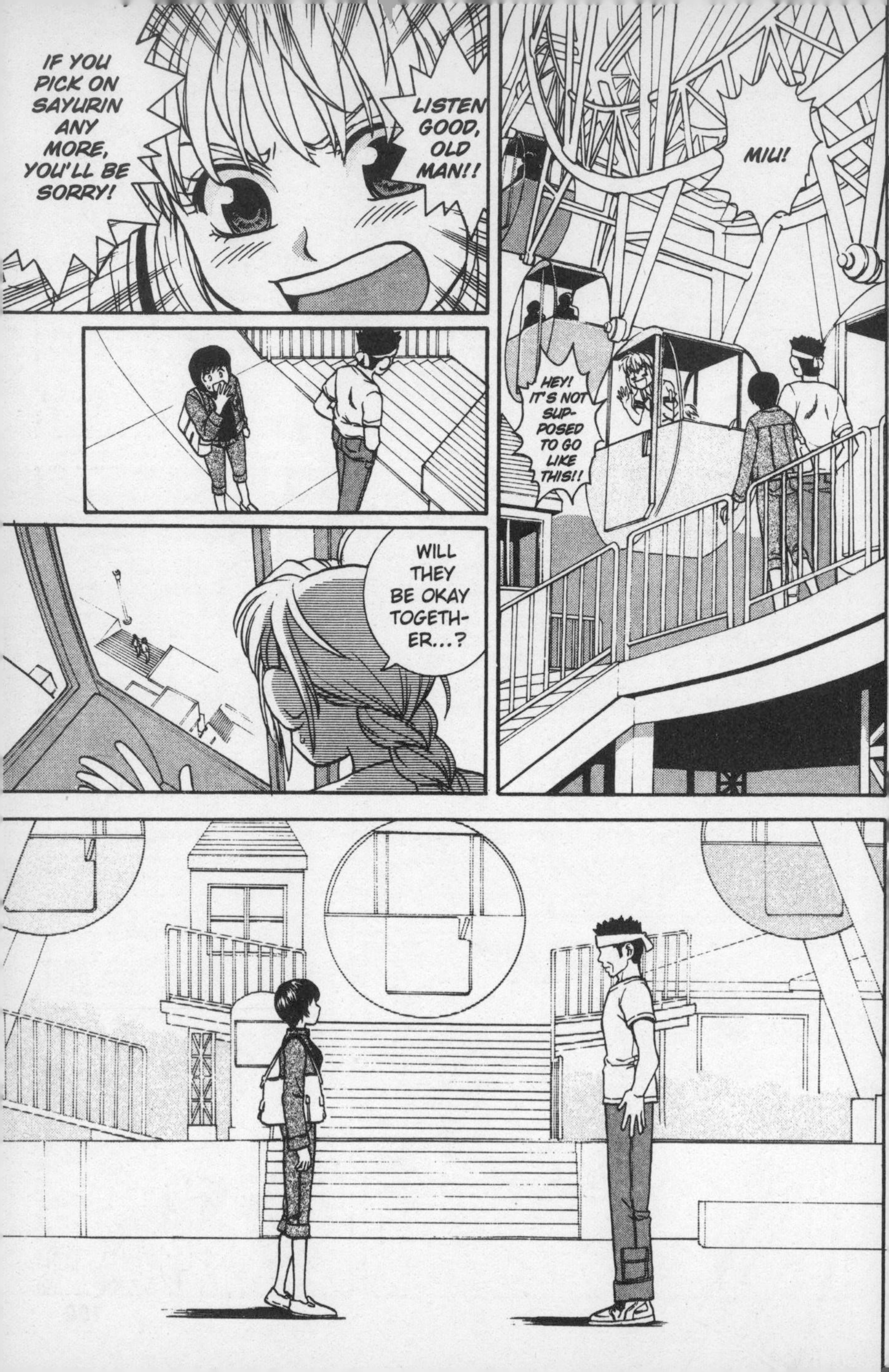
MIU!
HEY! IT'S NOT SUP-POSED TO GO LIKE THIS!!
LISTEN GOOD, OLD MAN!!
IF YOU PICK ON SAYURIN ANY MORE, YOU'LL BE SORRY!
WILL THEY BE OKAY TOGETH-ER...?

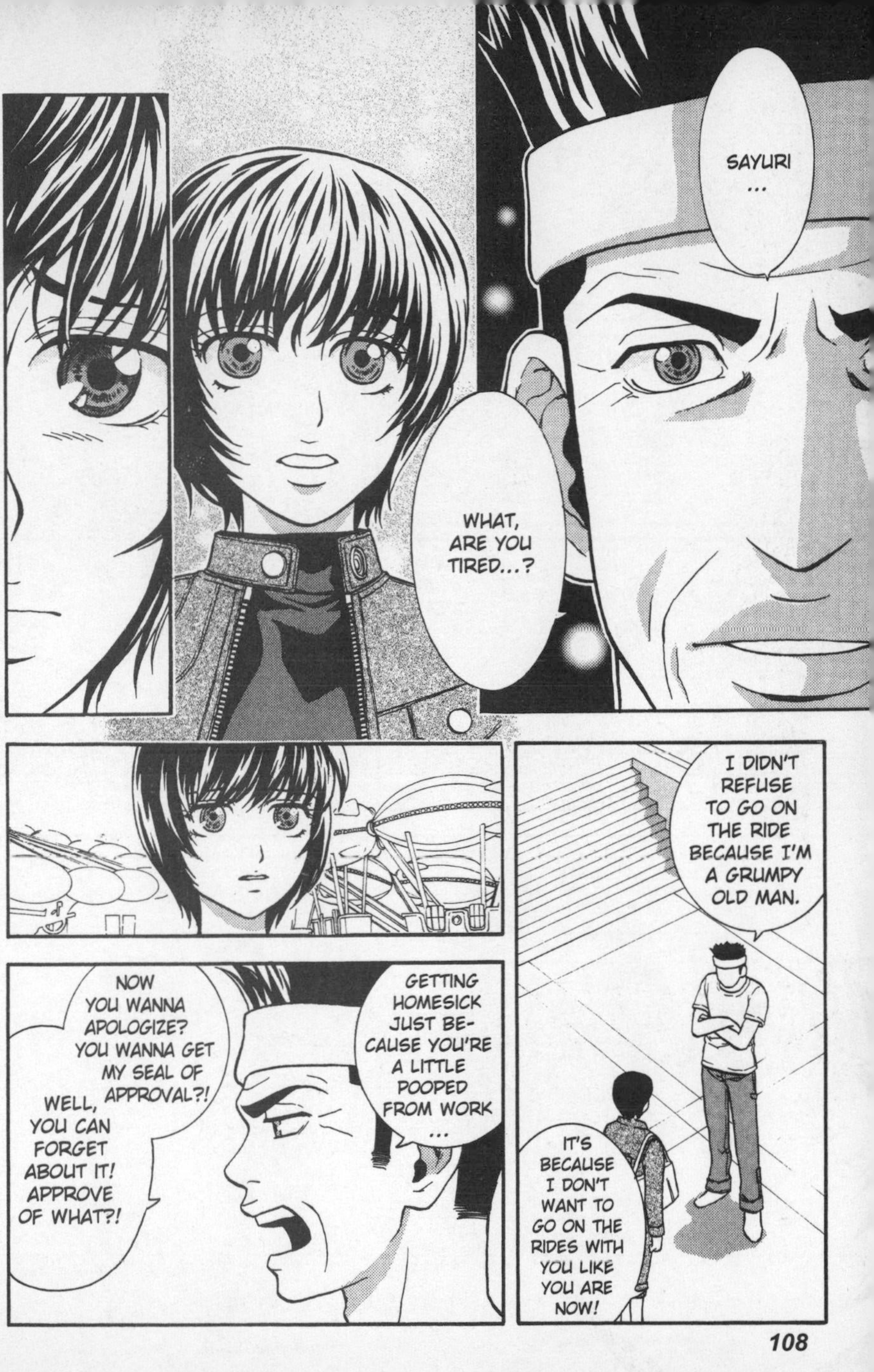
SAYURI ...
WHAT, ARE YOU TIRED...?
I DIDN'T REFUSE TO GO ON THE RIDE BECAUSE I'M A GRUMPY OLD MAN.
IT'S BECAUSE I DON'T WANT TO GO ON THE RIDES WITH YOU LIKE YOU ARE NOW!
GETTING HOMESICK JUST BE- CAUSE YOU'RE A LITTLE POOPED FROM WORK ...
NOW YOU WANNA APOLOGIZE? YOU WANNA GET MY SEAL OF APPROVAL?!
WELL, YOU CAN FORGET ABOUT IT! APPROVE OF WHAT?!

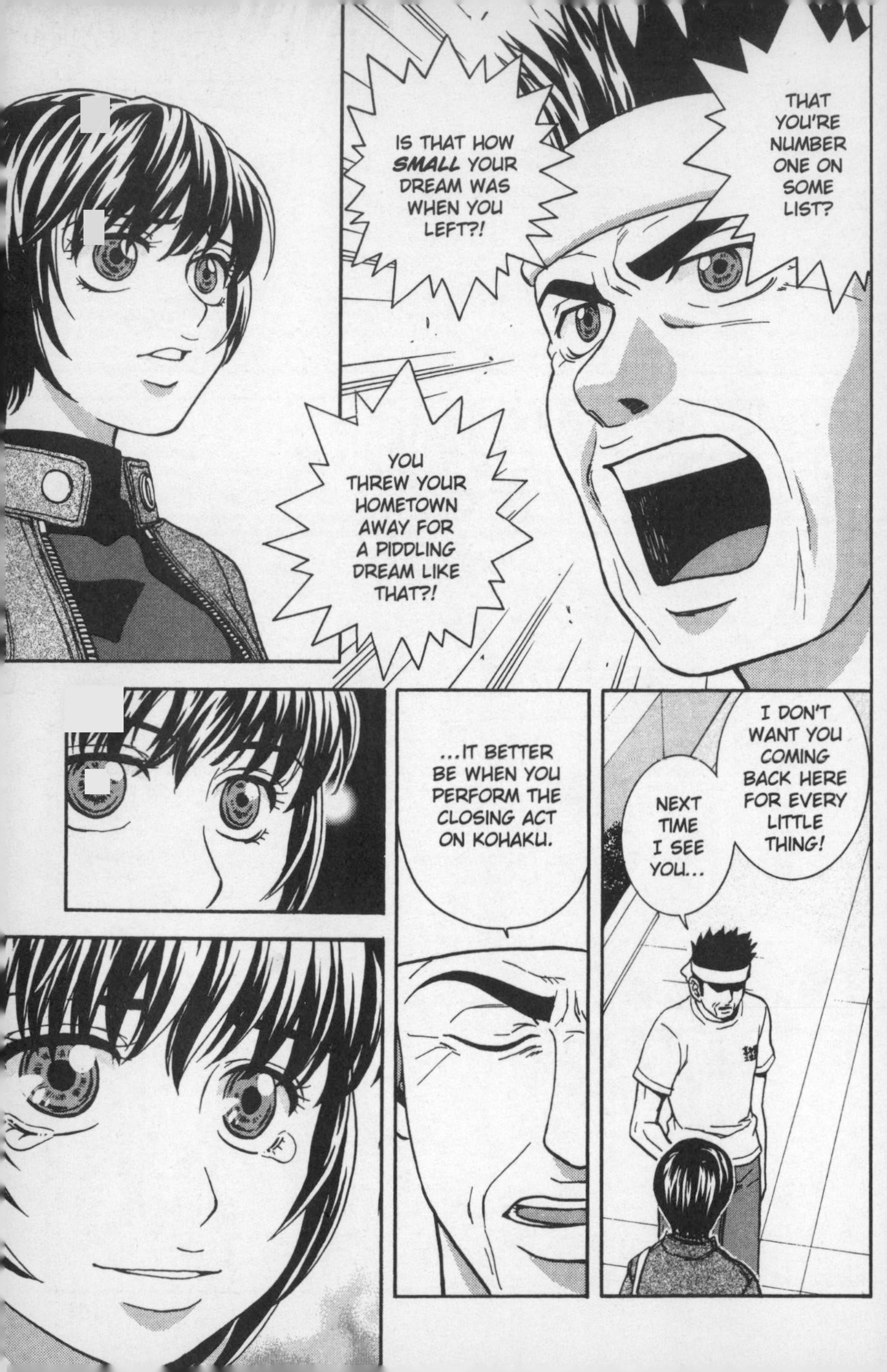
THAT YOU'RE NUMBER ONE ON SOME LIST?
IS THAT HOW **SMALL** YOUR DREAM WAS WHEN YOU LEFT?!
YOU THREW YOUR HOMETOWN AWAY FOR A PIDDLING DREAM LIKE THAT?!
I DON'T WANT YOU COMING BACK HERE FOR EVERY LITTLE THING!
NEXT TIME I SEE YOU...
...IT BETTER BE WHEN YOU PERFORM THE CLOSING ACT ON KOHAKU.

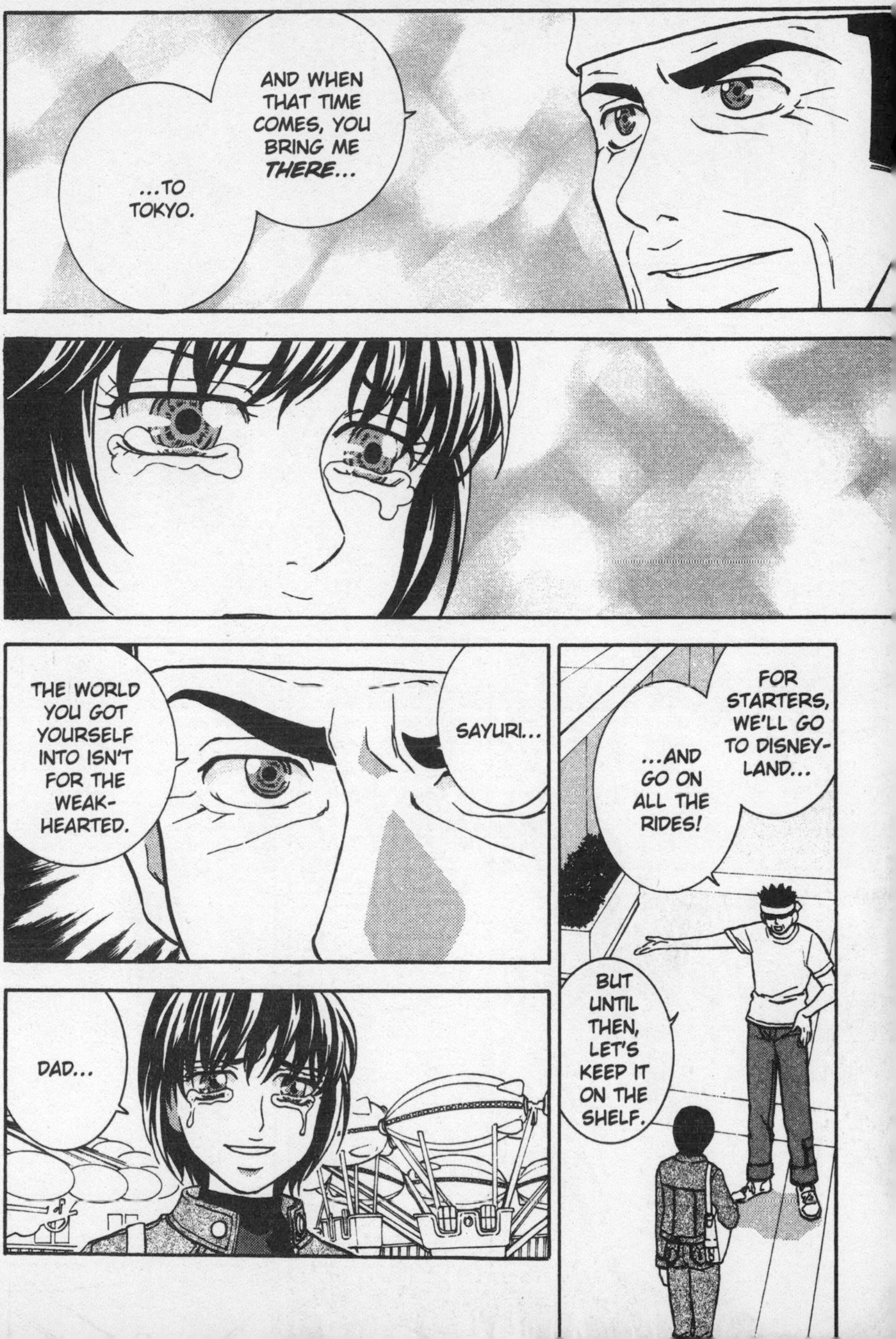
AND WHEN THAT TIME COMES, YOU BRING ME *THERE*...
...TO TOKYO.
FOR STARTERS, WE'LL GO TO DISNEY-LAND...
...AND GO ON ALL THE RIDES!
BUT UNTIL THEN, LET'S KEEP IT ON THE SHELF.
SAYURI...
THE WORLD YOU GOT YOURSELF INTO ISN'T FOR THE WEAK-HEARTED.
DAD...

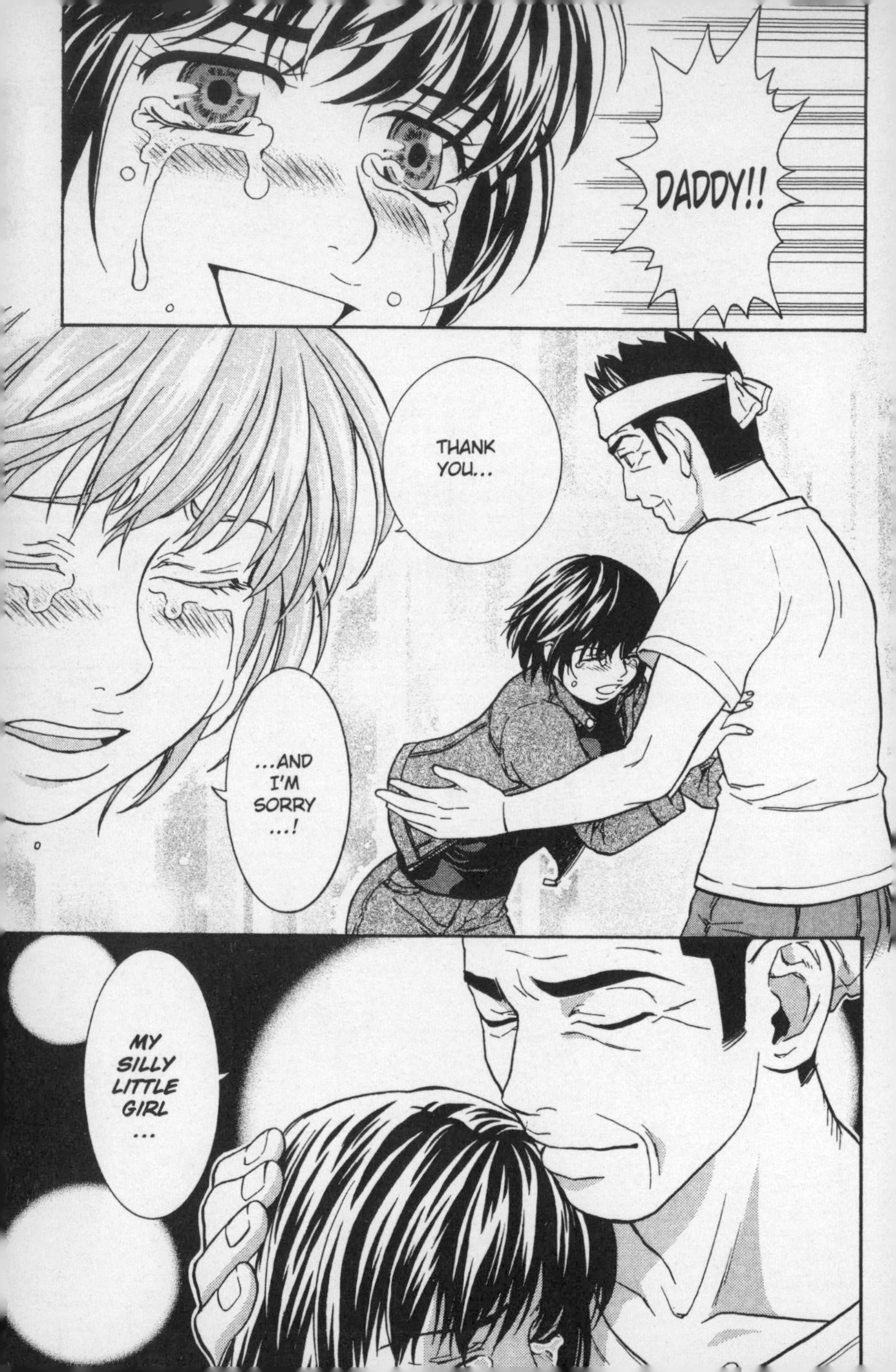
DADDY!!
THANK YOU...
...AND I'M SORRY ...!
MY SILLY LITTLE GIRL ...

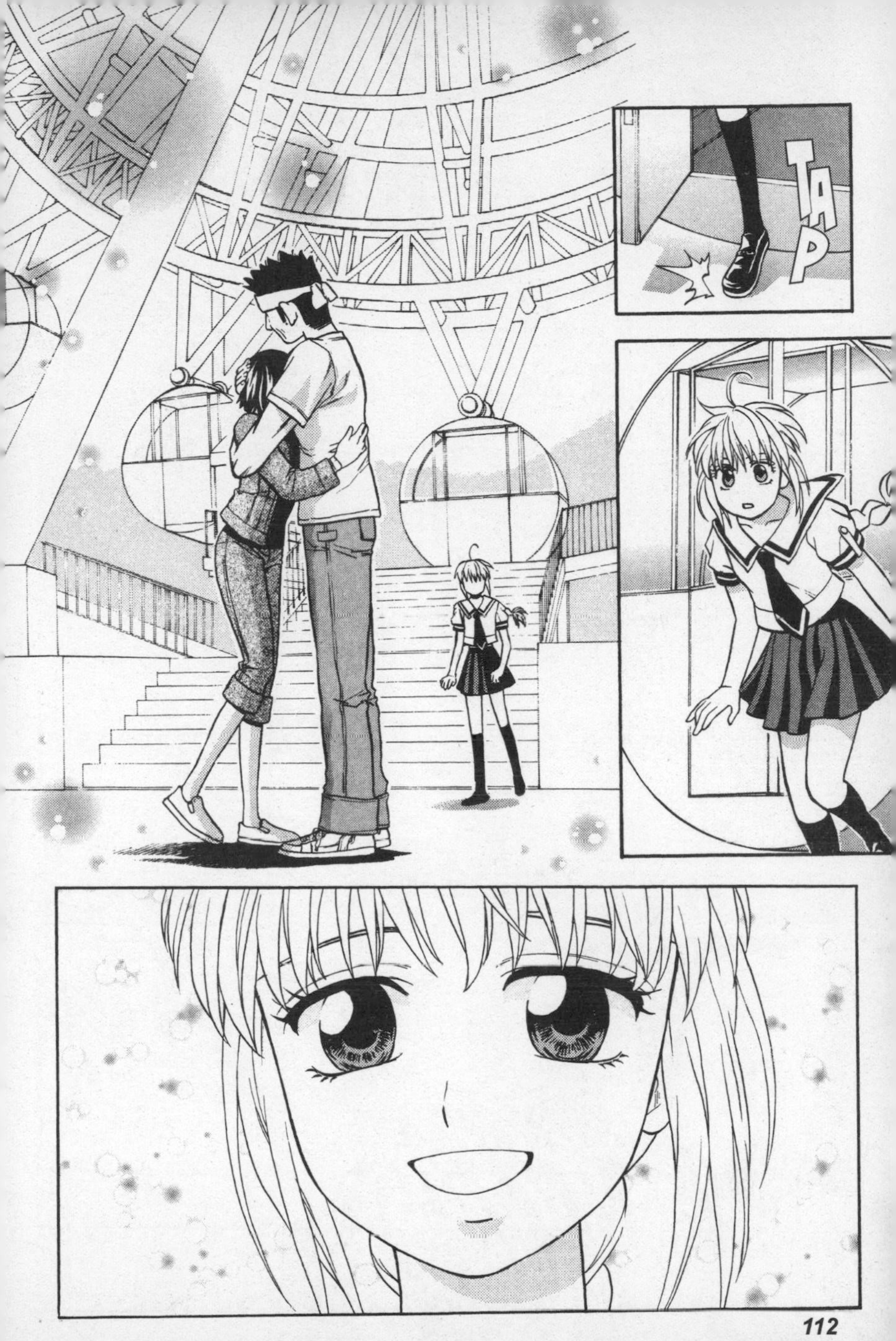
TAP

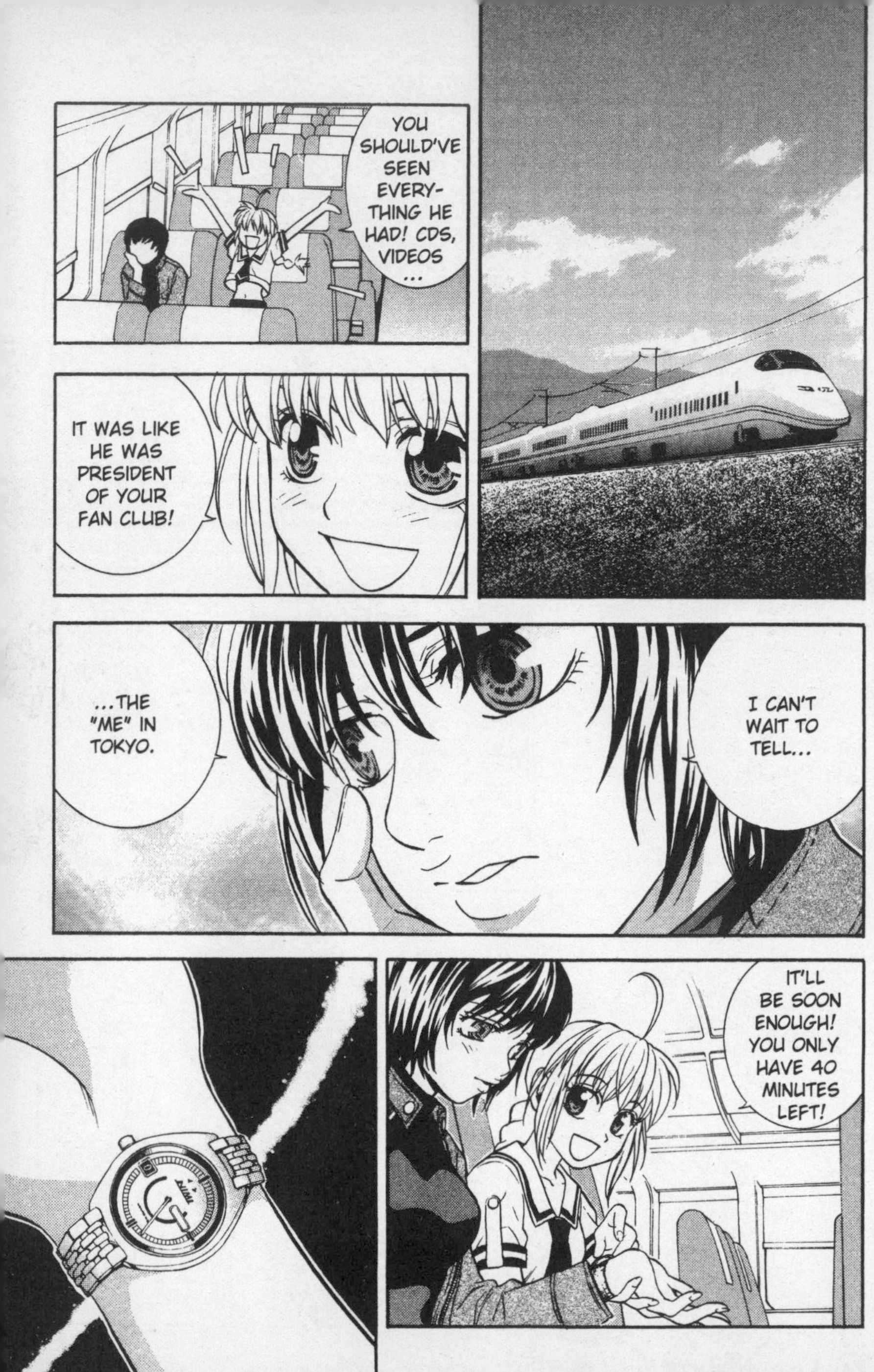
YOU SHOULD'VE SEEN EVERY-THING HE HAD! CDS, VIDEOS ...
IT WAS LIKE HE WAS PRESIDENT OF YOUR FAN CLUB!
I CAN'T WAIT TO TELL...
...THE "ME" IN TOKYO.
IT'LL BE SOON ENOUGH! YOU ONLY HAVE 40 MINUTES LEFT!

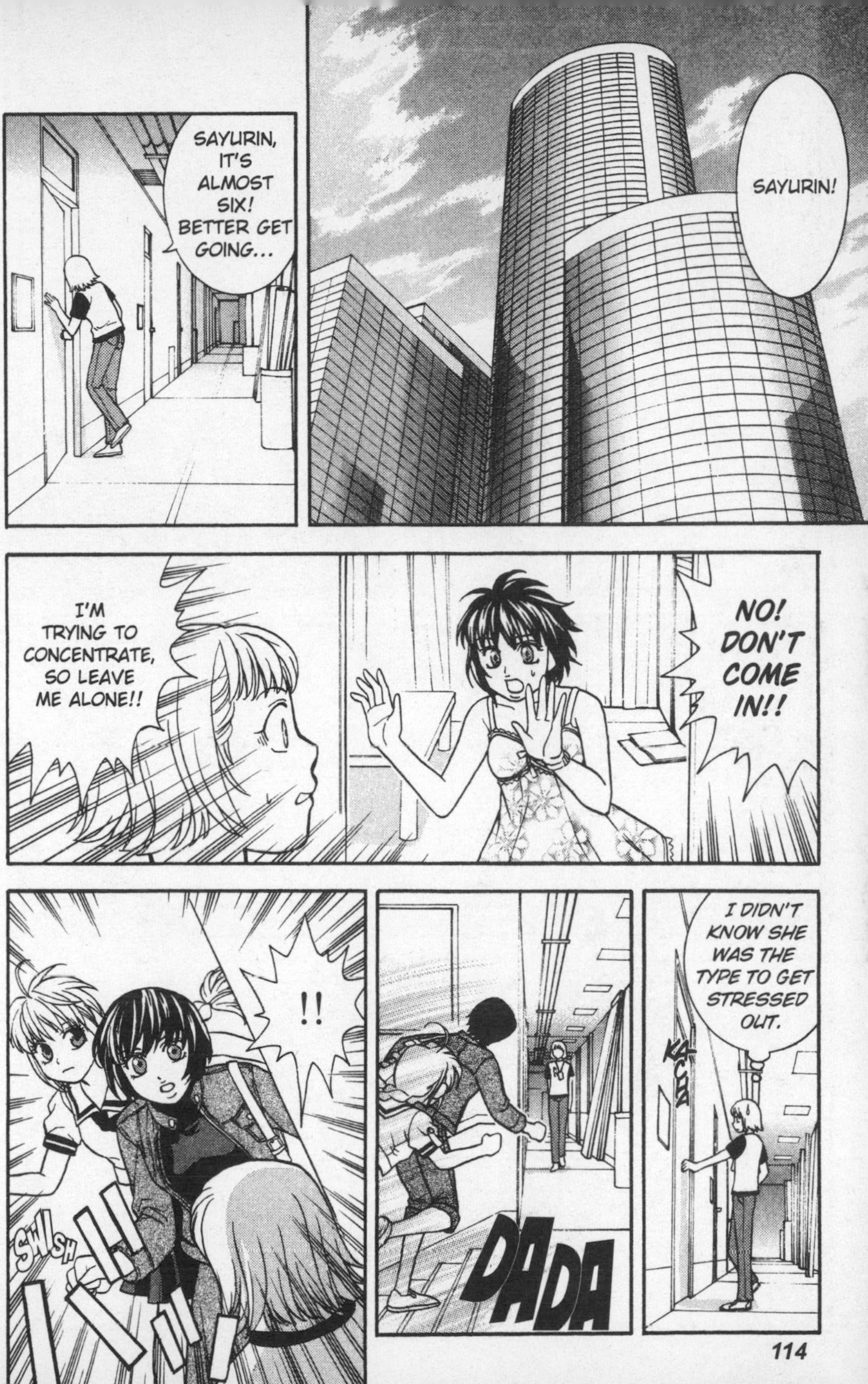
SAYURIN!
SAYURIN, IT'S ALMOST SIX! BETTER GET GOING...
NO! DON'T COME IN!!
I'M TRYING TO CONCENTRATE, SO LEAVE ME ALONE!!
I DIDN'T KNOW SHE WAS THE TYPE TO GET STRESSED OUT.
DADA
!!
SWISH

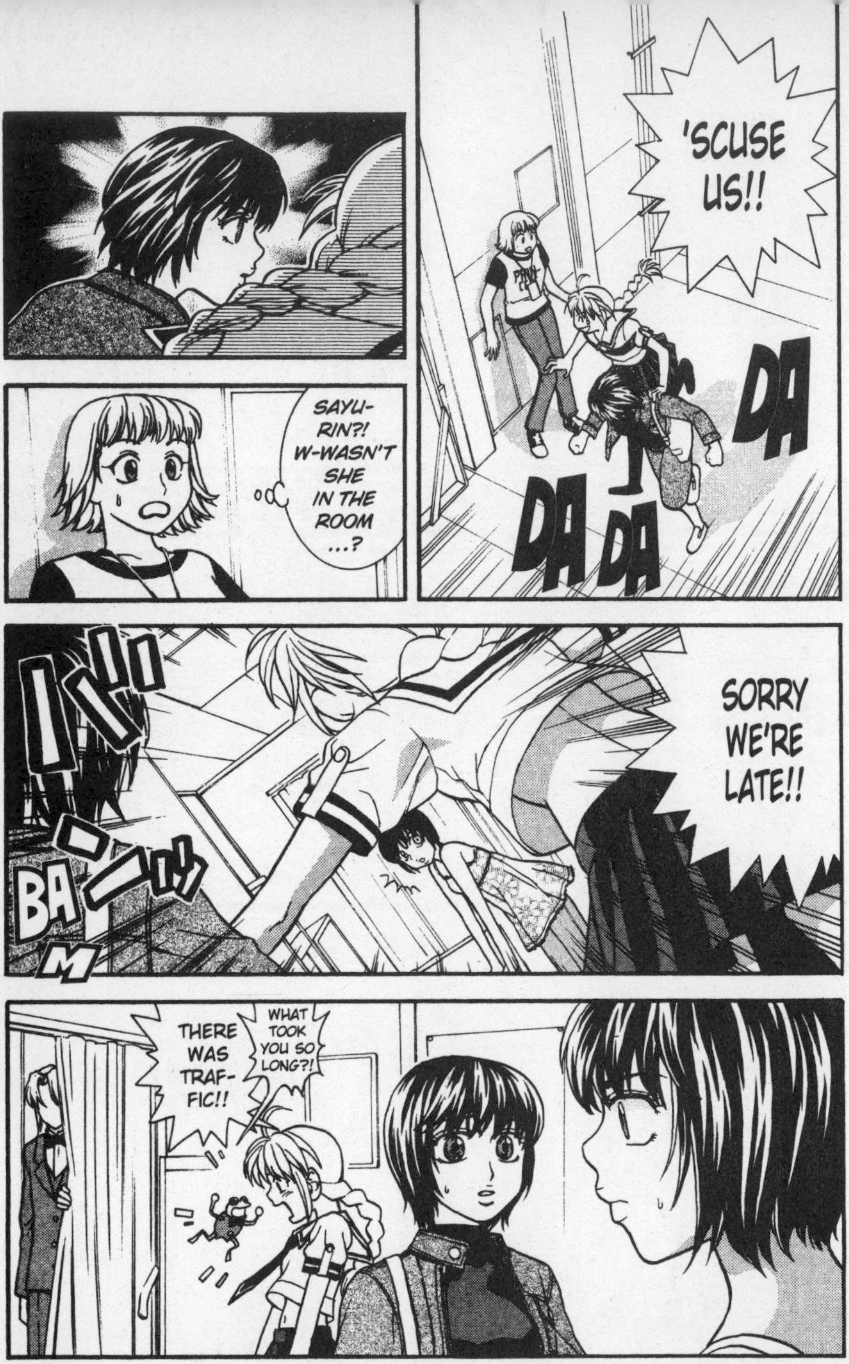
'SCUSE US!!
DA
DA
DA
DA
SAYU-RIN?! W-WASN'T SHE IN THE ROOM ...?
SORRY WE'RE LATE!!
BAM
WHAT TOOK YOU SO LONG?!
THERE WAS TRAF-FIC!!

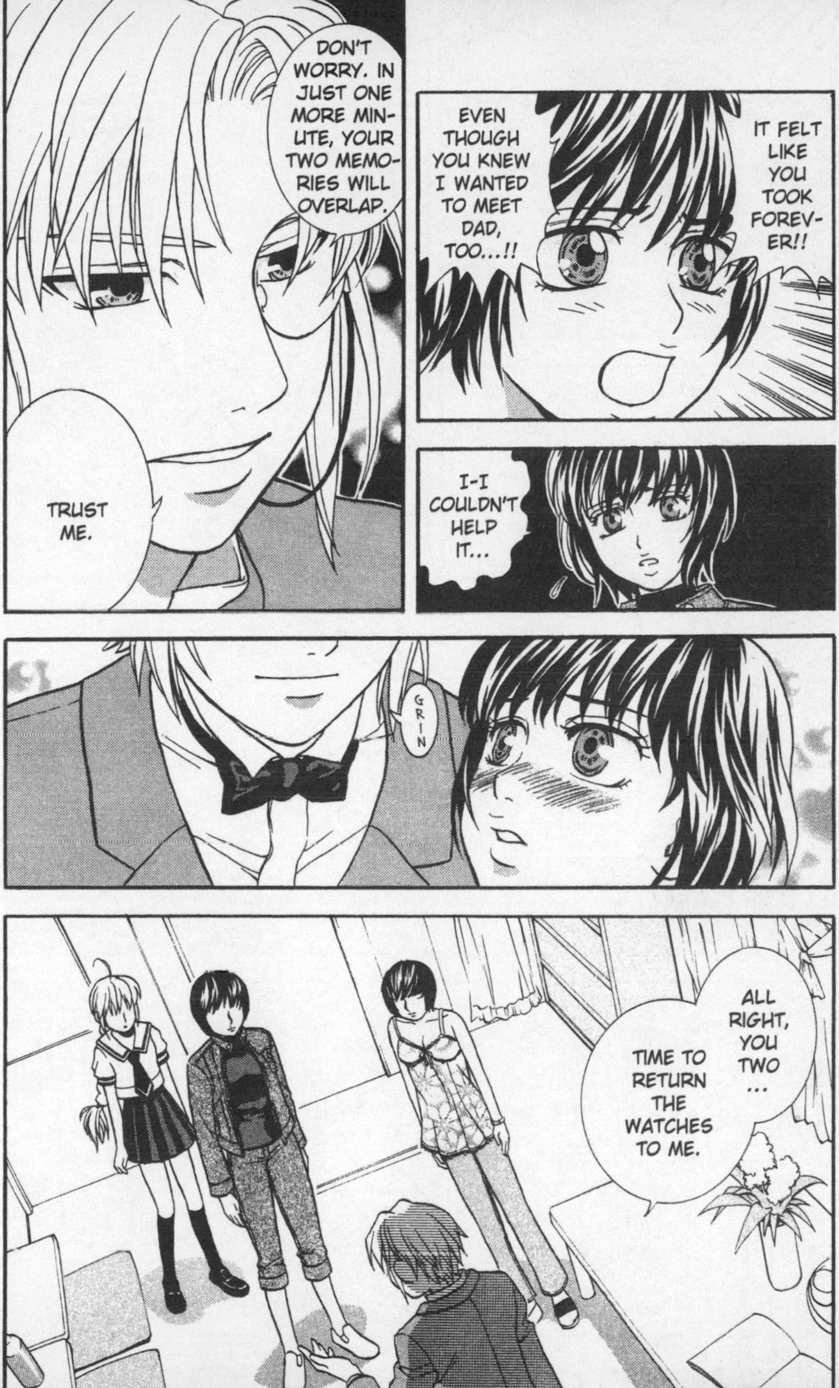
IT FELT LIKE YOU TOOK FOREV-ER!!
EVEN THOUGH YOU KNEW I WANTED TO MEET DAD, TOO...!!
I-I COULDN'T HELP IT...
DON'T WORRY. IN JUST ONE MORE MIN-UTE, YOUR TWO MEMO-RIES WILL OVERLAP.
TRUST ME.
GRIN
ALL RIGHT, YOU TWO...
TIME TO RETURN THE WATCHES TO ME.

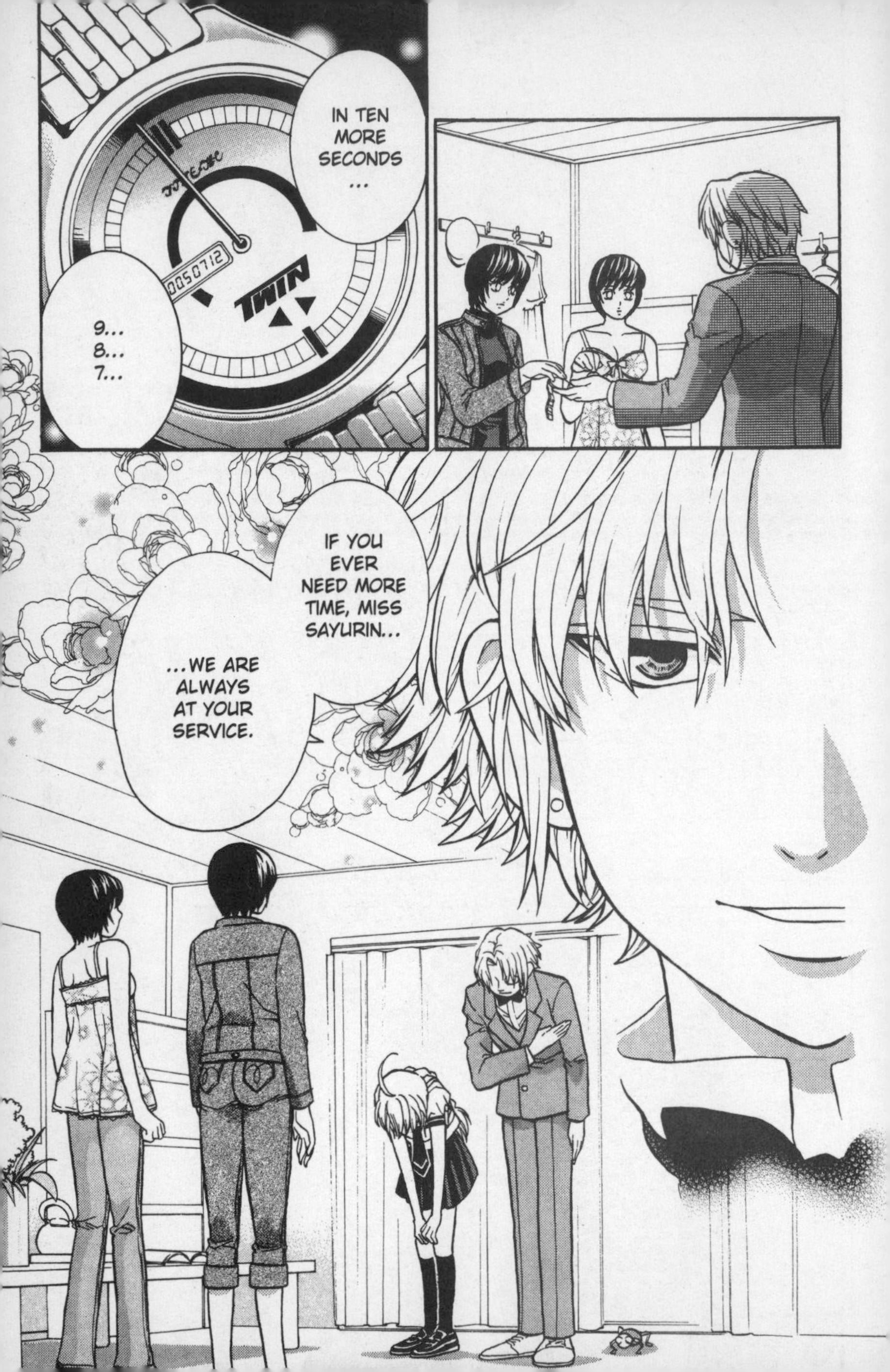
IN TEN MORE SECONDS...
9... 8... 7...
IF YOU EVER NEED MORE TIME, MISS SAYURIN...
...WE ARE ALWAYS AT YOUR SERVICE.

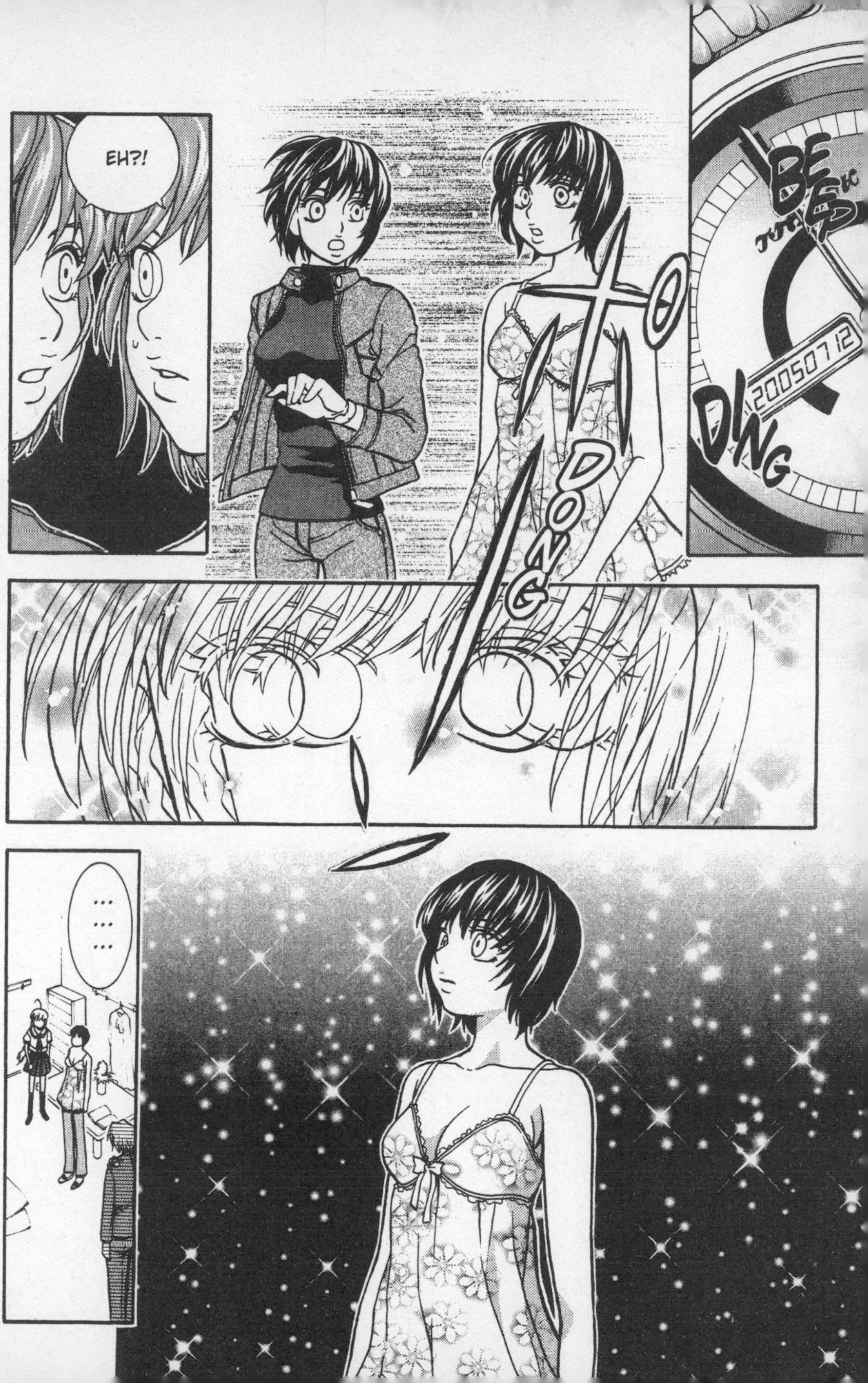
BEEP
20050712
DING
DONG
EH?!
...
...
...

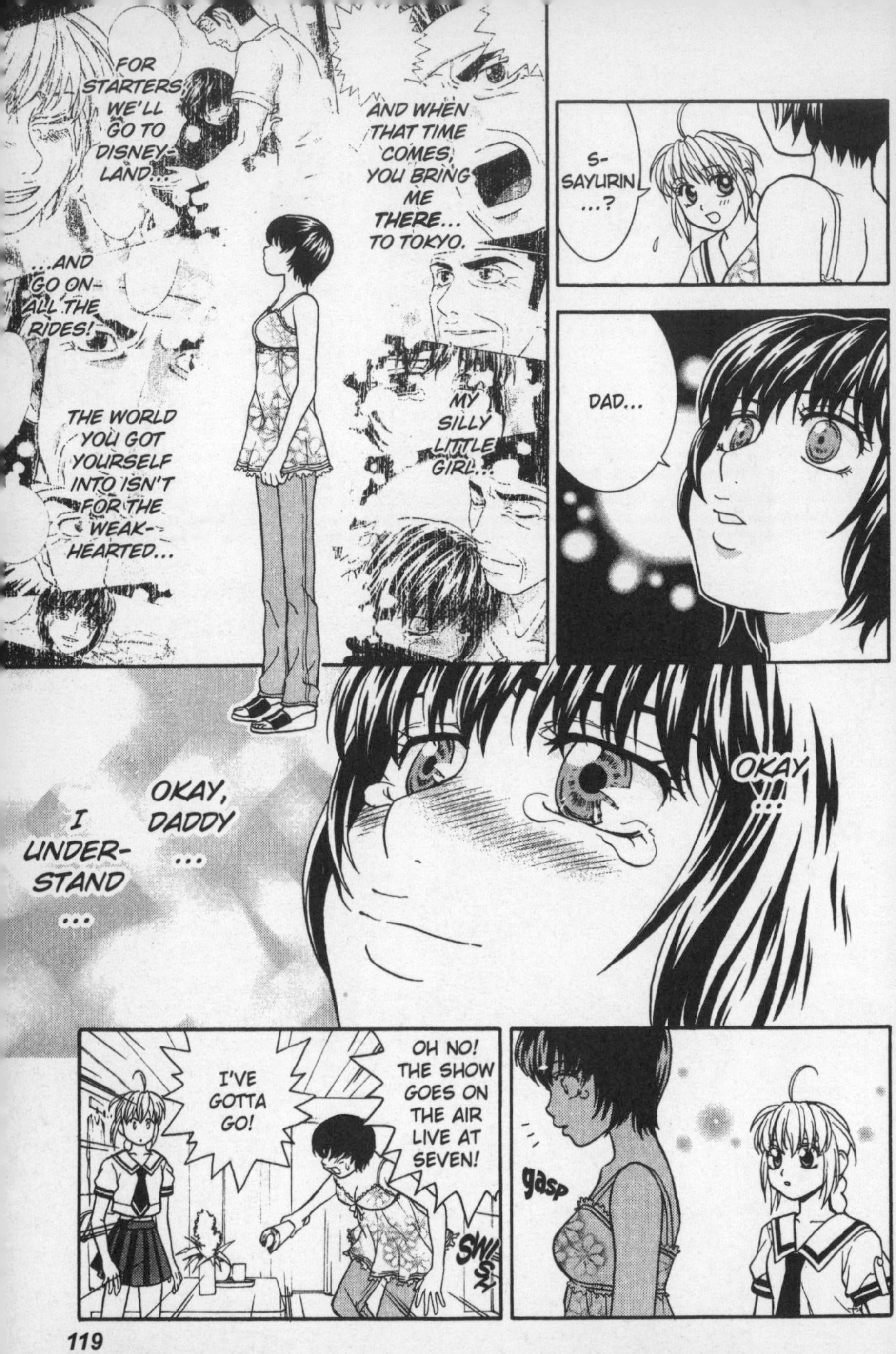
S-SAYURIN ...?
DAD...
AND WHEN THAT TIME COMES, YOU BRING ME THERE... TO TOKYO.
FOR STARTERS WE'LL GO TO DISNEY-LAND...
...AND GO ON ALL THE RIDES!
MY SILLY LITTLE GIRL...
THE WORLD YOU GOT YOURSELF INTO ISN'T FOR THE WEAK-HEARTED...
OKAY ...
OKAY, DADDY ...
I UNDER-STAND ...
gasp
OH NO! THE SHOW GOES ON THE AIR LIVE AT SEVEN!
I'VE GOTTA GO!
SWISH

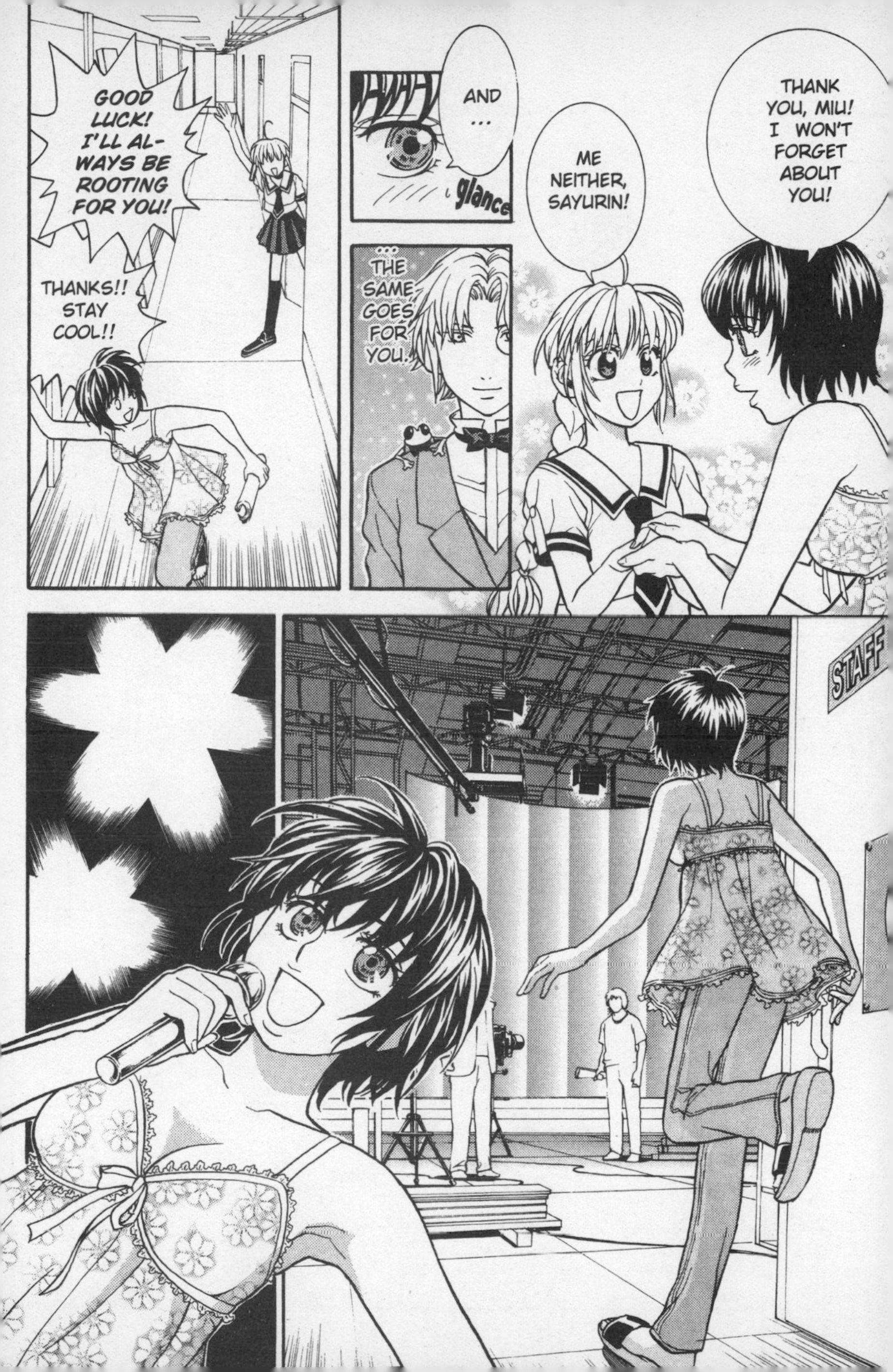
THANK YOU, MIU! I WON'T FORGET ABOUT YOU!
ME NEITHER, SAYURIN!
AND ...
glance
... THE SAME GOES FOR YOU.
GOOD LUCK! I'LL AL-WAYS BE ROOTING FOR YOU!
THANKS!! STAY COOL!!
STAFF

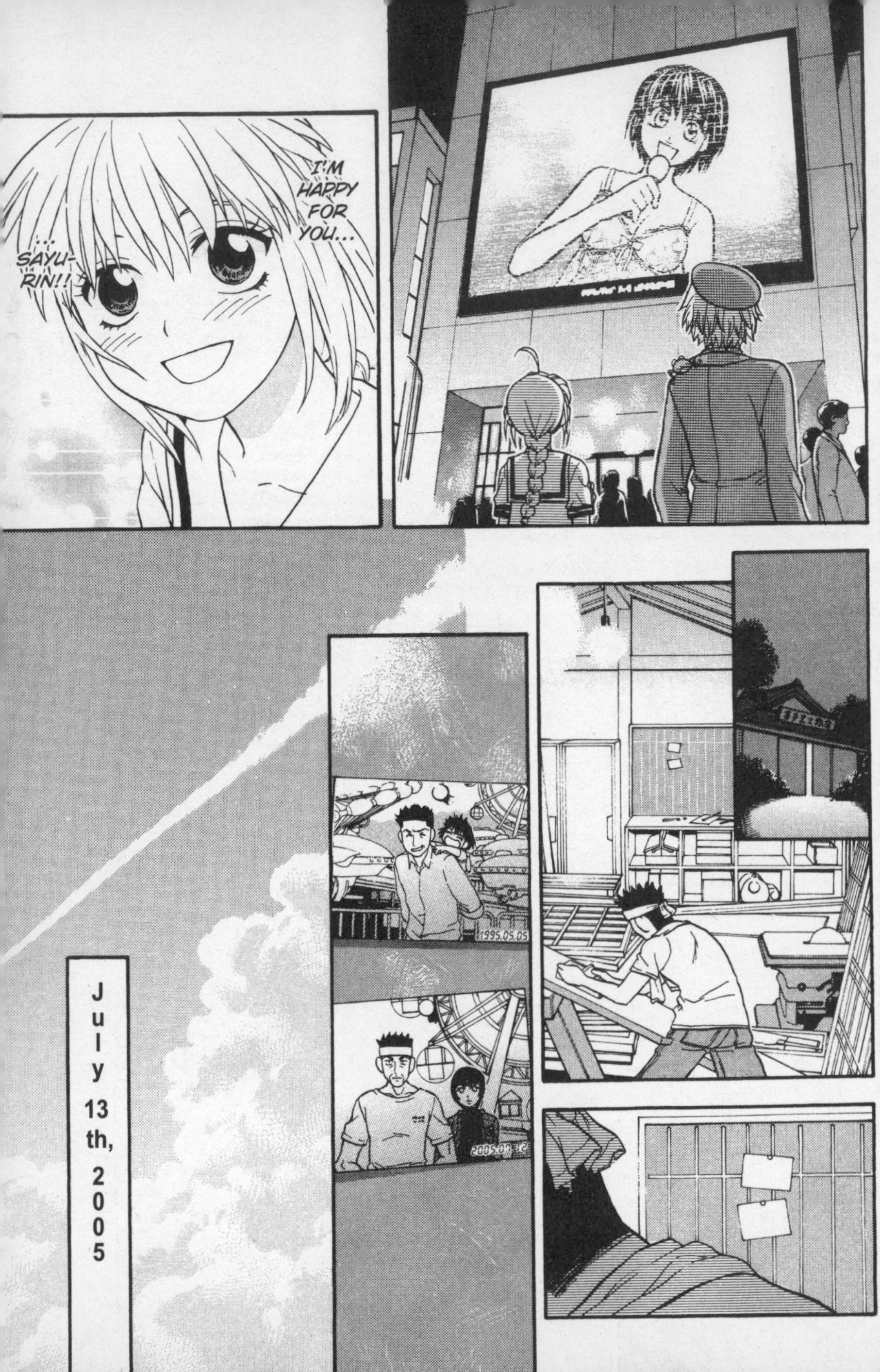
I'M HAPPY FOR YOU...
...SAYU-RIN!!
1995.05.05
July 13th, 2005

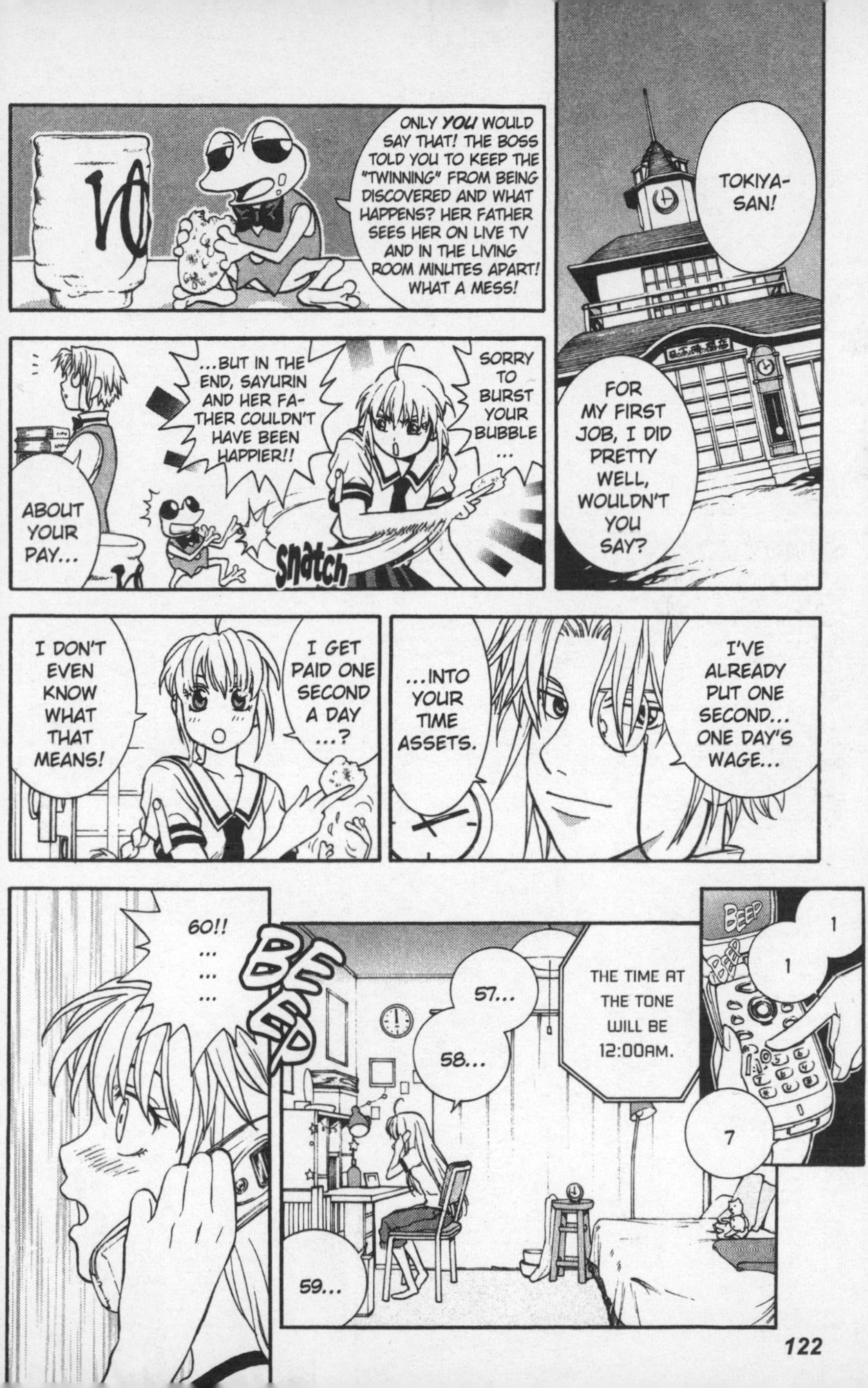
TOKIYA-SAN!
FOR MY FIRST JOB, I DID PRETTY WELL, WOULDN'T YOU SAY?
ONLY YOU WOULD SAY THAT! THE BOSS TOLD YOU TO KEEP THE "TWINNING" FROM BEING DISCOVERED AND WHAT HAPPENS? HER FATHER SEES HER ON LIVE TV AND IN THE LIVING ROOM MINUTES APART! WHAT A MESS!
SORRY TO BURST YOUR BUBBLE...
...BUT IN THE END, SAYURIN AND HER FATHER COULDN'T HAVE BEEN HAPPIER!!
SNATCH
ABOUT YOUR PAY...
I'VE ALREADY PUT ONE SECOND... ONE DAY'S WAGE...
...INTO YOUR TIME ASSETS.
I GET PAID ONE SECOND A DAY ...?
I DON'T EVEN KNOW WHAT THAT MEANS!
BEEP
BEEP
1
1
7
THE TIME AT THE TONE WILL BE 12:00AM.
57...
58...
59...
BEEP
60!! ... ...

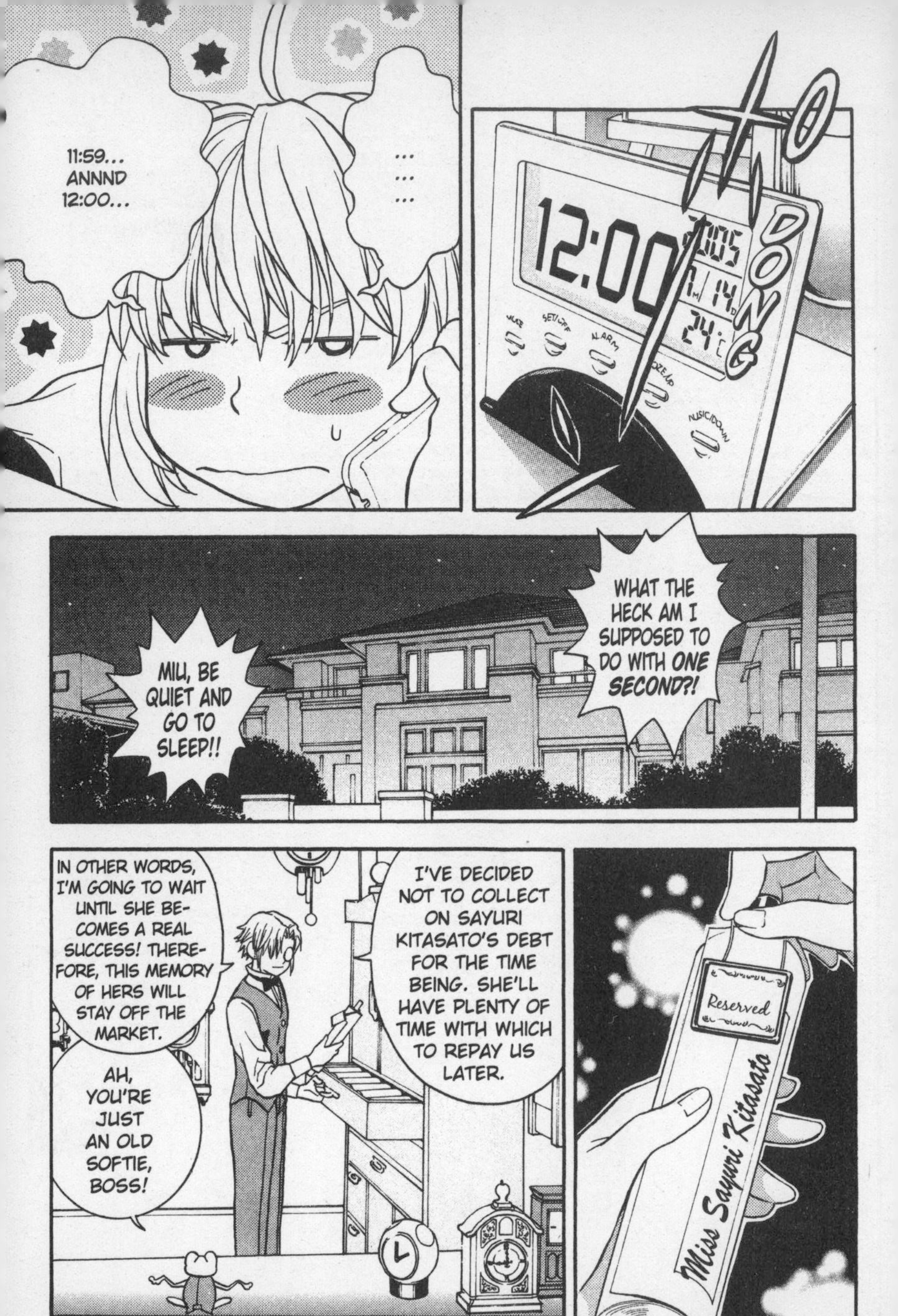
DONG
12:00
ALARM
SET/OFF
MUSIC/DOWN
...
...
...
11:59...
ANNND
12:00...
WHAT THE HECK AM I SUPPOSED TO DO WITH ONE SECOND?!
MIU, BE QUIET AND GO TO SLEEP!!
Reserved
Miss Sayuri Kitasato
I'VE DECIDED NOT TO COLLECT ON SAYURI KITASATO'S DEBT FOR THE TIME BEING. SHE'LL HAVE PLENTY OF TIME WITH WHICH TO REPAY US LATER.
IN OTHER WORDS, I'M GOING TO WAIT UNTIL SHE BECOMES A REAL SUCCESS! THEREFORE, THIS MEMORY OF HERS WILL STAY OFF THE MARKET.
AH, YOU'RE JUST AN OLD SOFTIE, BOSS!

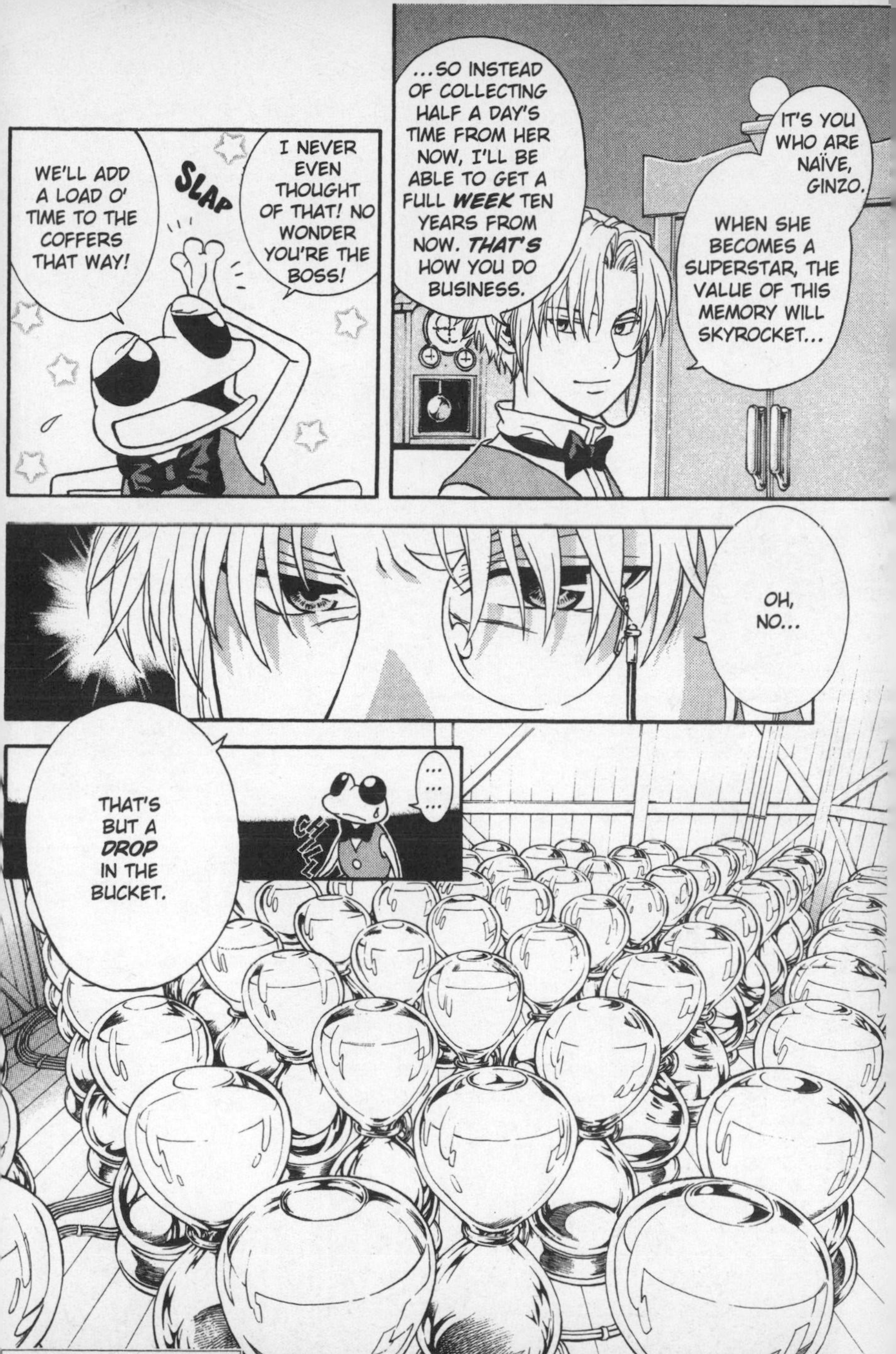
IT'S YOU WHO ARE NAÏVE, GINZO.
WHEN SHE BECOMES A SUPERSTAR, THE VALUE OF THIS MEMORY WILL SKYROCKET...
...SO INSTEAD OF COLLECTING HALF A DAY'S TIME FROM HER NOW, I'LL BE ABLE TO GET A FULL ***WEEK*** TEN YEARS FROM NOW. ***THAT'S*** HOW YOU DO BUSINESS.
I NEVER EVEN THOUGHT OF THAT! NO WONDER YOU'RE THE BOSS!
SLAP
WE'LL ADD A LOAD O' TIME TO THE COFFERS THAT WAY!
OH, NO...
......
CHILL
THAT'S BUT A ***DROP*** IN THE BUCKET.
Episode 3 Two Times (Part Two): The End

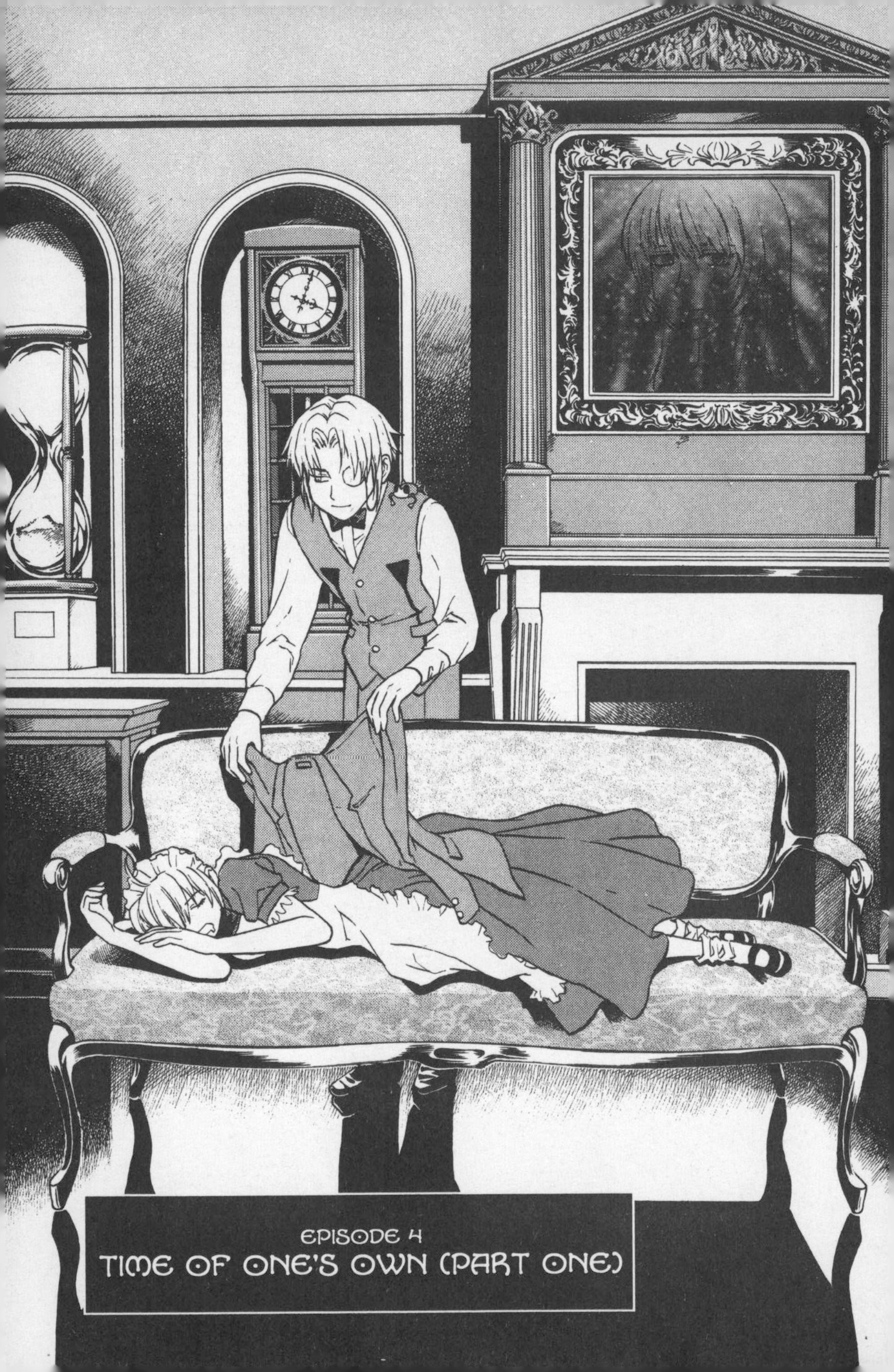
EPISODE 4
TIME OF ONE'S OWN (PART ONE)

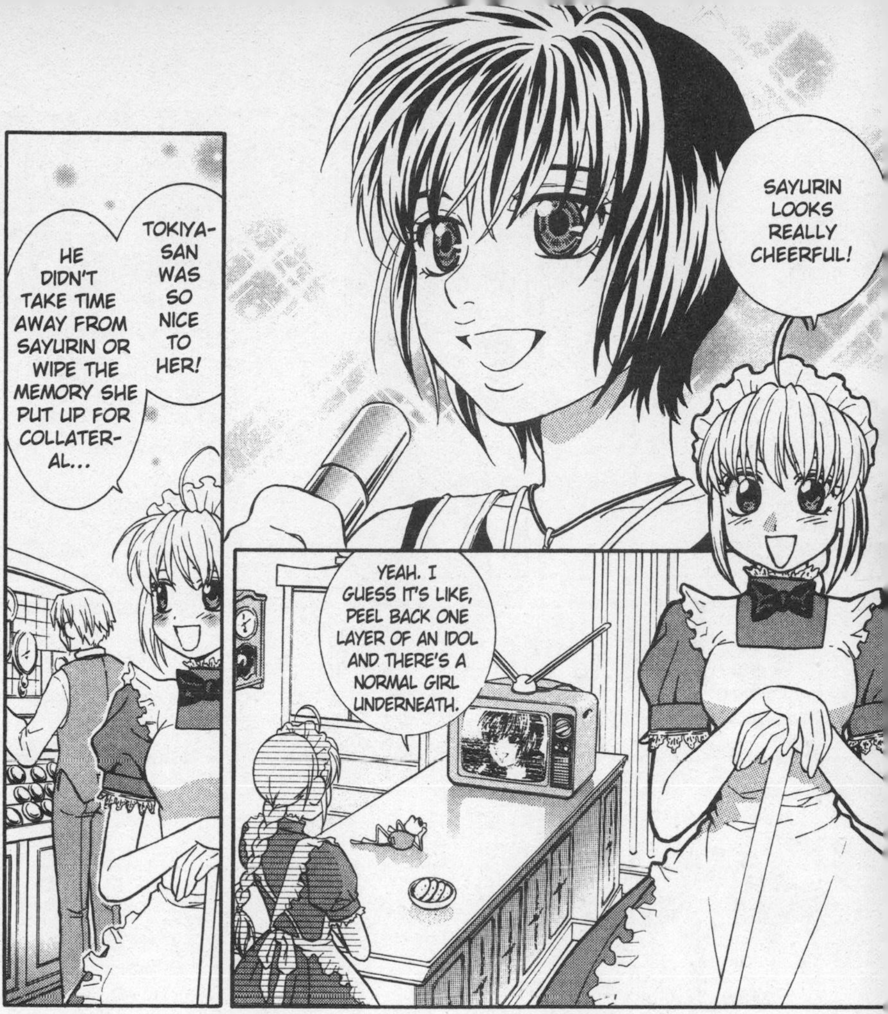
SAYURIN LOOKS REALLY CHEERFUL!
YEAH. I GUESS IT'S LIKE, PEEL BACK ONE LAYER OF AN IDOL AND THERE'S A NORMAL GIRL UNDERNEATH.
TOKIYA-SAN WAS SO NICE TO HER!
HE DIDN'T TAKE TIME AWAY FROM SAYURIN OR WIPE THE MEMORY SHE PUT UP FOR COLLATERAL...
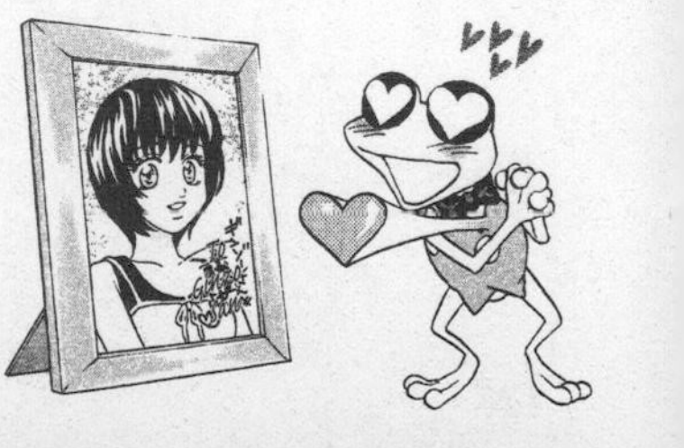

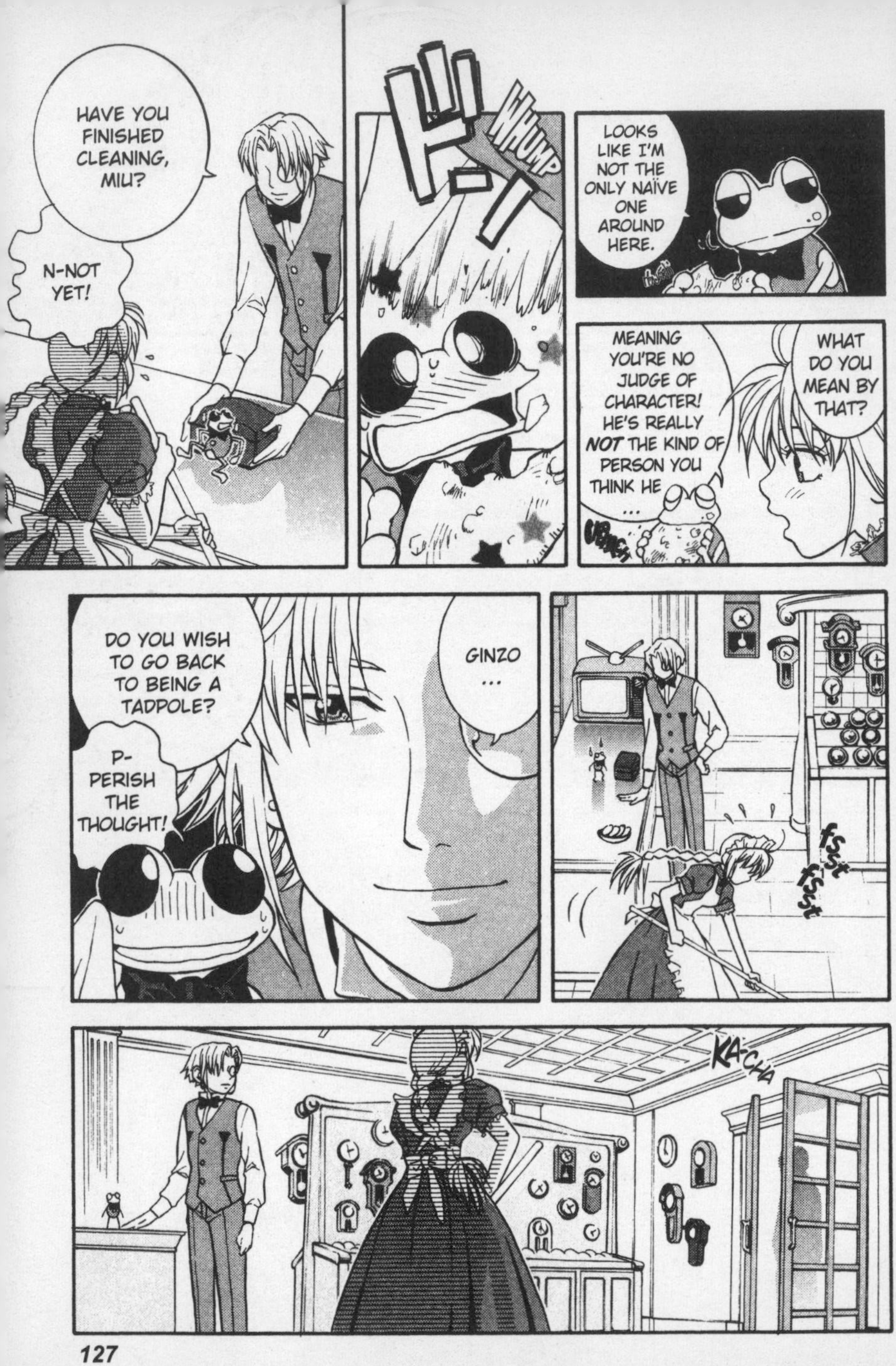
LOOKS LIKE I'M NOT THE ONLY NAÏVE ONE AROUND HERE.
WHAT DO YOU MEAN BY THAT?
MEANING YOU'RE NO JUDGE OF CHARACTER! HE'S REALLY *NOT* THE KIND OF PERSON YOU THINK HE ...
WHUMP
HAVE YOU FINISHED CLEANING, MIU?
N-NOT YET!
fsst
fsst
GINZO ...
DO YOU WISH TO GO BACK TO BEING A TADPOLE?
P-PERISH THE THOUGHT!
KA-CHA

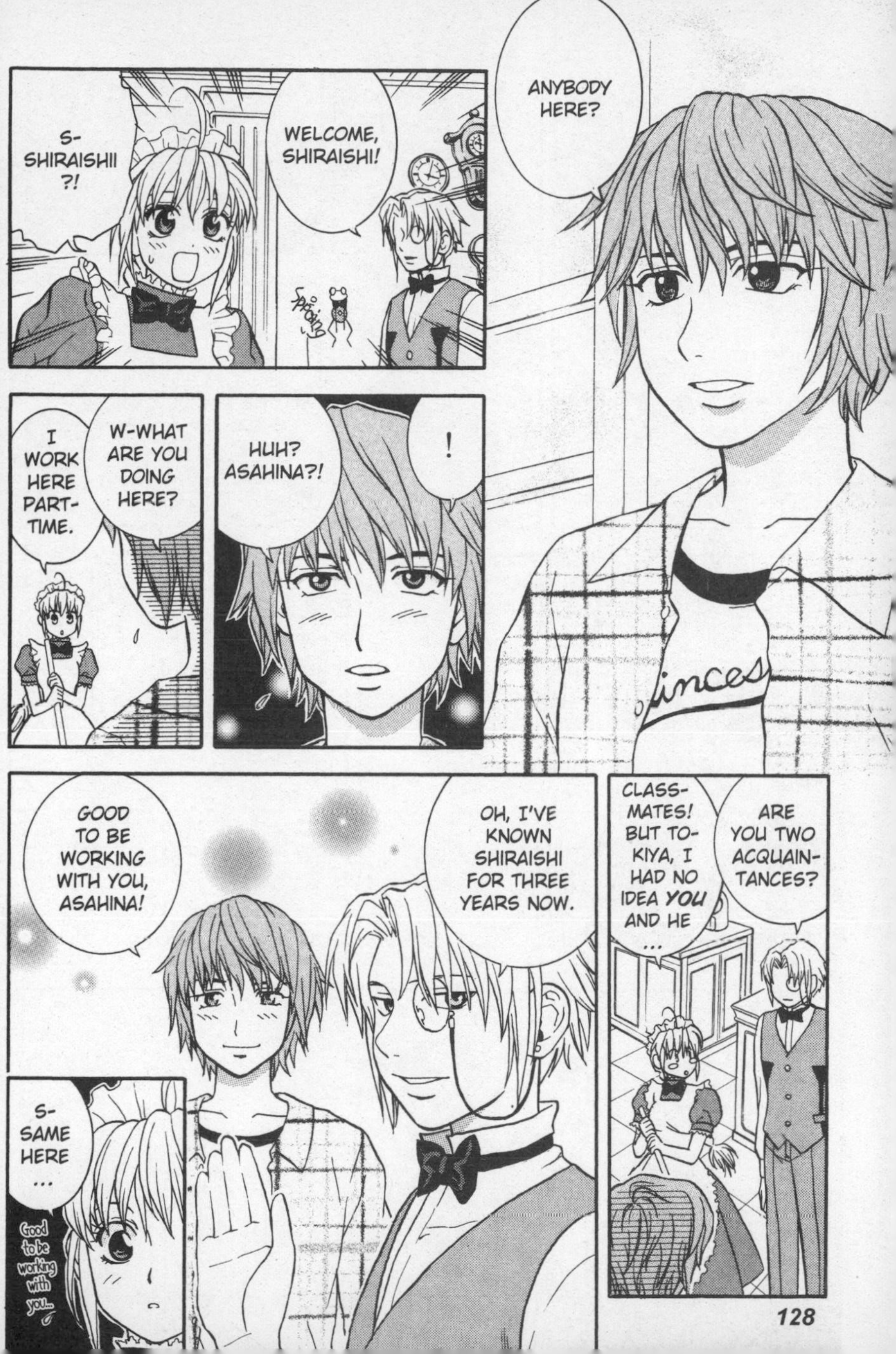
ANYBODY HERE?
WELCOME, SHIRAISHI!
S-SHIRAISHII?!
Spproing
!
HUH? ASAHINA?!
W-WHAT ARE YOU DOING HERE?
I WORK HERE PART-TIME.
ARE YOU TWO ACQUAINTANCES?
CLASSMATES! BUT TO-KIYA, I HAD NO IDEA *YOU* AND HE ...
OH, I'VE KNOWN SHIRAISHI FOR THREE YEARS NOW.
GOOD TO BE WORKING WITH YOU, ASAHINA!
S-SAME HERE ...
Good to be working with you...

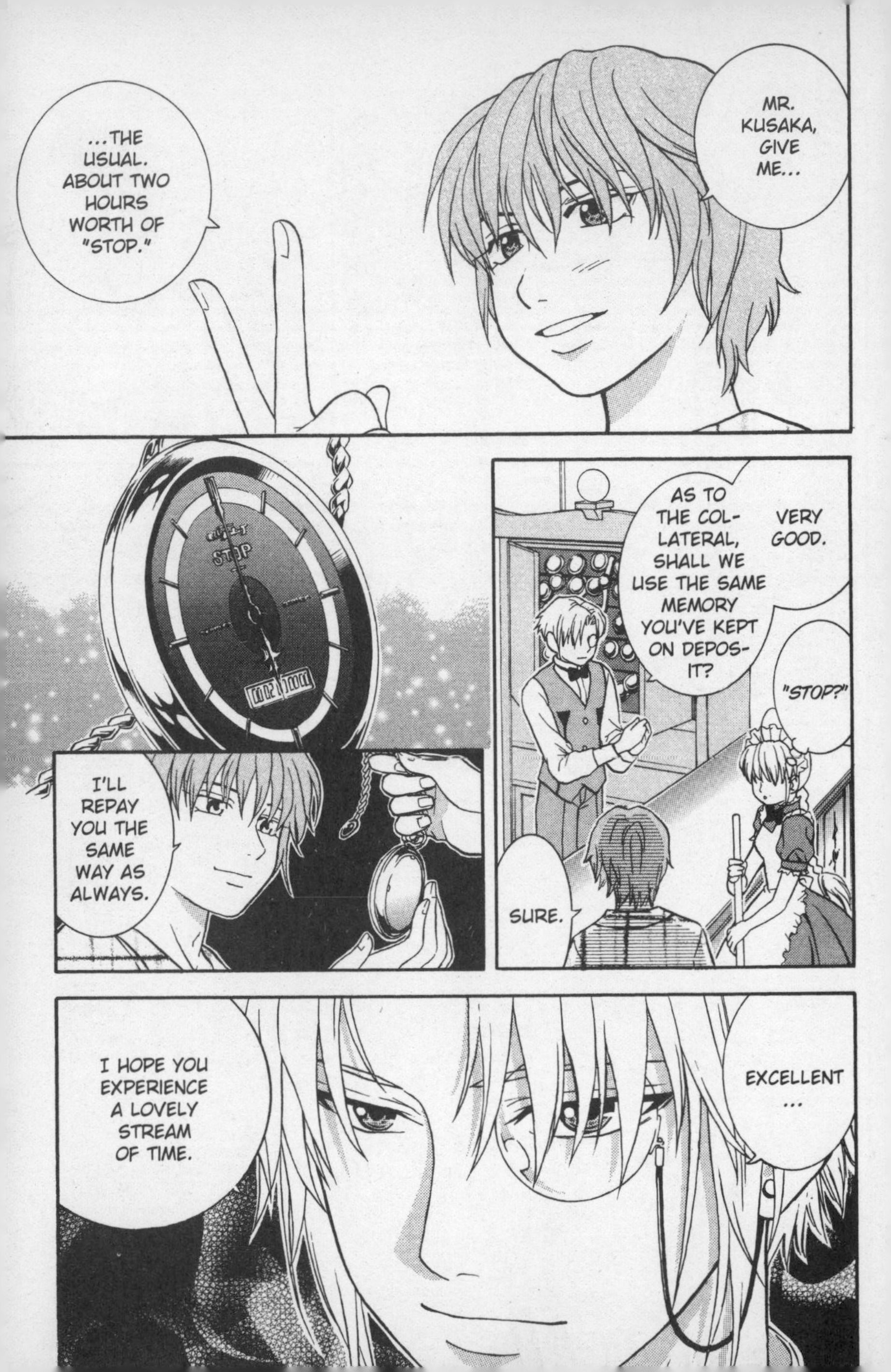
MR. KUSAKA, GIVE ME...
...THE USUAL. ABOUT TWO HOURS WORTH OF "STOP."
VERY GOOD.
AS TO THE COL-LATERAL, SHALL WE USE THE SAME MEMORY YOU'VE KEPT ON DEPOS-IT?
"STOP?"
SURE.
STOP
I'LL REPAY YOU THE SAME WAY AS ALWAYS.
EXCELLENT ...
I HOPE YOU EXPERIENCE A LOVELY STREAM OF TIME.

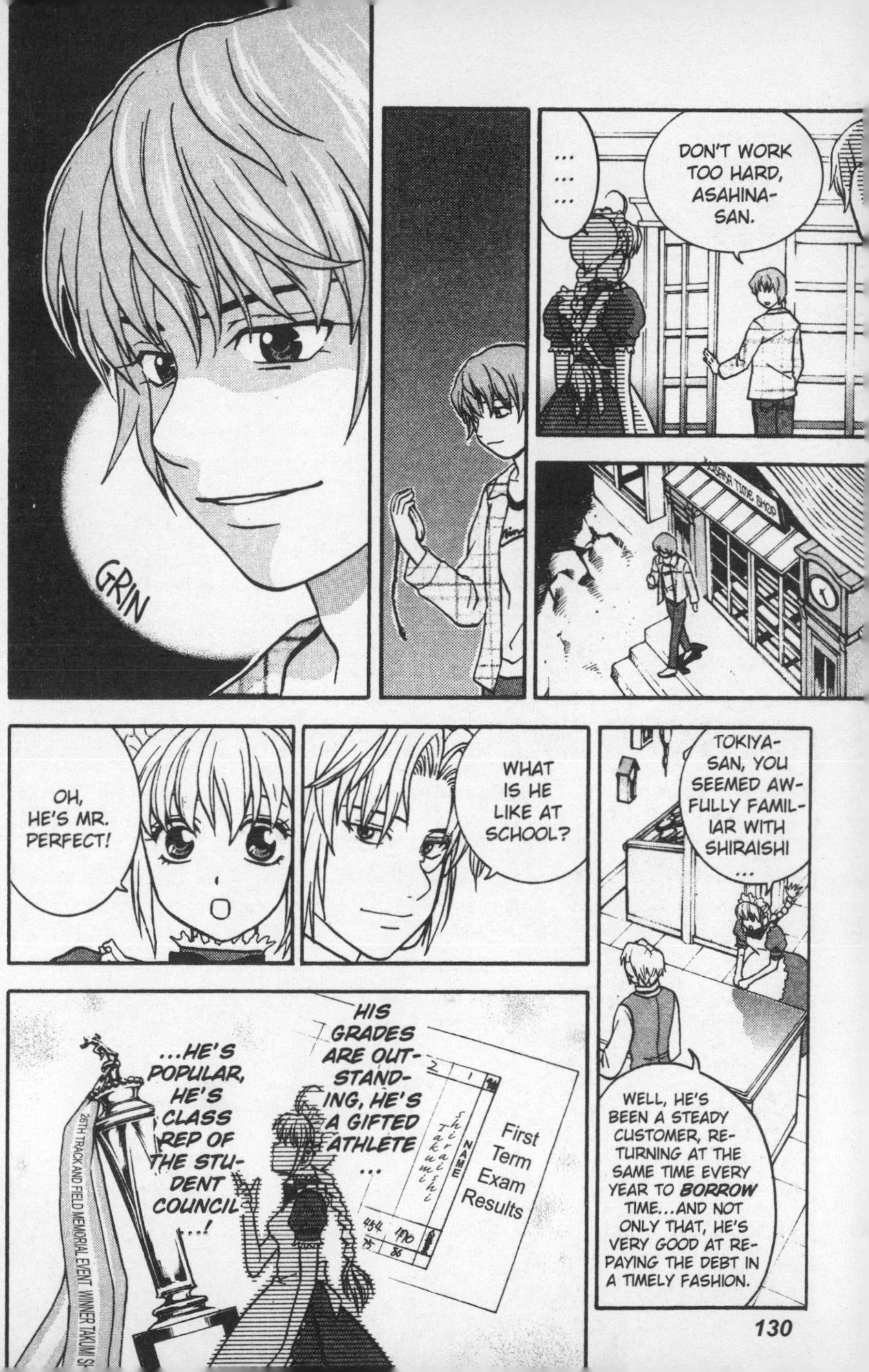
DON'T WORK TOO HARD, ASAHINA-SAN.
... ...
GRIN
TOKIYA-SAN, YOU SEEMED AWFULLY FAMILIAR WITH SHIRAISHI ...
WELL, HE'S BEEN A STEADY CUSTOMER, RETURNING AT THE SAME TIME EVERY YEAR TO ***BORROW*** TIME...AND NOT ONLY THAT, HE'S VERY GOOD AT REPAYING THE DEBT IN A TIMELY FASHION.
WHAT IS HE LIKE AT SCHOOL?
OH, HE'S MR. PERFECT!
HIS GRADES ARE OUTSTANDING, HE'S A GIFTED ATHLETE ...
...HE'S POPULAR, HE'S CLASS REP OF THE STUDENT COUNCIL ...!
First Term Exam Results
NAME Shiraishi Takumi
28TH TRACK AND FIELD MEMORIAL EVENT WINNER TAKUMI S

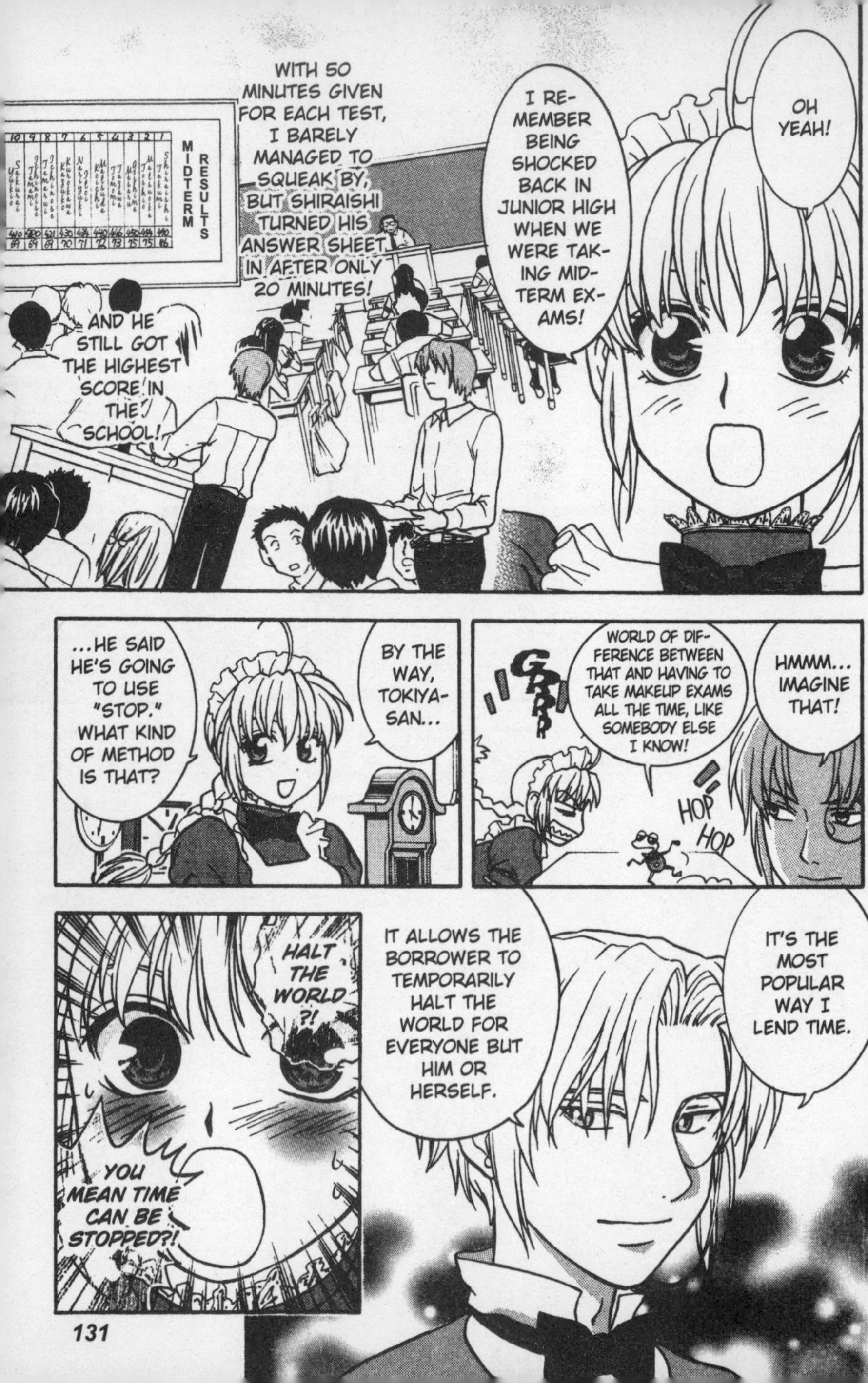
OH YEAH!
I RE-MEMBER BEING SHOCKED BACK IN JUNIOR HIGH WHEN WE WERE TAK-ING MID-TERM EX-AMS!
WITH 50 MINUTES GIVEN FOR EACH TEST, I BARELY MANAGED TO SQUEAK BY, BUT SHIRAISHI TURNED HIS ANSWER SHEET IN AFTER ONLY 20 MINUTES!
MIDTERM RESULTS
AND HE STILL GOT THE HIGHEST SCORE IN THE SCHOOL!
HMMM... IMAGINE THAT!
WORLD OF DIF-FERENCE BETWEEN THAT AND HAVING TO TAKE MAKEUP EXAMS ALL THE TIME, LIKE SOMEBODY ELSE I KNOW!
GRRR
HOP HOP
BY THE WAY, TOKIYA-SAN...
...HE SAID HE'S GOING TO USE "STOP." WHAT KIND OF METHOD IS THAT?
IT'S THE MOST POPULAR WAY I LEND TIME.
IT ALLOWS THE BORROWER TO TEMPORARILY HALT THE WORLD FOR EVERYONE BUT HIM OR HERSELF.
HALT THE WORLD ?!
YOU MEAN TIME CAN BE STOPPED?!

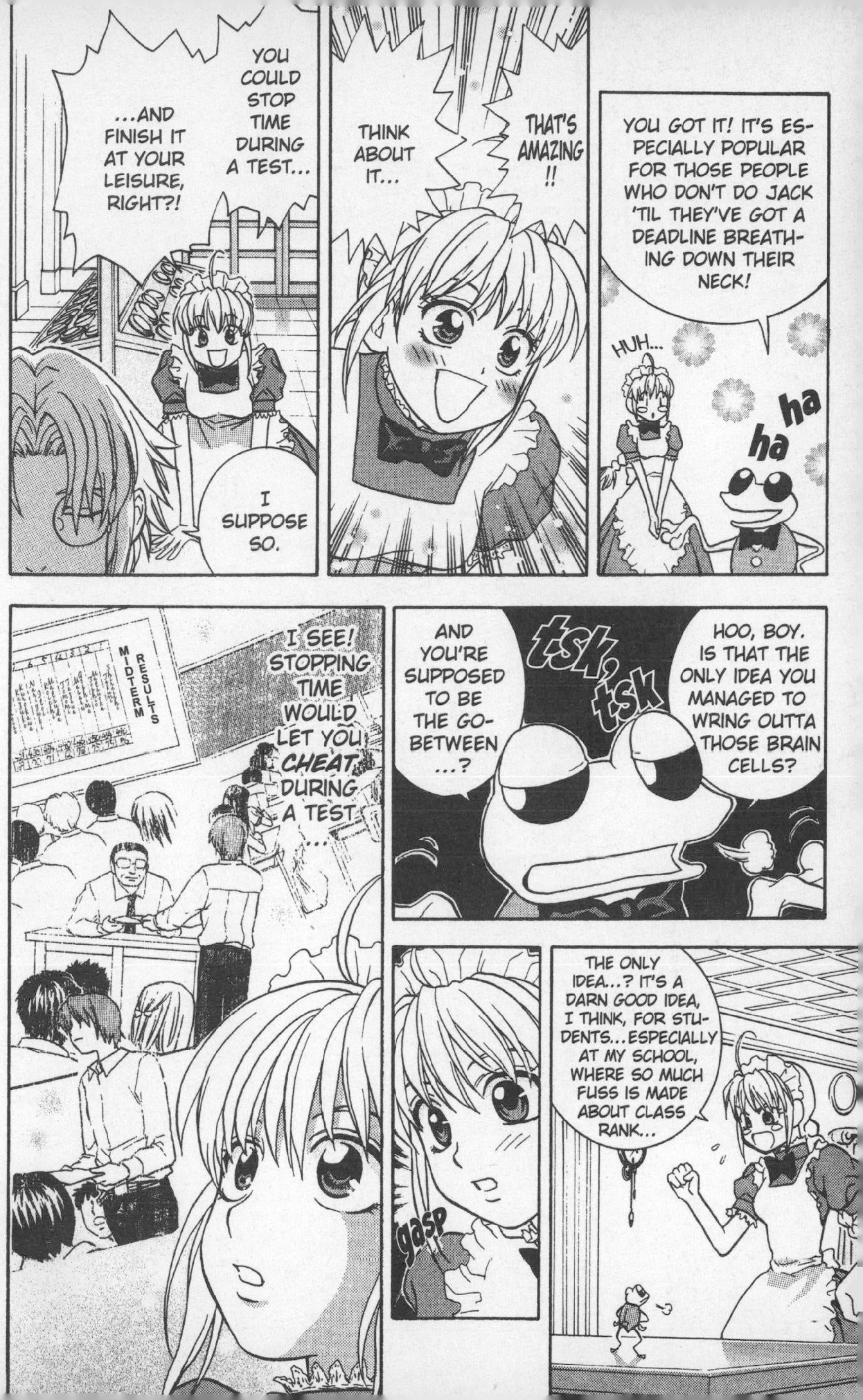
YOU COULD STOP TIME DURING A TEST...
...AND FINISH IT AT YOUR LEISURE, RIGHT?!
I SUPPOSE SO.
THINK ABOUT IT...
THAT'S AMAZING!!
YOU GOT IT! IT'S ES-PECIALLY POPULAR FOR THOSE PEOPLE WHO DON'T DO JACK 'TIL THEY'VE GOT A DEADLINE BREATH-ING DOWN THEIR NECK!
HUH...
ha ha
MIDTERM RESULTS
I SEE! STOPPING TIME WOULD LET YOU CHEAT DURING A TEST...
HOO, BOY. IS THAT THE ONLY IDEA YOU MANAGED TO WRING OUTTA THOSE BRAIN CELLS?
tsk, tsk
AND YOU'RE SUPPOSED TO BE THE GO-BETWEEN...?
gasp
THE ONLY IDEA...? IT'S A DARN GOOD IDEA, I THINK, FOR STU-DENTS...ESPECIALLY AT MY SCHOOL, WHERE SO MUCH FUSS IS MADE ABOUT CLASS RANK...

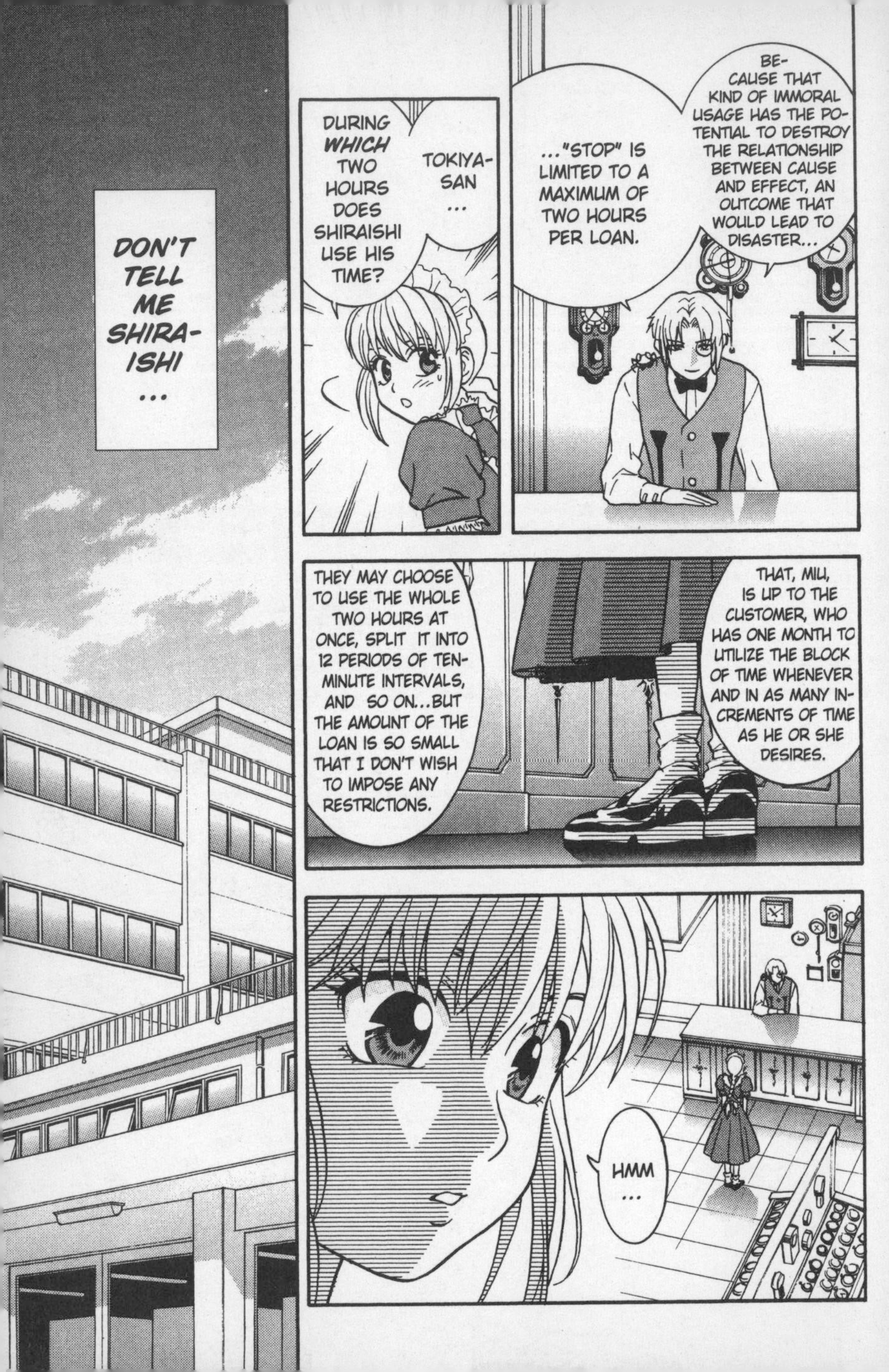
..."STOP" IS LIMITED TO A MAXIMUM OF TWO HOURS PER LOAN.
BE-CAUSE THAT KIND OF IMMORAL USAGE HAS THE PO-TENTIAL TO DESTROY THE RELATIONSHIP BETWEEN CAUSE AND EFFECT, AN OUTCOME THAT WOULD LEAD TO DISASTER...
TOKIYA-SAN ...
DURING *WHICH* TWO HOURS DOES SHIRAISHI USE HIS TIME?
THAT, MIU, IS UP TO THE CUSTOMER, WHO HAS ONE MONTH TO UTILIZE THE BLOCK OF TIME WHENEVER AND IN AS MANY IN-CREMENTS OF TIME AS HE OR SHE DESIRES.
THEY MAY CHOOSE TO USE THE WHOLE TWO HOURS AT ONCE, SPLIT IT INTO 12 PERIODS OF TEN-MINUTE INTERVALS, AND SO ON...BUT THE AMOUNT OF THE LOAN IS SO SMALL THAT I DON'T WISH TO IMPOSE ANY RESTRICTIONS.
HMM ...
DON'T TELL ME SHIRA-ISHI ...

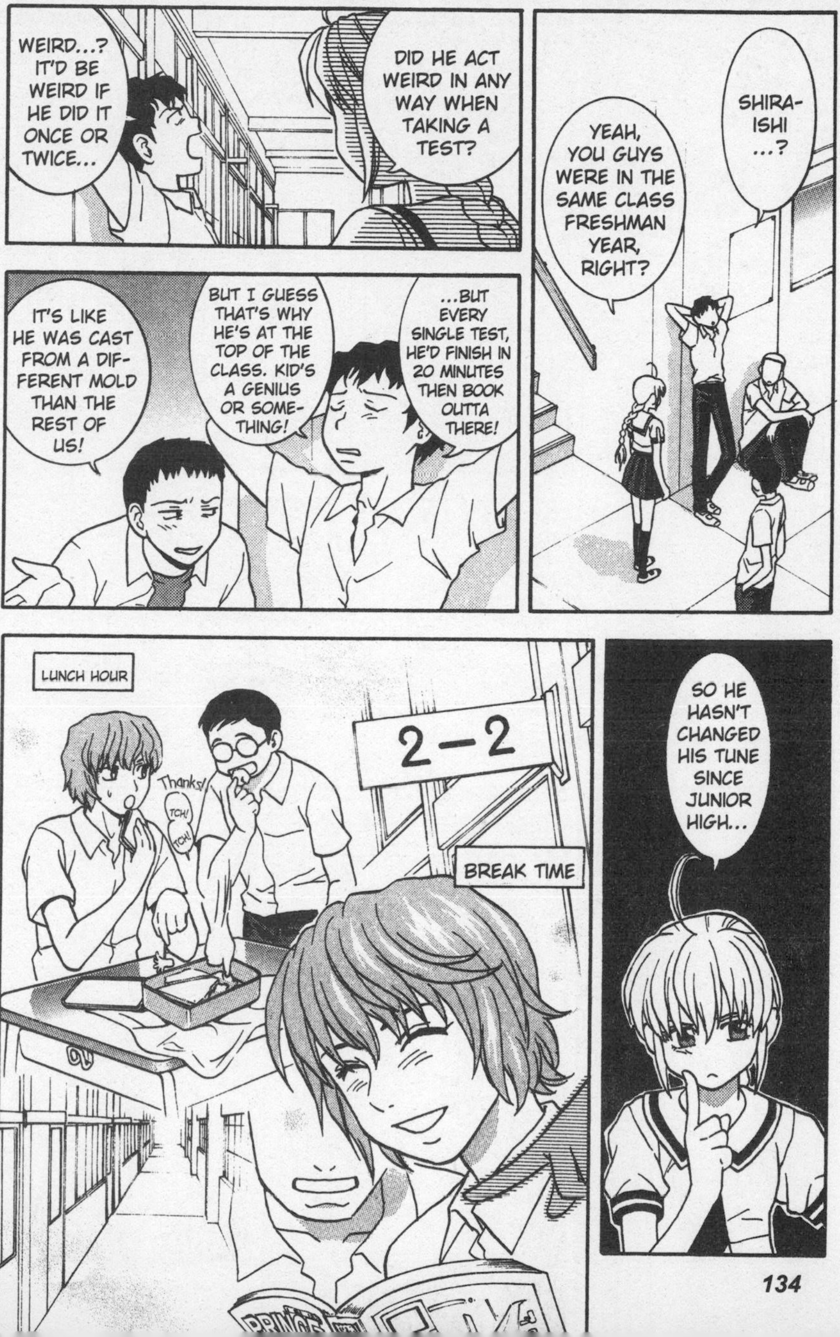
SHIRA-ISHI ...?
YEAH, YOU GUYS WERE IN THE SAME CLASS FRESHMAN YEAR, RIGHT?
DID HE ACT WEIRD IN ANY WAY WHEN TAKING A TEST?
WEIRD...? IT'D BE WEIRD IF HE DID IT ONCE OR TWICE...
...BUT EVERY SINGLE TEST, HE'D FINISH IN 20 MINUTES THEN BOOK OUTTA THERE!
BUT I GUESS THAT'S WHY HE'S AT THE TOP OF THE CLASS. KID'S A GENIUS OR SOME-THING!
IT'S LIKE HE WAS CAST FROM A DIF-FERENT MOLD THAN THE REST OF US!
SO HE HASN'T CHANGED HIS TUNE SINCE JUNIOR HIGH...
LUNCH HOUR
Thanks!
TCH! TCH!
2-2
BREAK TIME

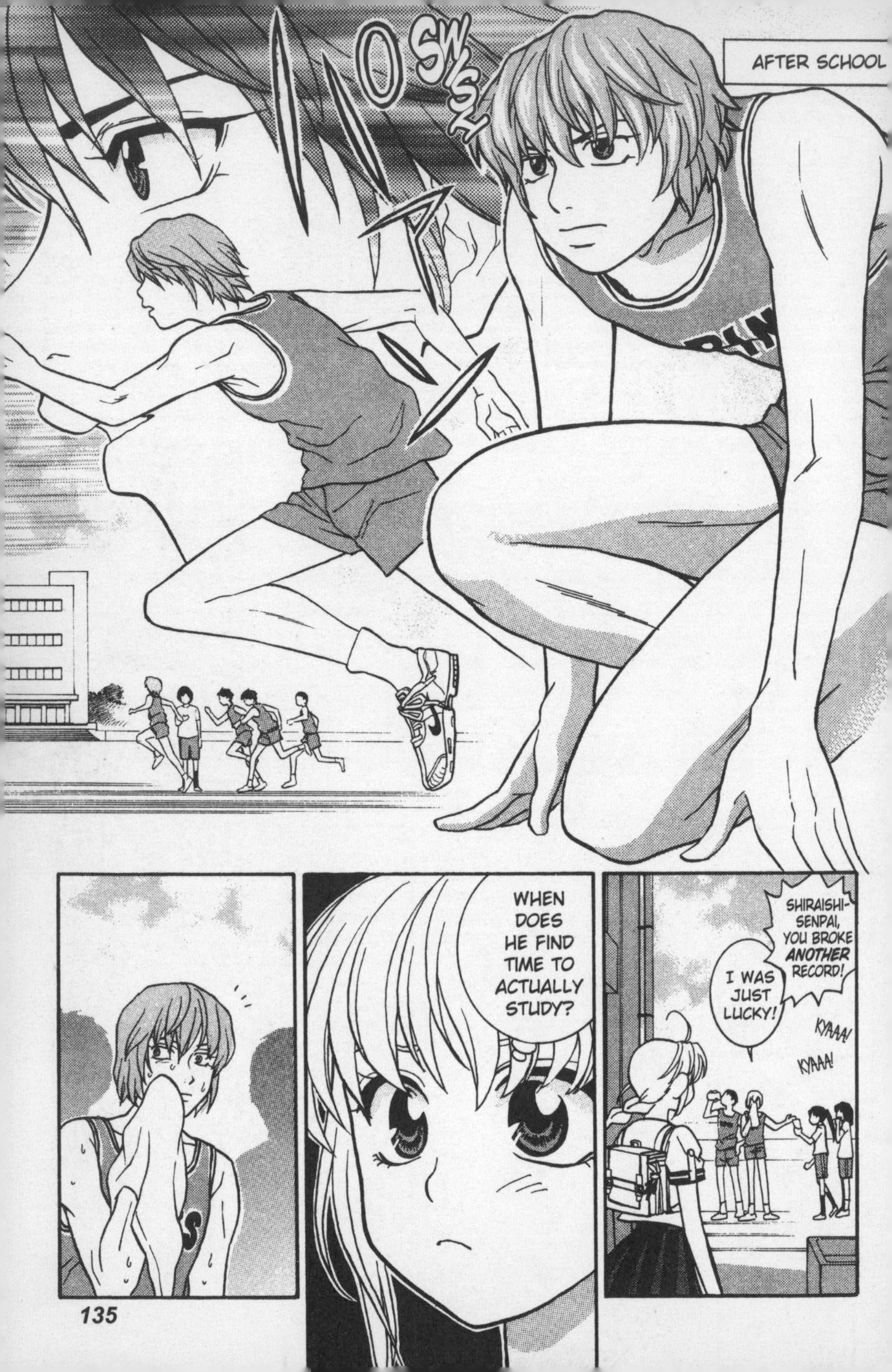
AFTER SCHOOL
SWISH
SHIRAISHI-SENPAI, YOU BROKE ANOTHER RECORD!
I WAS JUST LUCKY!
KYAAA!
KYAAA!
WHEN DOES HE FIND TIME TO ACTUALLY STUDY?

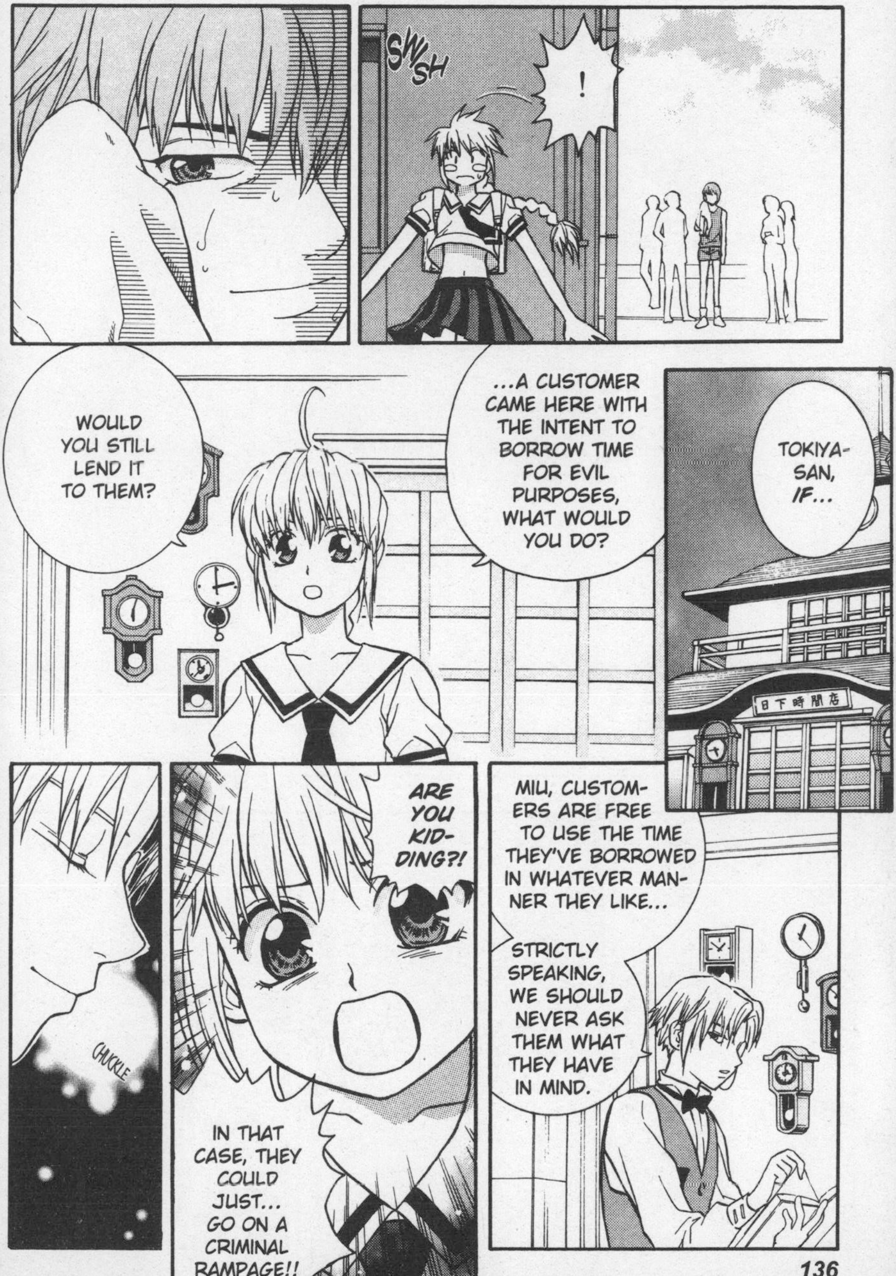
SWISH
!
TOKIYA-SAN, IF...
日下時間店
...A CUSTOMER CAME HERE WITH THE INTENT TO BORROW TIME FOR EVIL PURPOSES, WHAT WOULD YOU DO?
WOULD YOU STILL LEND IT TO THEM?
MIU, CUSTOMERS ARE FREE TO USE THE TIME THEY'VE BORROWED IN WHATEVER MANNER THEY LIKE...
STRICTLY SPEAKING, WE SHOULD NEVER ASK THEM WHAT THEY HAVE IN MIND.
ARE YOU KIDDING?!
IN THAT CASE, THEY COULD JUST... GO ON A CRIMINAL RAMPAGE!!
CHUCKLE

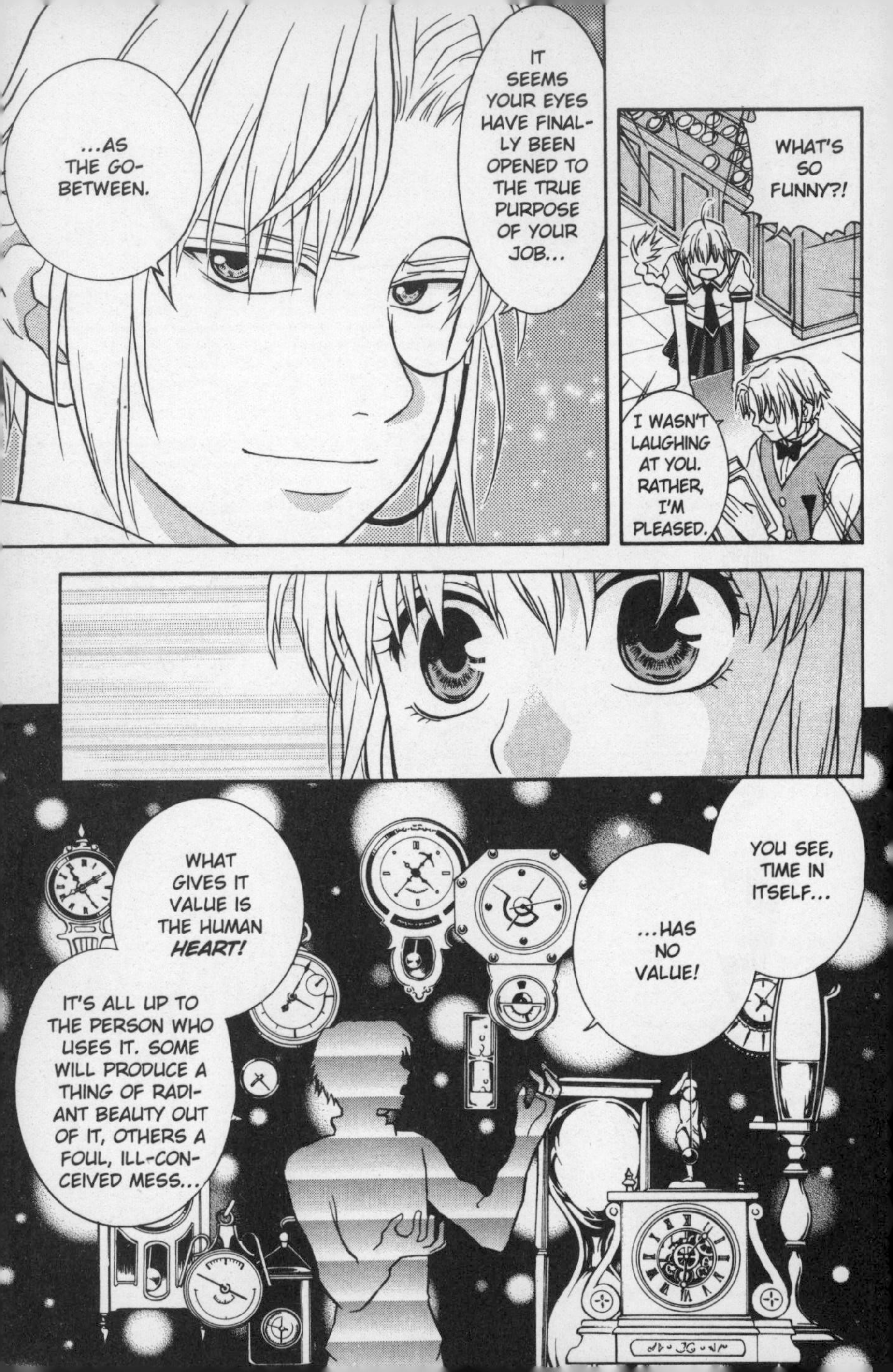
WHAT'S SO FUNNY?!
I WASN'T LAUGHING AT YOU. RATHER, I'M PLEASED.
IT SEEMS YOUR EYES HAVE FINAL-LY BEEN OPENED TO THE TRUE PURPOSE OF YOUR JOB...
...AS THE GO-BETWEEN.
YOU SEE, TIME IN ITSELF...
...HAS NO VALUE!
WHAT GIVES IT VALUE IS THE HUMAN ***HEART!***
IT'S ALL UP TO THE PERSON WHO USES IT. SOME WILL PRODUCE A THING OF RADI-ANT BEAUTY OUT OF IT, OTHERS A FOUL, ILL-CON-CEIVED MESS...

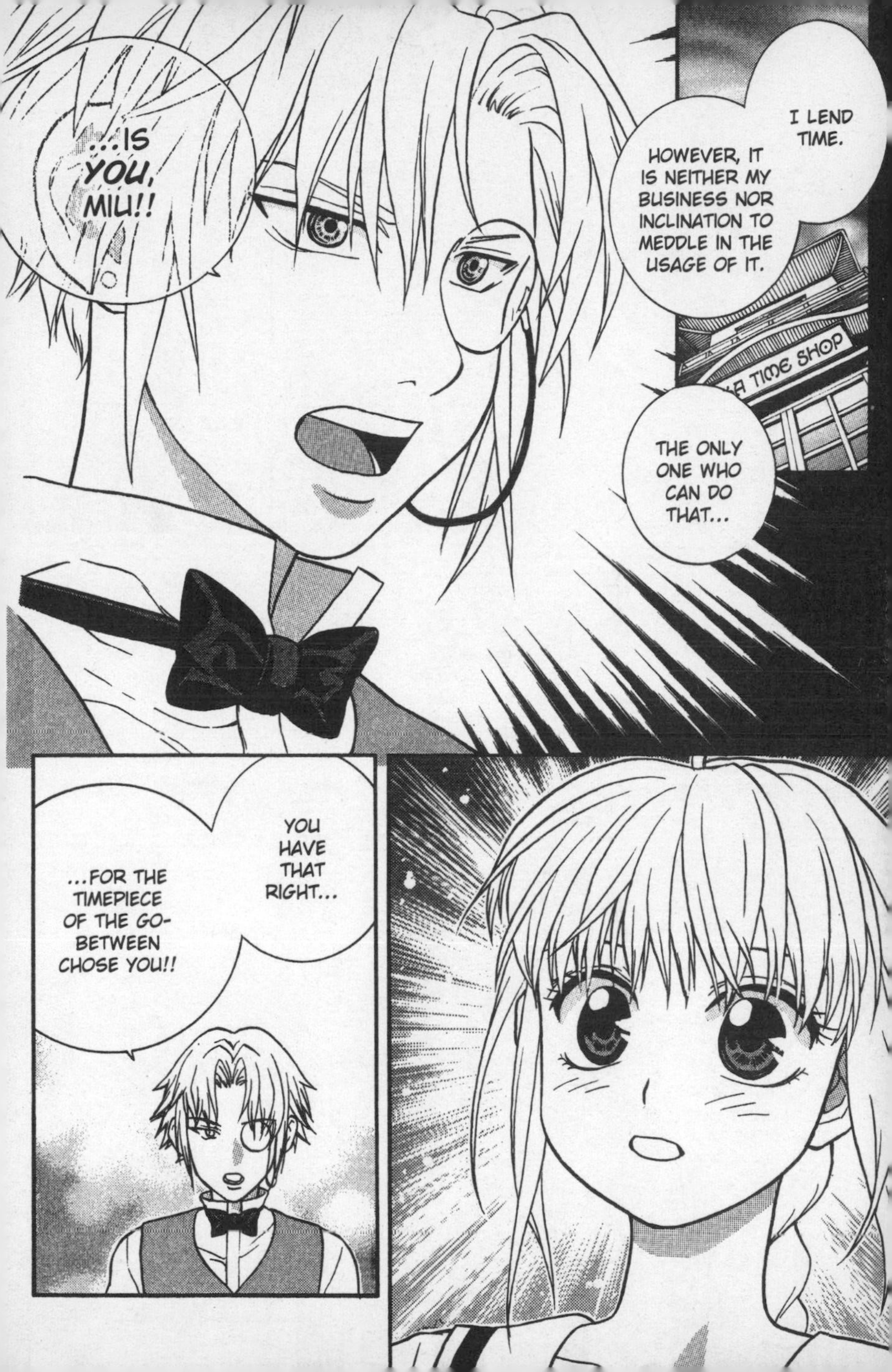
I LEND TIME.
HOWEVER, IT IS NEITHER MY BUSINESS NOR INCLINATION TO MEDDLE IN THE USAGE OF IT.
A TIME SHOP
THE ONLY ONE WHO CAN DO THAT...
...IS YOU, MIU!!
YOU HAVE THAT RIGHT...
...FOR THE TIMEPIECE OF THE GO-BETWEEN CHOSE YOU!!

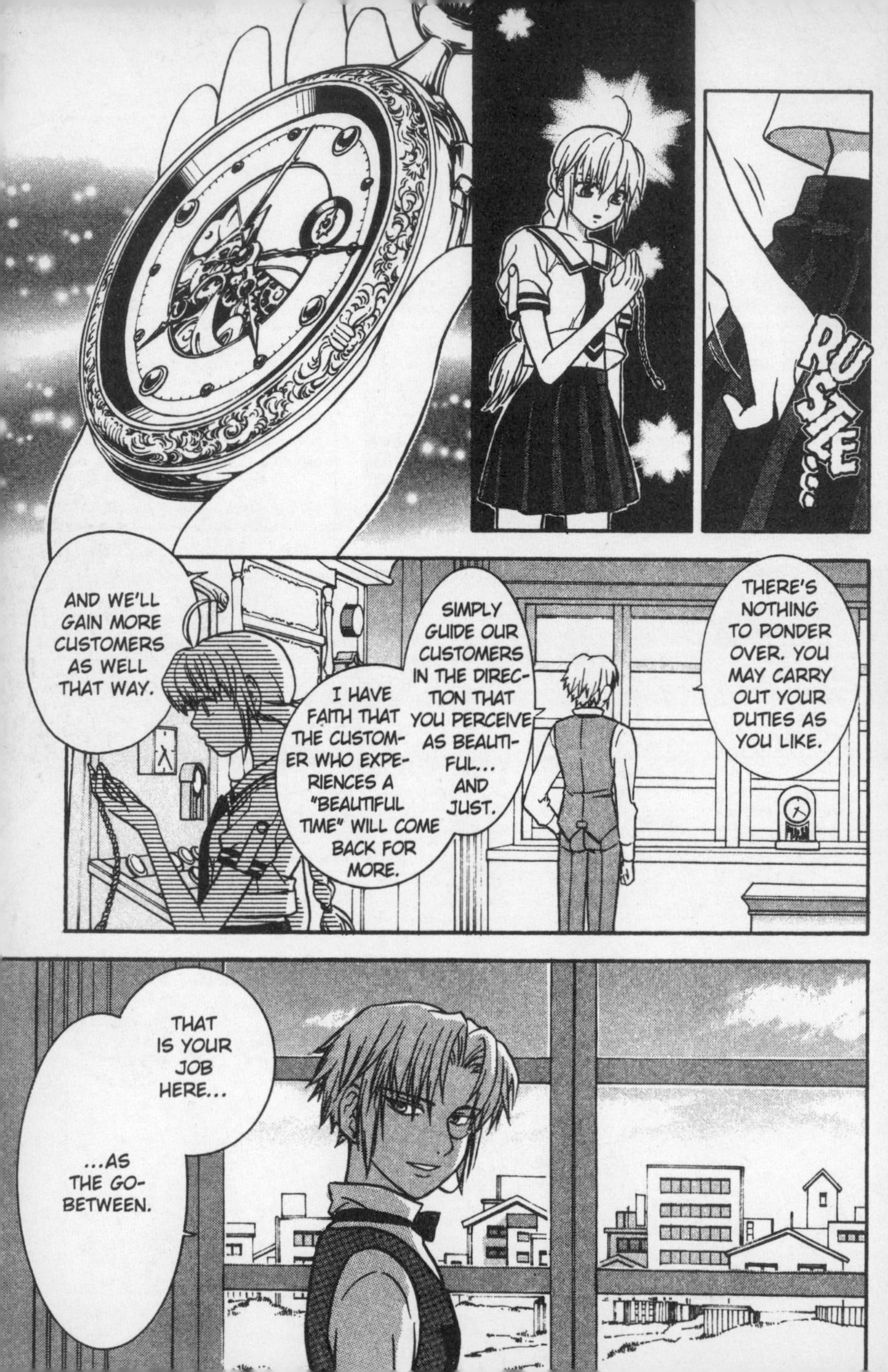
RUSTLE...
THERE'S NOTHING TO PONDER OVER. YOU MAY CARRY OUT YOUR DUTIES AS YOU LIKE.
SIMPLY GUIDE OUR CUSTOMERS IN THE DIRECTION THAT YOU PERCEIVE AS BEAUTIFUL... AND JUST.
I HAVE FAITH THAT THE CUSTOMER WHO EXPERIENCES A "BEAUTIFUL TIME" WILL COME BACK FOR MORE.
AND WE'LL GAIN MORE CUSTOMERS AS WELL THAT WAY.
THAT IS YOUR JOB HERE...
...AS THE GO-BETWEEN.

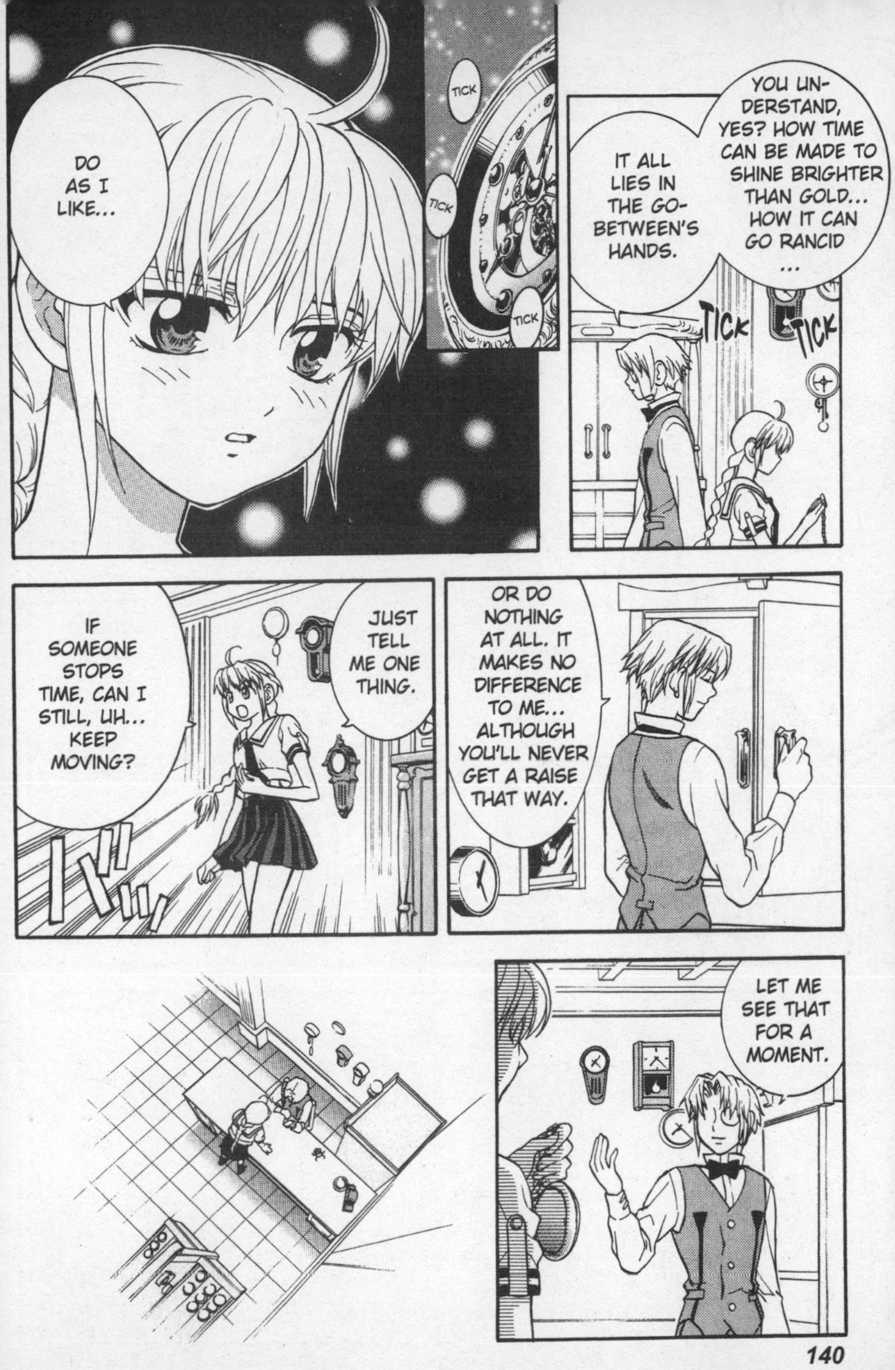
YOU UN-DERSTAND, YES? HOW TIME CAN BE MADE TO SHINE BRIGHTER THAN GOLD... HOW IT CAN GO RANCID ...
IT ALL LIES IN THE GO-BETWEEN'S HANDS.
TICK
TICK
TICK
TICK
TICK
DO AS I LIKE...
OR DO NOTHING AT ALL. IT MAKES NO DIFFERENCE TO ME... ALTHOUGH YOU'LL NEVER GET A RAISE THAT WAY.
JUST TELL ME ONE THING.
IF SOMEONE STOPS TIME, CAN I STILL, UH... KEEP MOVING?
LET ME SEE THAT FOR A MOMENT.

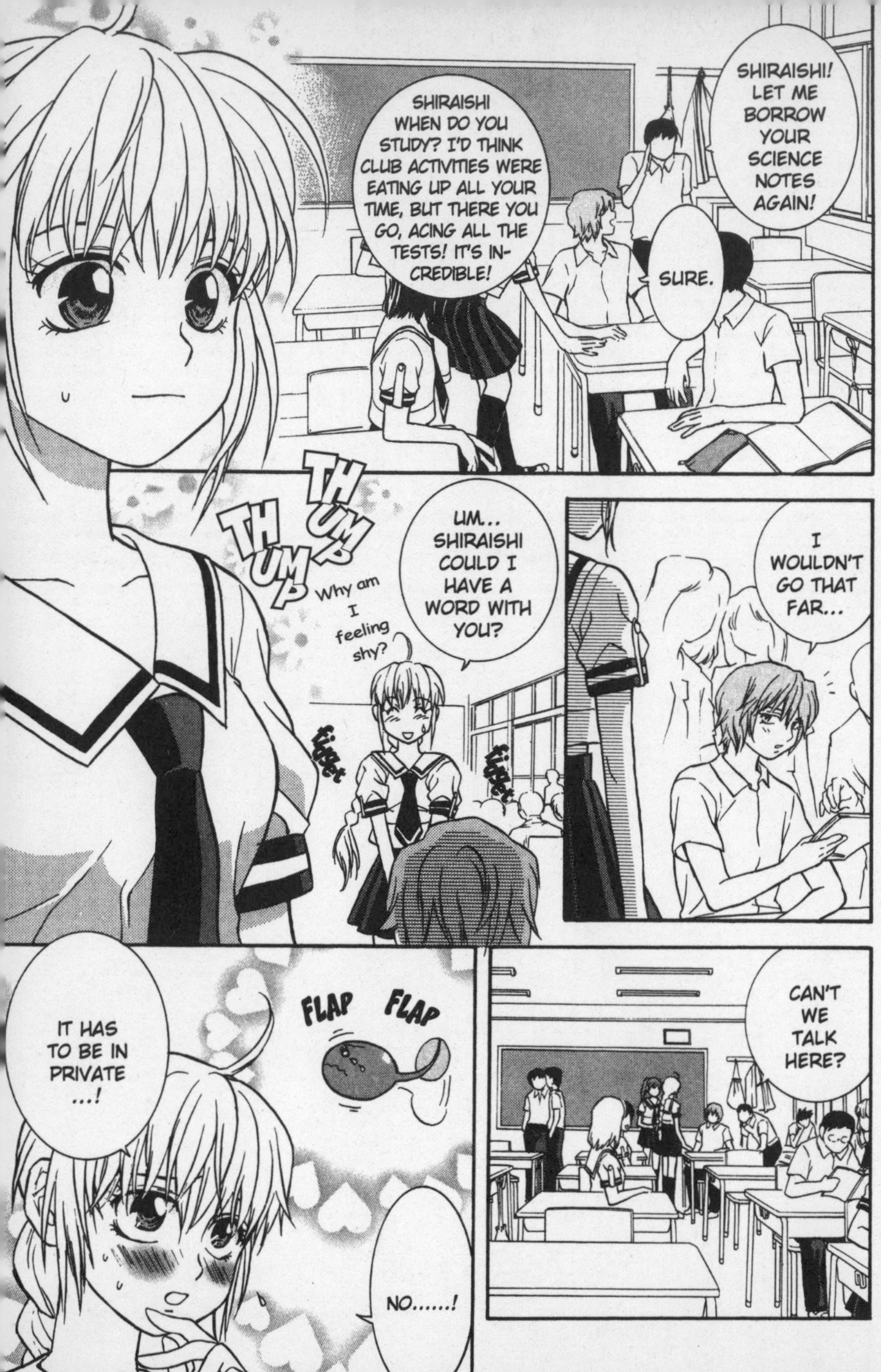
SHIRAISHI! LET ME BORROW YOUR SCIENCE NOTES AGAIN!
SURE.
SHIRAISHI WHEN DO YOU STUDY? I'D THINK CLUB ACTIVITIES WERE EATING UP ALL YOUR TIME, BUT THERE YOU GO, ACING ALL THE TESTS! IT'S IN-CREDIBLE!
I WOULDN'T GO THAT FAR...
THUMP
THUMP
UM... SHIRAISHI COULD I HAVE A WORD WITH YOU?
Why am I feeling shy?
fidget
fidget
CAN'T WE TALK HERE?
NO......!
FLAP FLAP
IT HAS TO BE IN PRIVATE ...!

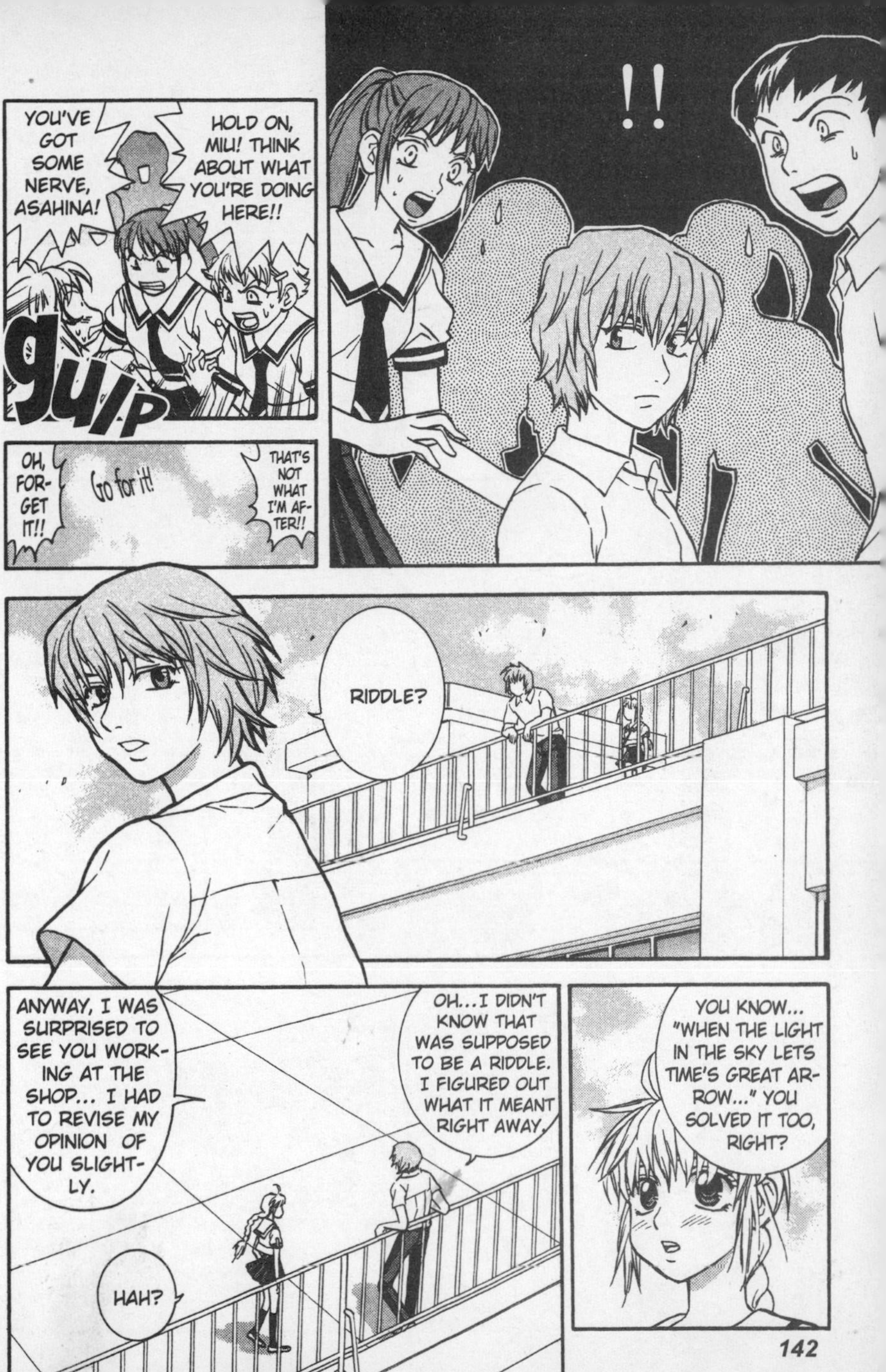
!!
HOLD ON, MIU! THINK ABOUT WHAT YOU'RE DOING HERE!!
YOU'VE GOT SOME NERVE, ASAHINA!
gulp
THAT'S NOT WHAT I'M AF-TER!!
Go for it!
OH, FOR-GET IT!!
RIDDLE?
YOU KNOW... "WHEN THE LIGHT IN THE SKY LETS TIME'S GREAT AR-ROW..." YOU SOLVED IT TOO, RIGHT?
OH...I DIDN'T KNOW THAT WAS SUPPOSED TO BE A RIDDLE. I FIGURED OUT WHAT IT MEANT RIGHT AWAY.
ANYWAY, I WAS SURPRISED TO SEE YOU WORK-ING AT THE SHOP... I HAD TO REVISE MY OPINION OF YOU SLIGHT-LY.
HAH?

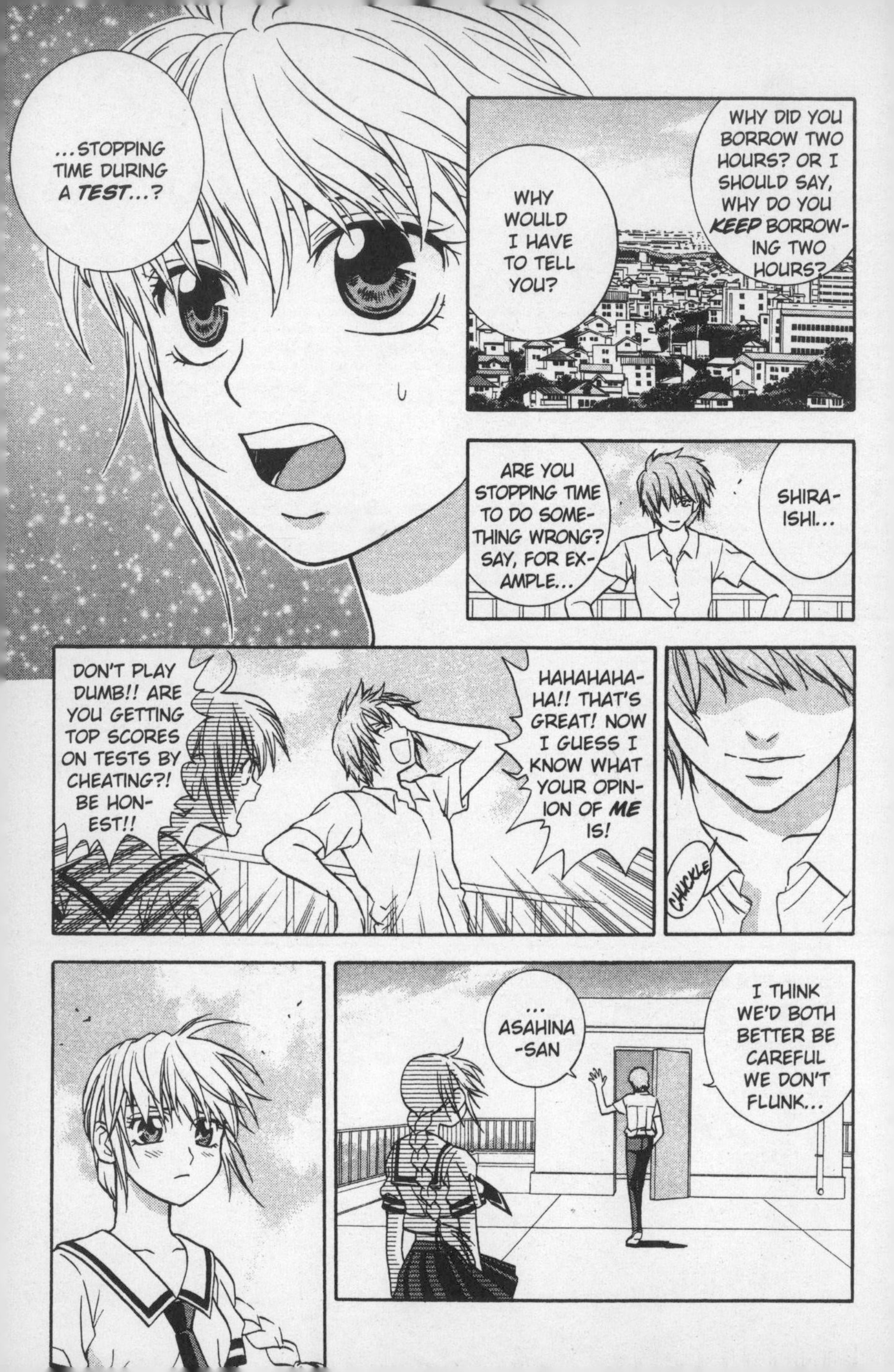

WHY DID YOU BORROW TWO HOURS? OR I SHOULD SAY, WHY DO YOU KEEP BORROWING TWO HOURS?
WHY WOULD I HAVE TO TELL YOU?
SHIRAISHI...
ARE YOU STOPPING TIME TO DO SOMETHING WRONG? SAY, FOR EXAMPLE...
...STOPPING TIME DURING A TEST...?
CHUCKLE
HAHAHAHAHA!! THAT'S GREAT! NOW I GUESS I KNOW WHAT YOUR OPINION OF ME IS!
DON'T PLAY DUMB!! ARE YOU GETTING TOP SCORES ON TESTS BY CHEATING?! BE HONEST!!
I THINK WE'D BOTH BETTER BE CAREFUL WE DON'T FLUNK...
... ASAHINA -SAN

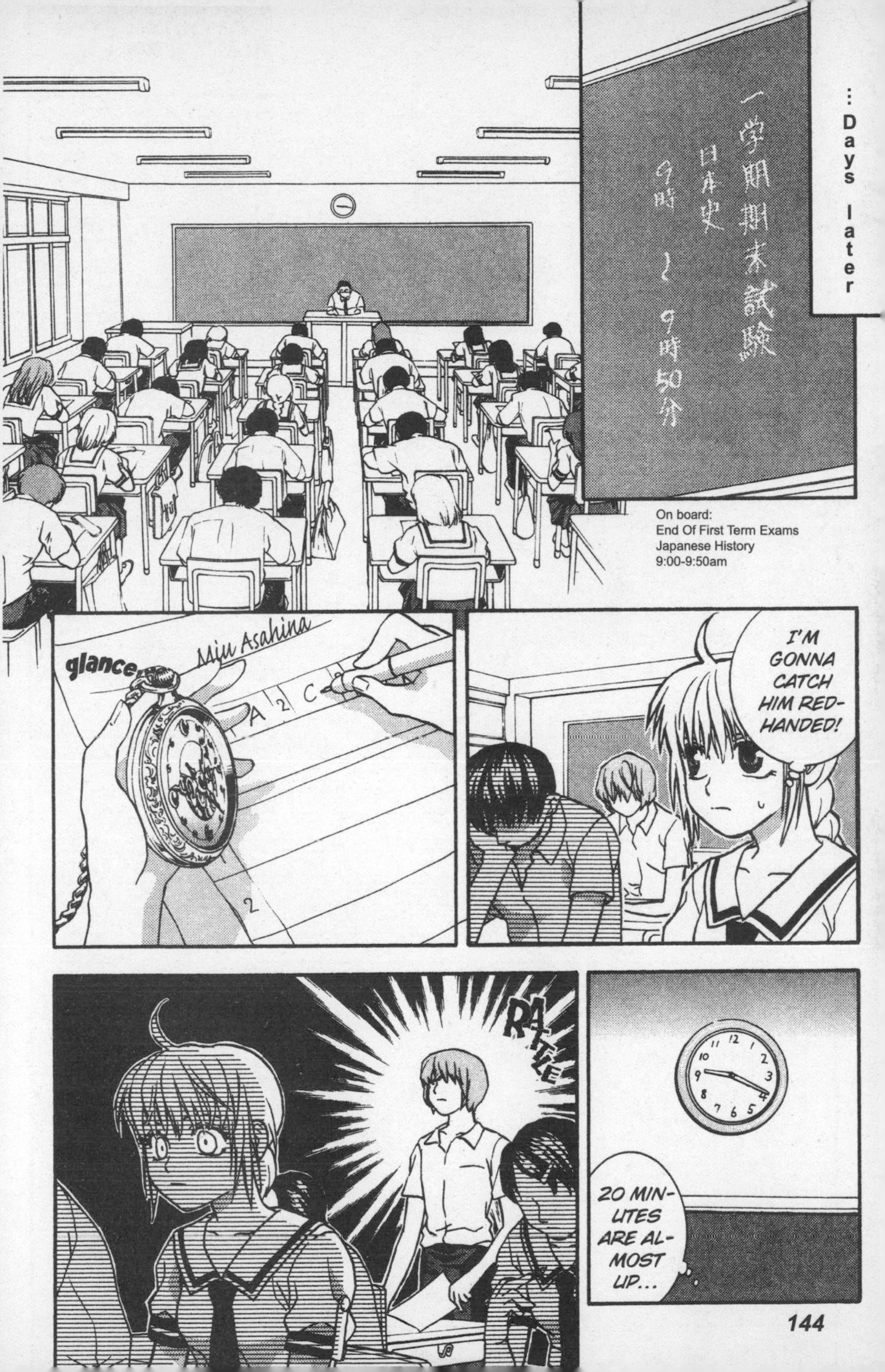

…Days later
一学期期末試験
日本史
9時～9時50分
On board:
End Of First Term Exams
Japanese History
9:00-9:50am
I'M GONNA CATCH HIM RED-HANDED!
glance
Miu Asahina
RATTLE
20 MINUTES ARE ALMOST UP…

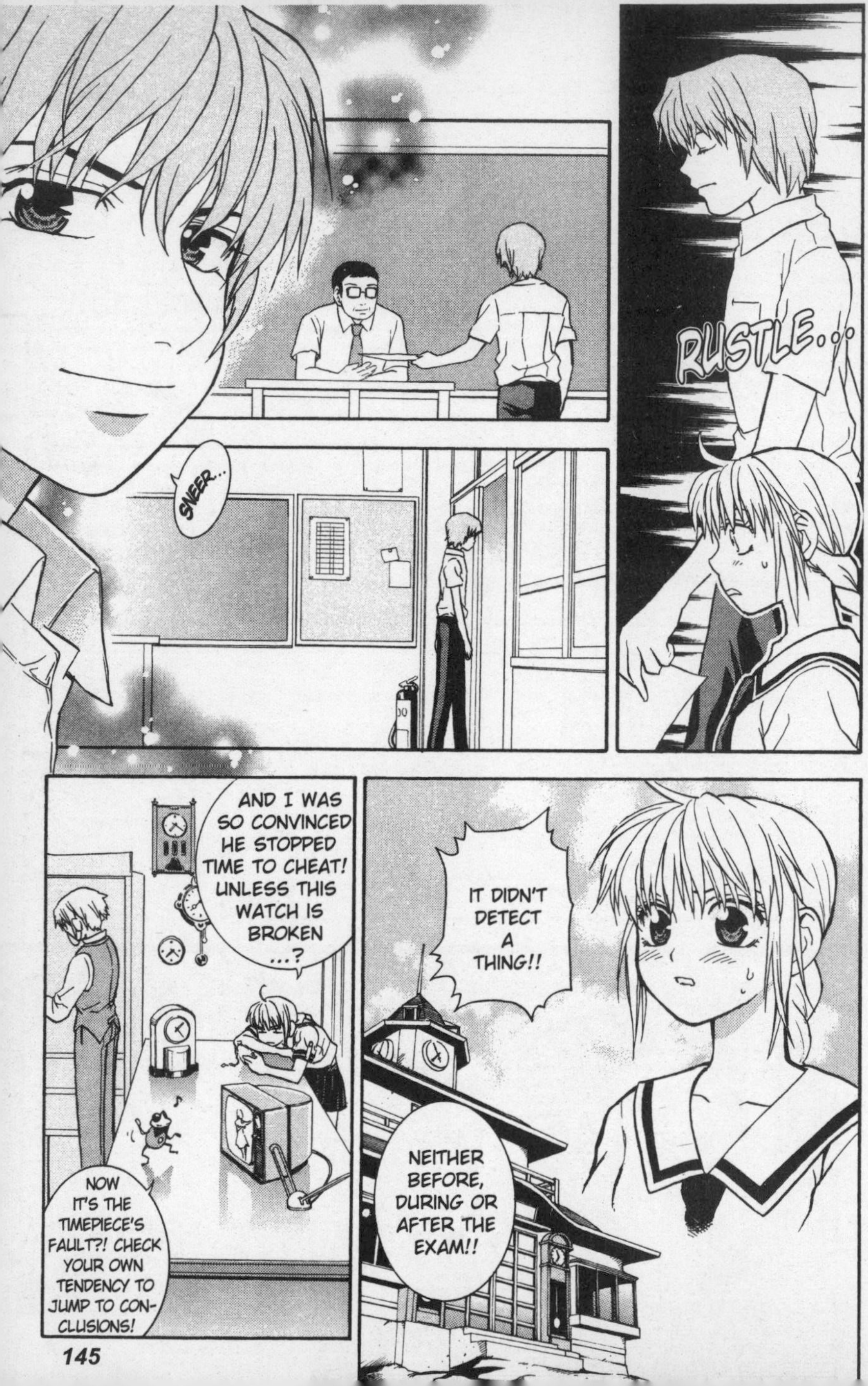
RUSTLE...
SNEER...
IT DIDN'T DETECT A THING!!
NEITHER BEFORE, DURING OR AFTER THE EXAM!!
AND I WAS SO CONVINCED HE STOPPED TIME TO CHEAT! UNLESS THIS WATCH IS BROKEN ...?
NOW IT'S THE TIMEPIECE'S FAULT?! CHECK YOUR OWN TENDENCY TO JUMP TO CON-CLUSIONS!

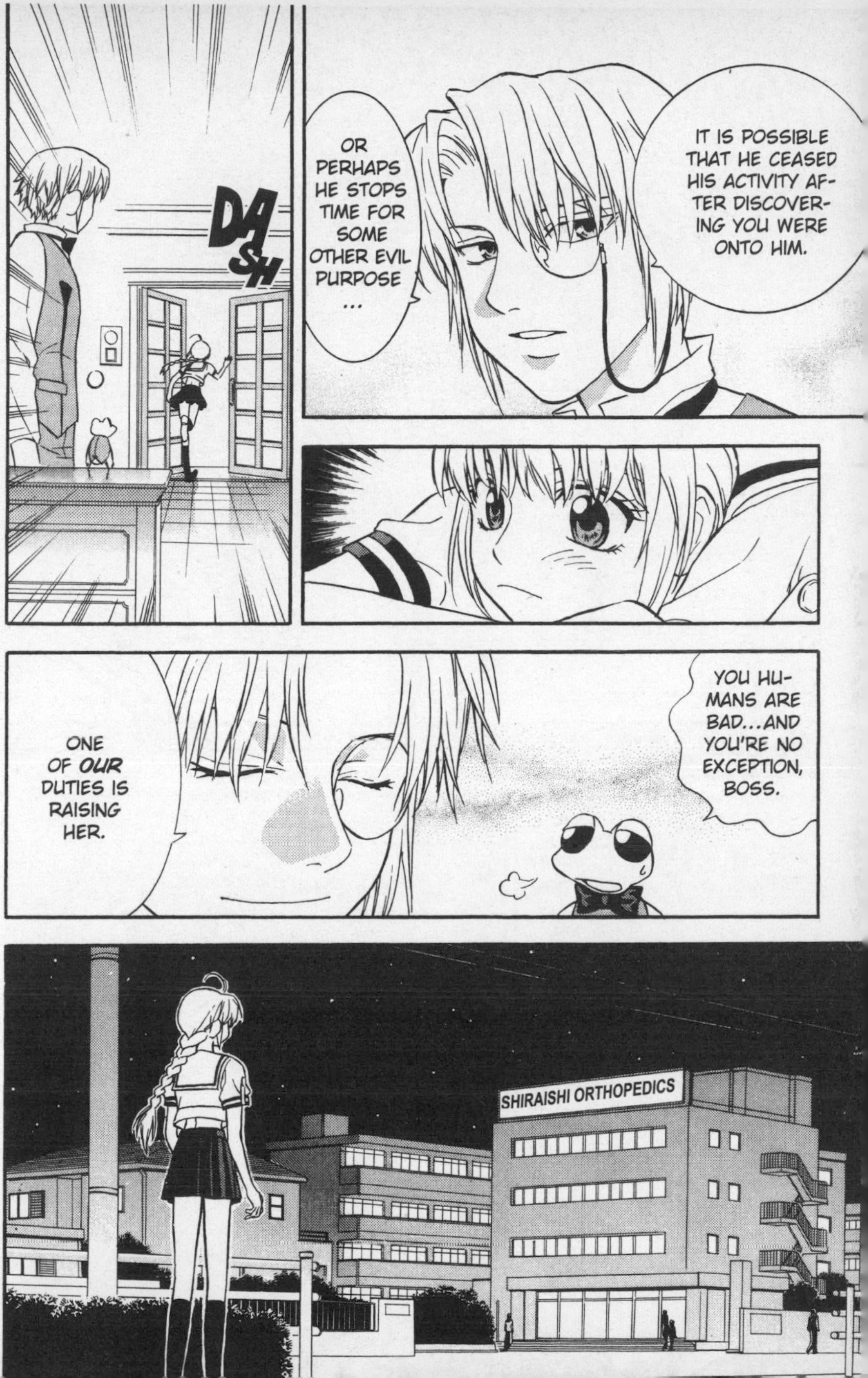
IT IS POSSIBLE THAT HE CEASED HIS ACTIVITY AF-TER DISCOVER-ING YOU WERE ONTO HIM.
OR PERHAPS HE STOPS TIME FOR SOME OTHER EVIL PURPOSE ...
DASH
YOU HU-MANS ARE BAD...AND YOU'RE NO EXCEPTION, BOSS.
ONE OF OUR DUTIES IS RAISING HER.
SHIRAISHI ORTHOPEDICS

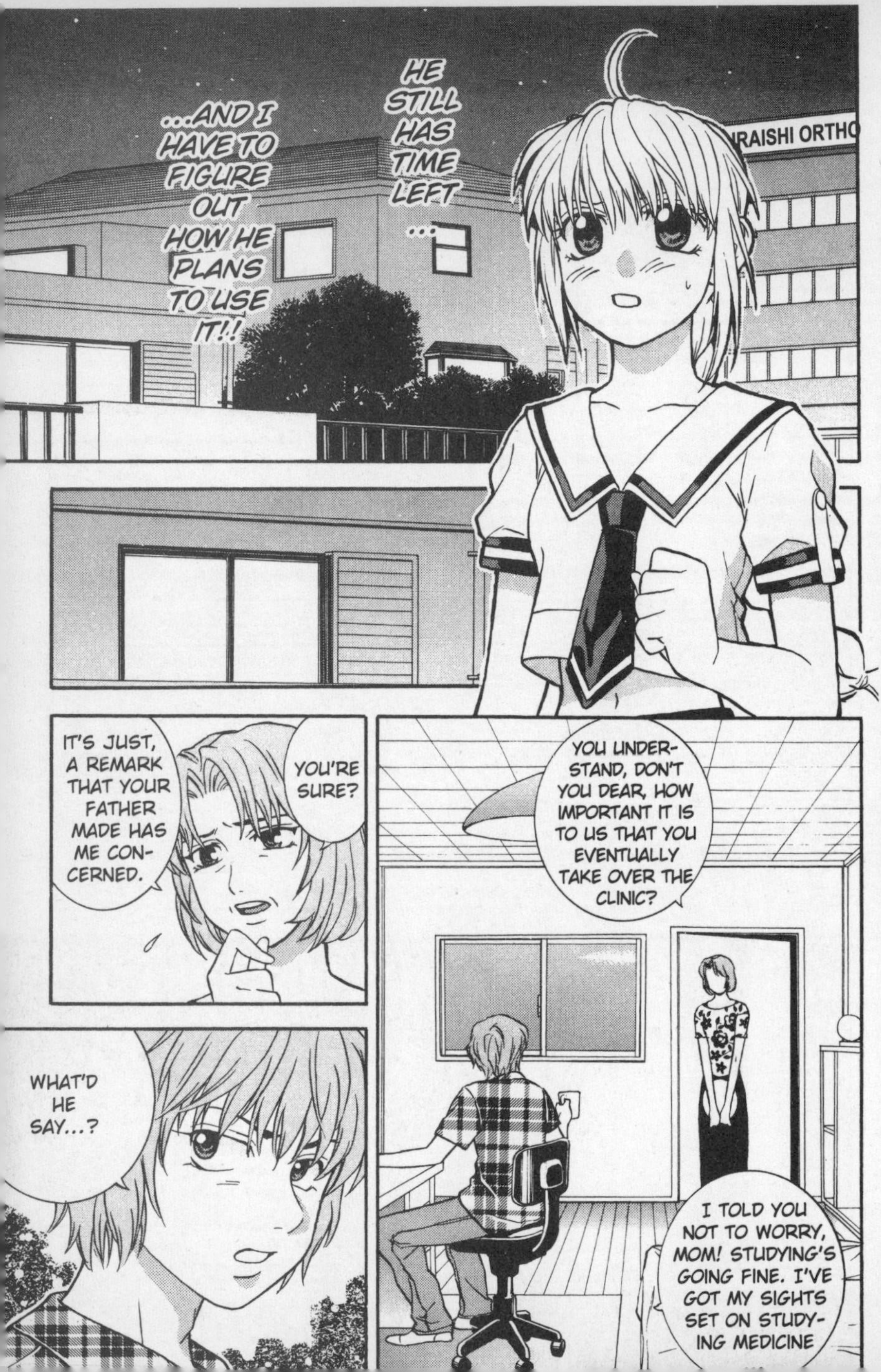
RAISHI ORTHO
HE STILL HAS TIME LEFT...
...AND I HAVE TO FIGURE OUT HOW HE PLANS TO USE IT!!
YOU UNDER-STAND, DON'T YOU DEAR, HOW IMPORTANT IT IS TO US THAT YOU EVENTUALLY TAKE OVER THE CLINIC?
I TOLD YOU NOT TO WORRY, MOM! STUDYING'S GOING FINE. I'VE GOT MY SIGHTS SET ON STUDY-ING MEDICINE
YOU'RE SURE?
IT'S JUST, A REMARK THAT YOUR FATHER MADE HAS ME CON-CERNED.
WHAT'D HE SAY...?

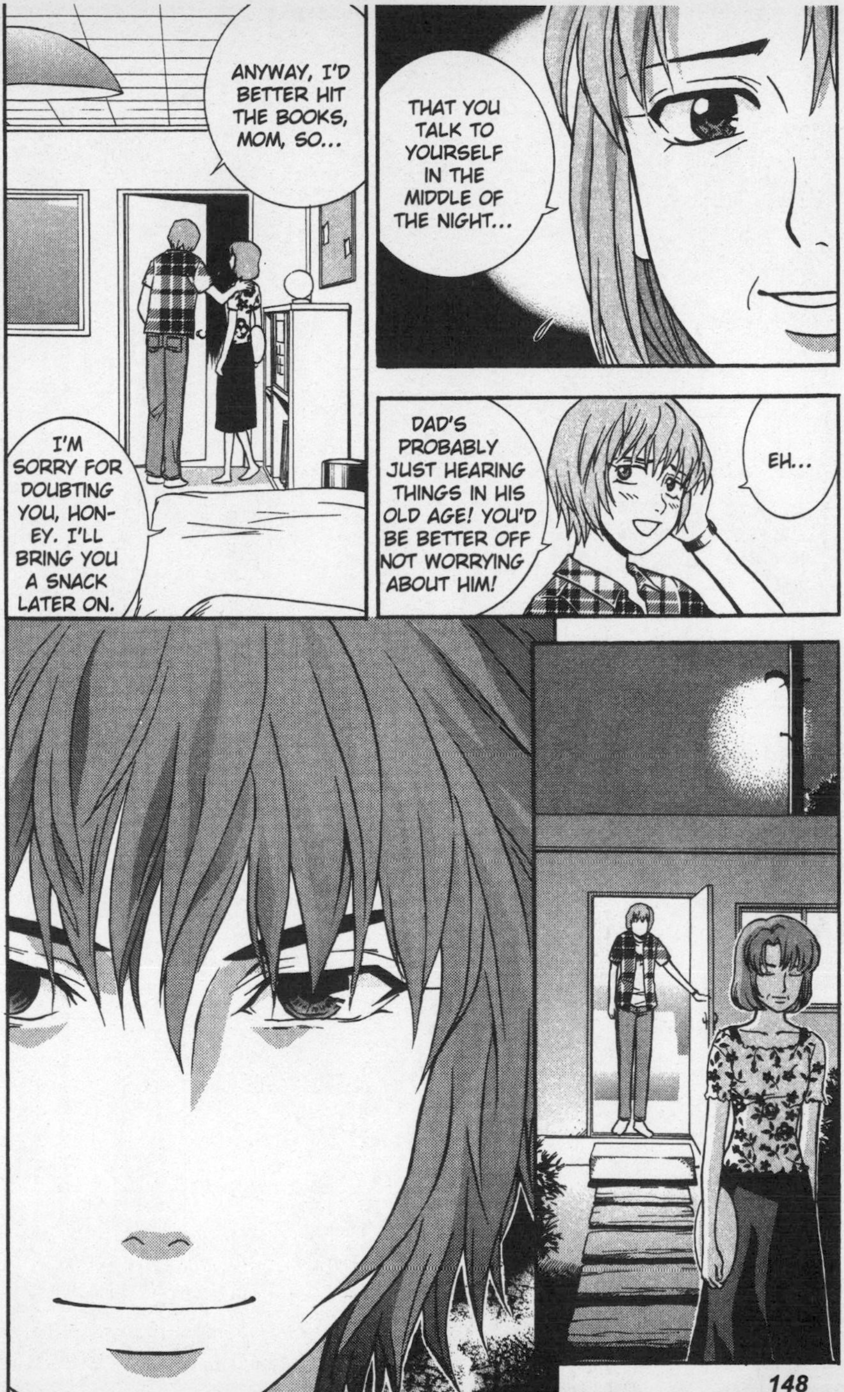
THAT YOU TALK TO YOURSELF IN THE MIDDLE OF THE NIGHT...
EH...
DAD'S PROBABLY JUST HEARING THINGS IN HIS OLD AGE! YOU'D BE BETTER OFF NOT WORRYING ABOUT HIM!
ANYWAY, I'D BETTER HIT THE BOOKS, MOM, SO...
I'M SORRY FOR DOUBTING YOU, HON-EY. I'LL BRING YOU A SNACK LATER ON.

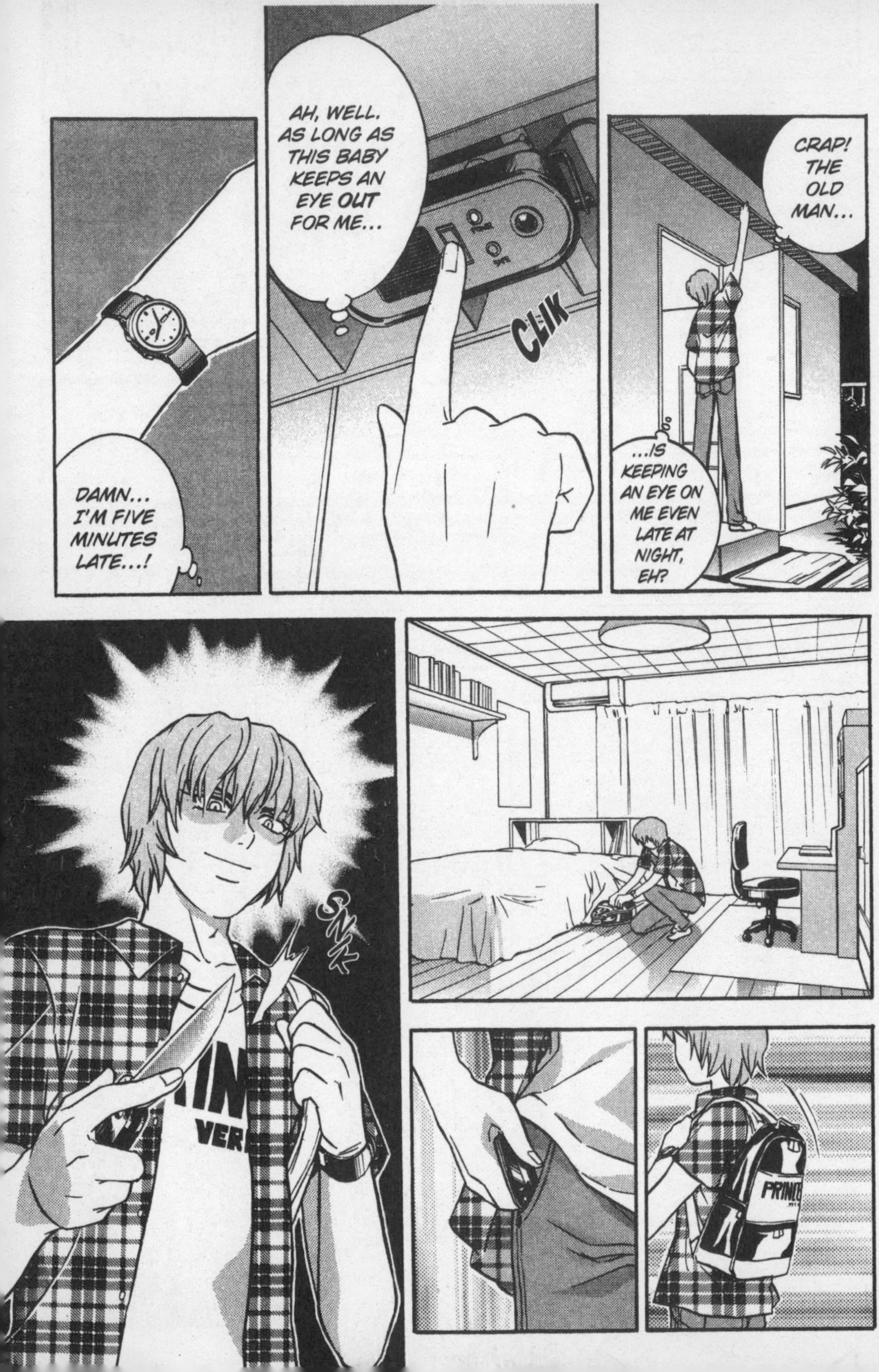
CRAP! THE OLD MAN...
...IS KEEPING AN EYE ON ME EVEN LATE AT NIGHT, EH?
AH, WELL. AS LONG AS THIS BABY KEEPS AN EYE OUT FOR ME...
CLIK
DAMN... I'M FIVE MINUTES LATE...!
SNIK

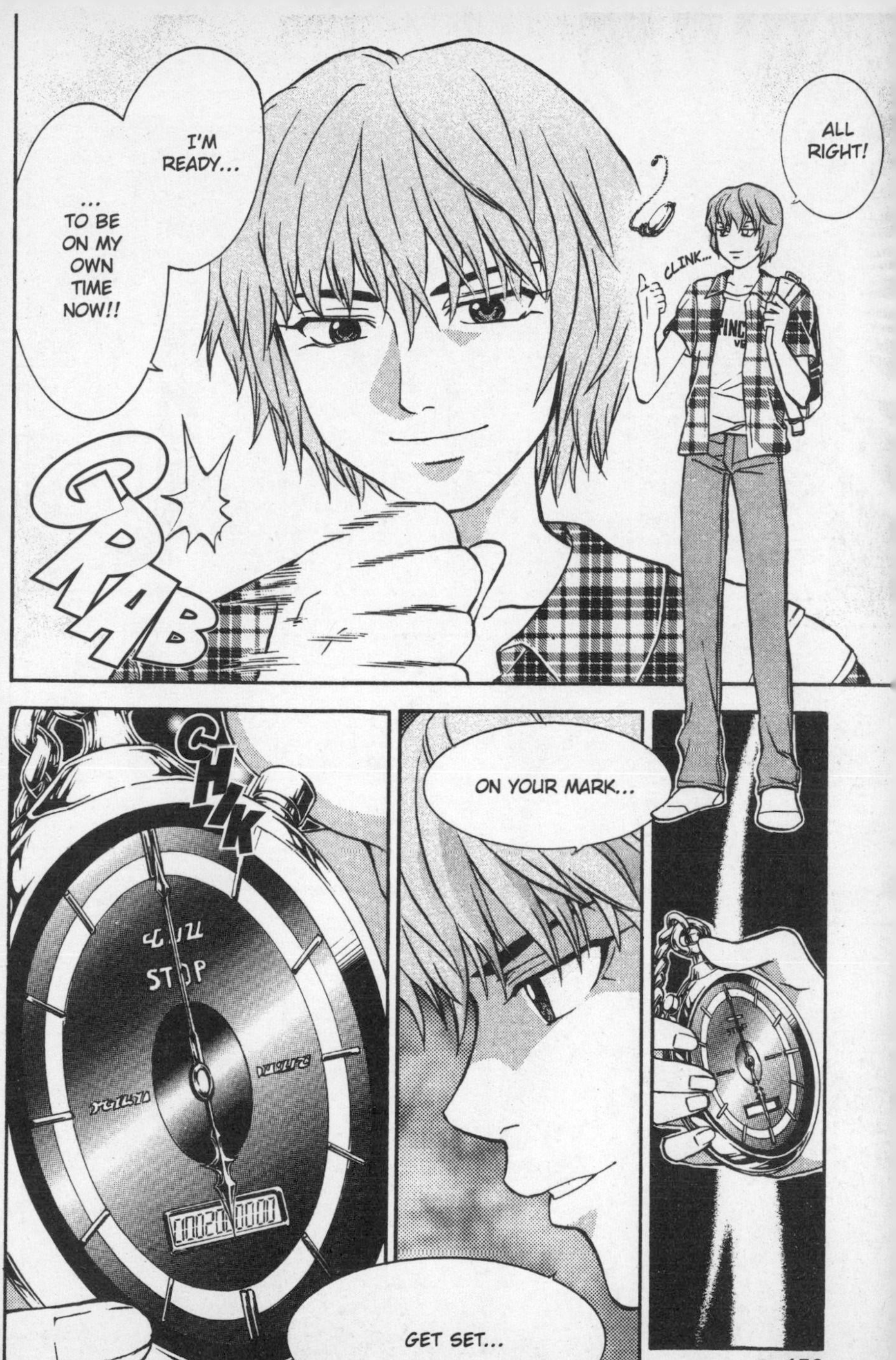

ALL RIGHT!
CLINK...
I'M READY...
... TO BE ON MY OWN TIME NOW!!
GRAB
ON YOUR MARK...
CHIK
STOP
GET SET...

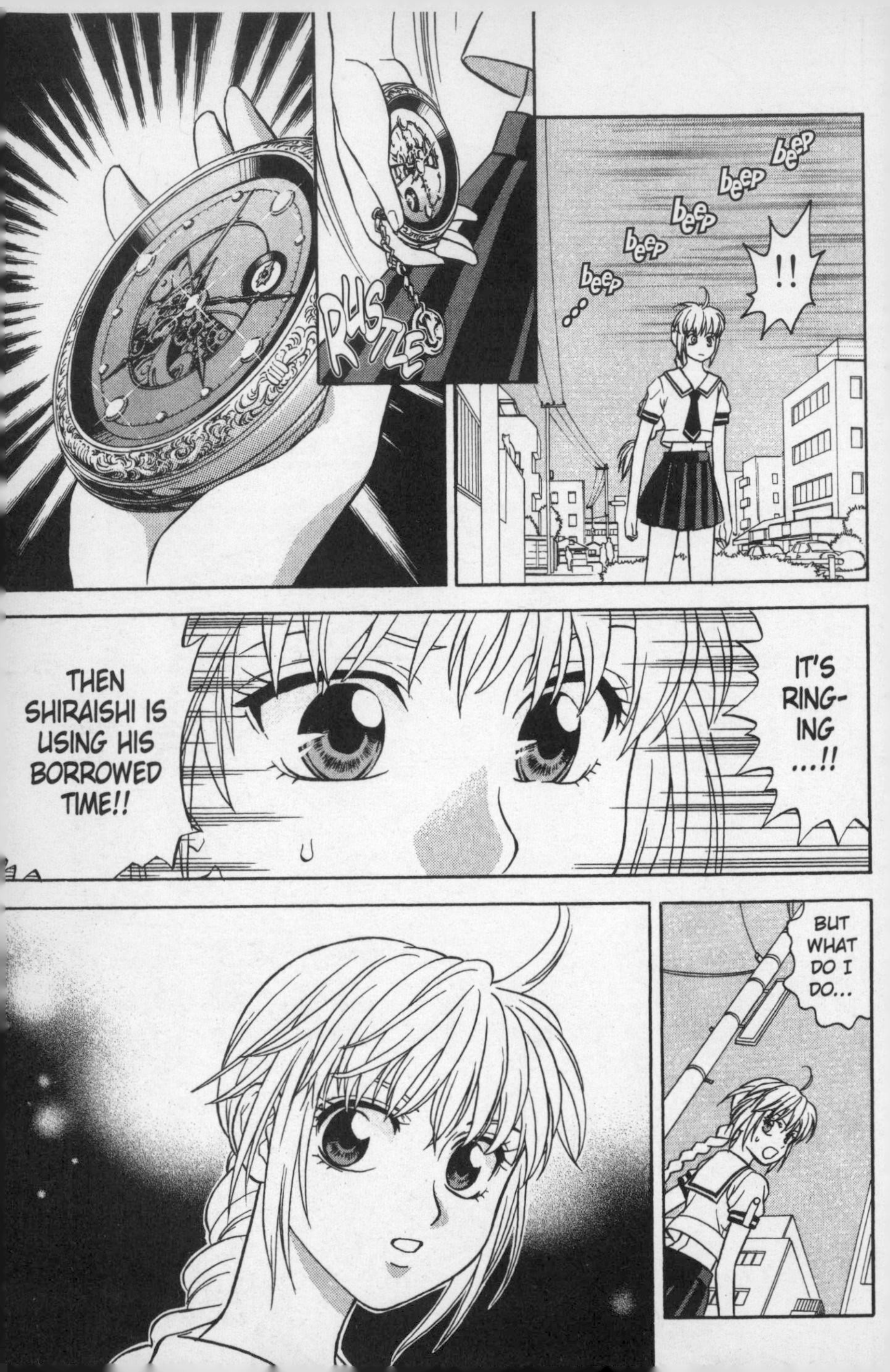

beep
beep
beep
beep
beep
!!
RUSTLE
IT'S RINGING...!!
THEN SHIRAISHI IS USING HIS BORROWED TIME!!
BUT WHAT DO I DO...

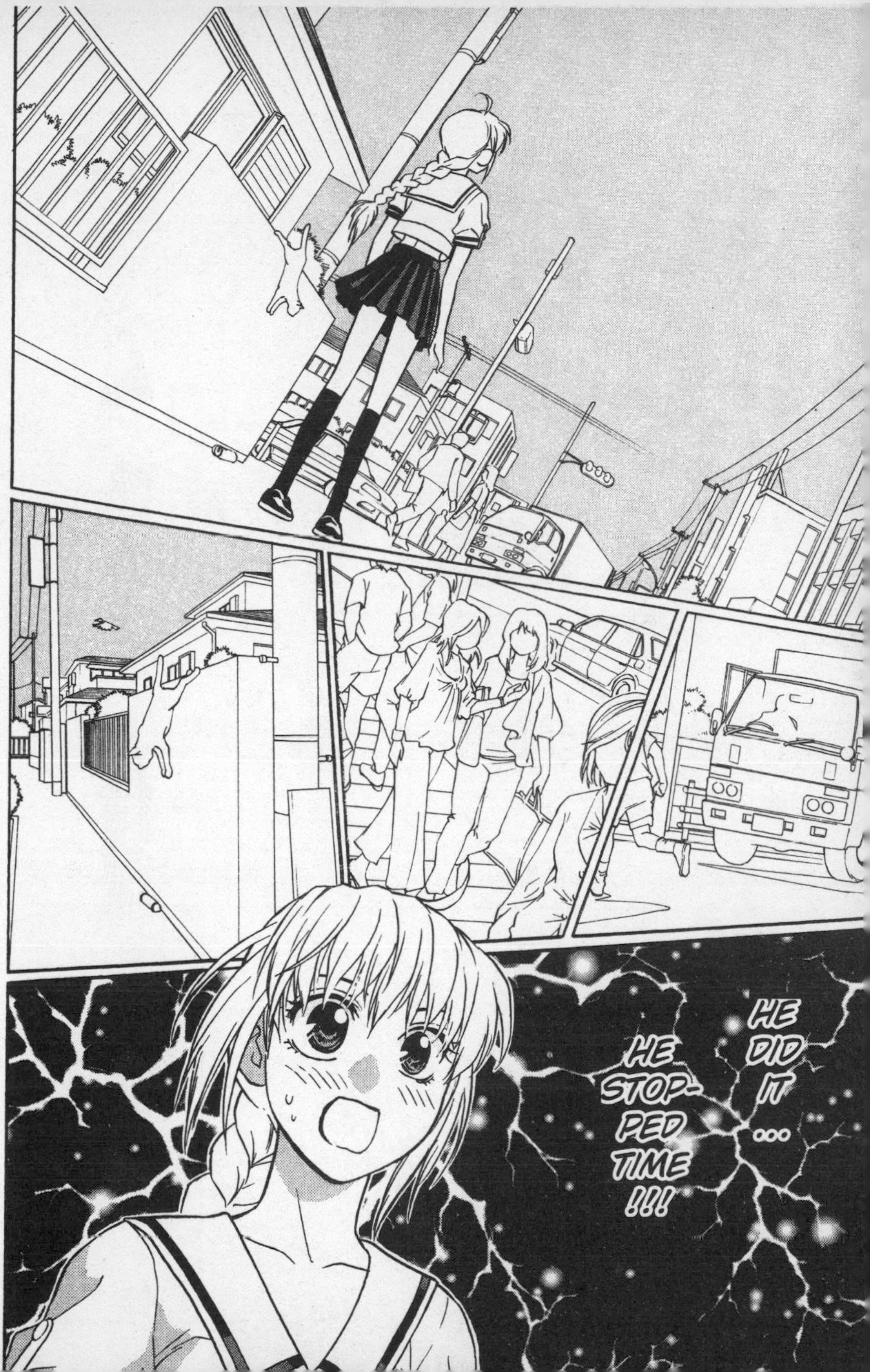
HE DID IT...
HE STOP-PED TIME!!!

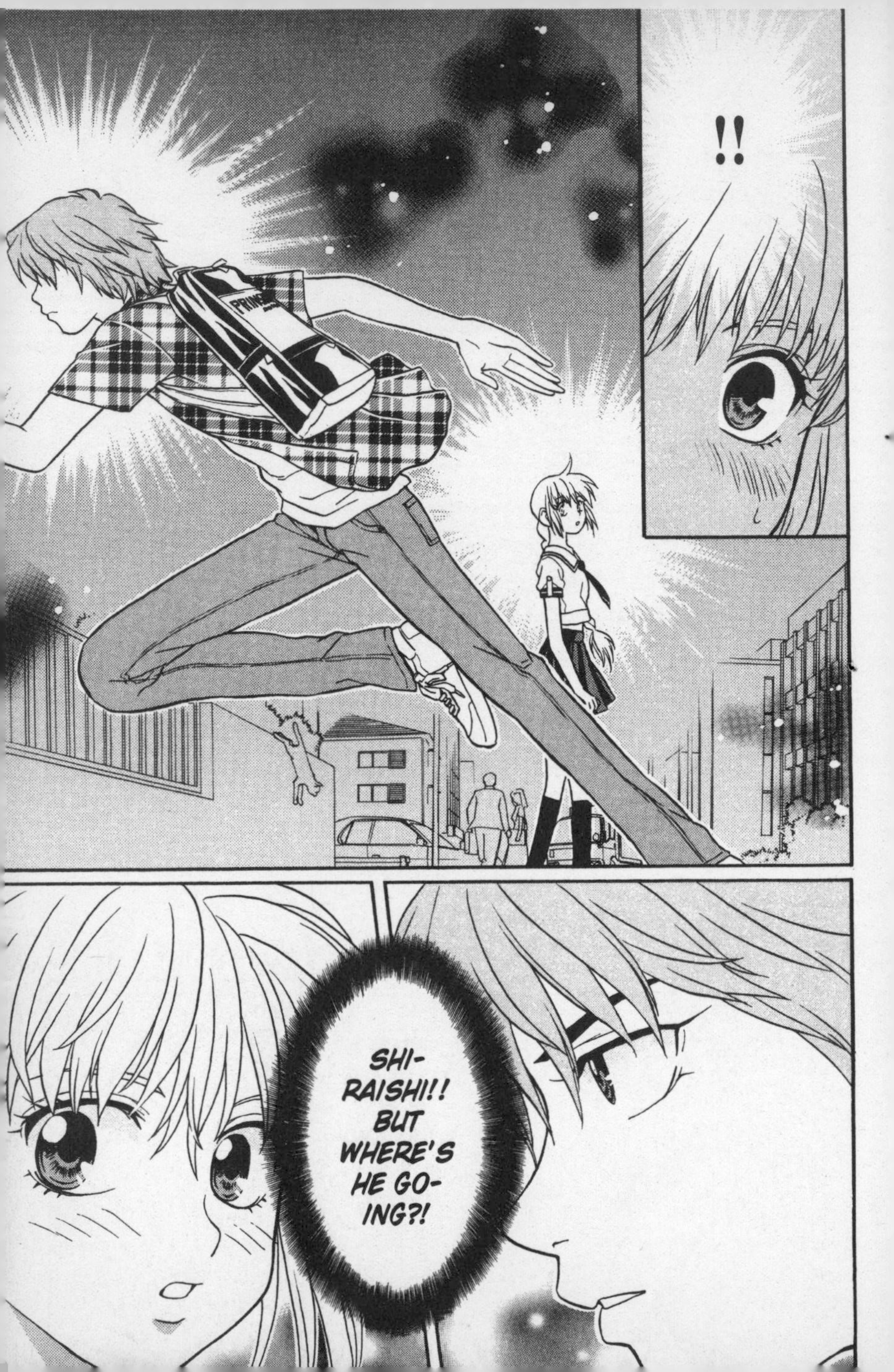
!!
SHI-RAISHI!! BUT WHERE'S HE GO-ING?!

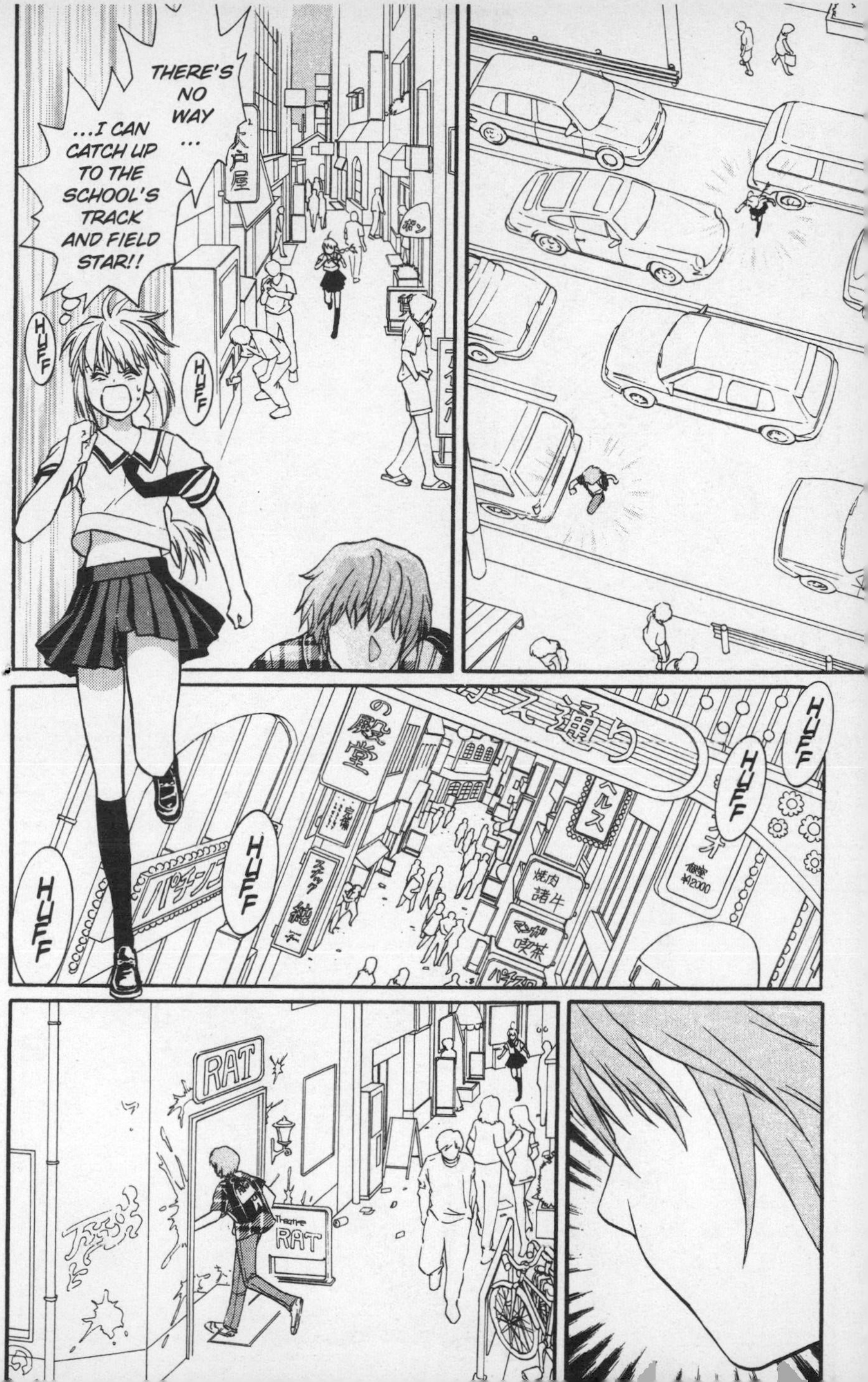
THERE'S NO WAY ...
...I CAN CATCH UP TO THE SCHOOL'S TRACK AND FIELD STAR!!
HUFF
HUFF
HUFF
HUFF
HUFF
HUFF
RAT
Theatre RAT

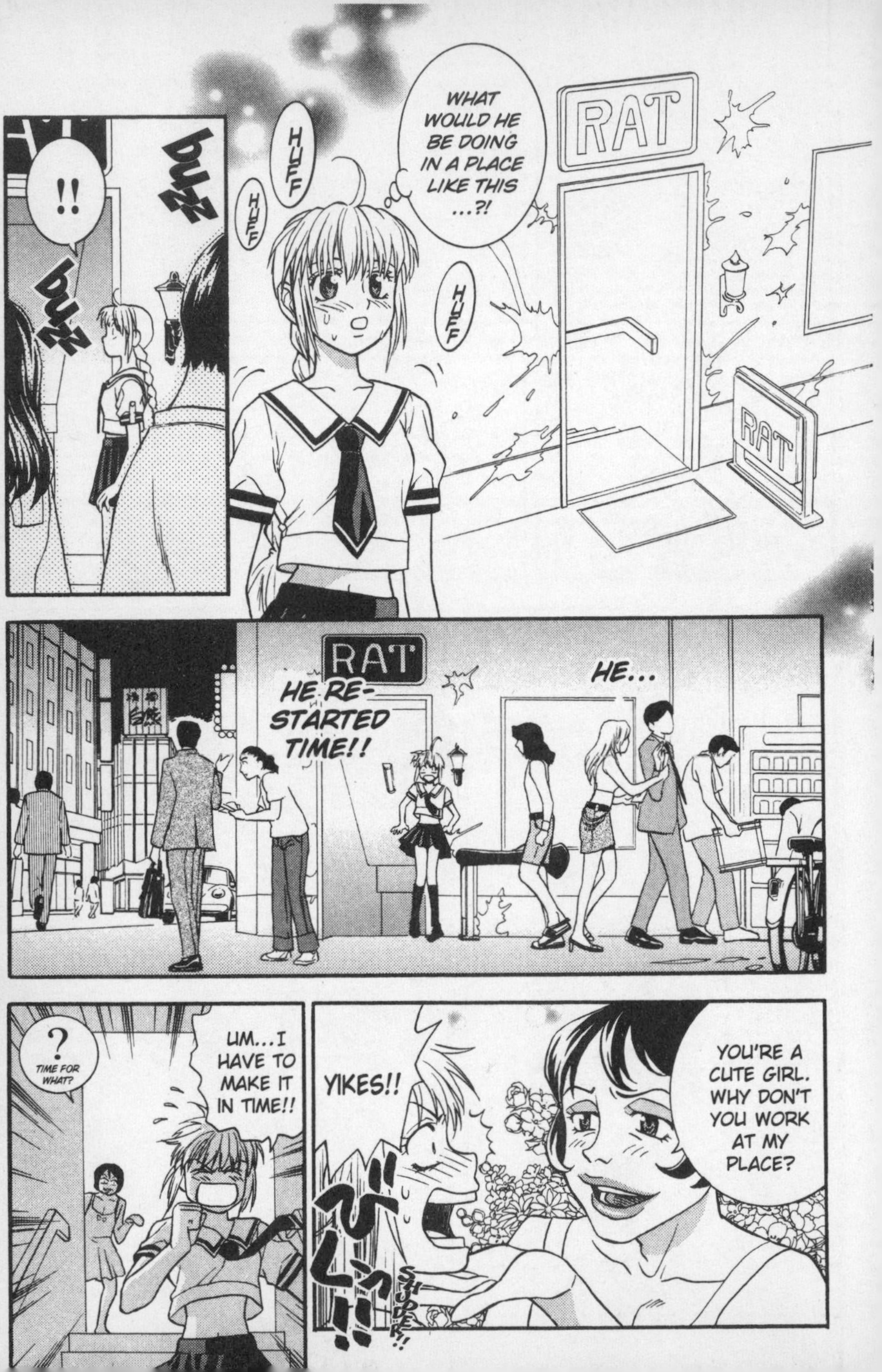
RAT
HUFF
HUFF
WHAT WOULD HE BE DOING IN A PLACE LIKE THIS ...?!
HUFF
RAT
!!
BUNN
BUNN
RAT
HE...
HE RE-STARTED TIME!!
YOU'RE A CUTE GIRL. WHY DON'T YOU WORK AT MY PLACE?
YIKES!!
SHUDDER!!
UM...I HAVE TO MAKE IT IN TIME!!
?
TIME FOR WHAT?

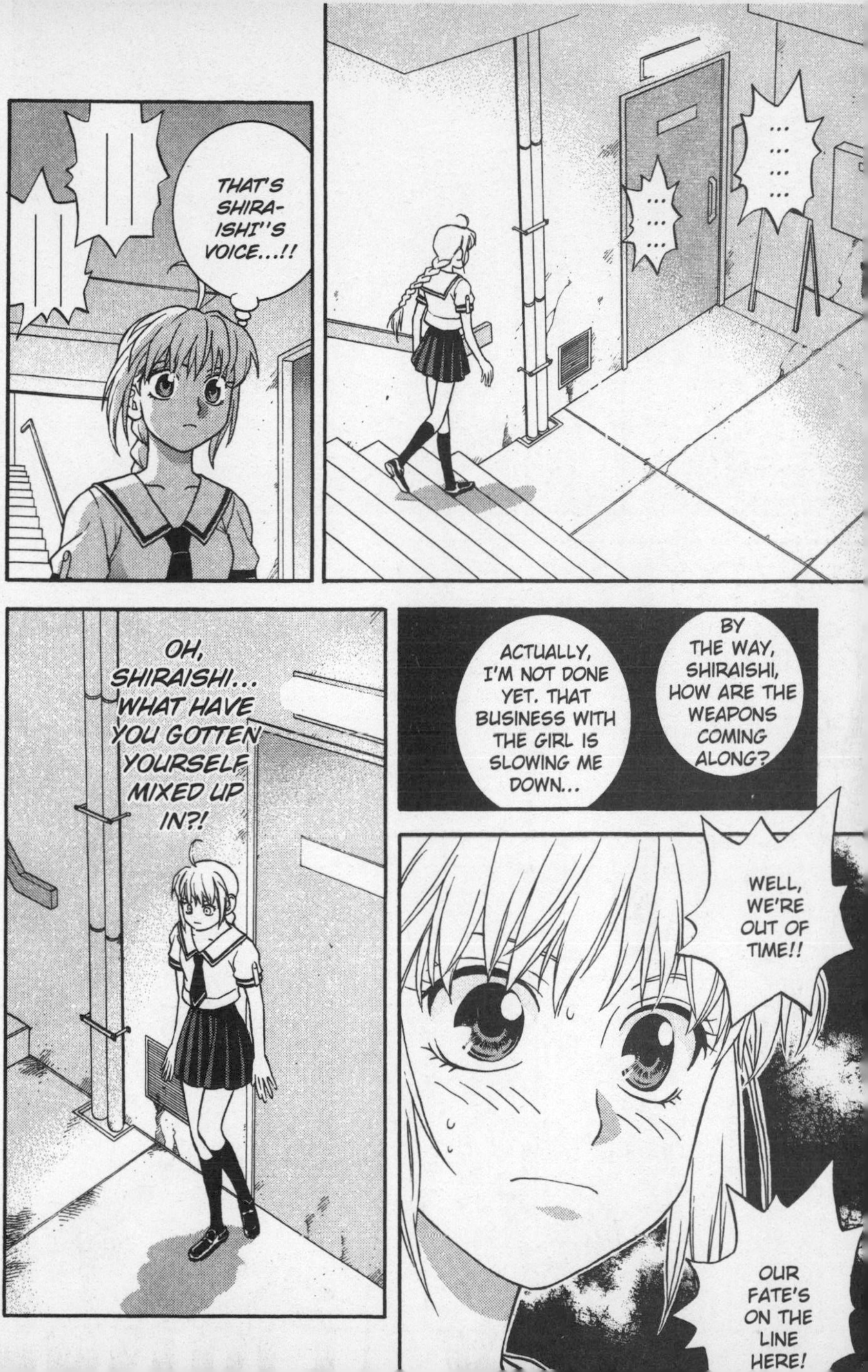
... ...
... ...
THAT'S SHIRAISHI''S VOICE...!!
BY THE WAY, SHIRAISHI, HOW ARE THE WEAPONS COMING ALONG?
ACTUALLY, I'M NOT DONE YET. THAT BUSINESS WITH THE GIRL IS SLOWING ME DOWN...
WELL, WE'RE OUT OF TIME!!
OUR FATE'S ON THE LINE HERE!
OH, SHIRAISHI... WHAT HAVE YOU GOTTEN YOURSELF MIXED UP IN?!

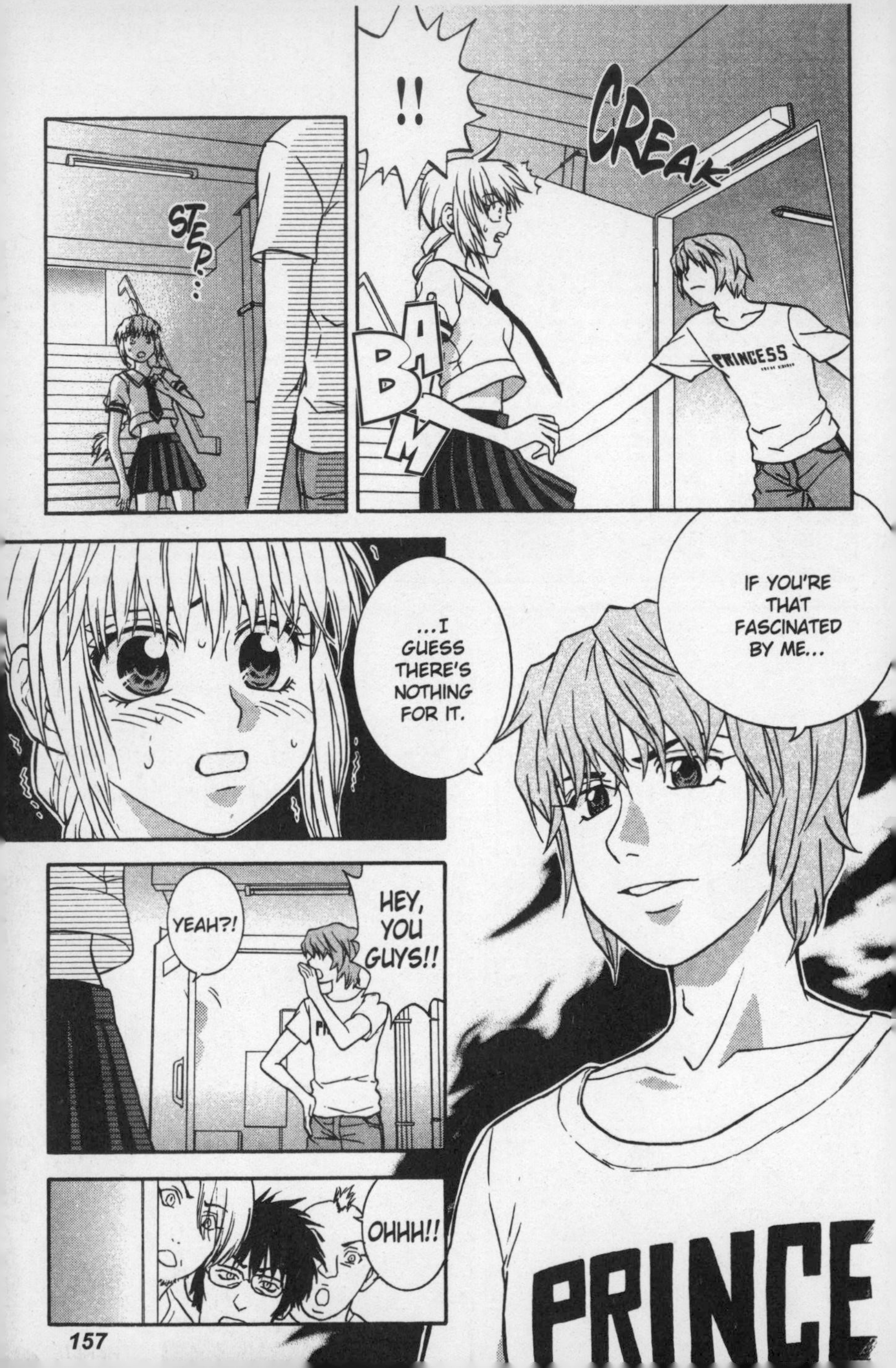
!!
CREAK
BAM
PRINCESS
STEP...
IF YOU'RE THAT FASCINATED BY ME...
PRINCE
...I GUESS THERE'S NOTHING FOR IT.
HEY, YOU GUYS!!
YEAH?!
OHHH!!

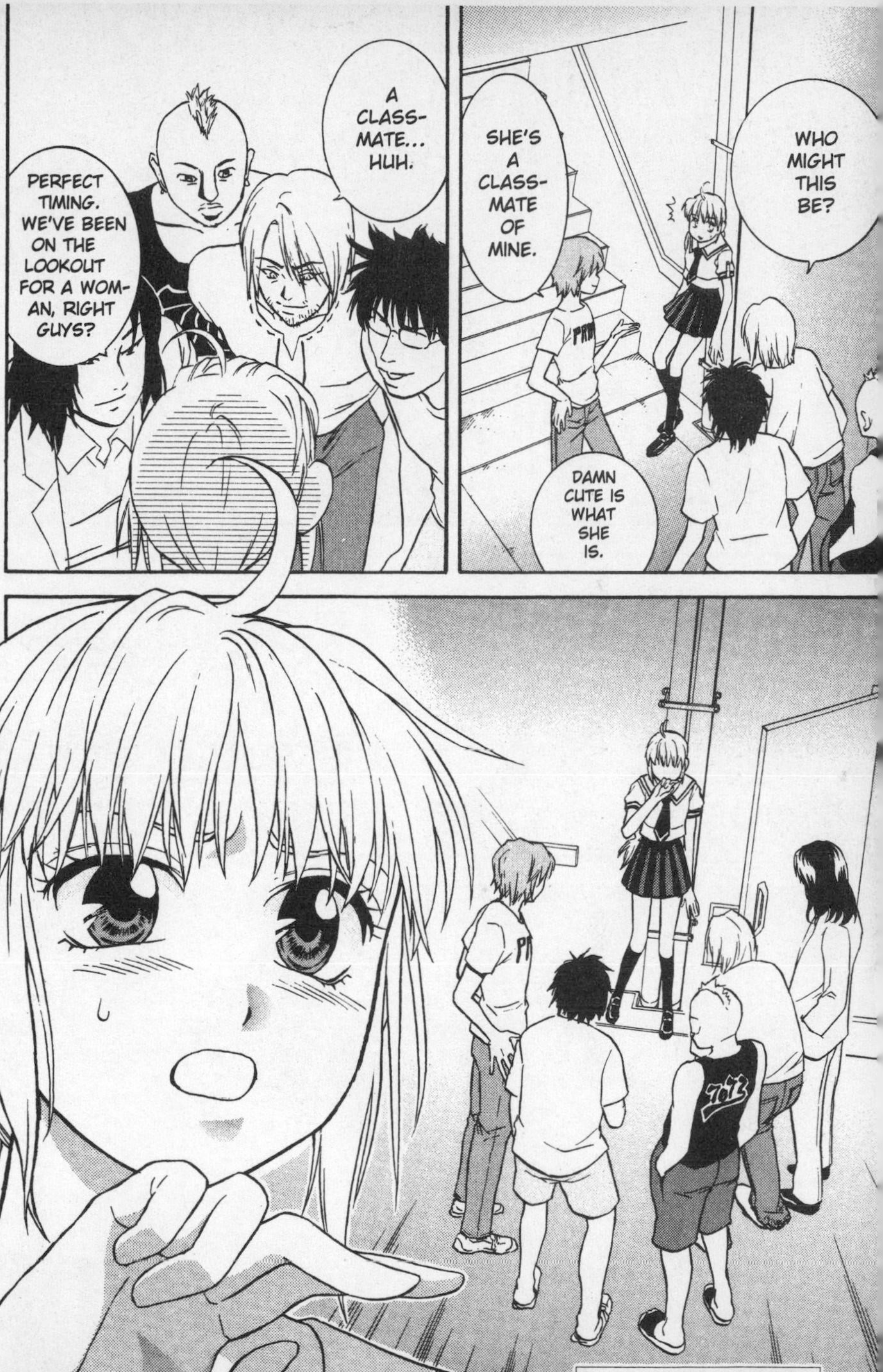
WHO MIGHT THIS BE?
SHE'S A CLASS-MATE OF MINE.
DAMN CUTE IS WHAT SHE IS.
A CLASS-MATE... HUH.
PERFECT TIMING. WE'VE BEEN ON THE LOOKOUT FOR A WOM-AN, RIGHT GUYS?

Episode 4 Time Of One's Own (Part One): The End

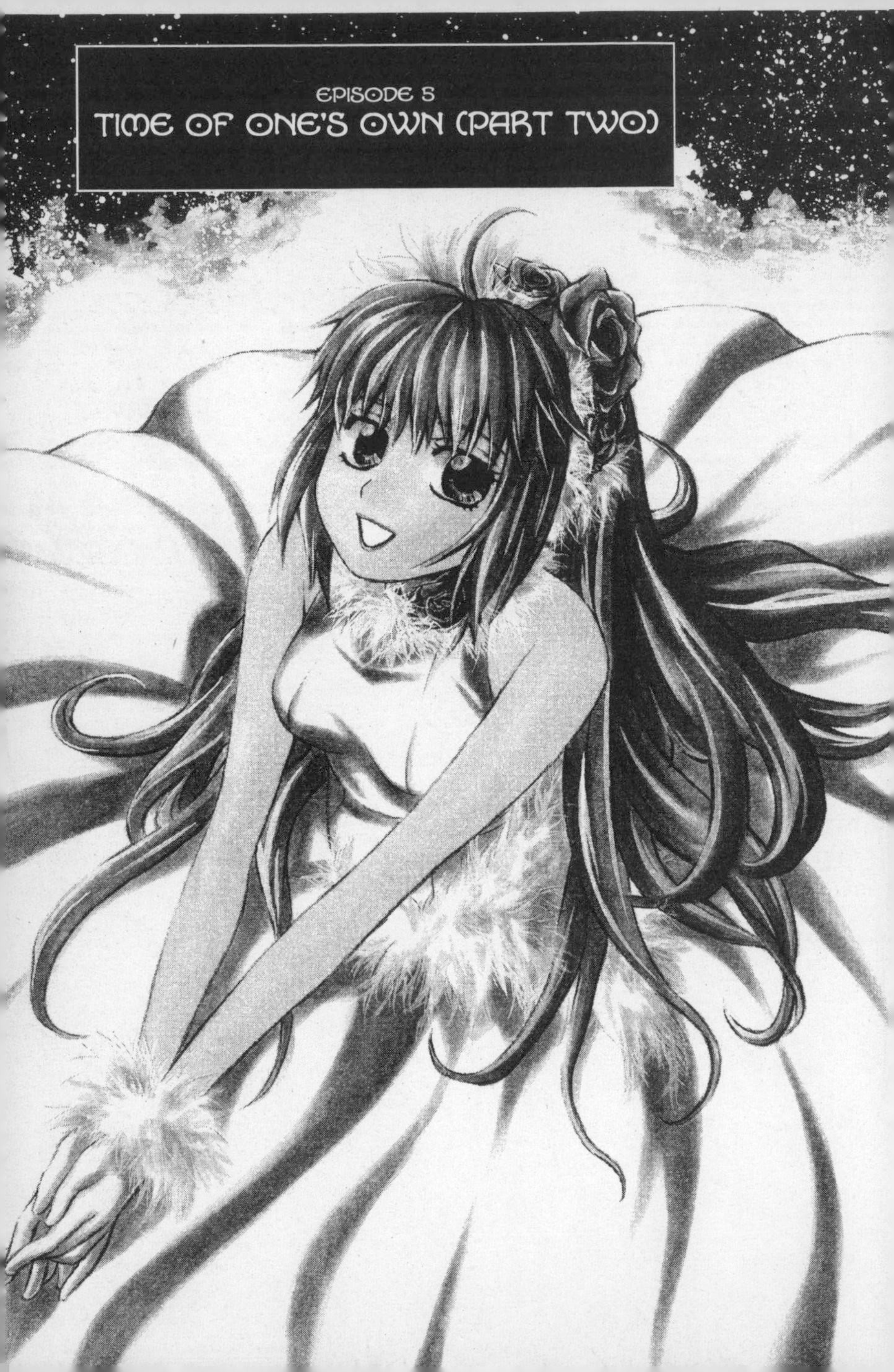
EPISODE 5
TIME OF ONE'S OWN (PART TWO)

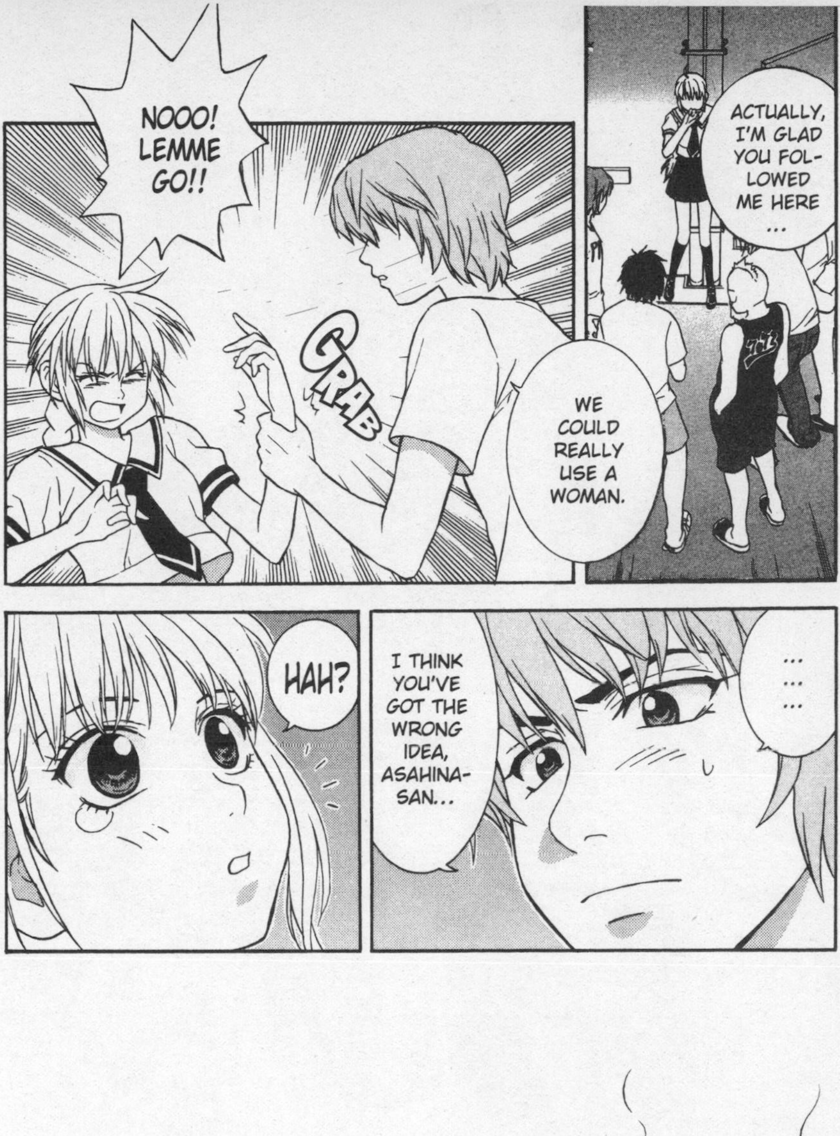
ACTUALLY, I'M GLAD YOU FOL-LOWED ME HERE ...
WE COULD REALLY USE A WOMAN.
NOOO! LEMME GO!!
GRAB
... ...
I THINK YOU'VE GOT THE WRONG IDEA, ASAHINA-SAN...
HAH?

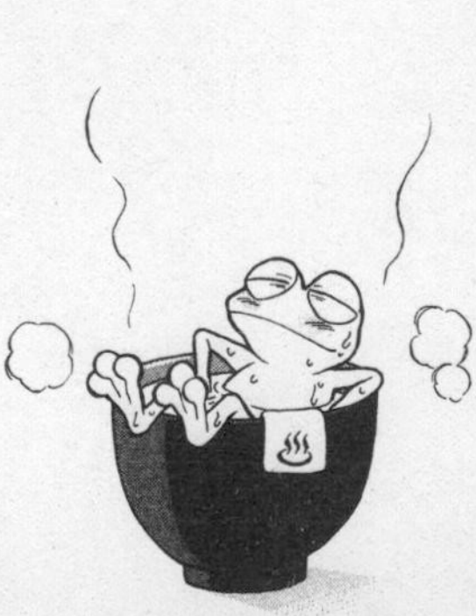

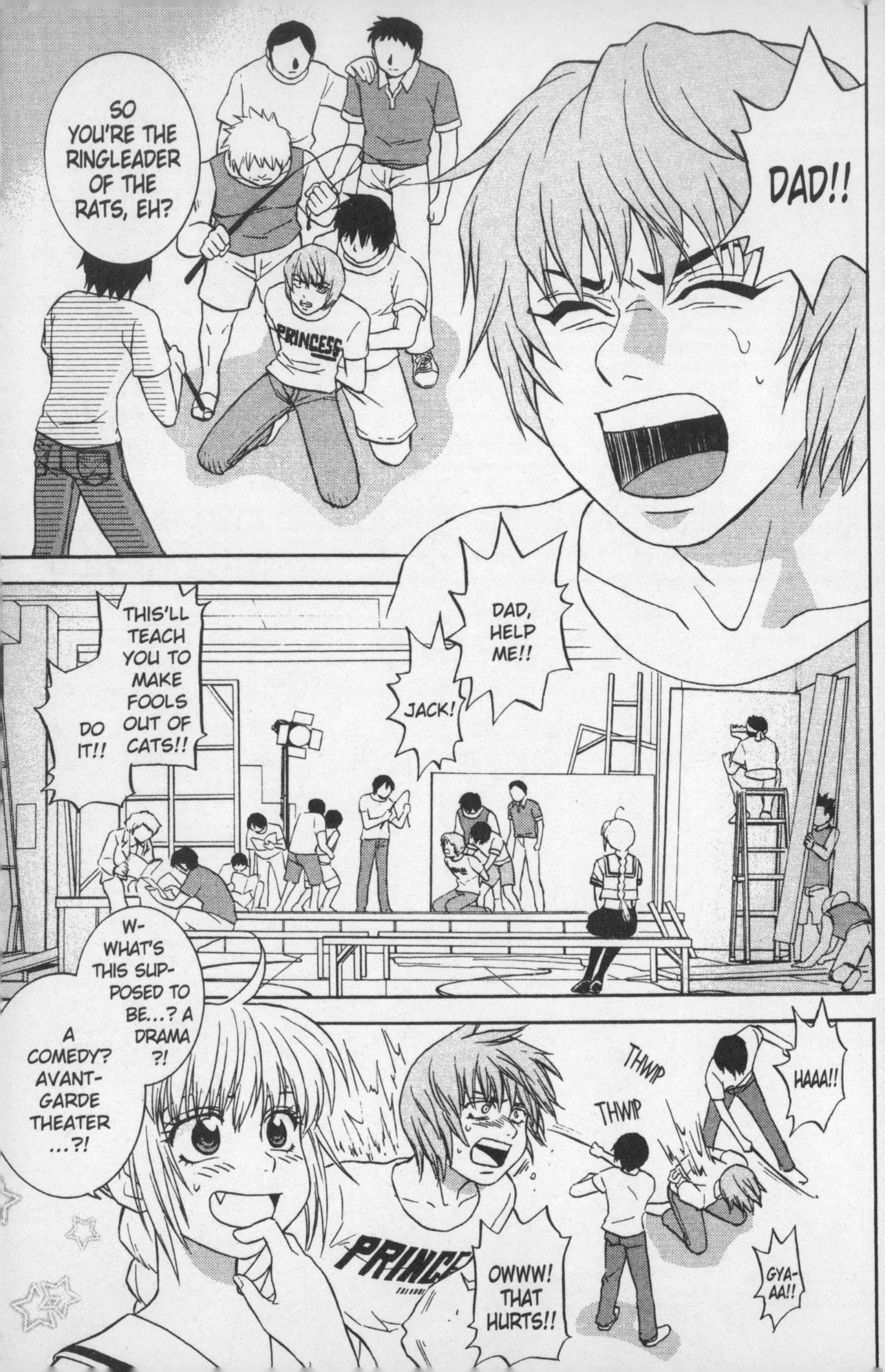

DAD!!
SO YOU'RE THE RINGLEADER OF THE RATS, EH?
PRINCESS
DAD, HELP ME!!
JACK!
THIS'LL TEACH YOU TO MAKE FOOLS OUT OF CATS!!
DO IT!!
HAAA!!
THWIP
THWIP
GYA-AA!!
OWWW! THAT HURTS!!
W-WHAT'S THIS SUP-POSED TO BE...? A DRAMA?!
A COMEDY? AVANT-GARDE THEATER...?!

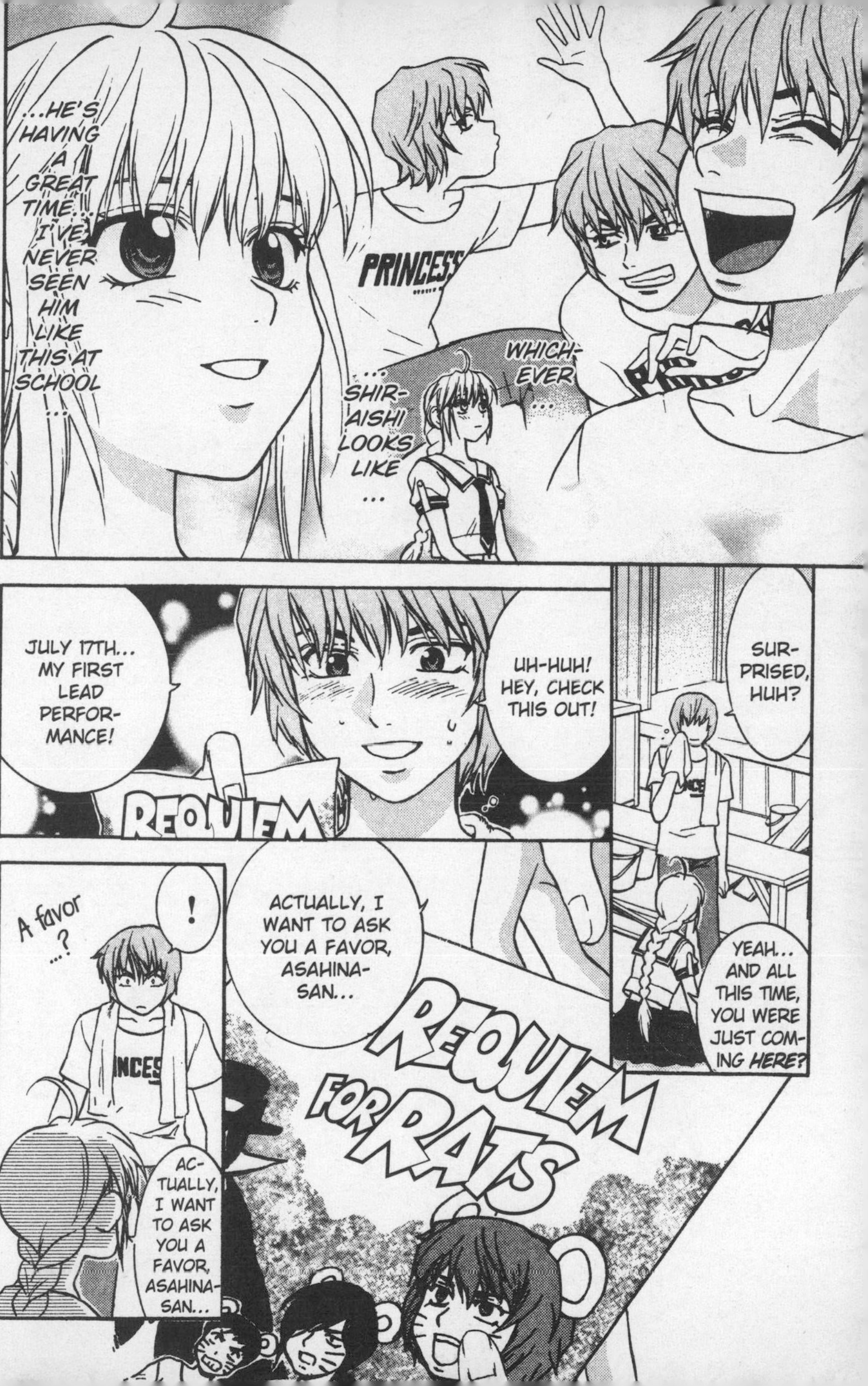
WHICH-EVER...
...SHIRAISHI LOOKS LIKE...
...HE'S HAVING A GREAT TIME... I'VE NEVER SEEN HIM LIKE THIS AT SCHOOL...
PRINCESS
SUR-PRISED, HUH?
YEAH... AND ALL THIS TIME, YOU WERE JUST COMING HERE?
UH-HUH! HEY, CHECK THIS OUT!
JULY 17TH... MY FIRST LEAD PERFORMANCE!
REQUIEM
ACTUALLY, I WANT TO ASK YOU A FAVOR, ASAHINA-SAN...
REQUIEM FOR RATS
!
A favor ...?
ACTUALLY, I WANT TO ASK YOU A FAVOR, ASAHINA-SAN...

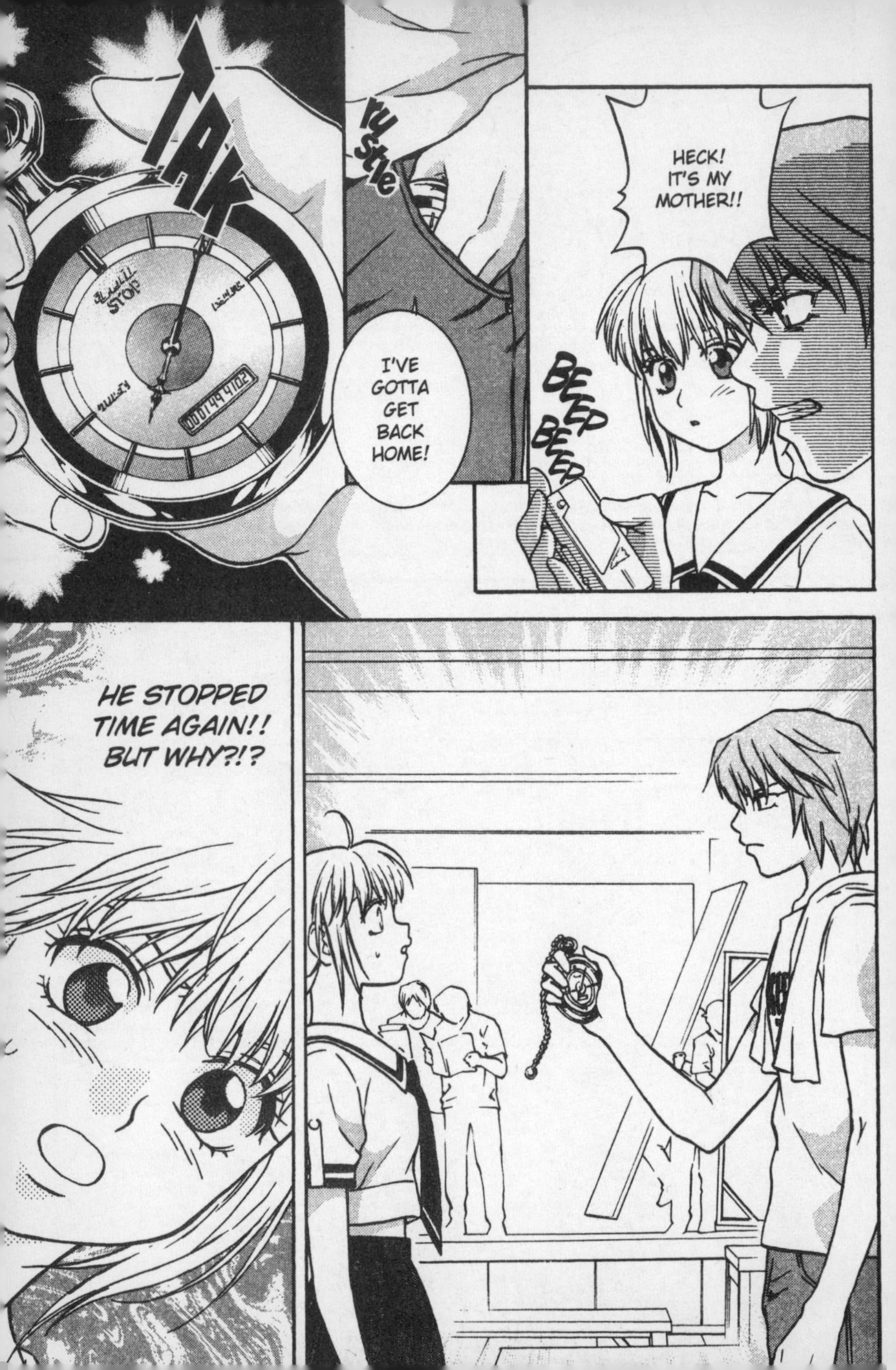
HECK! IT'S MY MOTHER!!
BEEP BEEP
I'VE GOTTA GET BACK HOME!
TAK
STOP
HE STOPPED TIME AGAIN!! BUT WHY?!?

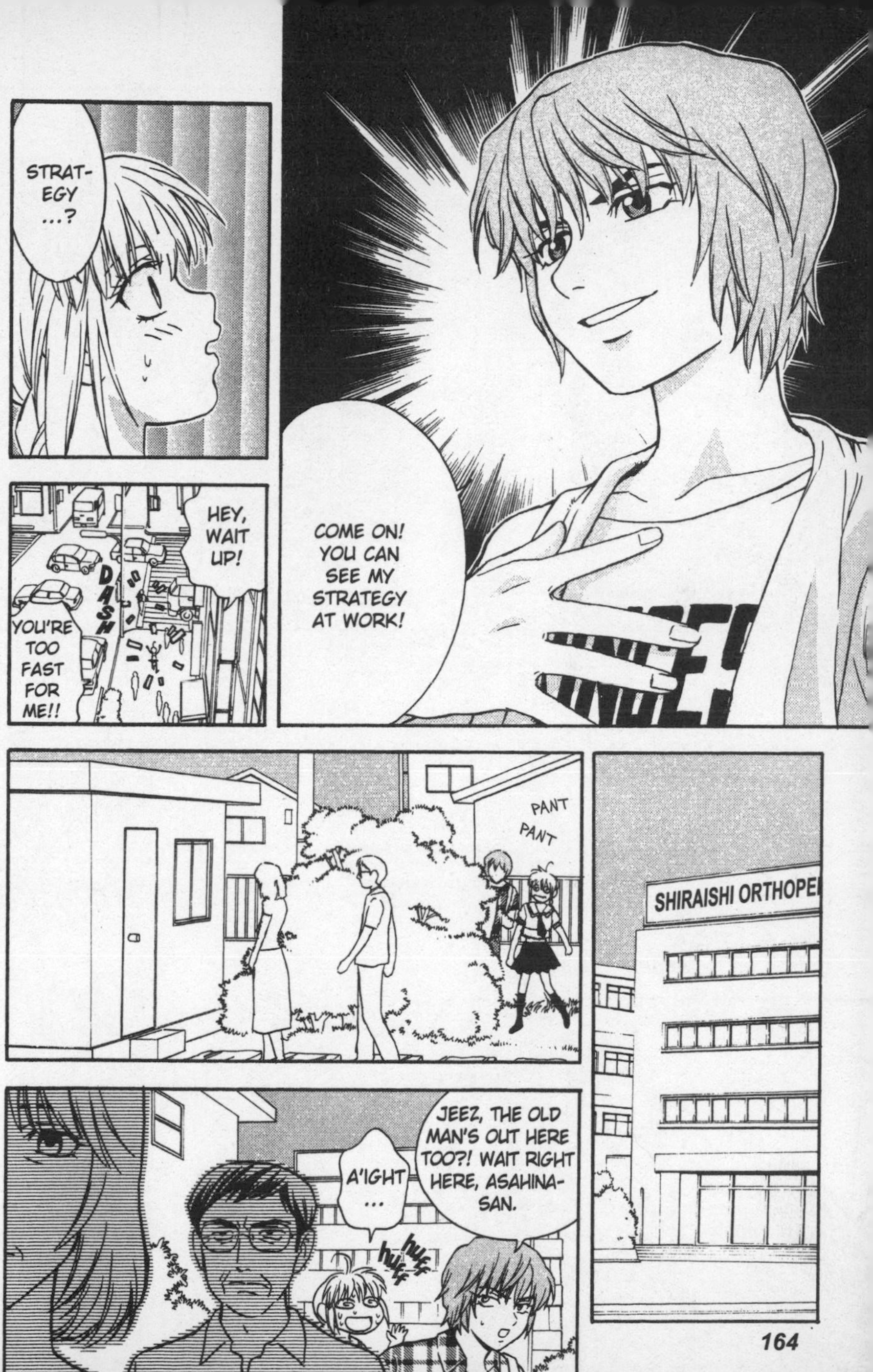
COME ON! YOU CAN SEE MY STRATEGY AT WORK!
STRAT-EGY ...?
HEY, WAIT UP!
DASH
YOU'RE TOO FAST FOR ME!!
SHIRAISHI ORTHOPE
PANT PANT
JEEZ, THE OLD MAN'S OUT HERE TOO?! WAIT RIGHT HERE, ASAHINA-SAN.
A'IGHT ...
huff huff

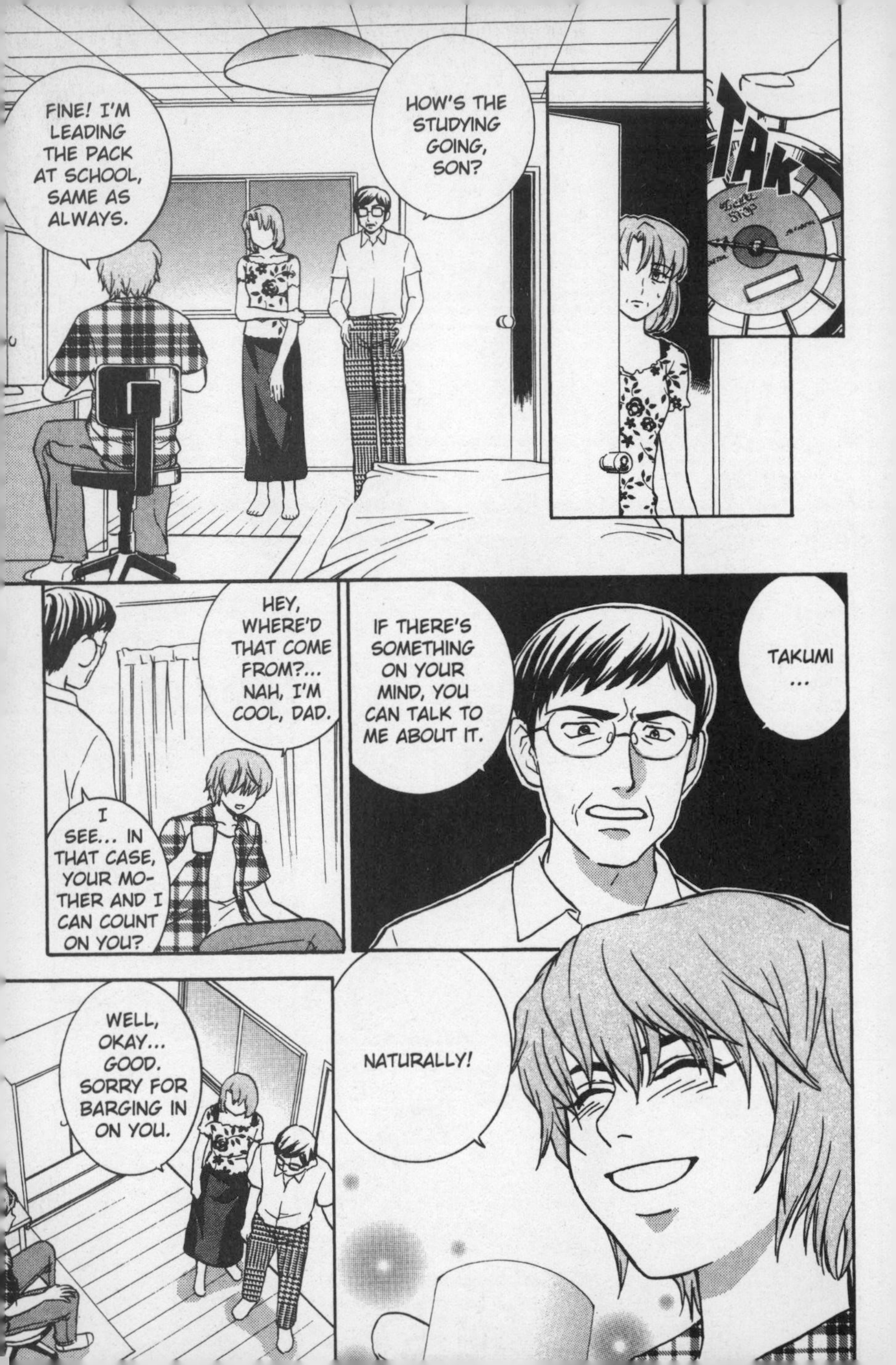
TAK
HOW'S THE STUDYING GOING, SON?
FINE! I'M LEADING THE PACK AT SCHOOL, SAME AS ALWAYS.
TAKUMI ...
IF THERE'S SOMETHING ON YOUR MIND, YOU CAN TALK TO ME ABOUT IT.
HEY, WHERE'D THAT COME FROM?... NAH, I'M COOL, DAD.
I SEE... IN THAT CASE, YOUR MO-THER AND I CAN COUNT ON YOU?
NATURALLY!
WELL, OKAY... GOOD. SORRY FOR BARGING IN ON YOU.

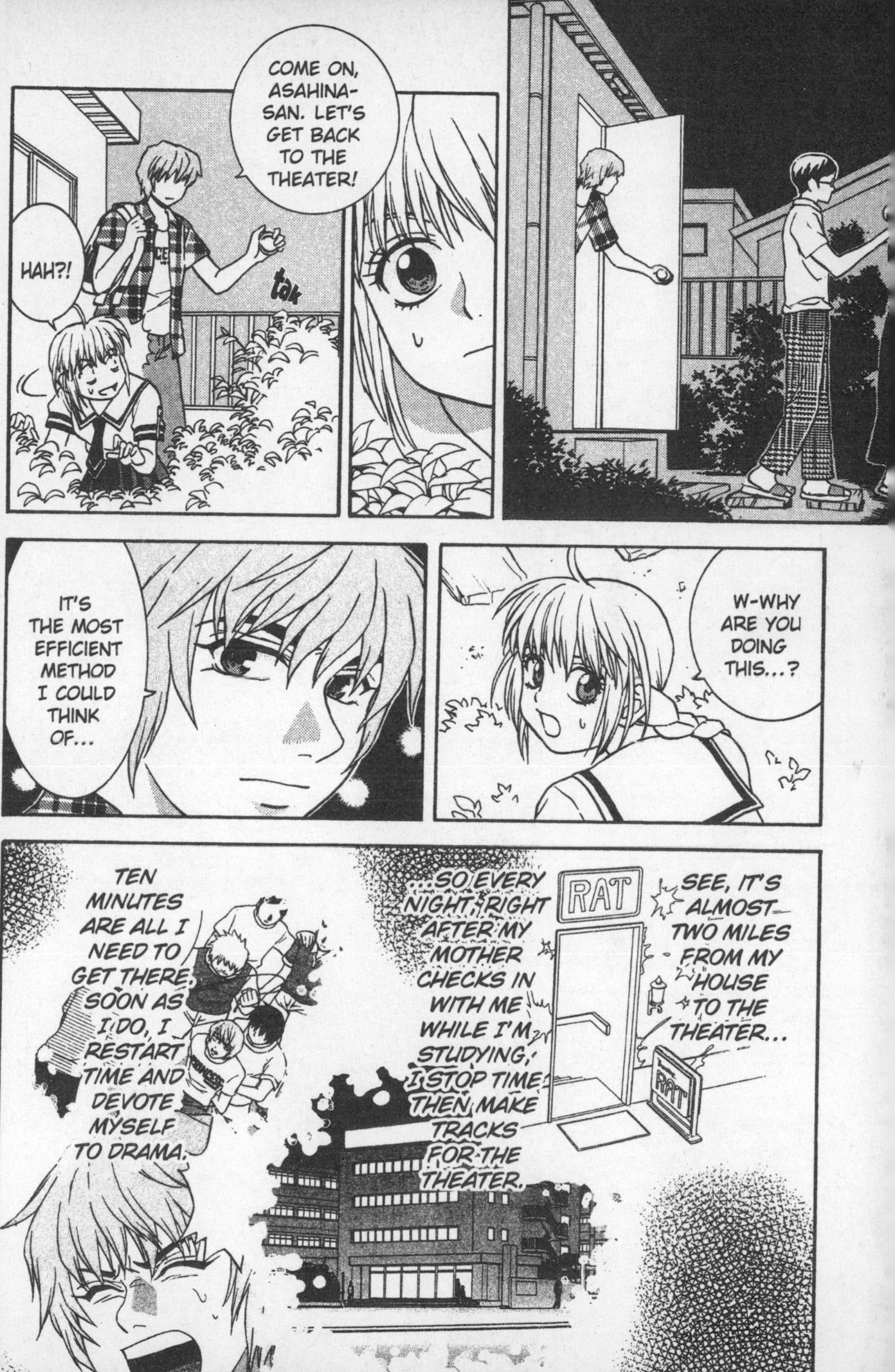

COME ON, ASAHINA-SAN. LET'S GET BACK TO THE THEATER!
tak
HAH?!
W-WHY ARE YOU DOING THIS...?
IT'S THE MOST EFFICIENT METHOD I COULD THINK OF...
SEE, IT'S ALMOST TWO MILES FROM MY HOUSE TO THE THEATER...
RAT
RAT
...SO EVERY NIGHT, RIGHT AFTER MY MOTHER CHECKS IN WITH ME WHILE I'M STUDYING, I STOP TIME, THEN MAKE TRACKS FOR THE THEATER.
TEN MINUTES ARE ALL I NEED TO GET THERE. SOON AS I DO, I RESTART TIME AND DEVOTE MYSELF TO DRAMA.

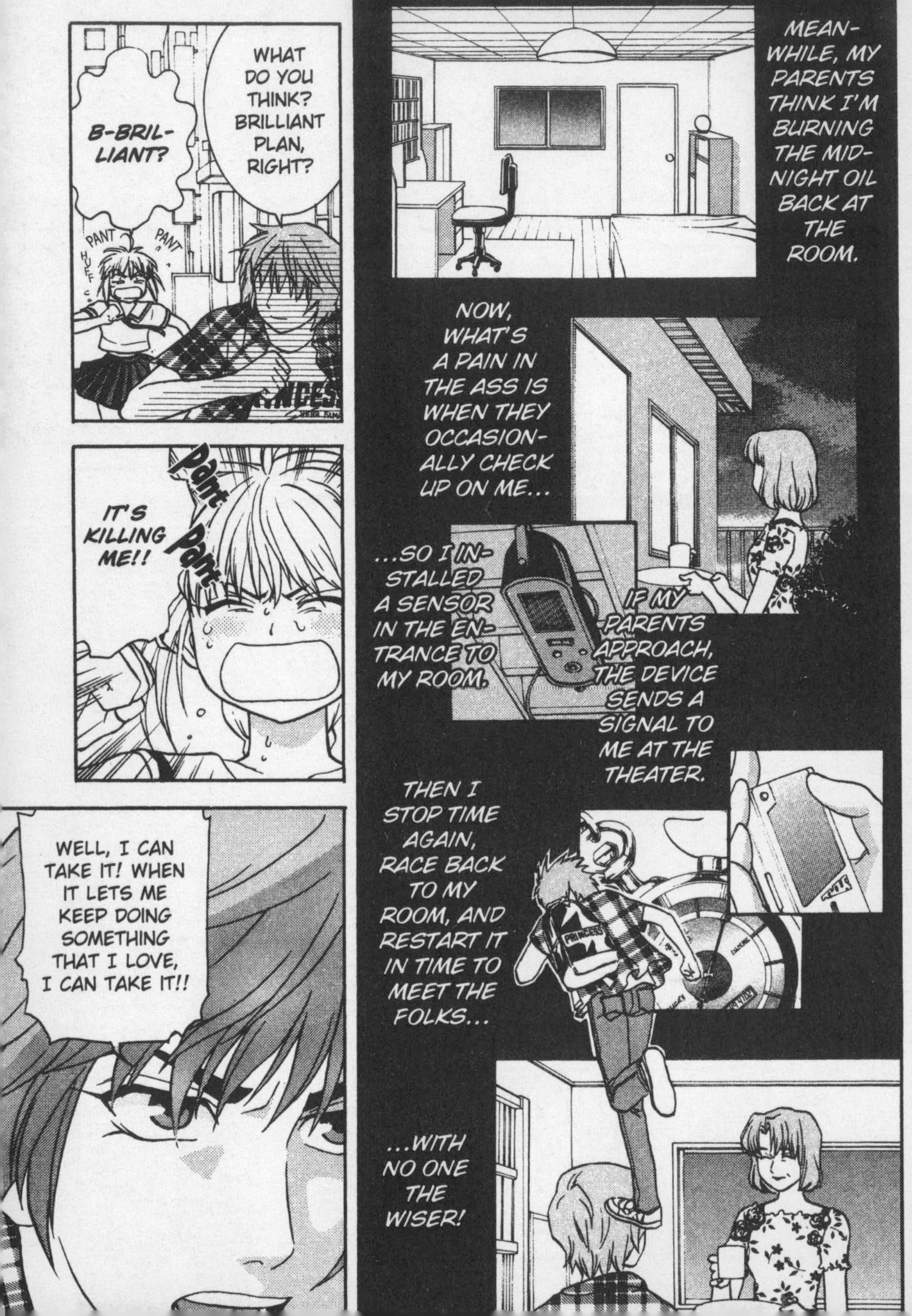
MEAN-WHILE, MY PARENTS THINK I'M BURNING THE MID-NIGHT OIL BACK AT THE ROOM.
NOW, WHAT'S A PAIN IN THE ASS IS WHEN THEY OCCASION-ALLY CHECK UP ON ME...
...SO I IN-STALLED A SENSOR IN THE EN-TRANCE TO MY ROOM.
IF MY PARENTS APPROACH, THE DEVICE SENDS A SIGNAL TO ME AT THE THEATER.
THEN I STOP TIME AGAIN, RACE BACK TO MY ROOM, AND RESTART IT IN TIME TO MEET THE FOLKS...
PRINCESS
...WITH NO ONE THE WISER!
WHAT DO YOU THINK? BRILLIANT PLAN, RIGHT?
B-BRIL-LIANT?
PANT
PANT
HUFF
PRINCESS
Pant
Pant
IT'S KILLING ME!!
WELL, I CAN TAKE IT! WHEN IT LETS ME KEEP DOING SOMETHING THAT I LOVE, I CAN TAKE IT!!

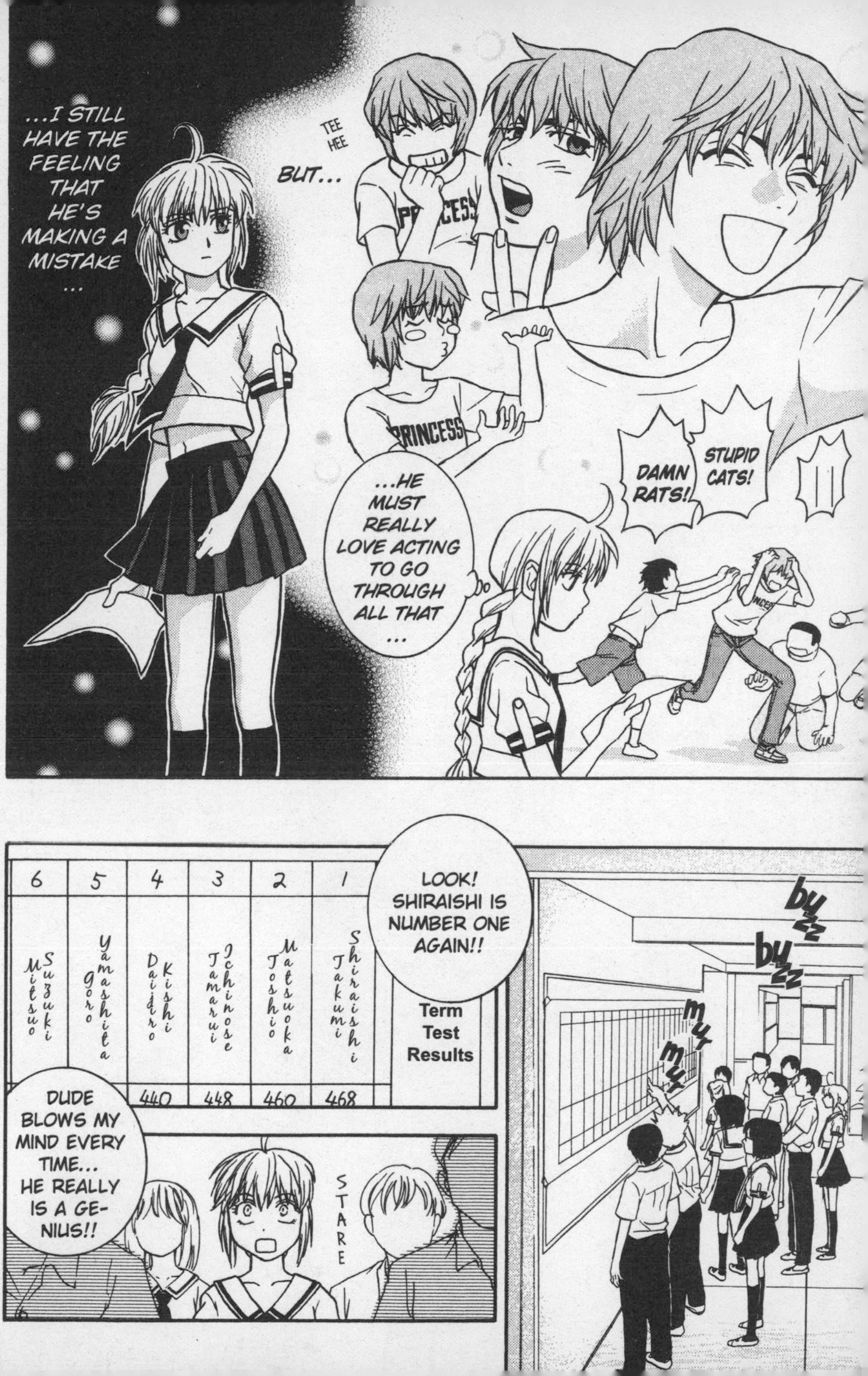
TEE HEE
BUT...
STUPID CATS!
DAMN RATS!
...HE MUST REALLY LOVE ACTING TO GO THROUGH ALL THAT ...
...I STILL HAVE THE FEELING THAT HE'S MAKING A MISTAKE ...
buzz buzz
mur mur
LOOK! SHIRAISHI IS NUMBER ONE AGAIN!!
Term Test Results
1 Shiraishi Takumi 468
2 Matsuoka Toshio 460
3 Ichinose Tamarui 448
4 Kishi Daijiro 440
5 Yamashita Goro
6 Suzuki Mitsuo
DUDE BLOWS MY MIND EVERY TIME... HE REALLY IS A GE-NIUS!!
STARE

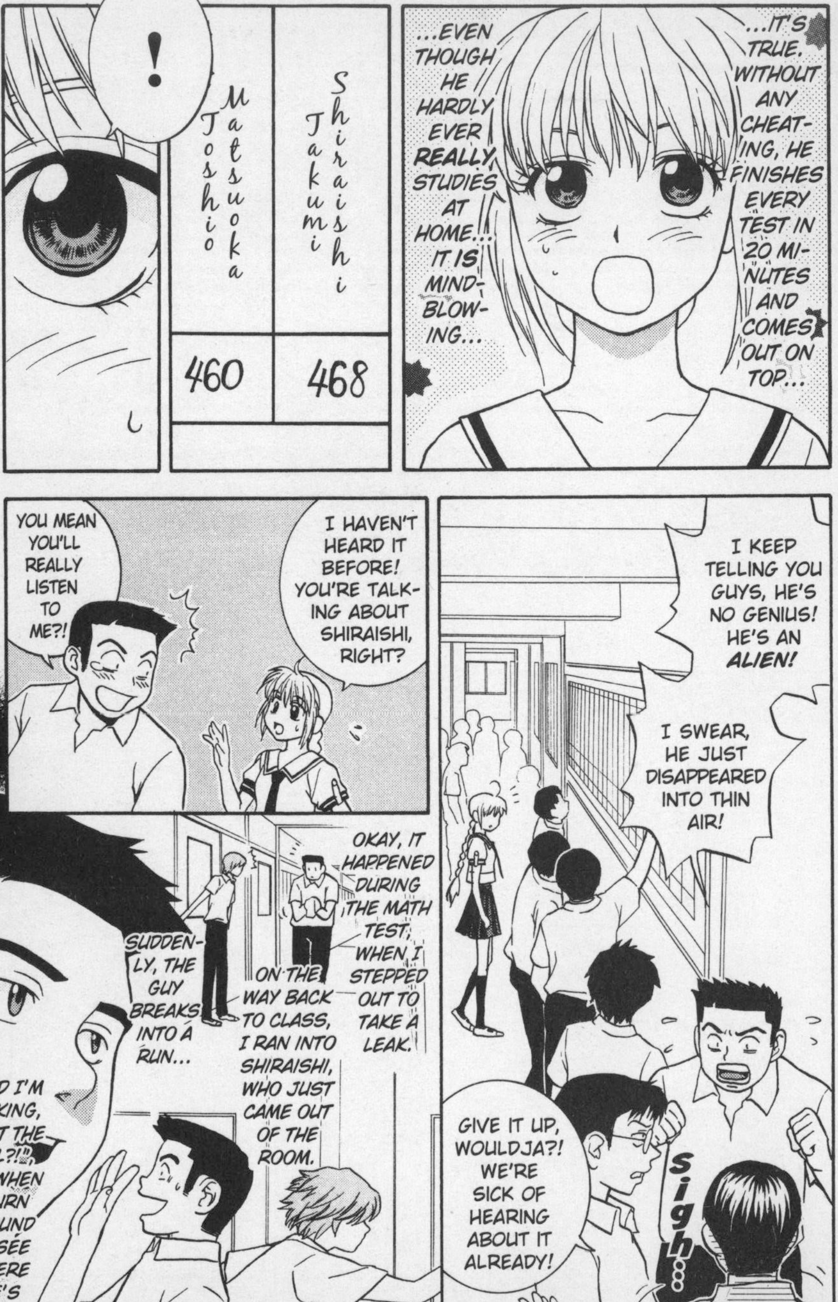
...IT'S TRUE. WITHOUT ANY CHEATING, HE FINISHES EVERY TEST IN 20 MINUTES AND COMES OUT ON TOP...
...EVEN THOUGH HE HARDLY EVER REALLY STUDIES AT HOME... IT IS MIND-BLOWING...
Shiraishi Takumi
468
Matsuoka Toshio
460
!
I KEEP TELLING YOU GUYS, HE'S NO GENIUS! HE'S AN ALIEN!
I SWEAR, HE JUST DISAPPEARED INTO THIN AIR!
GIVE IT UP, WOULDJA?! WE'RE SICK OF HEARING ABOUT IT ALREADY!
Sigh...
I HAVEN'T HEARD IT BEFORE! YOU'RE TALKING ABOUT SHIRAISHI, RIGHT?
YOU MEAN YOU'LL REALLY LISTEN TO ME?!
OKAY, IT HAPPENED DURING THE MATH TEST, WHEN I STEPPED OUT TO TAKE A LEAK.
ON THE WAY BACK TO CLASS, I RAN INTO SHIRAISHI, WHO JUST CAME OUT OF THE ROOM.
SUDDENLY, THE GUY BREAKS INTO A RUN...
...AND I'M THINKING, "WHAT THE HELL?!", BUT WHEN I TURN AROUND TO SEE WHERE HE'S GOIN'...

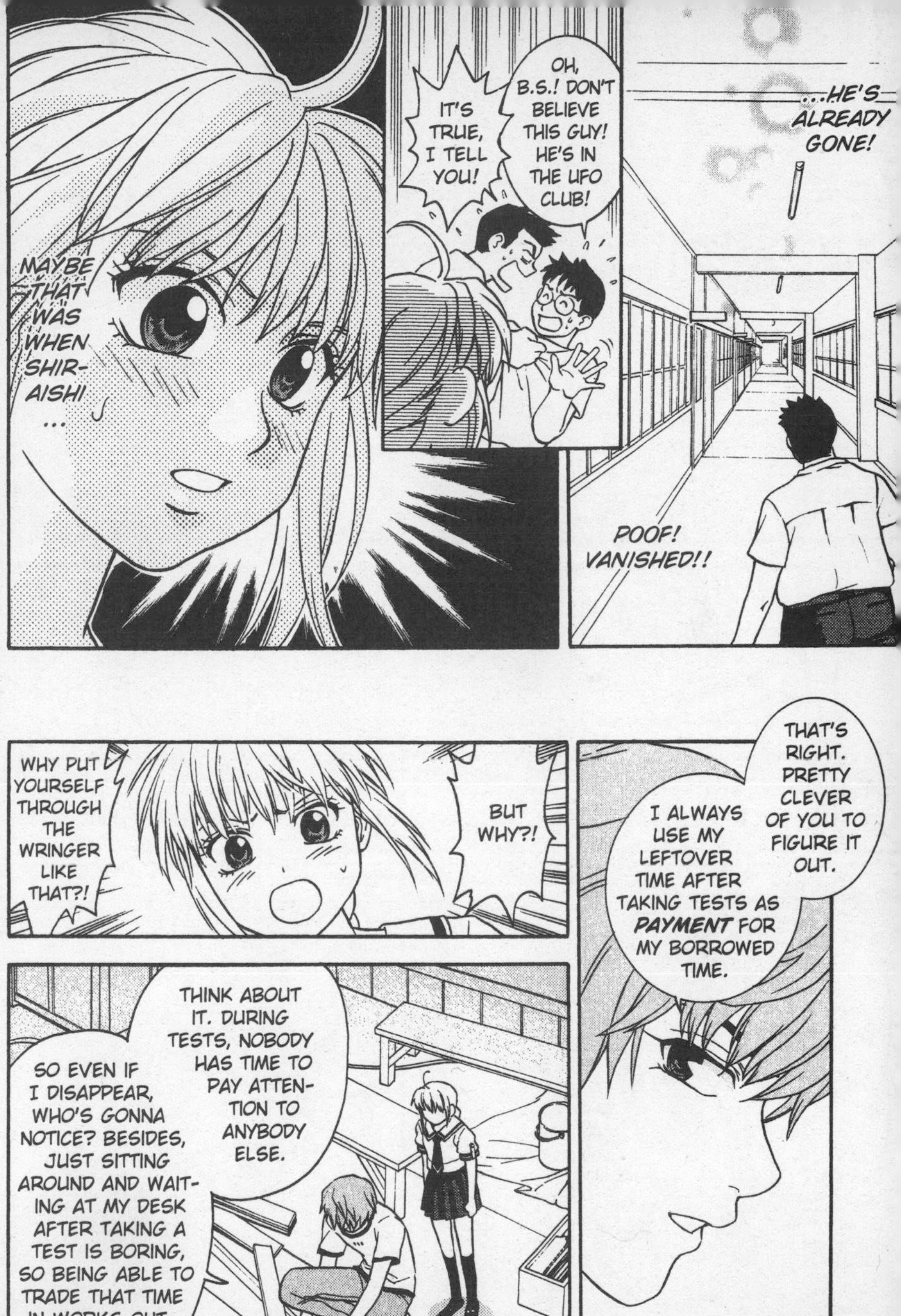
...HE'S ALREADY GONE!
POOF! VANISHED!!
OH, B.S.! DON'T BELIEVE THIS GUY! HE'S IN THE UFO CLUB!
IT'S TRUE, I TELL YOU!
MAYBE THAT WAS WHEN SHIRAISHI ...
THAT'S RIGHT. PRETTY CLEVER OF YOU TO FIGURE IT OUT.
I ALWAYS USE MY LEFTOVER TIME AFTER TAKING TESTS AS ***PAYMENT*** FOR MY BORROWED TIME.
BUT WHY?!
WHY PUT YOURSELF THROUGH THE WRINGER LIKE THAT?!
THINK ABOUT IT. DURING TESTS, NOBODY HAS TIME TO PAY ATTENTION TO ANYBODY ELSE.
SO EVEN IF I DISAPPEAR, WHO'S GONNA NOTICE? BESIDES, JUST SITTING AROUND AND WAITING AT MY DESK AFTER TAKING A TEST IS BORING, SO BEING ABLE TO TRADE THAT TIME IN WORKS OUT PERFECTLY.

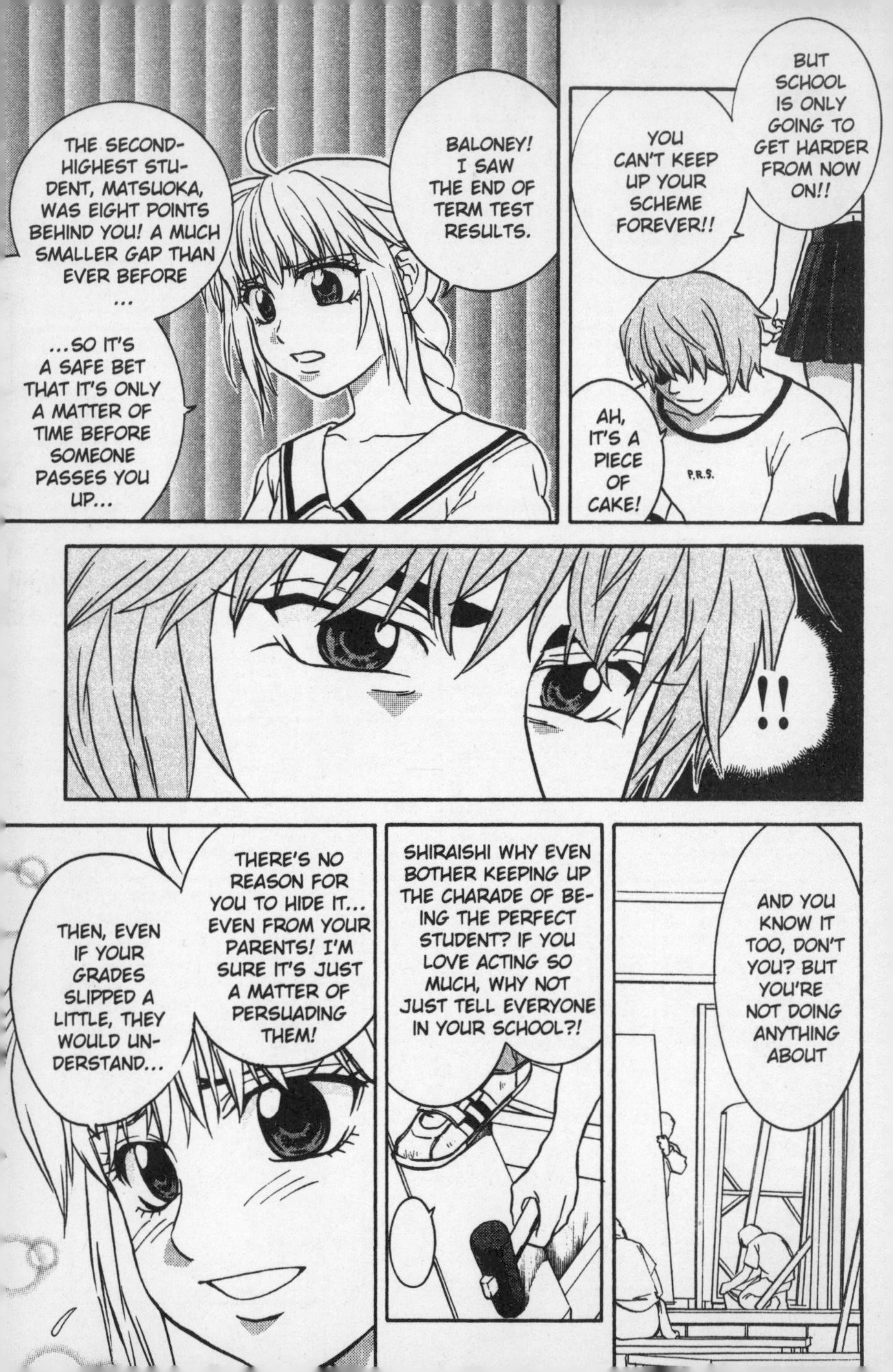
BUT SCHOOL IS ONLY GOING TO GET HARDER FROM NOW ON!!
YOU CAN'T KEEP UP YOUR SCHEME FOREVER!!
AH, IT'S A PIECE OF CAKE!
P.R.S.
BALONEY! I SAW THE END OF TERM TEST RESULTS.
THE SECOND-HIGHEST STUDENT, MATSUOKA, WAS EIGHT POINTS BEHIND YOU! A MUCH SMALLER GAP THAN EVER BEFORE ...
...SO IT'S A SAFE BET THAT IT'S ONLY A MATTER OF TIME BEFORE SOMEONE PASSES YOU UP...
!!
AND YOU KNOW IT TOO, DON'T YOU? BUT YOU'RE NOT DOING ANYTHING ABOUT
SHIRAISHI WHY EVEN BOTHER KEEPING UP THE CHARADE OF BEING THE PERFECT STUDENT? IF YOU LOVE ACTING SO MUCH, WHY NOT JUST TELL EVERYONE IN YOUR SCHOOL?!
THERE'S NO REASON FOR YOU TO HIDE IT... EVEN FROM YOUR PARENTS! I'M SURE IT'S JUST A MATTER OF PERSUADING THEM!
THEN, EVEN IF YOUR GRADES SLIPPED A LITTLE, THEY WOULD UNDERSTAND...

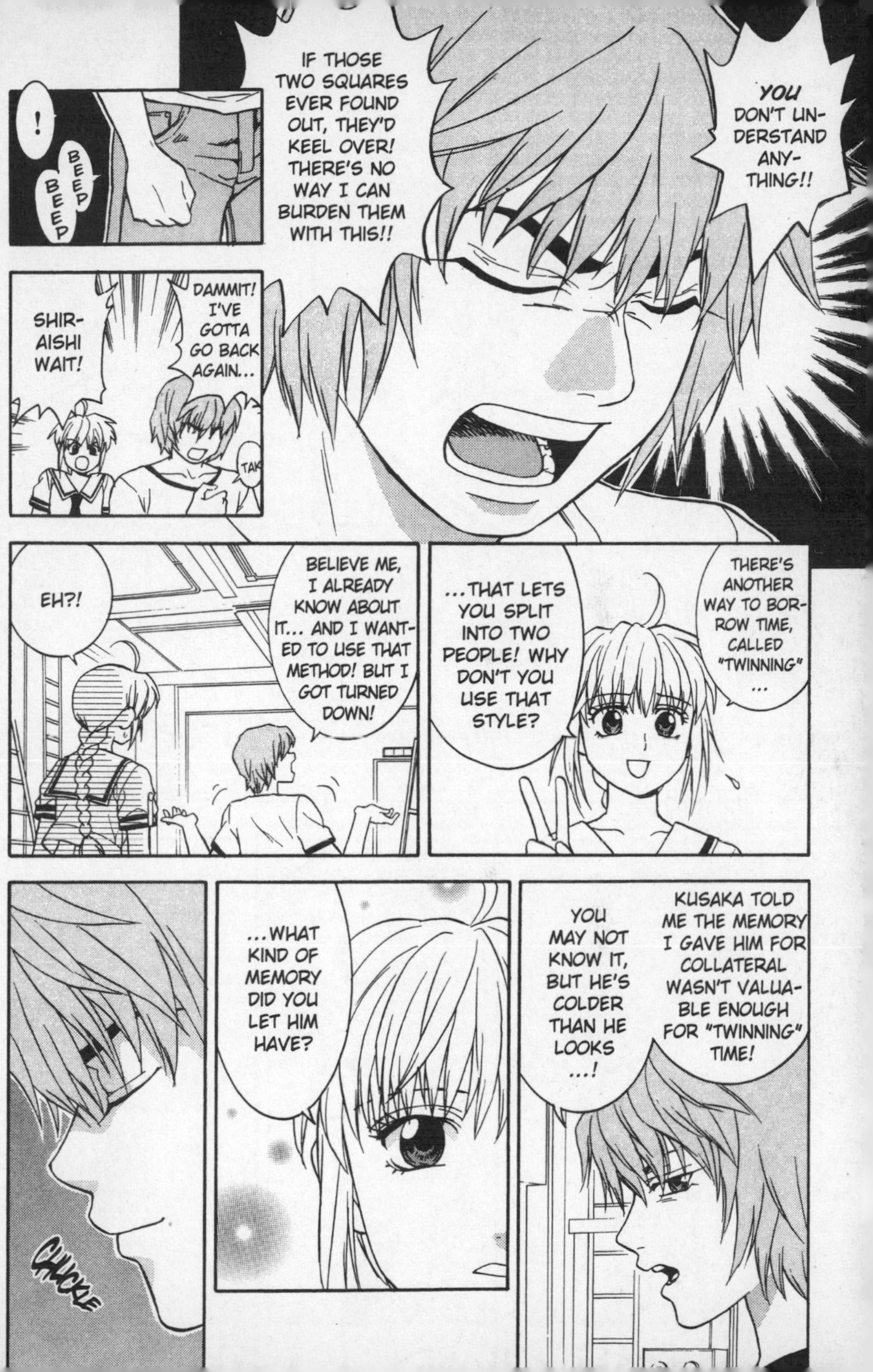
YOU DON'T UNDERSTAND ANYTHING!!
IF THOSE TWO SQUARES EVER FOUND OUT, THEY'D KEEL OVER! THERE'S NO WAY I CAN BURDEN THEM WITH THIS!!
!
BEEP BEEP
DAMMIT! I'VE GOTTA GO BACK AGAIN...
SHIRAISHI WAIT!
TAK
THERE'S ANOTHER WAY TO BORROW TIME, CALLED "TWINNING"...
...THAT LETS YOU SPLIT INTO TWO PEOPLE! WHY DON'T YOU USE THAT STYLE?
BELIEVE ME, I ALREADY KNOW ABOUT IT... AND I WANTED TO USE THAT METHOD! BUT I GOT TURNED DOWN!
EH?!
KUSAKA TOLD ME THE MEMORY I GAVE HIM FOR COLLATERAL WASN'T VALUABLE ENOUGH FOR "TWINNING" TIME!
YOU MAY NOT KNOW IT, BUT HE'S COLDER THAN HE LOOKS...!
...WHAT KIND OF MEMORY DID YOU LET HIM HAVE?
CHUCKLE

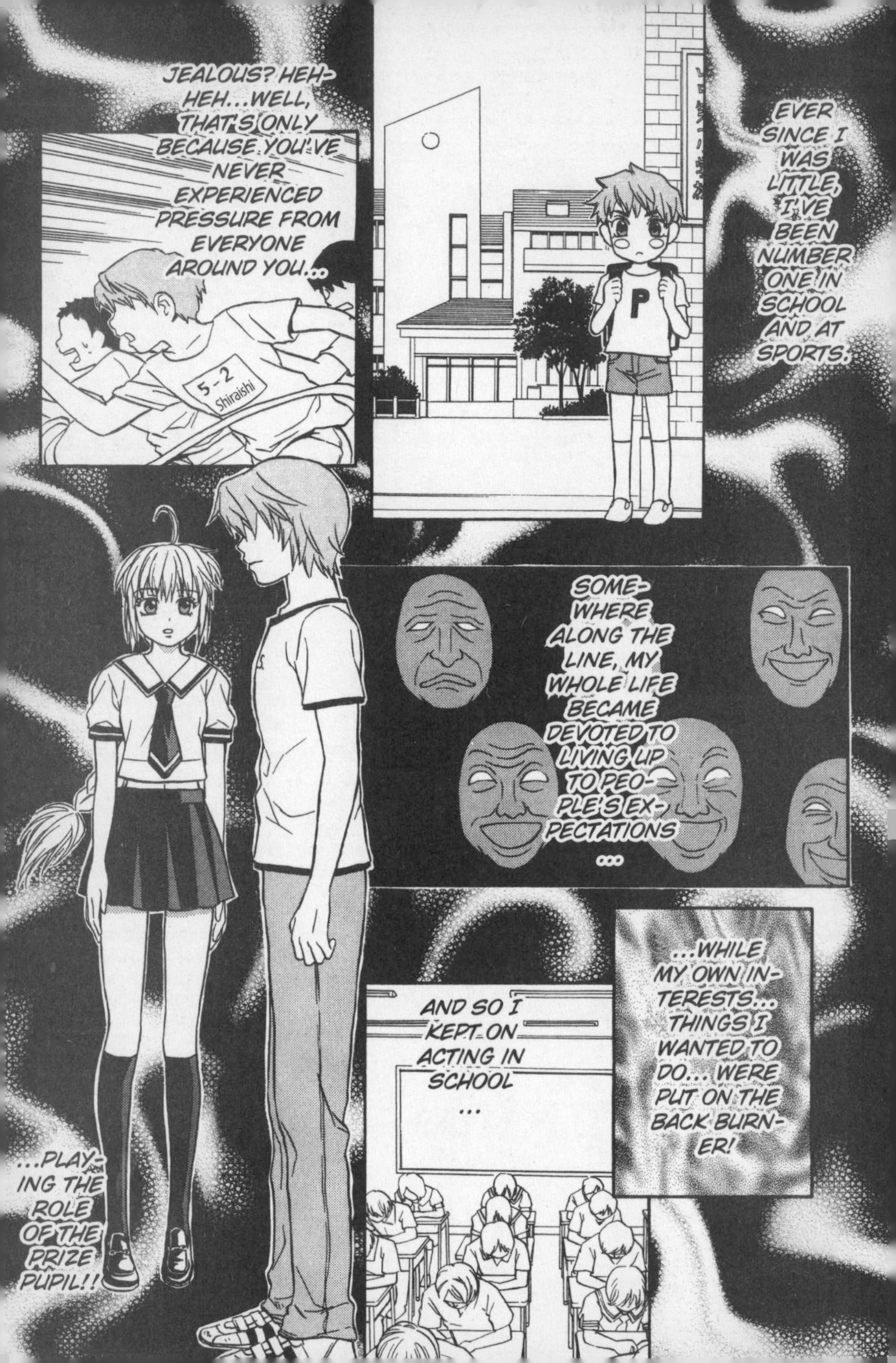
EVER SINCE I WAS LITTLE, I'VE BEEN NUMBER ONE IN SCHOOL AND AT SPORTS.
JEALOUS? HEH-HEH...WELL, THAT'S ONLY BECAUSE YOU'VE NEVER EXPERIENCED PRESSURE FROM EVERYONE AROUND YOU...
5-2
Shiraishi
P
SOME-WHERE ALONG THE LINE, MY WHOLE LIFE BECAME DEVOTED TO LIVING UP TO PEO-PLE'S EX-PECTATIONS...
...WHILE MY OWN IN-TERESTS... THINGS I WANTED TO DO... WERE PUT ON THE BACK BURN-ER!
AND SO I KEPT ON ACTING IN SCHOOL...
...PLAY-ING THE ROLE OF THE PRIZE PUPIL!!

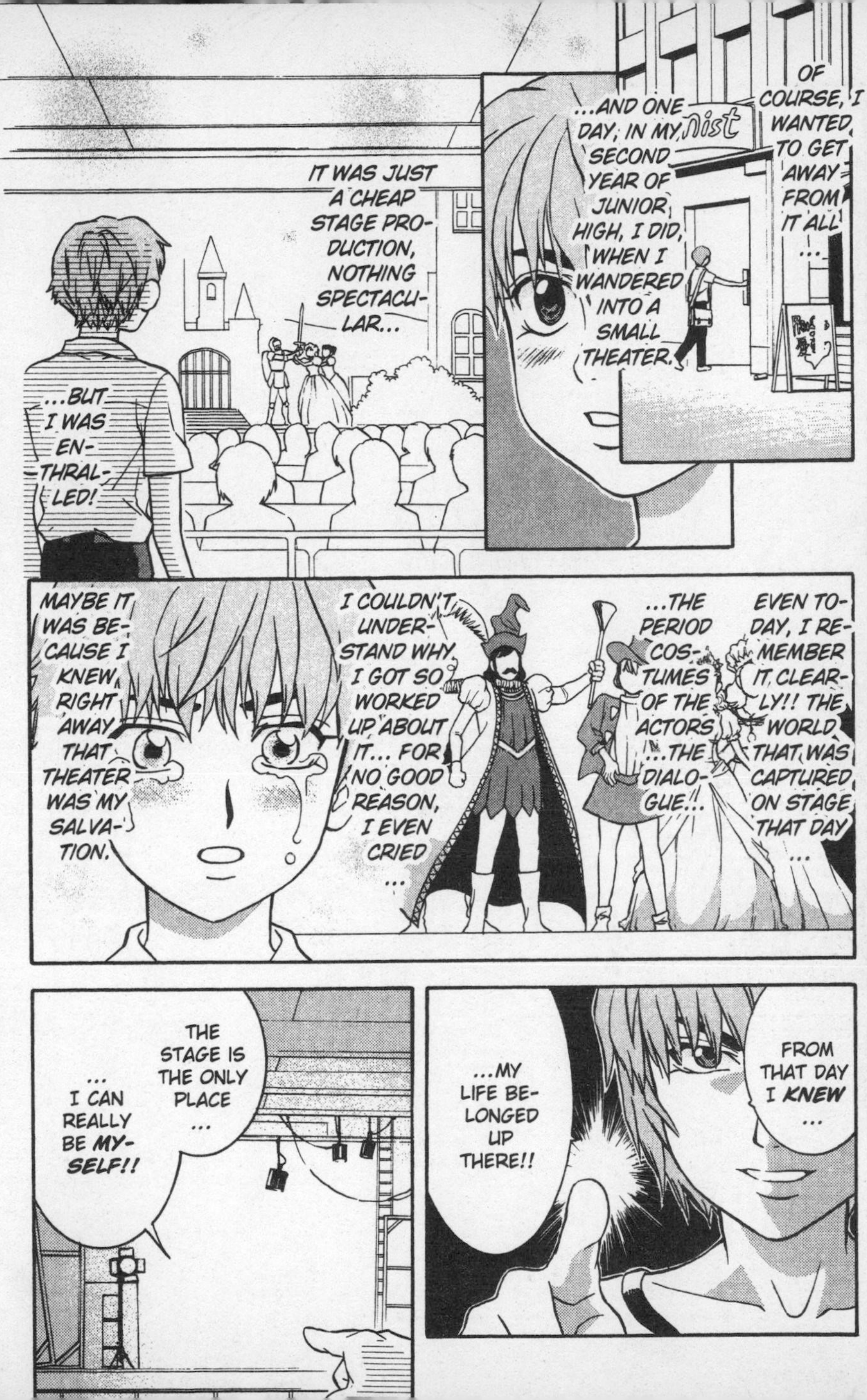
OF COURSE, I WANTED TO GET AWAY FROM IT ALL...
...AND ONE DAY, IN MY SECOND YEAR OF JUNIOR HIGH, I DID, WHEN I WANDERED INTO A SMALL THEATER.
nist
IT WAS JUST A CHEAP STAGE PRODUCTION, NOTHING SPECTACULAR...
...BUT I WAS ENTHRALLED!
EVEN TODAY, I REMEMBER IT CLEARLY!! THE WORLD THAT WAS CAPTURED ON STAGE THAT DAY...
...THE PERIOD COSTUMES OF THE ACTORS ...THE DIALOGUE...!
I COULDN'T UNDERSTAND WHY I GOT SO WORKED UP ABOUT IT... FOR NO GOOD REASON, I EVEN CRIED...
MAYBE IT WAS BECAUSE I KNEW RIGHT AWAY THAT THEATER WAS MY SALVATION.
FROM THAT DAY I *KNEW*...
...MY LIFE BELONGED UP THERE!!
THE STAGE IS THE ONLY PLACE...
...I CAN REALLY BE ***MYSELF!!***

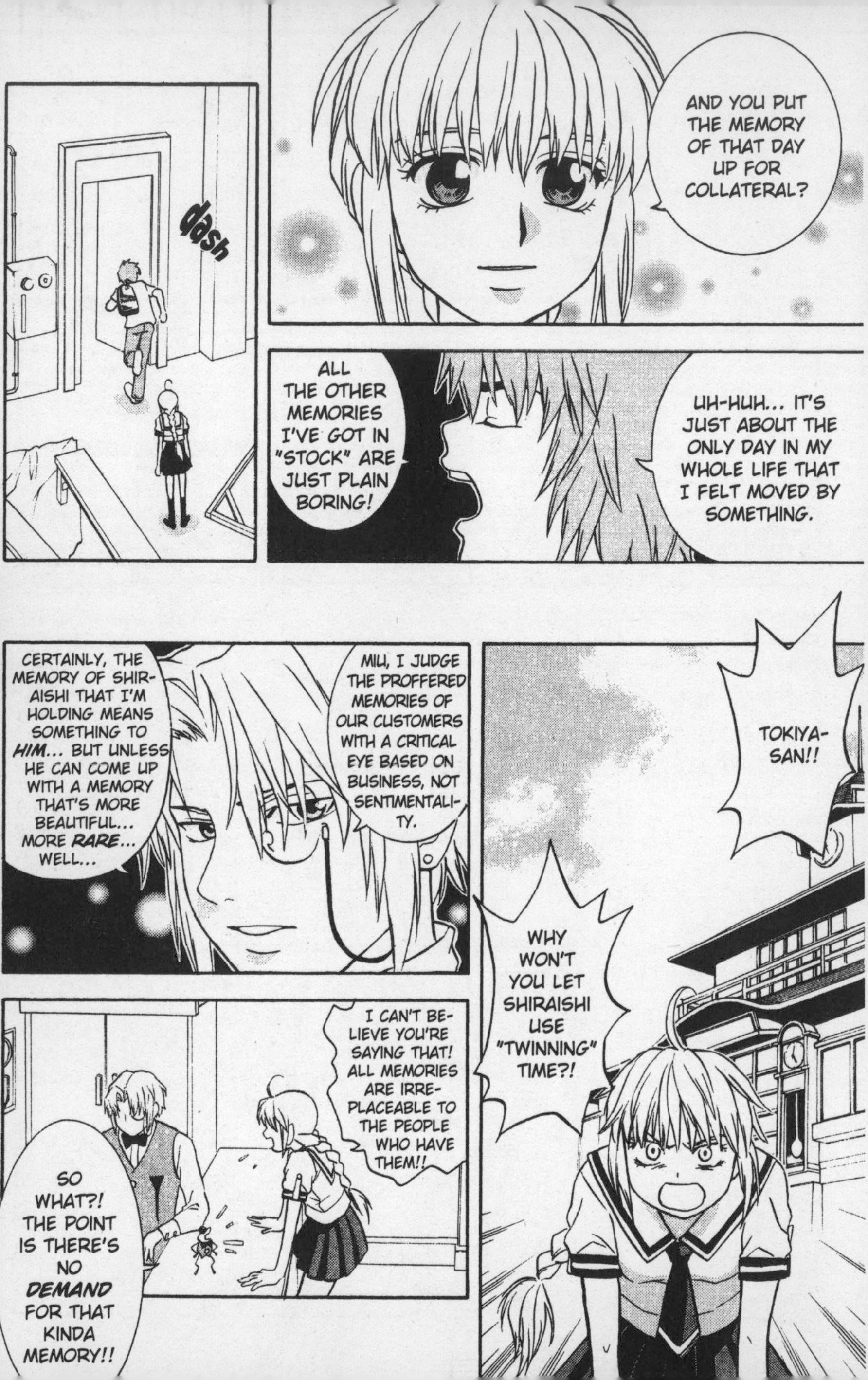
AND YOU PUT THE MEMORY OF THAT DAY UP FOR COLLATERAL?
UH-HUH... IT'S JUST ABOUT THE ONLY DAY IN MY WHOLE LIFE THAT I FELT MOVED BY SOMETHING.
ALL THE OTHER MEMORIES I'VE GOT IN "STOCK" ARE JUST PLAIN BORING!
dash
TOKIYA-SAN!!
WHY WON'T YOU LET SHIRAISHI USE "TWINNING" TIME?!
MIU, I JUDGE THE PROFFERED MEMORIES OF OUR CUSTOMERS WITH A CRITICAL EYE BASED ON BUSINESS, NOT SENTIMENTALI-TY.
CERTAINLY, THE MEMORY OF SHIRAISHI THAT I'M HOLDING MEANS SOMETHING TO *HIM*... BUT UNLESS HE CAN COME UP WITH A MEMORY THAT'S MORE BEAUTIFUL... MORE *RARE*... WELL...
I CAN'T BE-LIEVE YOU'RE SAYING THAT! ALL MEMORIES ARE IRRE-PLACEABLE TO THE PEOPLE WHO HAVE THEM!!
SO WHAT?! THE POINT IS THERE'S NO *DEMAND* FOR THAT KINDA MEMORY!!

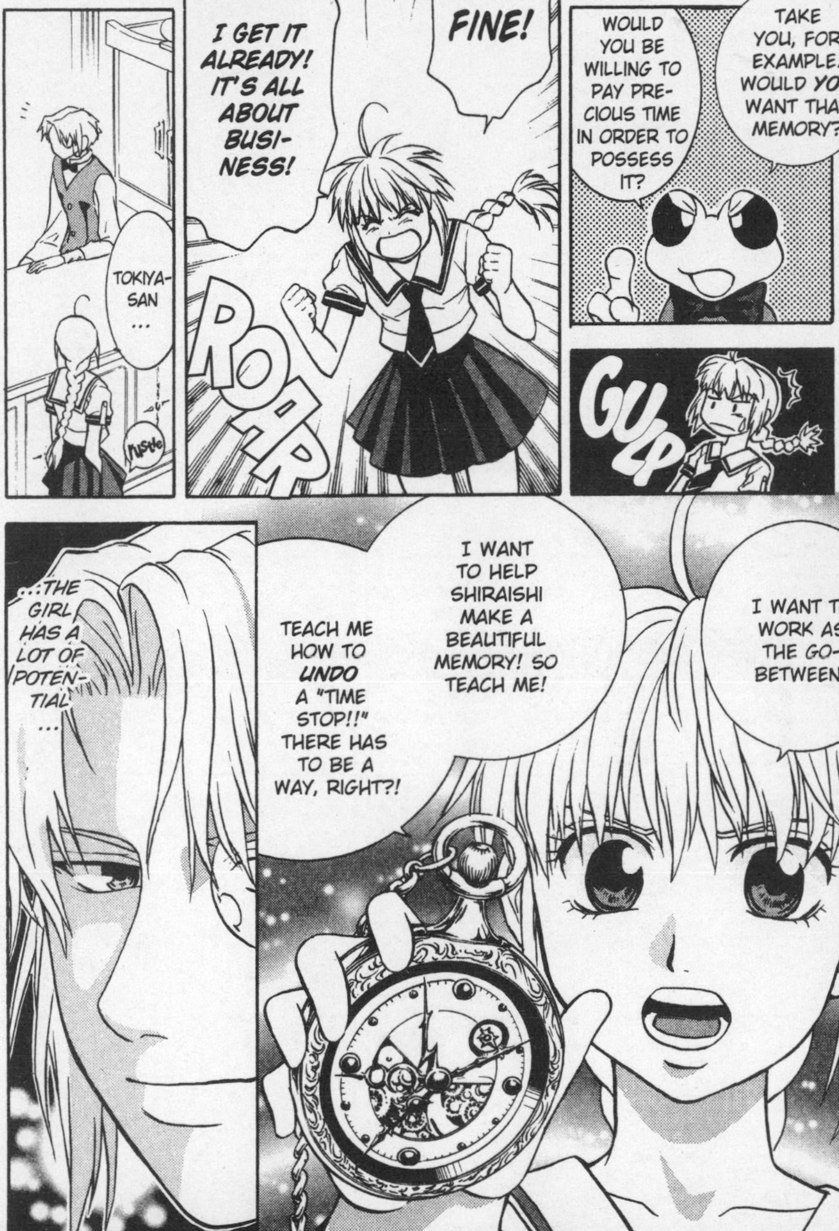
TAKE YOU, FOR EXAMPLE. WOULD YOU WANT THAT MEMORY?
WOULD YOU BE WILLING TO PAY PRECIOUS TIME IN ORDER TO POSSESS IT?
GULP
FINE!
I GET IT ALREADY! IT'S ALL ABOUT BUSINESS!
ROAR
TOKIYA-SAN ...
rustle
I WANT TO WORK AS THE GO-BETWEEN!
I WANT TO HELP SHIRAISHI MAKE A BEAUTIFUL MEMORY! SO TEACH ME!
TEACH ME HOW TO UNDO A "TIME STOP!!" THERE HAS TO BE A WAY, RIGHT?!
...THE GIRL HAS A LOT OF POTENTIAL ...

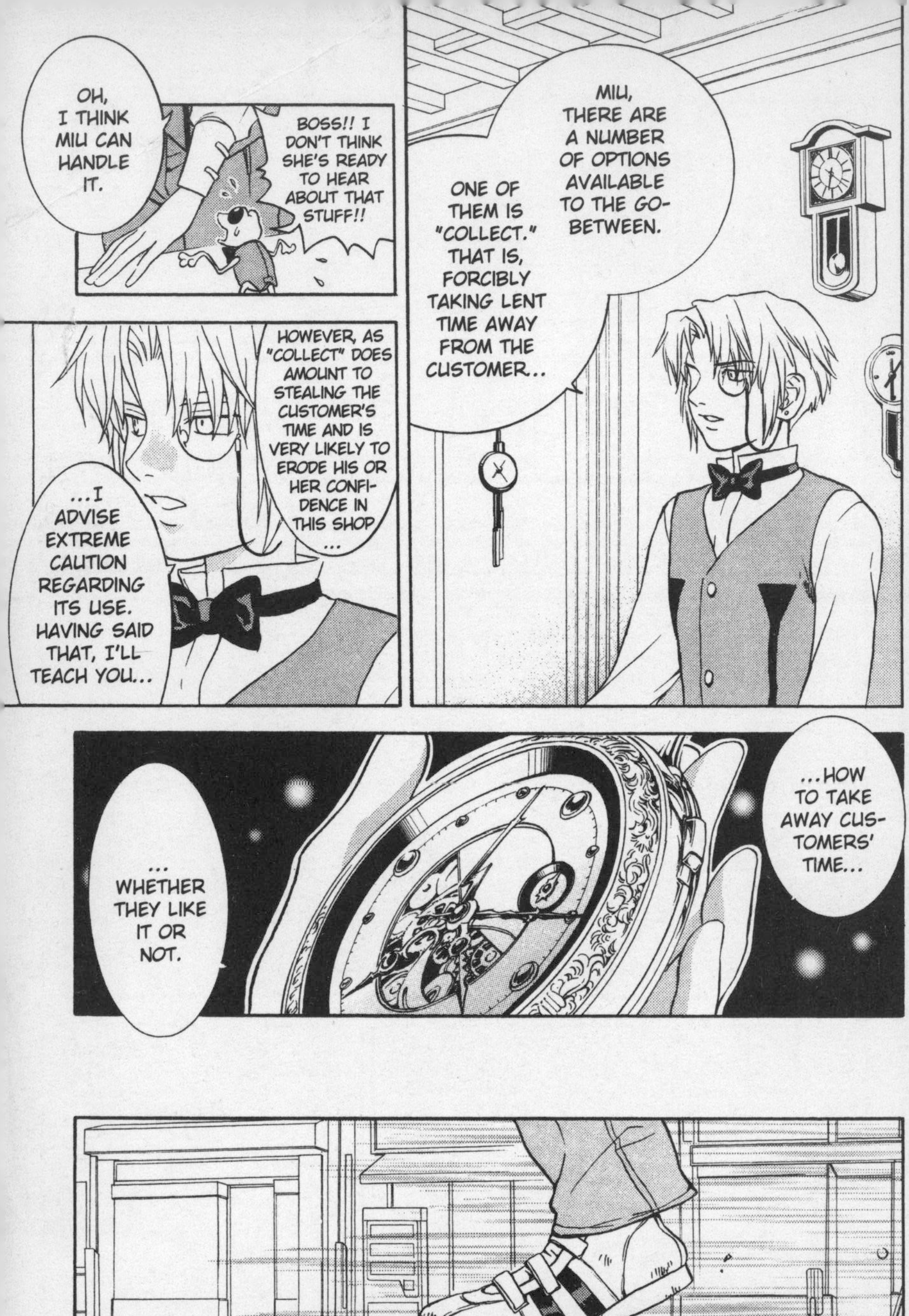
MIU, THERE ARE A NUMBER OF OPTIONS AVAILABLE TO THE GO-BETWEEN.
ONE OF THEM IS "COLLECT." THAT IS, FORCIBLY TAKING LENT TIME AWAY FROM THE CUSTOMER...
BOSS!! I DON'T THINK SHE'S READY TO HEAR ABOUT THAT STUFF!!
OH, I THINK MIU CAN HANDLE IT.
HOWEVER, AS "COLLECT" DOES AMOUNT TO STEALING THE CUSTOMER'S TIME AND IS VERY LIKELY TO ERODE HIS OR HER CONFIDENCE IN THIS SHOP...
...I ADVISE EXTREME CAUTION REGARDING ITS USE. HAVING SAID THAT, I'LL TEACH YOU...
...HOW TO TAKE AWAY CUSTOMERS' TIME...
...WHETHER THEY LIKE IT OR NOT.

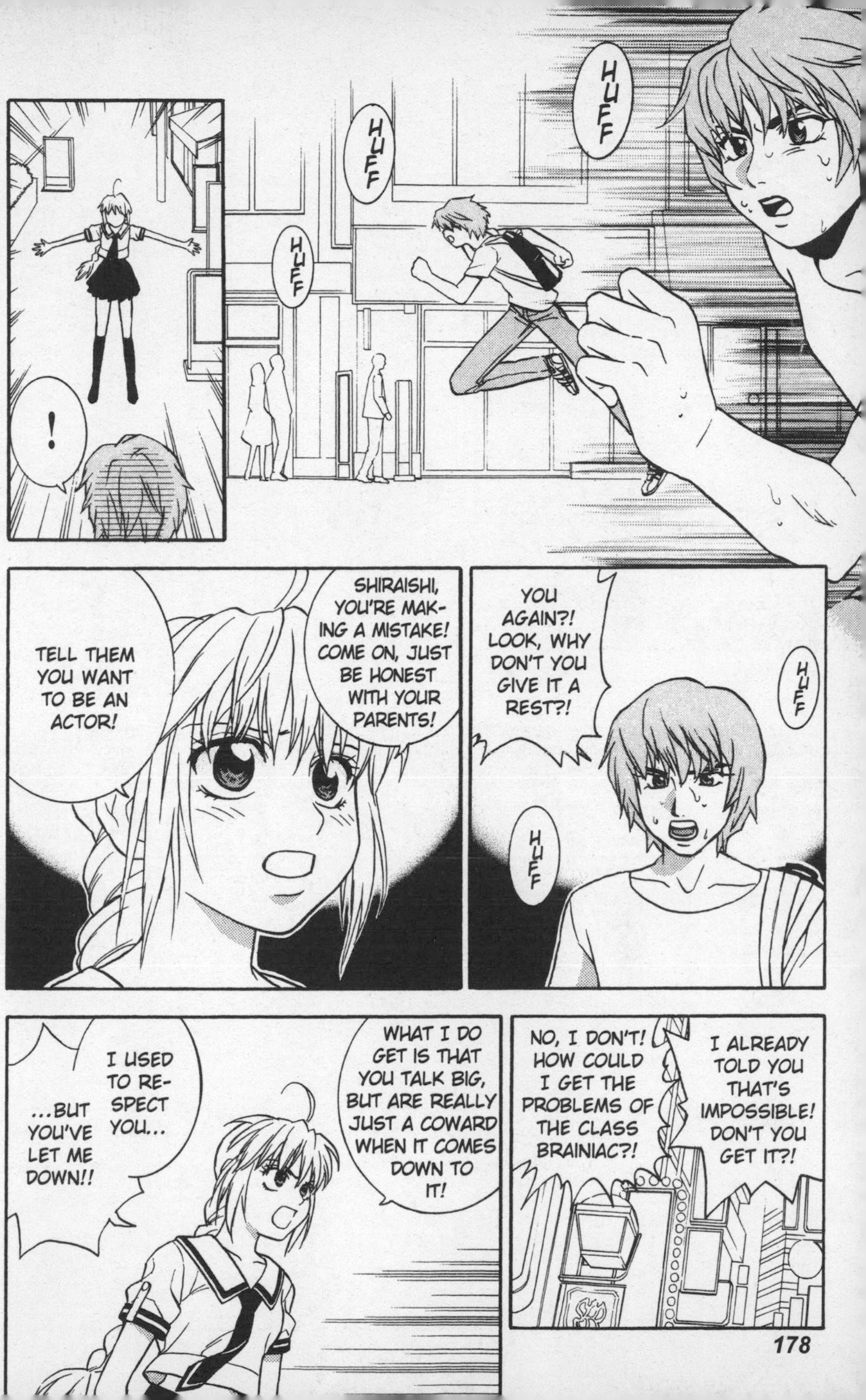
HUFF
HUFF
HUFF
!
HUFF
YOU AGAIN?! LOOK, WHY DON'T YOU GIVE IT A REST?!
HUFF
SHIRAISHI, YOU'RE MAKING A MISTAKE! COME ON, JUST BE HONEST WITH YOUR PARENTS!
TELL THEM YOU WANT TO BE AN ACTOR!
I ALREADY TOLD YOU THAT'S IMPOSSIBLE! DON'T YOU GET IT?!
NO, I DON'T! HOW COULD I GET THE PROBLEMS OF THE CLASS BRAINIAC?!
WHAT I DO GET IS THAT YOU TALK BIG, BUT ARE REALLY JUST A COWARD WHEN IT COMES DOWN TO IT!
I USED TO RESPECT YOU...
...BUT YOU'VE LET ME DOWN!!

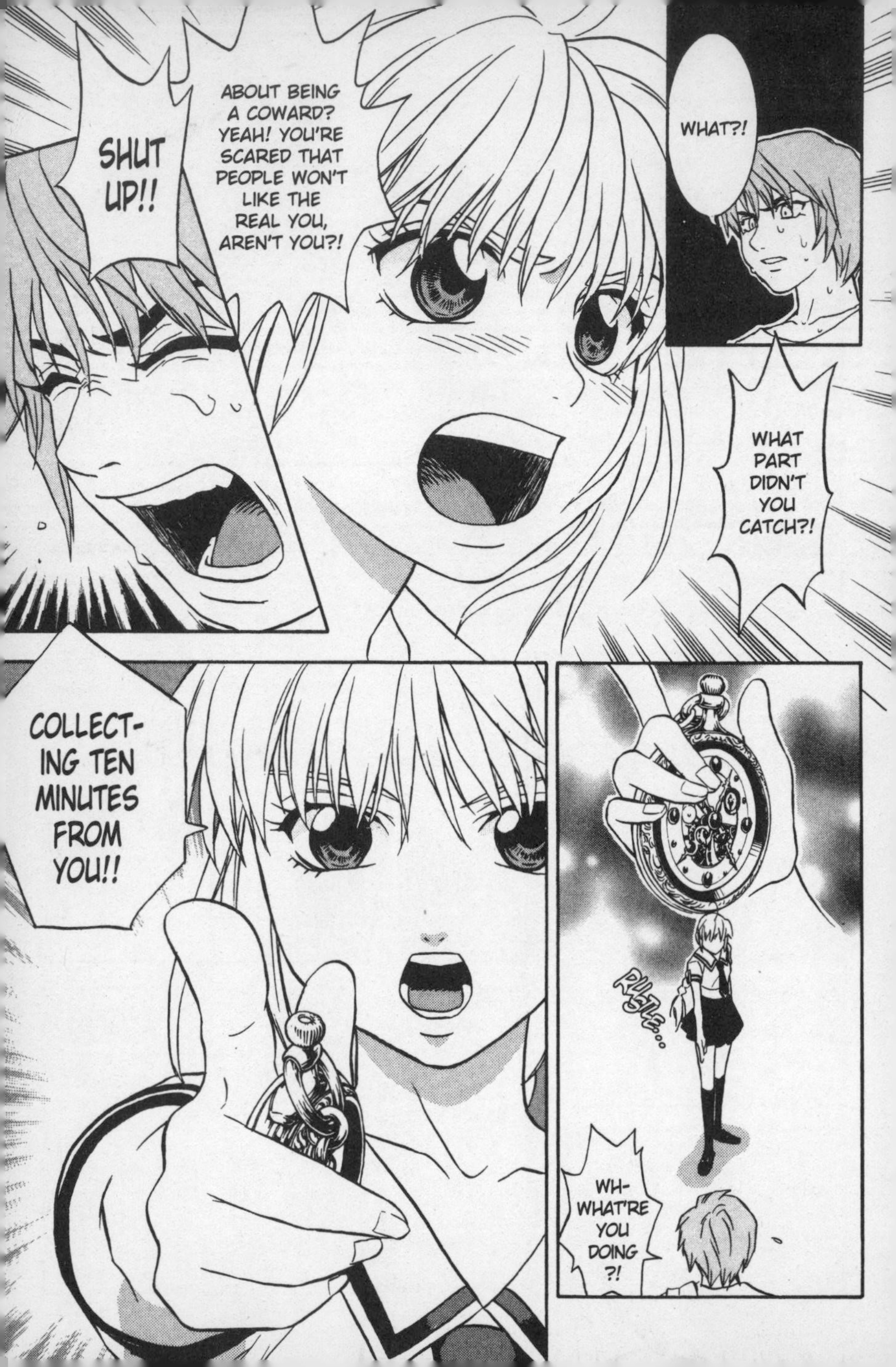
WHAT?!
WHAT PART DIDN'T YOU CATCH?!
ABOUT BEING A COWARD? YEAH! YOU'RE SCARED THAT PEOPLE WON'T LIKE THE REAL YOU, AREN'T YOU?!
SHUT UP!!
RUSTLE...
WH-WHAT'RE YOU DOING ?!
COLLECT-ING TEN MINUTES FROM YOU!!

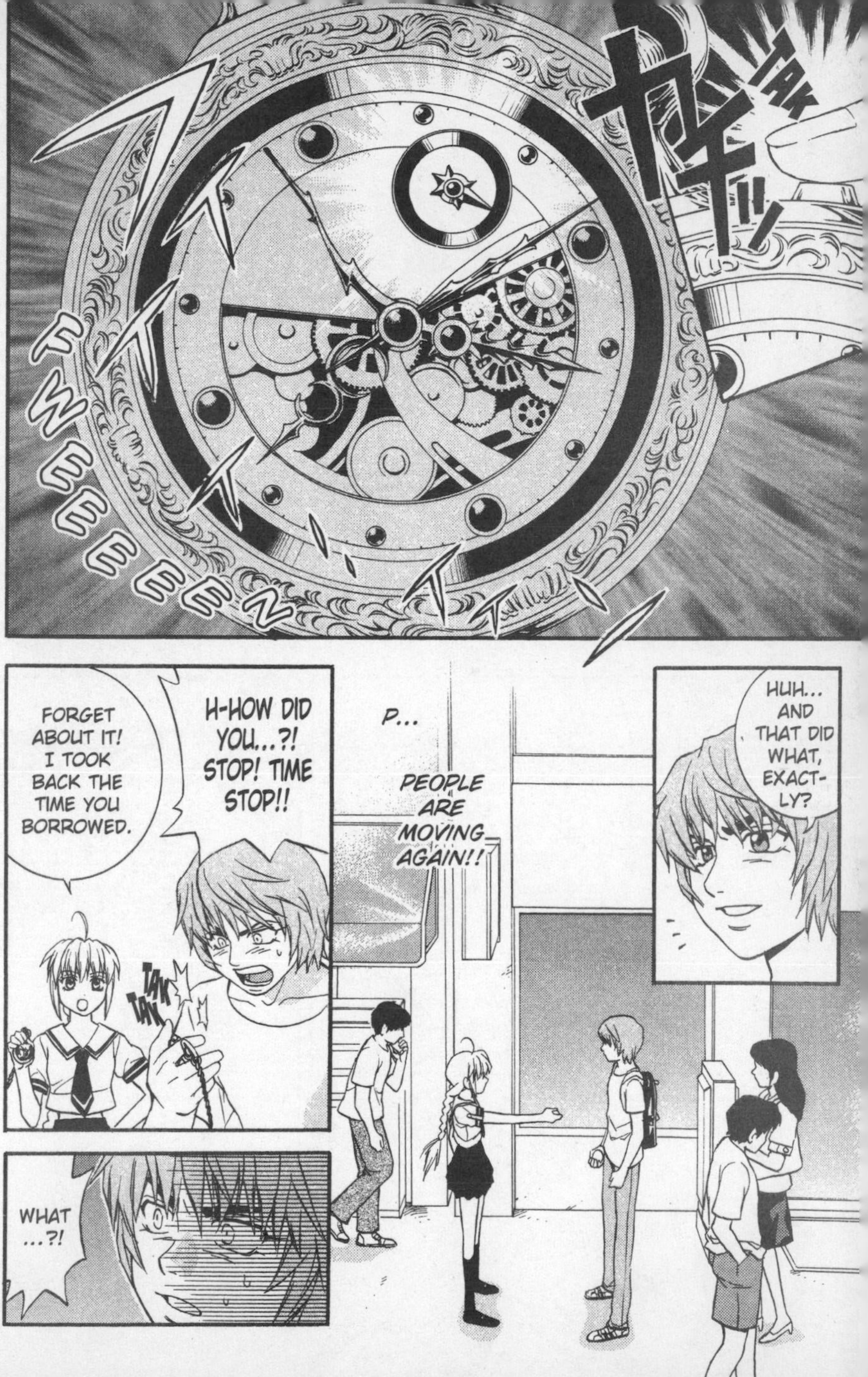
TAK
FWEEEEN
HUH... AND THAT DID WHAT, EXACTLY?
P...
PEOPLE ARE MOVING AGAIN!!
H-HOW DID YOU...?! STOP! TIME STOP!!
FORGET ABOUT IT! I TOOK BACK THE TIME YOU BORROWED.
TAK TAK
WHAT ...?!

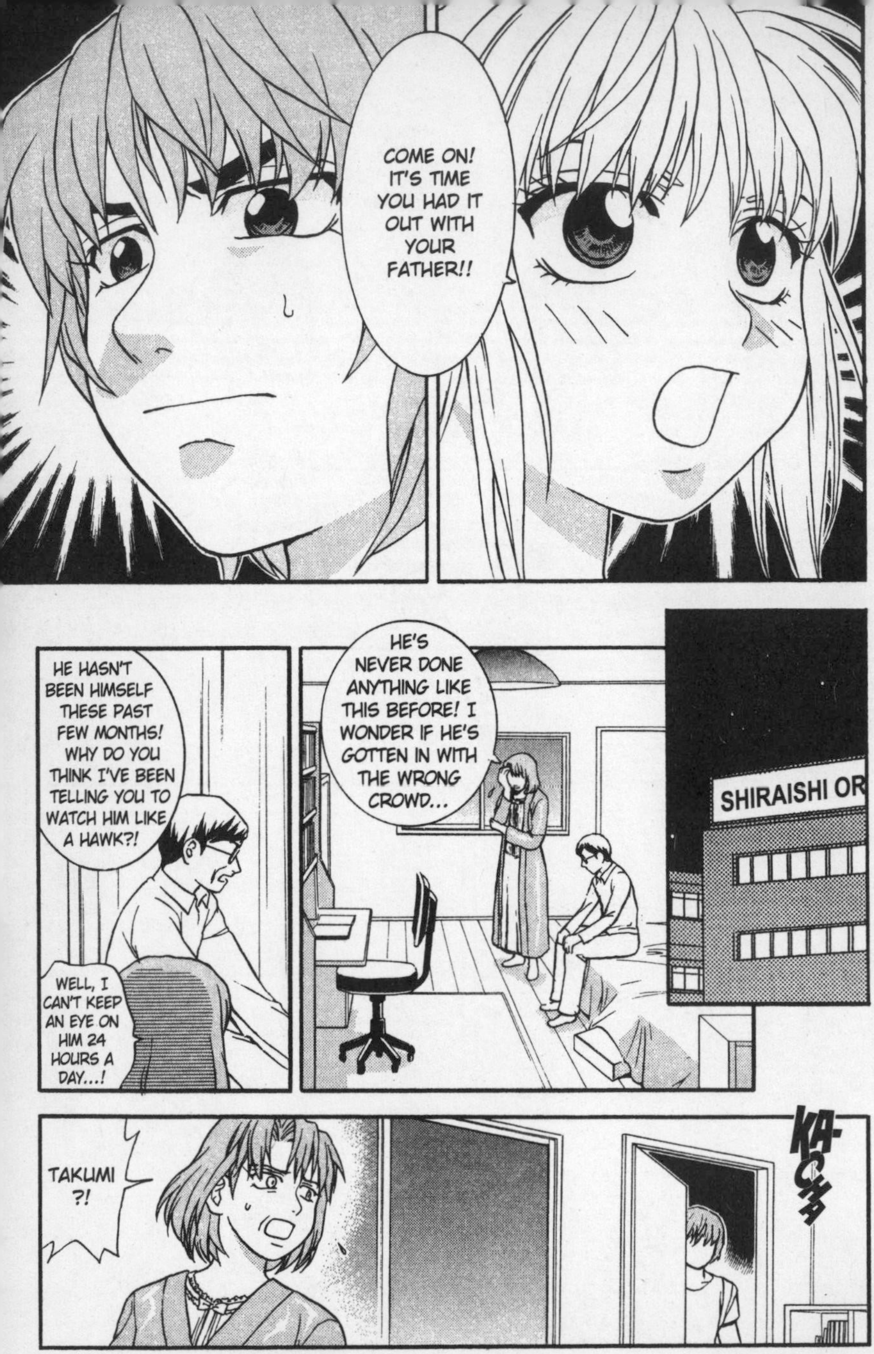
COME ON! IT'S TIME YOU HAD IT OUT WITH YOUR FATHER!!
SHIRAISHI OR
HE'S NEVER DONE ANYTHING LIKE THIS BEFORE! I WONDER IF HE'S GOTTEN IN WITH THE WRONG CROWD...
HE HASN'T BEEN HIMSELF THESE PAST FEW MONTHS! WHY DO YOU THINK I'VE BEEN TELLING YOU TO WATCH HIM LIKE A HAWK?!
WELL, I CAN'T KEEP AN EYE ON HIM 24 HOURS A DAY...!
KA-CHA
TAKUMI?!

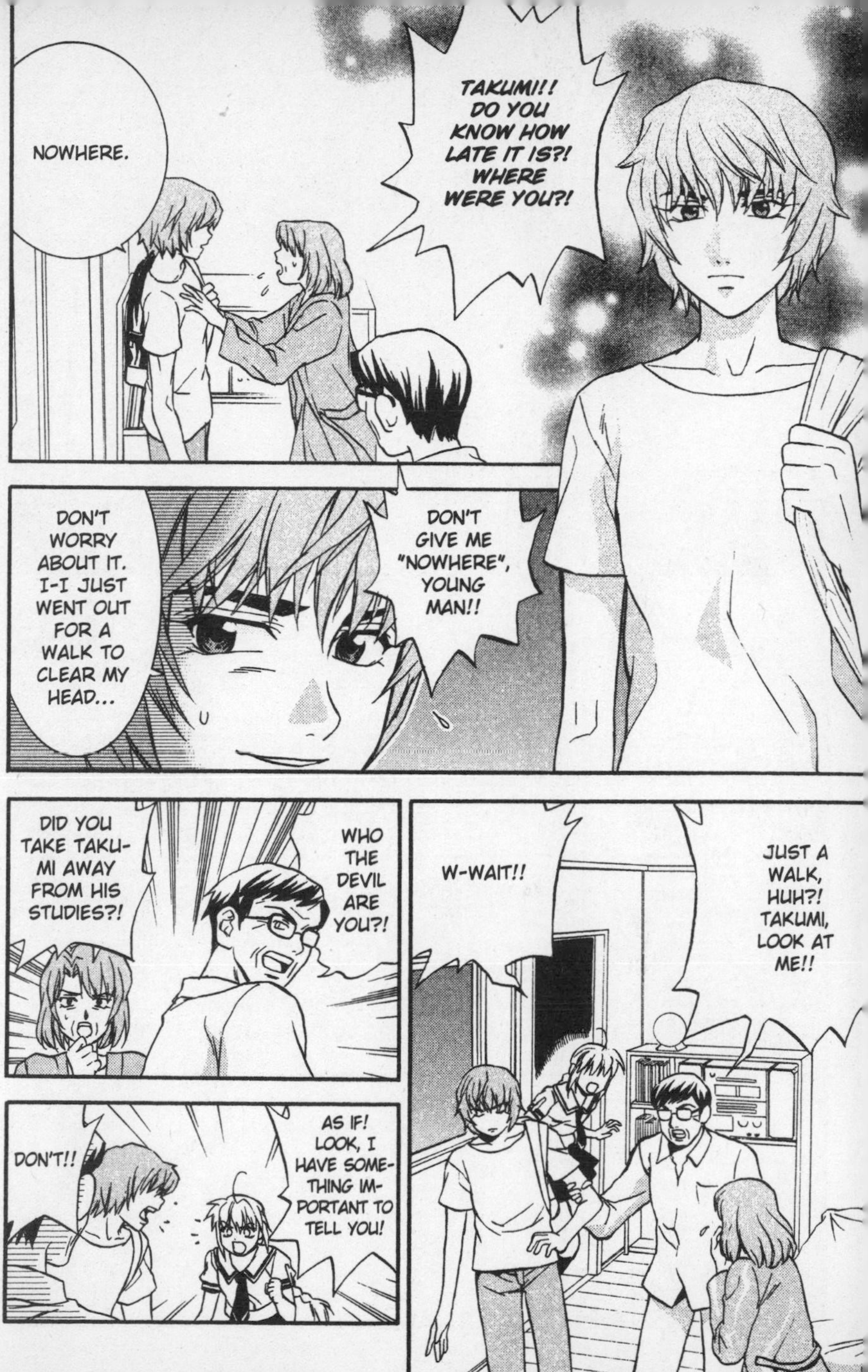
TAKUMI!! DO YOU KNOW HOW LATE IT IS?! WHERE WERE YOU?!
NOWHERE.
DON'T GIVE ME "NOWHERE", YOUNG MAN!!
DON'T WORRY ABOUT IT. I-I JUST WENT OUT FOR A WALK TO CLEAR MY HEAD...
JUST A WALK, HUH?! TAKUMI, LOOK AT ME!!
W-WAIT!!
WHO THE DEVIL ARE YOU?!
DID YOU TAKE TAKU-MI AWAY FROM HIS STUDIES?!
AS IF! LOOK, I HAVE SOME-THING IM-PORTANT TO TELL YOU!
DON'T!!

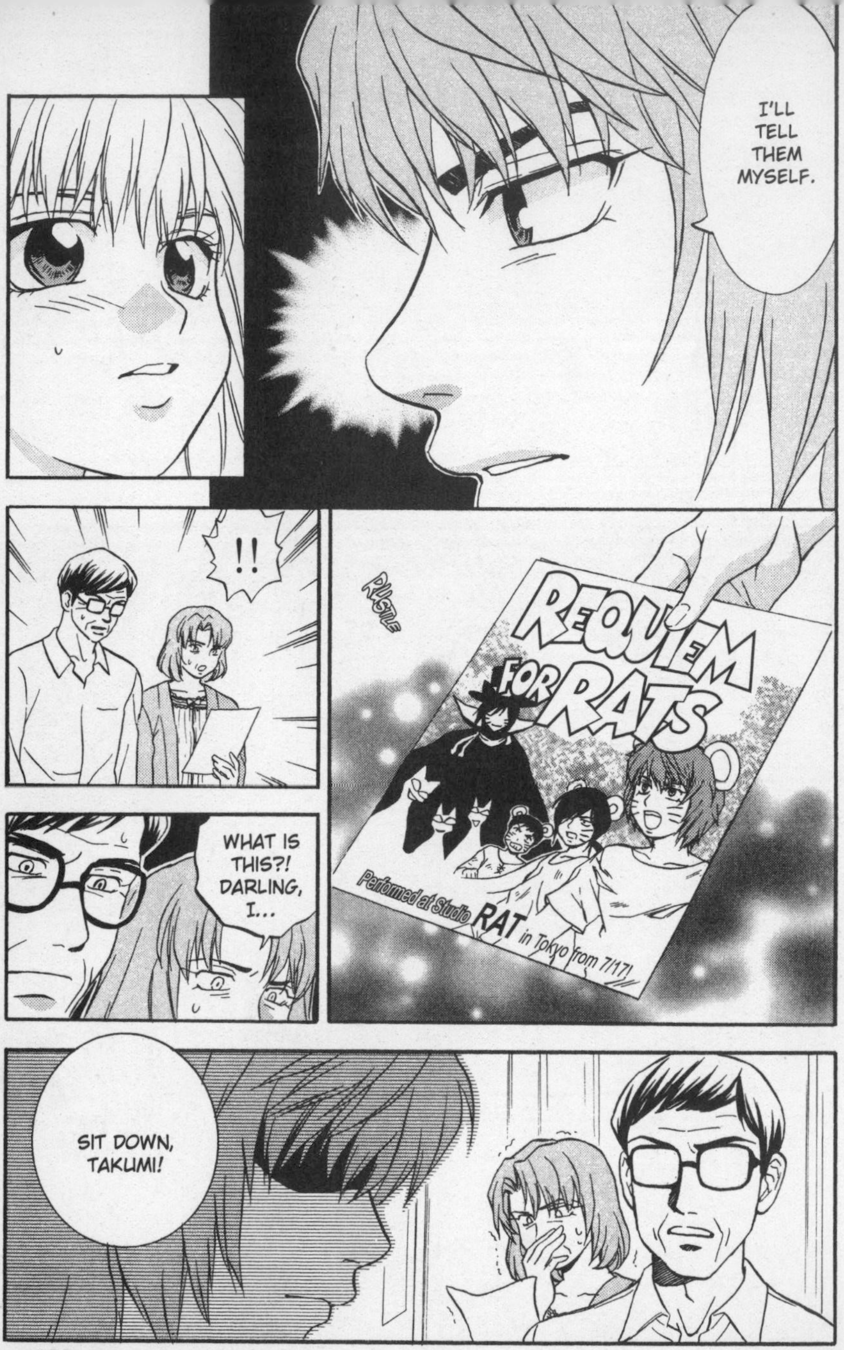
I'LL TELL THEM MYSELF.
RUSTLE
REQUIEM FOR RATS
Performed at Studio RAT in Tokyo from 7/17!
!!
WHAT IS THIS?! DARLING, I...
SIT DOWN, TAKUMI!

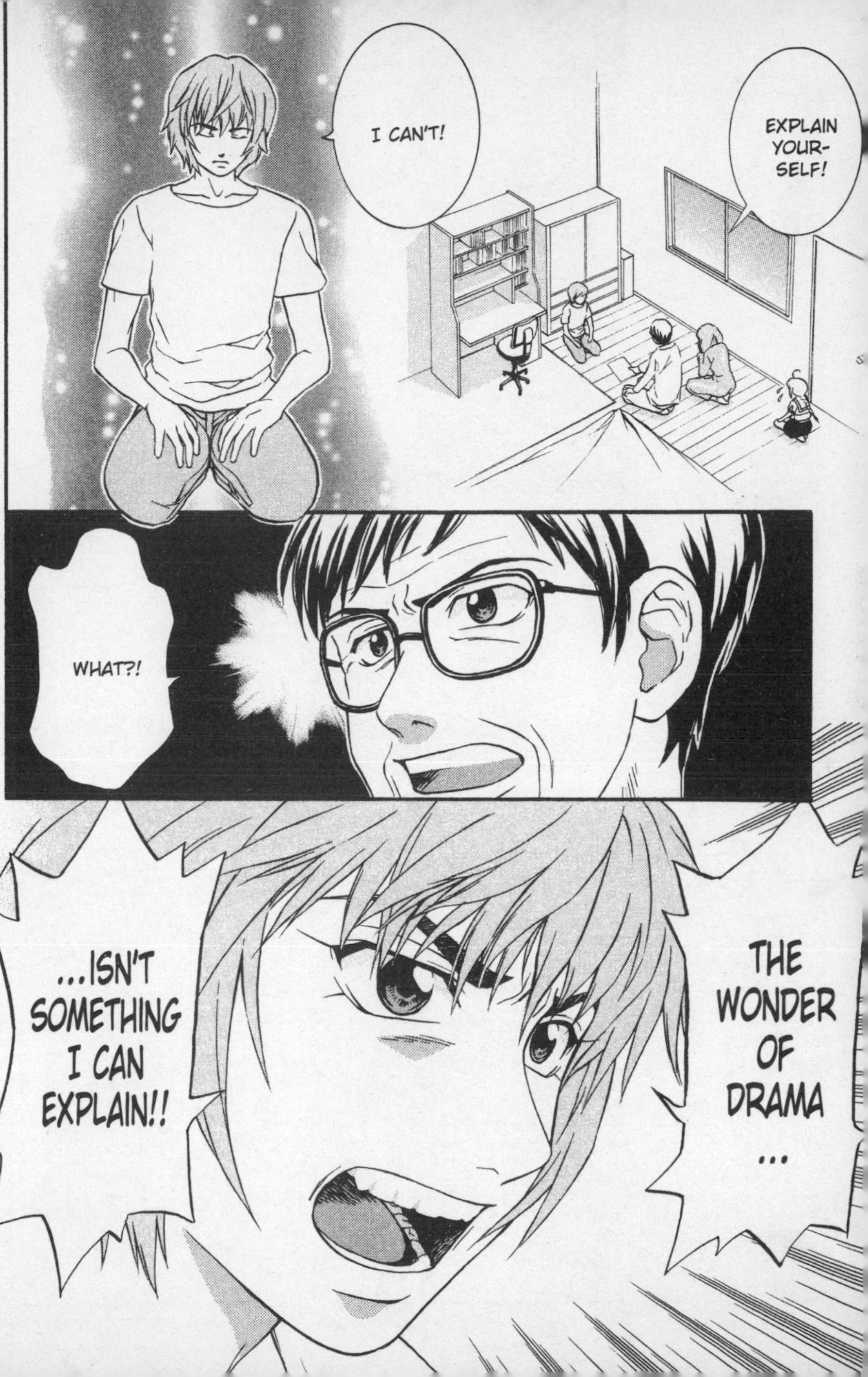
EXPLAIN YOUR-SELF!
I CAN'T!
WHAT?!
THE WONDER OF DRAMA...
...ISN'T SOMETHING I CAN EXPLAIN!!

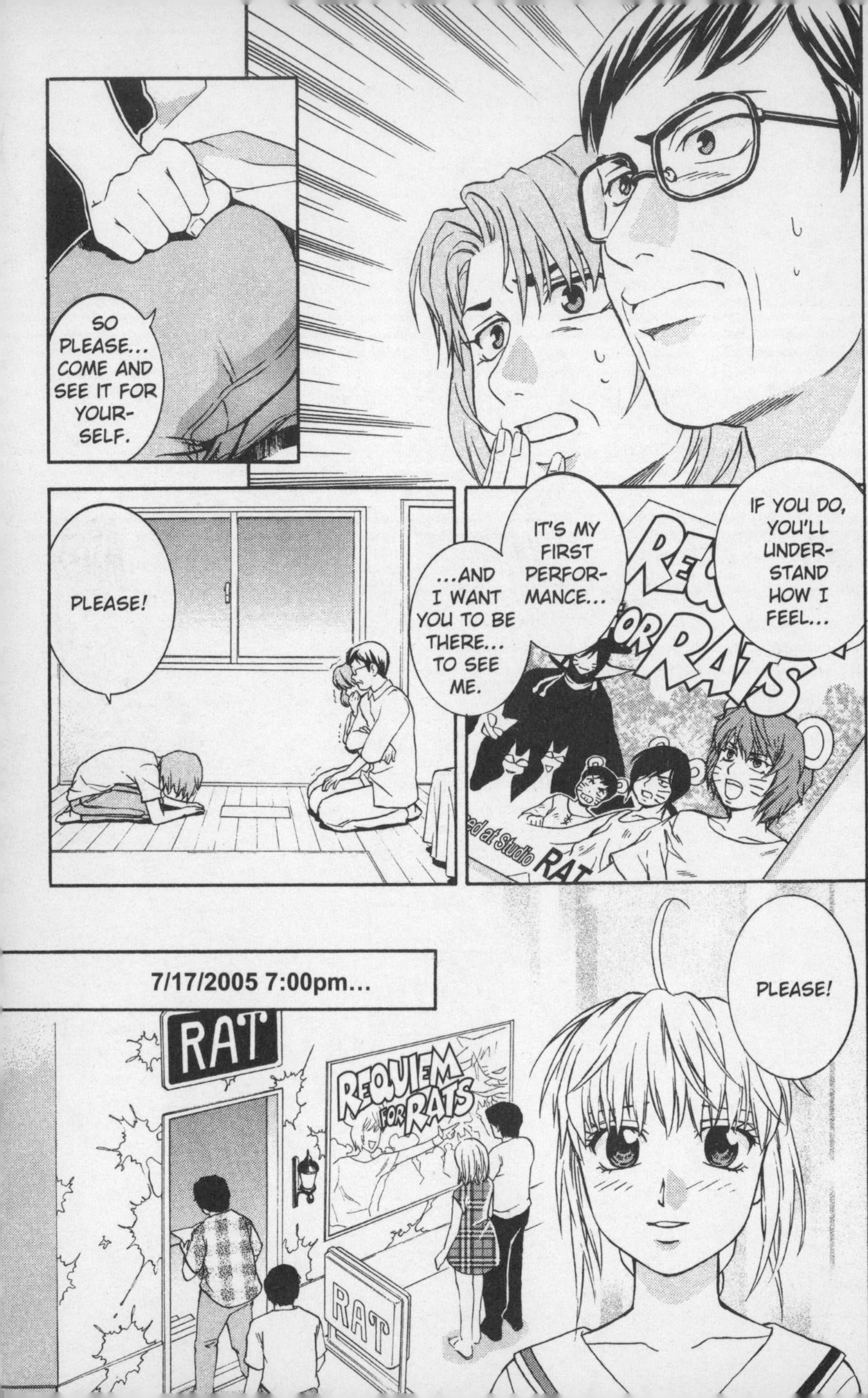

SO PLEASE... COME AND SEE IT FOR YOUR-SELF.
IF YOU DO, YOU'LL UNDER-STAND HOW I FEEL...
IT'S MY FIRST PERFOR-MANCE...
...AND I WANT YOU TO BE THERE... TO SEE ME.
REQUIEM FOR RATS
ed at Studio RAT
PLEASE!
PLEASE!
7/17/2005 7:00pm...
RAT
REQUIEM FOR RATS
RAT

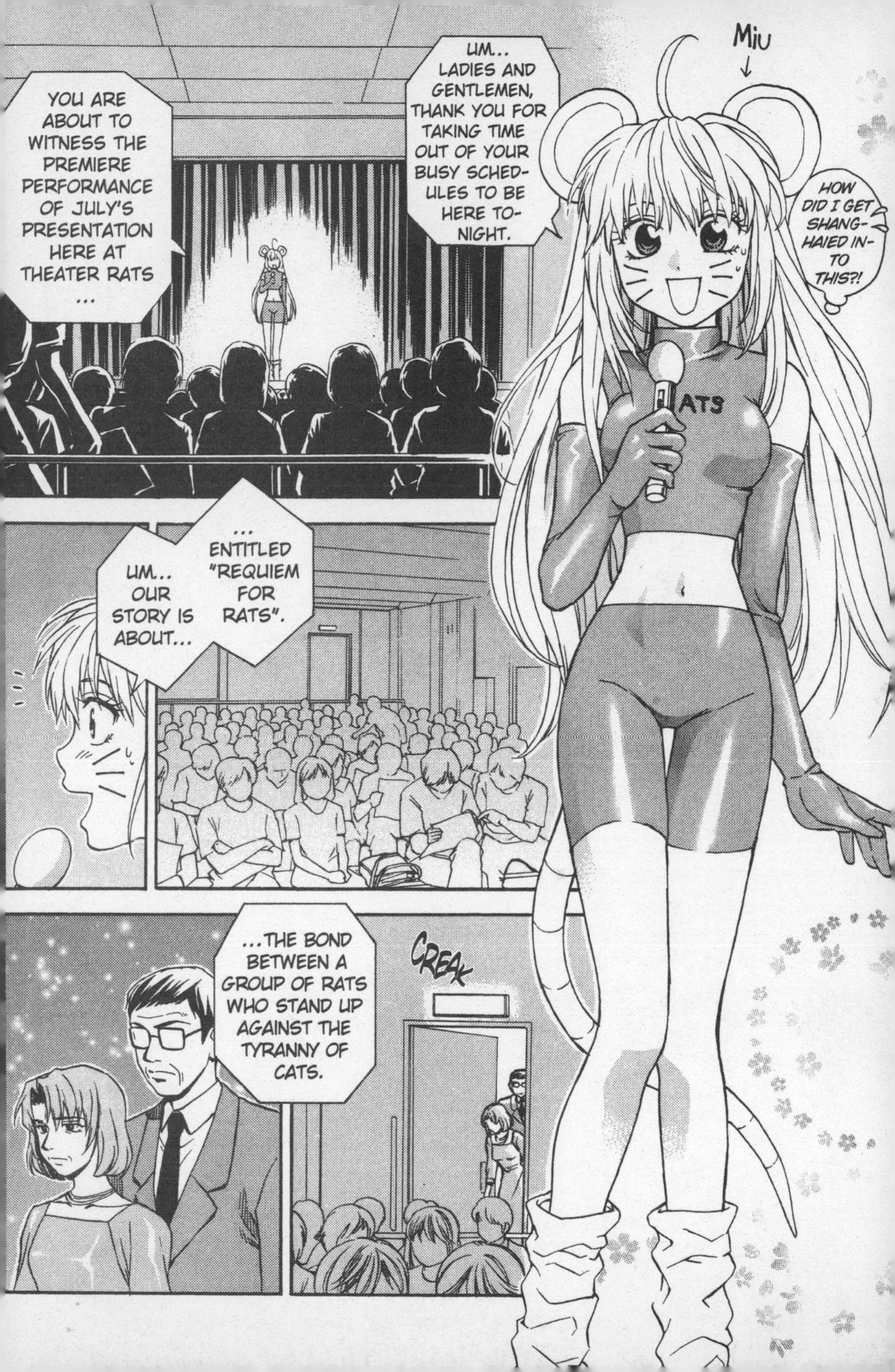

MIU
HOW DID I GET SHANGHAIED INTO THIS?!
UM... LADIES AND GENTLEMEN, THANK YOU FOR TAKING TIME OUT OF YOUR BUSY SCHEDULES TO BE HERE TONIGHT.
YOU ARE ABOUT TO WITNESS THE PREMIERE PERFORMANCE OF JULY'S PRESENTATION HERE AT THEATER RATS ...
... ENTITLED "REQUIEM FOR RATS".
UM... OUR STORY IS ABOUT...
CREAK
...THE BOND BETWEEN A GROUP OF RATS WHO STAND UP AGAINST THE TYRANNY OF CATS.

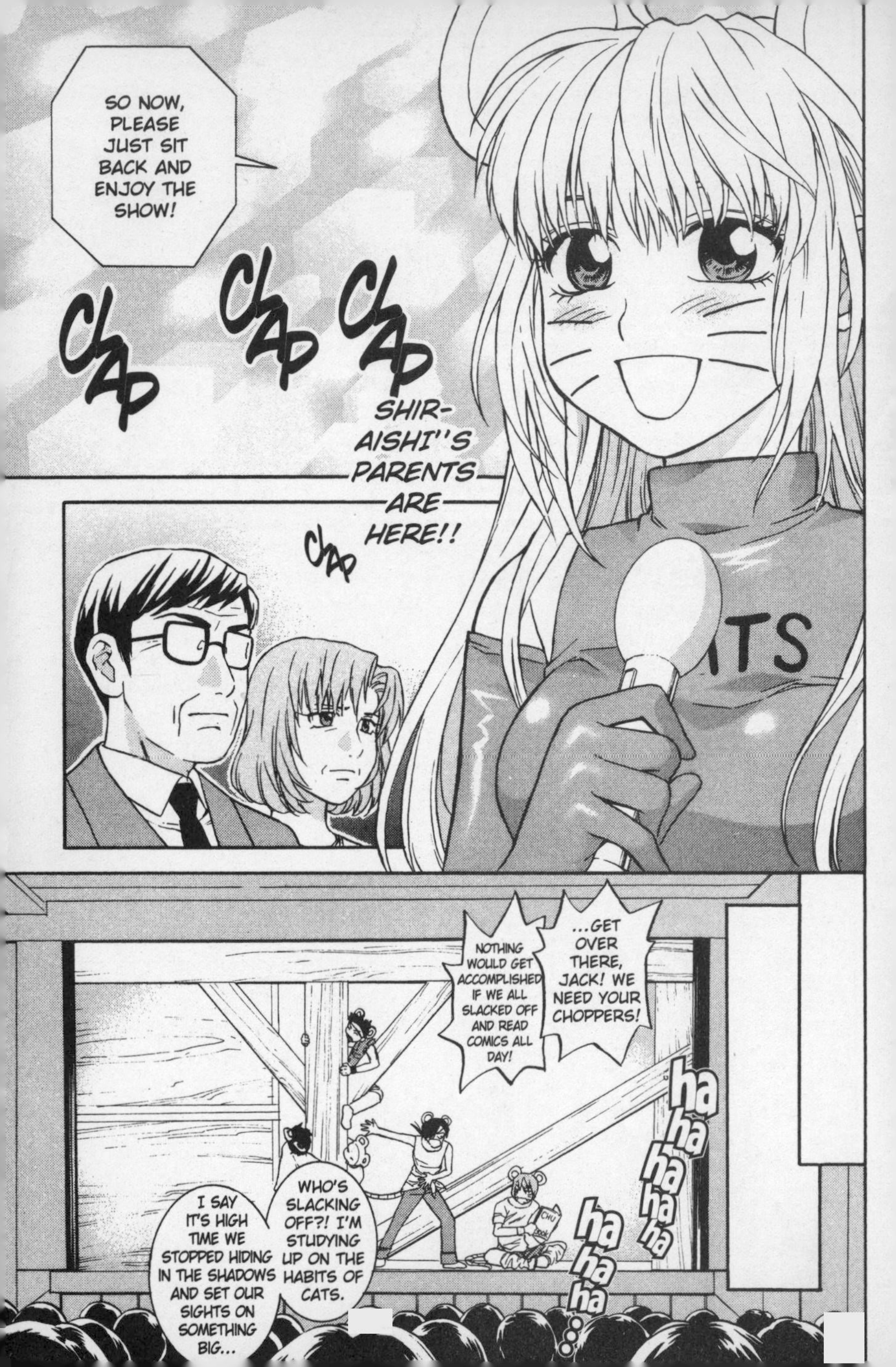
SO NOW, PLEASE JUST SIT BACK AND ENJOY THE SHOW!
CLAP CLAP CLAP
SHIR-AISHI''S PARENTS ARE HERE!!
CLAP
...GET OVER THERE, JACK! WE NEED YOUR CHOPPERS!
NOTHING WOULD GET ACCOMPLISHED IF WE ALL SLACKED OFF AND READ COMICS ALL DAY!
ha ha ha ha ha
ha ha ha...
WHO'S SLACKING OFF?! I'M STUDYING UP ON THE HABITS OF CATS.
I SAY IT'S HIGH TIME WE STOPPED HIDING IN THE SHADOWS AND SET OUR SIGHTS ON SOMETHING BIG...

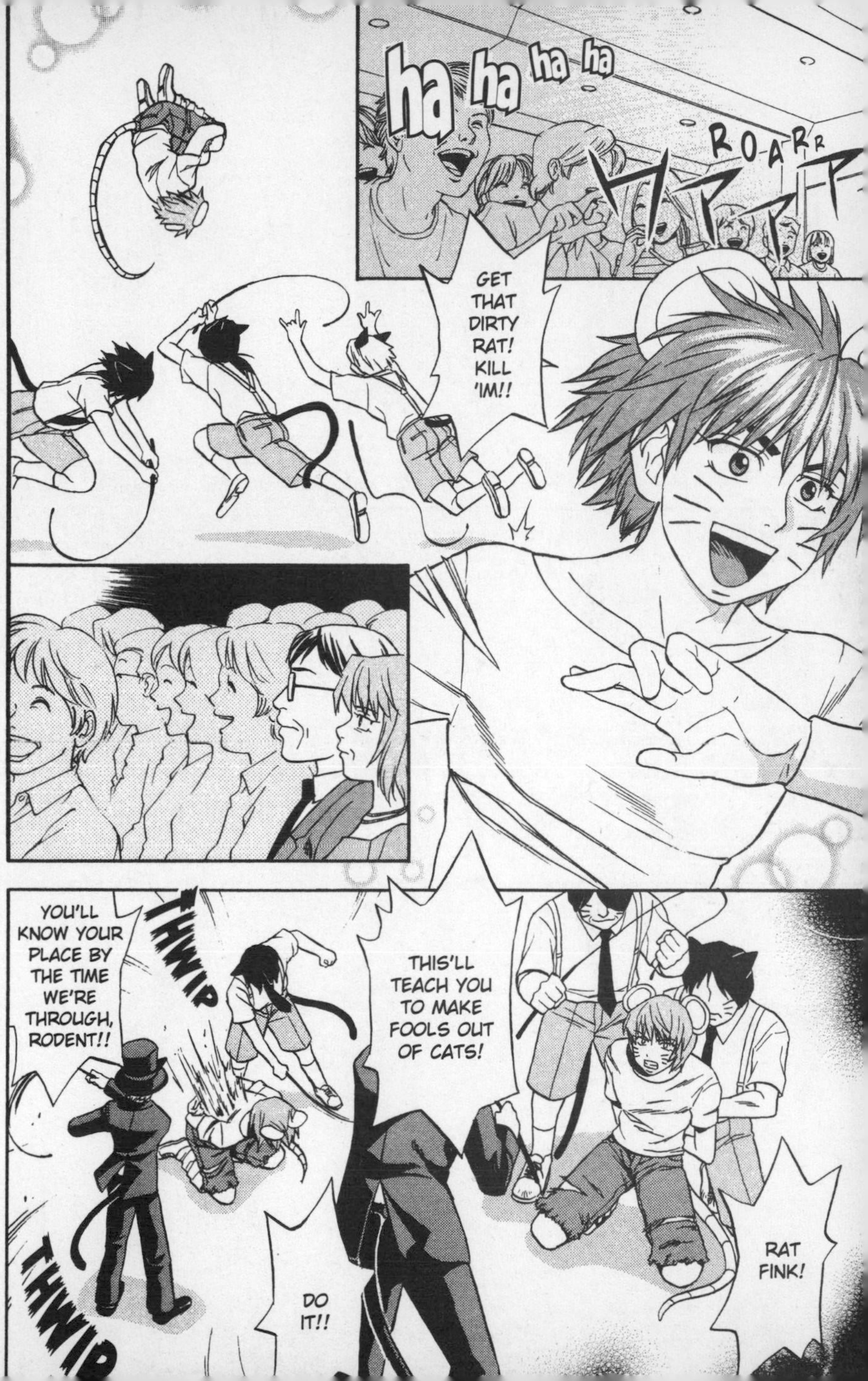

ha ha ha ha
ROARR
GET THAT DIRTY RAT! KILL 'IM!!
RAT FINK!
THIS'LL TEACH YOU TO MAKE FOOLS OUT OF CATS!
DO IT!!
THWIP
YOU'LL KNOW YOUR PLACE BY THE TIME WE'RE THROUGH, RODENT!!
THWIP

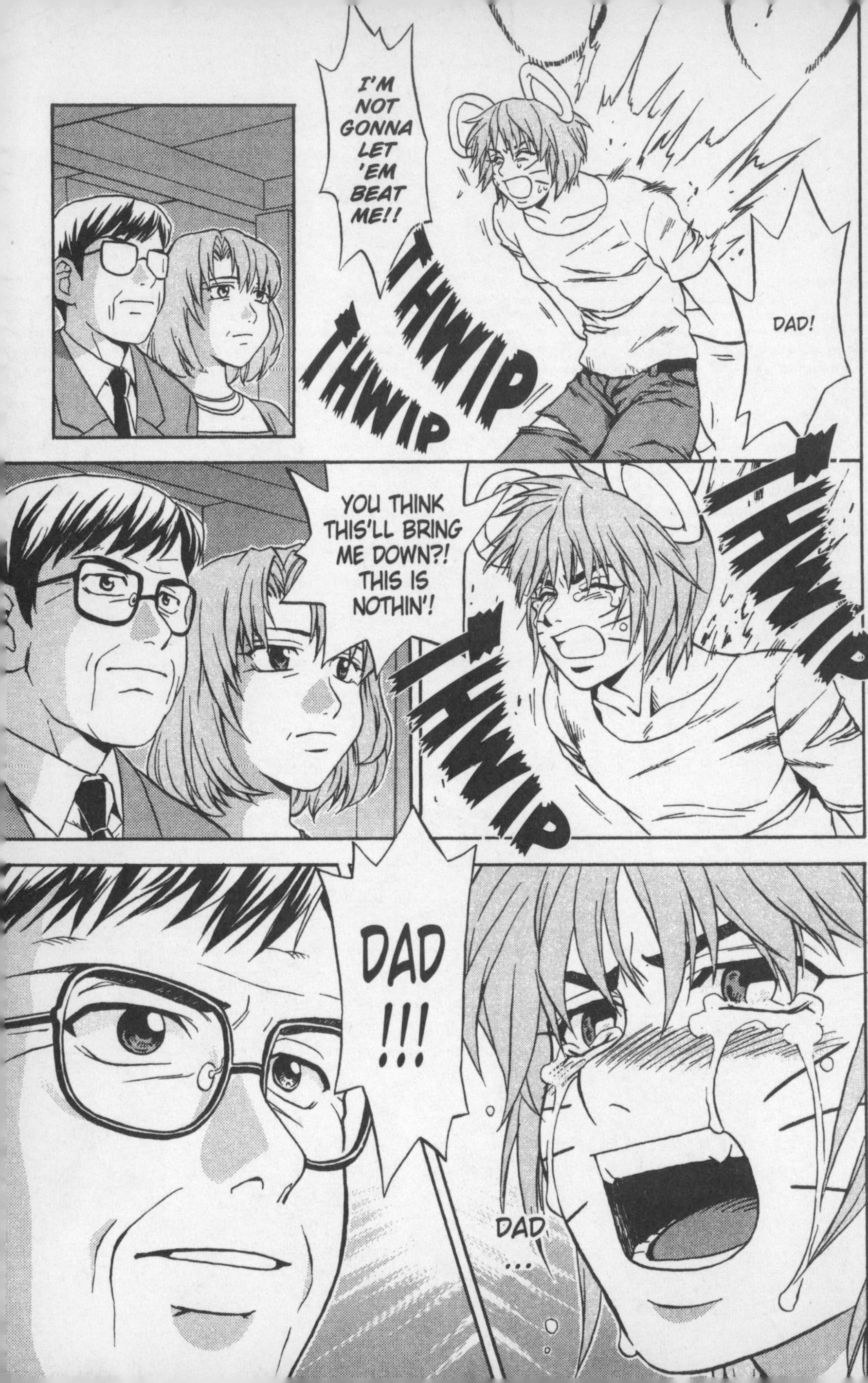
DAD!
I'M NOT GONNA LET 'EM BEAT ME!!
THWIP THWIP
THWIP THWIP
YOU THINK THIS'LL BRING ME DOWN?! THIS IS NOTHIN'!
DAD ...
DAD !!!

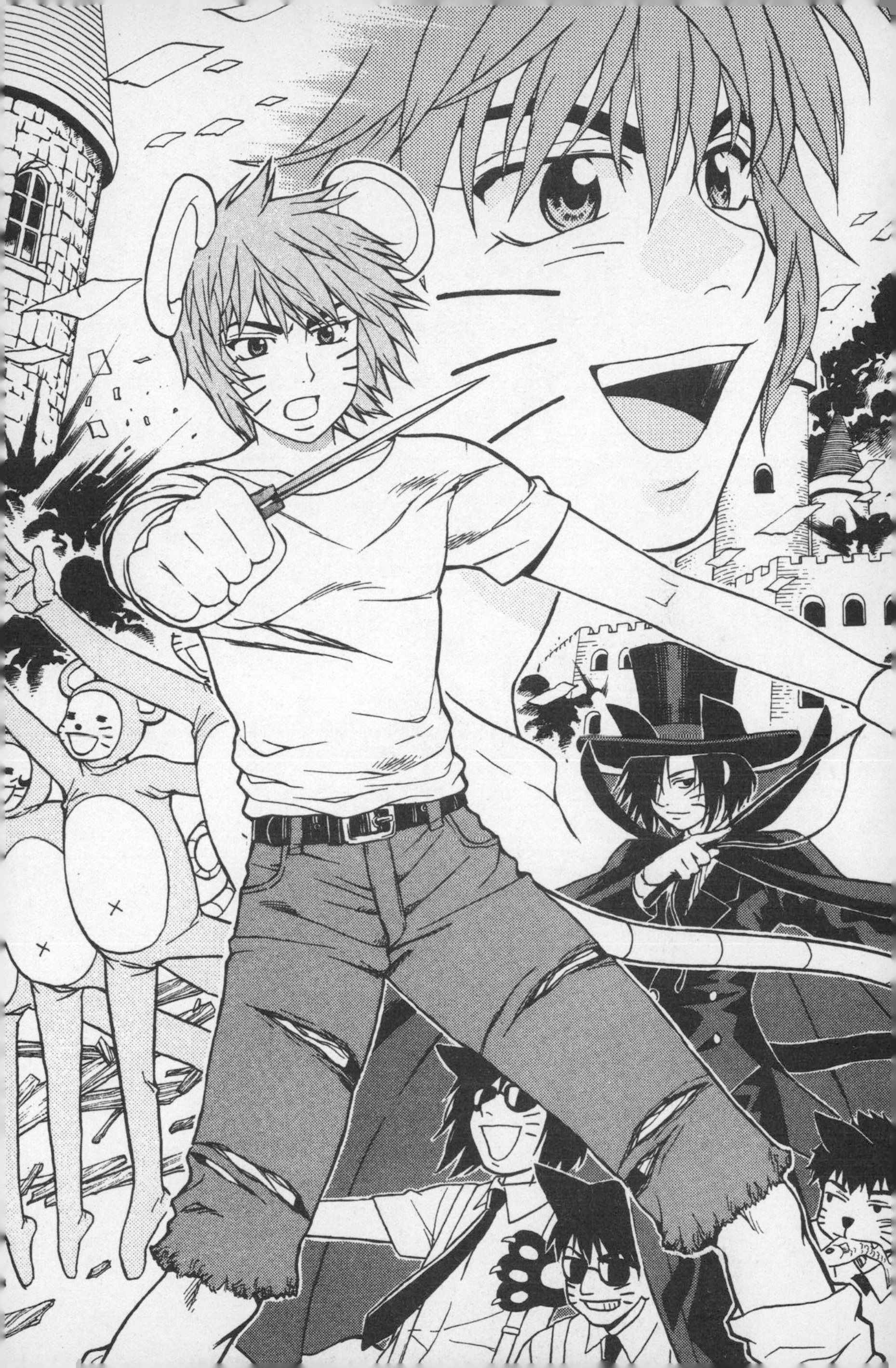

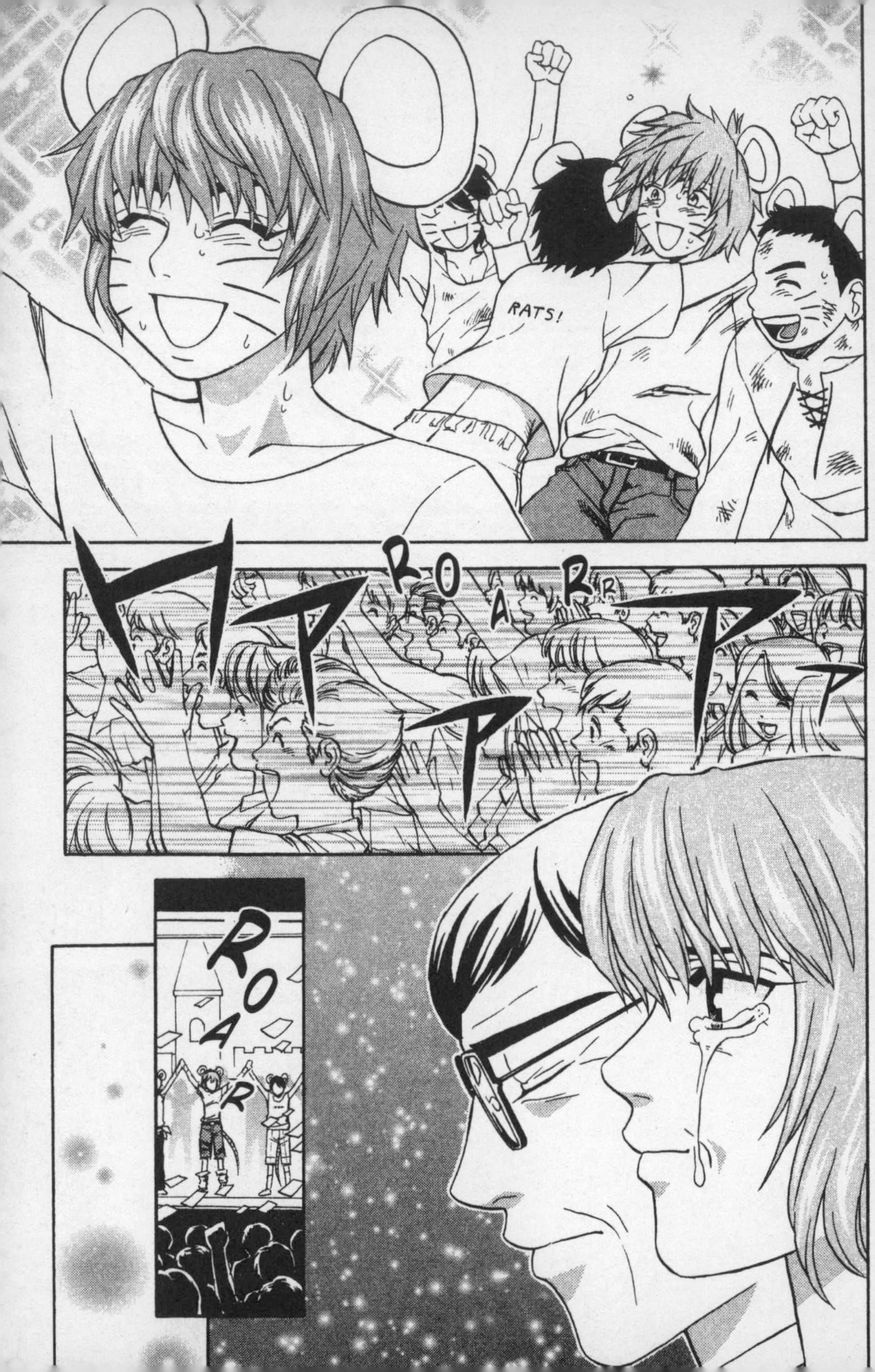
RATS!
ROARR
ROAR

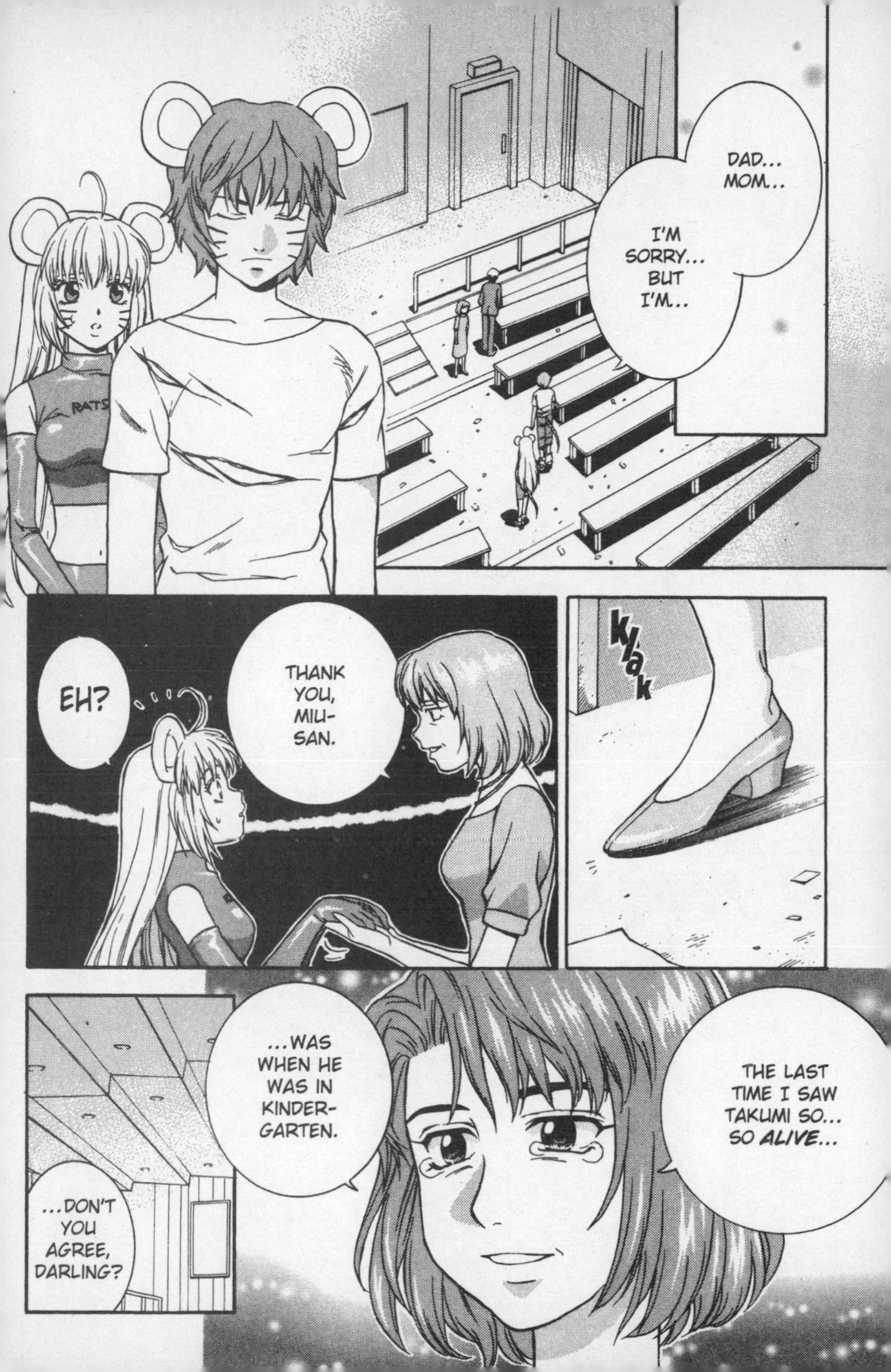
DAD... MOM...
I'M SORRY... BUT I'M...
KLAK
THANK YOU, MIU-SAN.
EH?
THE LAST TIME I SAW TAKUMI SO... SO ALIVE...
...WAS WHEN HE WAS IN KINDERGARTEN.
...DON'T YOU AGREE, DARLING?

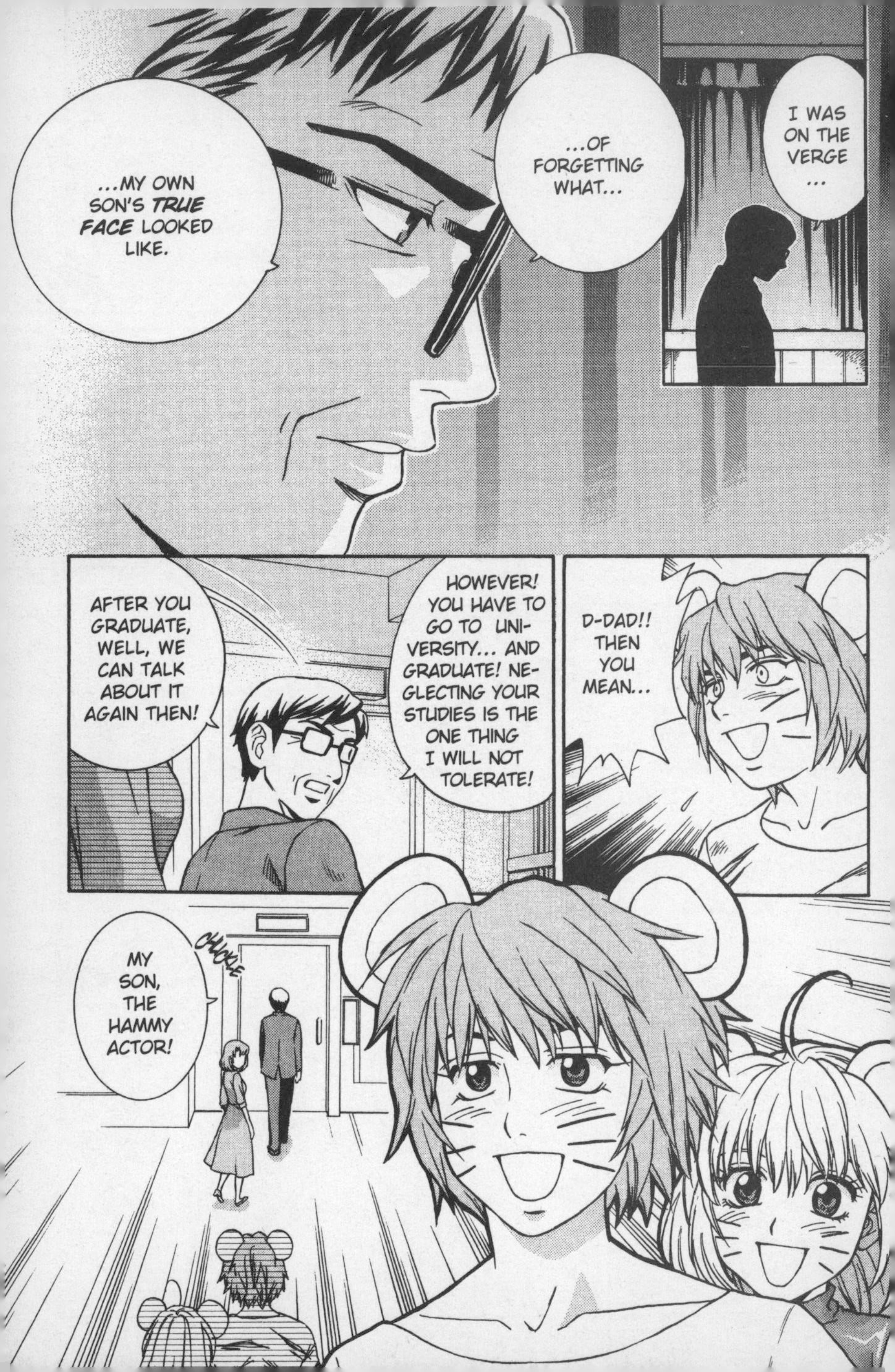
I WAS ON THE VERGE ...
...OF FORGETTING WHAT...
...MY OWN SON'S TRUE FACE LOOKED LIKE.
D-DAD!! THEN YOU MEAN...
HOWEVER! YOU HAVE TO GO TO UNI-VERSITY... AND GRADUATE! NE-GLECTING YOUR STUDIES IS THE ONE THING I WILL NOT TOLERATE!
AFTER YOU GRADUATE, WELL, WE CAN TALK ABOUT IT AGAIN THEN!
CHUCKLE
MY SON, THE HAMMY ACTOR!

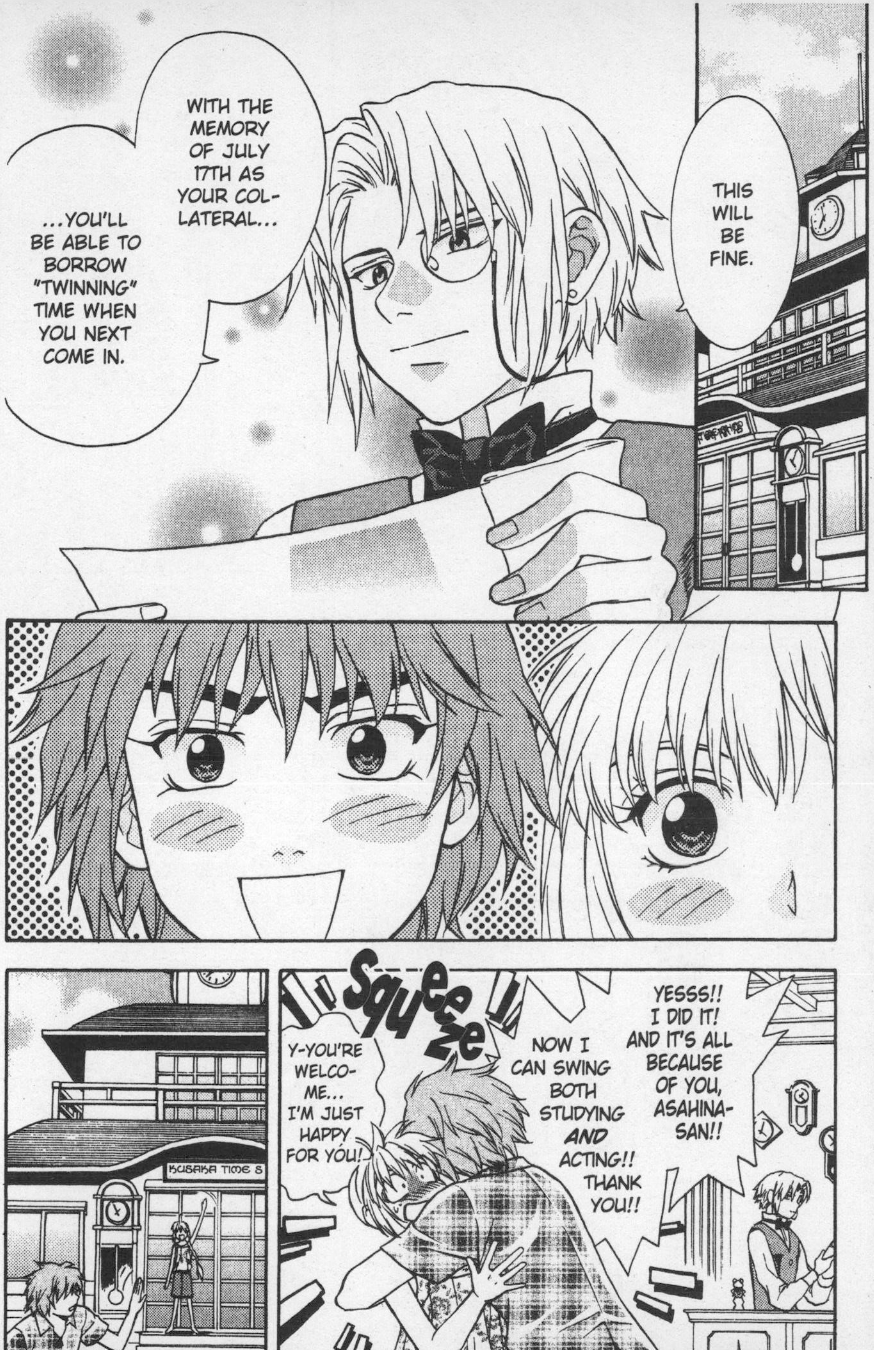
THIS WILL BE FINE.
WITH THE MEMORY OF JULY 17TH AS YOUR COL-LATERAL...
...YOU'LL BE ABLE TO BORROW "TWINNING" TIME WHEN YOU NEXT COME IN.
YESSS!! I DID IT! AND IT'S ALL BECAUSE OF YOU, ASAHINA-SAN!!
NOW I CAN SWING BOTH STUDYING AND ACTING!! THANK YOU!!
Squeeze
Y-YOU'RE WELCO-ME... I'M JUST HAPPY FOR YOU!
KUSAKA TIME S

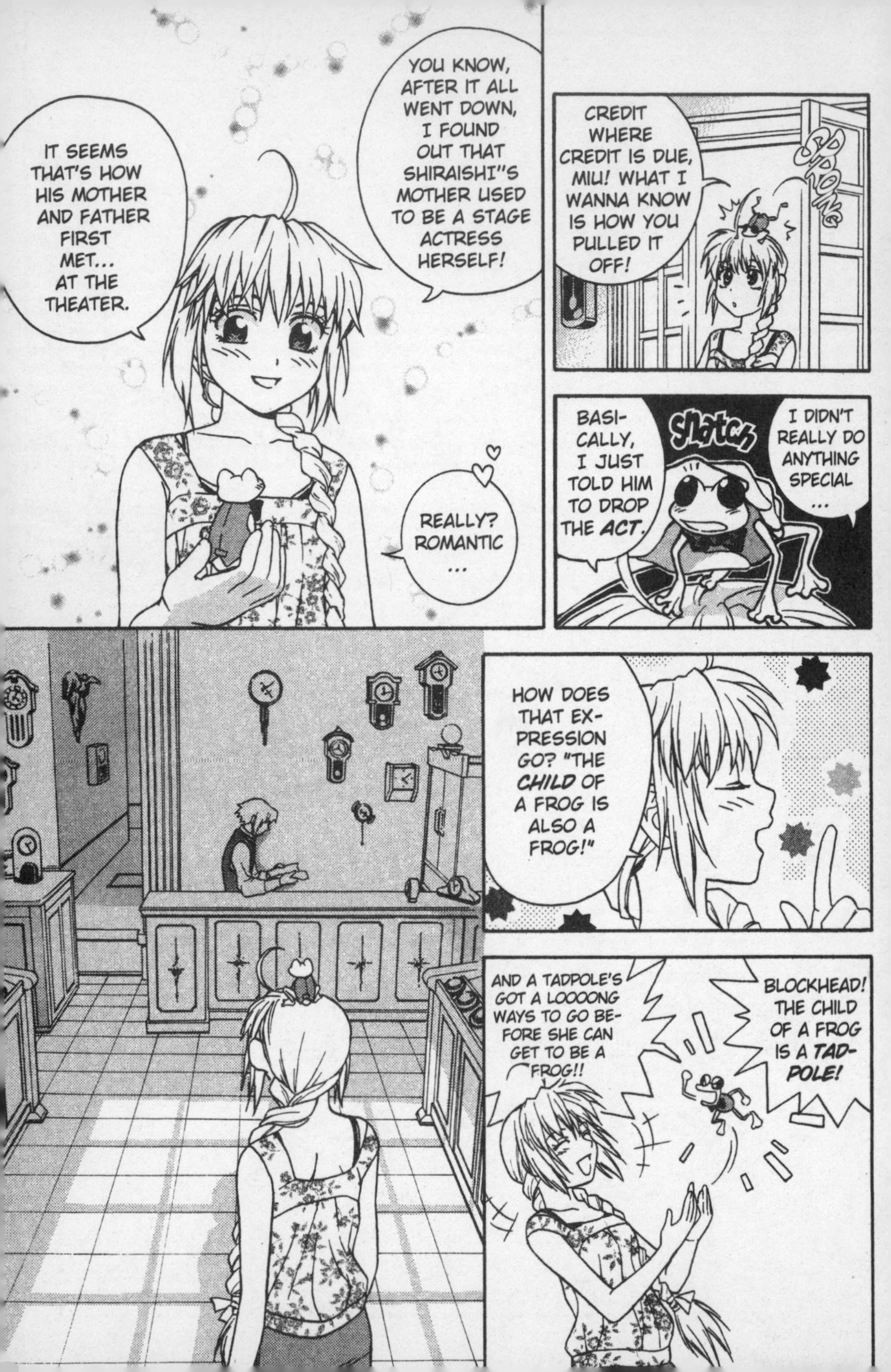
CREDIT WHERE CREDIT IS DUE, MIU! WHAT I WANNA KNOW IS HOW YOU PULLED IT OFF!
SPRONG
I DIDN'T REALLY DO ANYTHING SPECIAL ...
SNATCH
BASI-CALLY, I JUST TOLD HIM TO DROP THE ACT.
YOU KNOW, AFTER IT ALL WENT DOWN, I FOUND OUT THAT SHIRAISHI''S MOTHER USED TO BE A STAGE ACTRESS HERSELF!
IT SEEMS THAT'S HOW HIS MOTHER AND FATHER FIRST MET... AT THE THEATER.
REALLY? ROMANTIC ...
HOW DOES THAT EX-PRESSION GO? "THE CHILD OF A FROG IS ALSO A FROG!"
BLOCKHEAD! THE CHILD OF A FROG IS A TAD-POLE!
AND A TADPOLE'S GOT A LOOOONG WAYS TO GO BE-FORE SHE CAN GET TO BE A FROG!!

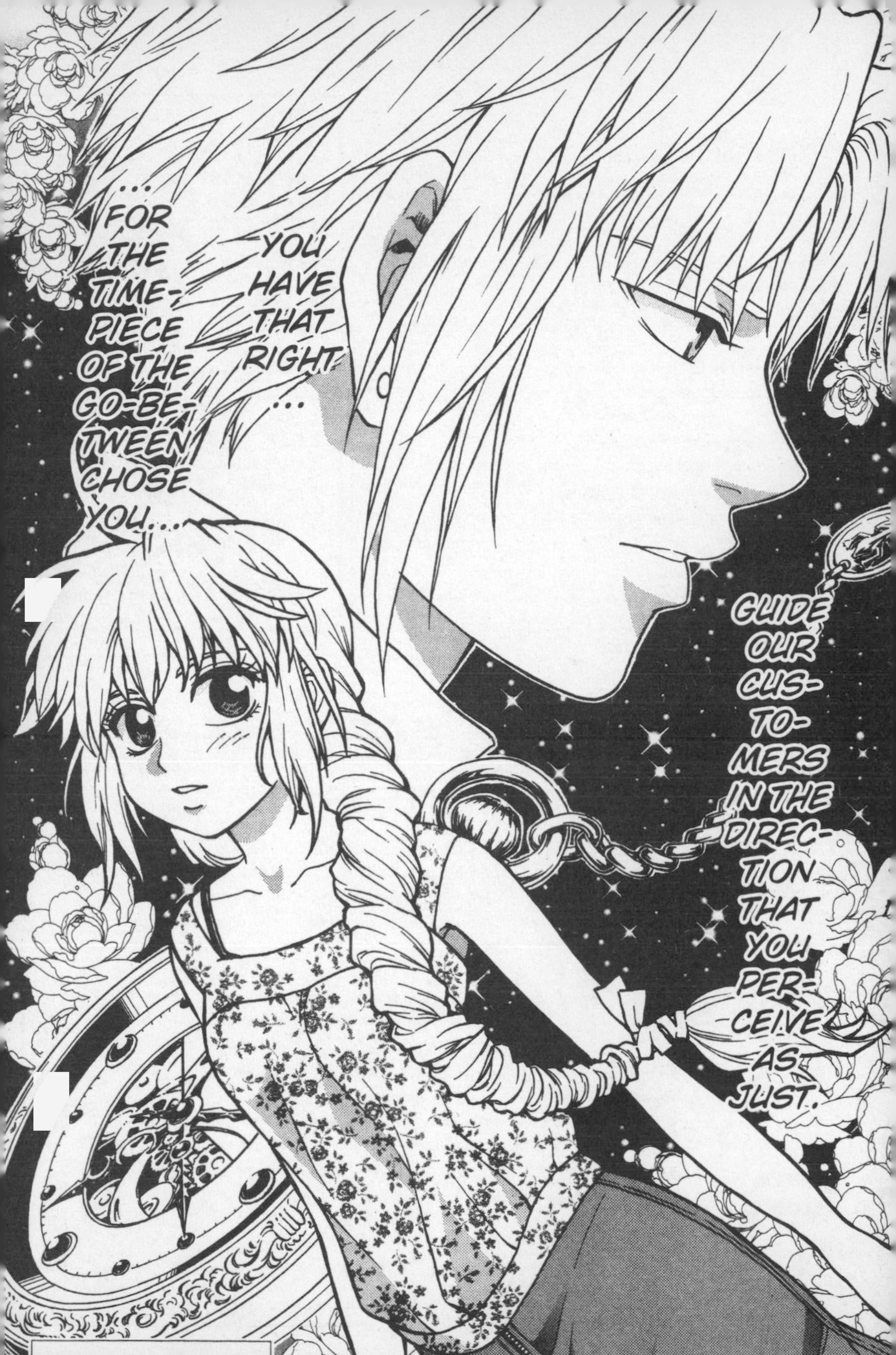
YOU HAVE THAT RIGHT...
...FOR THE TIME-PIECE OF THE GO-BE-TWEEN CHOSE YOU...
GUIDE OUR CUS-TO-MERS IN THE DIREC-TION THAT YOU PER-CEIVE AS JUST.

Episode 5: Time Of One's Own (Part Two) The End

Afterword...

or My Deep Dark Secrets...or...

This is my daily timetable.
Kind of weird, isn't it?
Yeah, I know...

It seems as though my body
clock counts 25 hours as being
one day. I bet everyone has
their own specific internal
clock as well, but most people
try to reset theirs to match
the traditional day/night cycle.

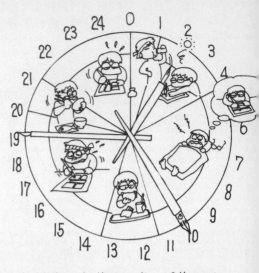

...Actually, it was thinking about that that led me to the creation of this series.
Hope you keep reading!!

05.09.17   5:40 am
Daimuro Kishi 9/17/05 5:40am

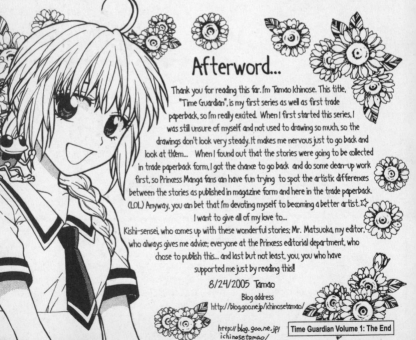

Afterword...

Thank you for reading this far. I'm Tamao Ichinose. This title,
"Time Guardian", is my first series as well as first trade
paperback, so I'm really excited. When I first started this series, I
was still unsure of myself and not used to drawing so much, so the
drawings don't look very steady. It makes me nervous just to go back and
look at them... When I found out that the stories were going to be collected
in trade paperback form, I got the chance to go back and do some clean-up work
first, so Princess Manga fans can have fun trying to spot the artistic differences
between the stories as published in magazine form and here in the trade paperback.
(LOL) Anyway, you can bet that I'm devoting myself to becoming a better artist. ☆
I want to give all of my love to...
Kishi-sensei, who comes up with these wonderful stories; Mr. Matsuoka, my editor,
who always gives me advice; everyone at the Princess editorial department, who
chose to publish this... and last but not least, you, you who have
supported me just by reading this!!

8/24/2005 Tamao

Blog address
http://blog.goo.ne.jp/ichinosetamao/

http://blog.goo.ne.jp/
ichinosetamao/

Time Guardian Volume 1: The End

IS THE TIME SHOP CLOSING FOR GOOD?!
FIND OUT IN JUNE!

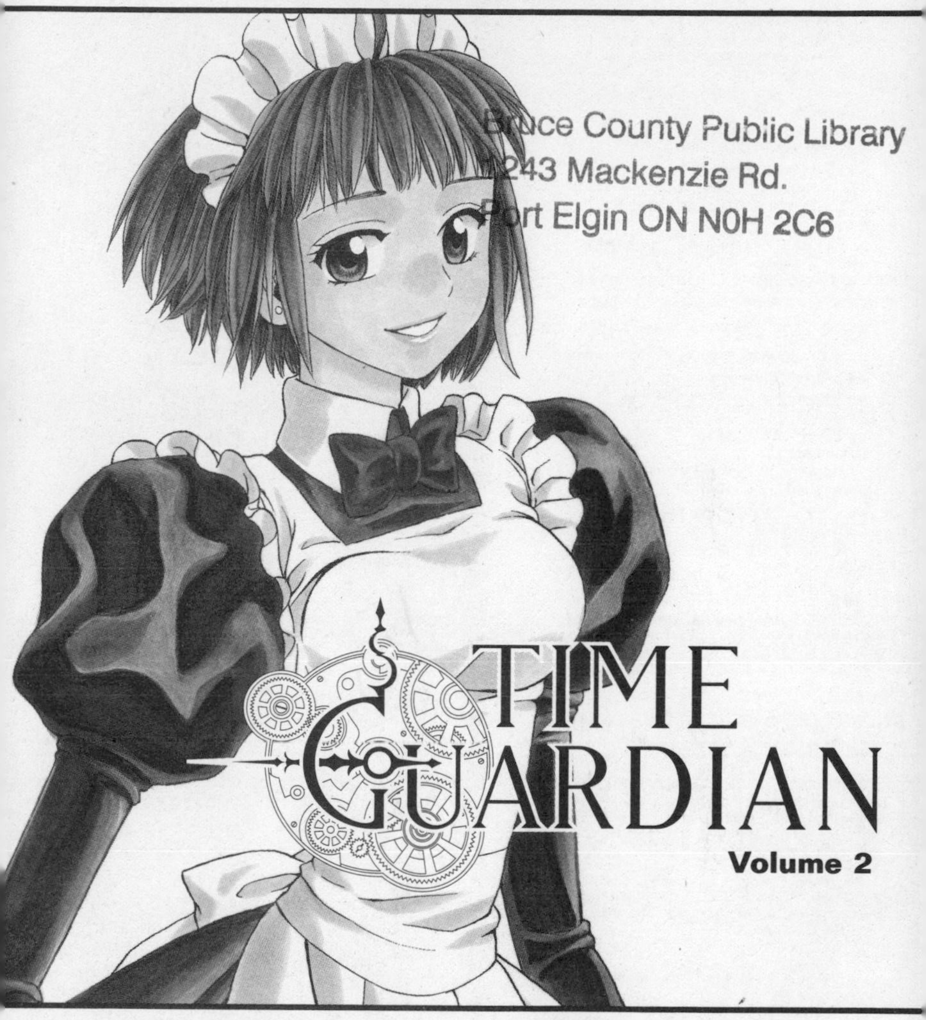
TIME
GUARDIAN
Volume 2

By Daimuro Kishi & Tamao Ichinose. Two former high school sweethearts trade in all of their memories as a couple in order to forget their relationship...but Miu thinks they still have feelings for each other. Then Mr. Kusaka announces that he's going to sell off all the memories held in collateral and close the time shop. When Miu tries to protest, she can't find him! Is she too late?!

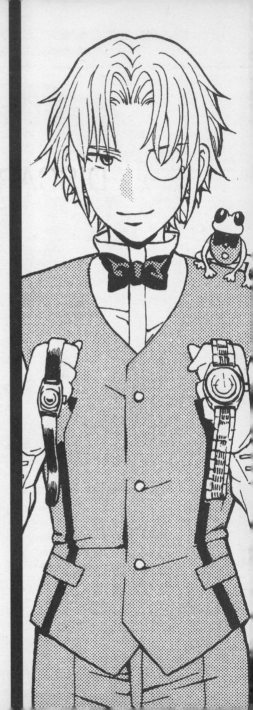

TIME GUARDIAN Vol. 1 © 2005 Daimuro Kishi, Tamao
Ichinose. All rights reserved. First published in Japan in
2005 by Akita Publishing Co., Ltd.

TIME GUARDIAN Volume 1, published by WildStorm
Productions, an imprint of DC Comics, 888 Prospect St.
#240, La Jolla, CA 92037. English Translation © 2007. All
Rights Reserved. English translation rights in U.S.A. And
Canada arranged with Akita Publishing Co., Ltd., through
Tuttle-Mori Agency, Inc., Tokyo. The stories, characters, and
incidents mentioned in this magazine are entirely fictional.
Printed on recyclable paper. WildStorm does not read or
accept unsolicited submissions of ideas, stories or artwork.
Printed in Canada.

DC Comics, a Warner Bros. Entertainment Company.

Sheldon Drzka – Translation and Adaptation
Kathryn Renta – Lettering
Larry Berry – Design
Jim Chadwick – Editor

ISBN:1-4012-1161-5
ISBN-13: 978-1-4012-1161-5

All the pages in this book were created—and are printed here—in Japanese RIGHT-to-LEFT format. No artwork has been reversed or altered, so you can read the stories the way the creators meant for them to be read.

FLIP IT!

RIGHT TO LEFT?!

Traditional Japanese manga starts at the upper right-hand corner, and moves right-to-left as it goes down the page. Follow this guide for an easy understanding.

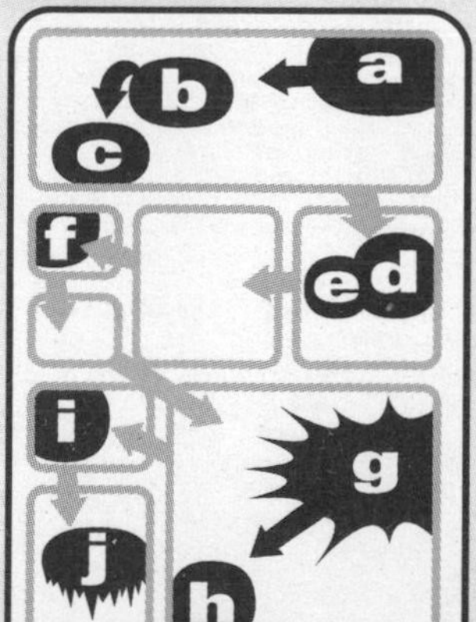
a
b
c
d
e
f
g
h
i
j

For more information and sneak previews, visit cmxmanga.com. Call 1-800-COMIC BOOK for the nearest comics shop or head to your local book store.